PROFESSIONAL ANGULARJS

PROFESSIONAL

AngularJS

PROFESSIONAL

AngularJS

Valeri Karpov
Diego Netto

wrox™
A Wiley Brand

Professional AngularJS

Published by
John Wiley & Sons, Inc.
10475 Crosspoint Boulevard
Indianapolis, IN 46256
www.wiley.com

Copyright © 2015 by John Wiley & Sons, Inc., Indianapolis, Indiana

Published simultaneously in Canada

ISBN: 978-1-118-83207-3

ISBN: 978-1-118-83209-7 (ebk)

ISBN: 978-1-118-83208-0 (ebk)

Manufactured in the United States of America

10 9 8 7 6 5 4 3 2

For general information on our other products and services please contact our Customer Care Department within the United States at (877) 762-2974, outside the United States at (317) 572-3993 or fax (317) 572-4002.

Wiley publishes in a variety of print and electronic formats and by print-on-demand. Some material included with standard print versions of this book may not be included in e-books or in print-on-demand. If this book refers to media such as a CD or DVD that is not included in the version you purchased, you may download this material at http://booksupport.wiley.com. For more information about Wiley products, visit www.wiley.com.

Library of Congress Control Number: 2014951014

For my father, the elder Valeri Karpov,
who taught me to never settle for "good enough."

—VALERI KARPOV

For my mother, Liliana, who showed me how to find
happiness by living each day like it might be your last.

—DIEGO NETTO

ABOUT THE AUTHORS

VALERI KARPOV is a NodeJS Engineer at MongoDB, where he focuses on maintaining the popular Mongoose ODM and numerous other MongoDB-related NodeJS modules. In addition, he's a Hacker in Residence at BookaLokal, a blogger for StrongLoop, and the person who gave the MEAN stack its name. He has been running production AngularJS apps since AngularJS v0.9.4 in 2010. Most recently, he used AngularJS to build out BookaLokal's mobile website and a web client for MongoDB's internal continuous integration framework.

DIEGO NETTO is a software consultant and open source evangelist. He wears the many hats of a full stack engineer and entrepreneur. Owner of a development shop operating out of Los Angeles and Dallas, Diego creates web and mobile applications for both startups and enterprise companies. Maintainer of the IonicFramework Yeoman generator, he has most recently used AngularJS and the IonicFramework to build the Prop mobile app for www.aboatapp.com, and is using Famo.us/Angular to build the mobile app for www.modelrevolt.com.

ABOUT THE TECHNICAL EDITOR

STÉPHANE BÉGAUDEAU graduated from the Faculty of Sciences and Technology of Nantes and is currently working as a web technology specialist and Eclipse modeling consultant at Obeo in France. He has contributed to several open source projects in the Eclipse Foundation, and he is the leader of Acceleo. He also worked on Dart Designer, an open source tooling for the Dart programming language.

CREDITS

PROJECT EDITOR
Kelly Talbot

TECHNICAL EDITOR
Stéphane Bégaudeau

PRODUCTION EDITOR
Christine O'Connor

COPY EDITOR
Karen Gill

**MANAGER OF CONTENT DEVELOPMENT
& ASSEMBLY**
Mary Beth Wakefield

MARKETING DIRECTOR
David Mayhew

MARKETING MANAGER
Carrie Sherrill

**PROFESSIONAL TECHNOLOGY &
STRATEGY DIRECTOR**
Barry Pruett

BUSINESS MANAGER
Amy Knies

ASSOCIATE PUBLISHER
Jim Minatel

PROJECT COORDINATOR, COVER
Brent Savage

PROOFREADER
Nancy Carrasco

INDEXER
Johnna VanHoose Dinse

COVER DESIGNER
Wiley

COVER IMAGE
iStock.com/Manuel Faba Ortega

ACKNOWLEDGMENTS

SOCRATES WROTE THAT "Education is the kindling of a flame, not the filling of a vessel." In that vein, I'm thankful that I have had teachers and mentors who made programming my lifelong passion rather than just a career. In particular, I'd like to thank Professors Kernighan and Tarjan from Princeton University; and Dr. Nevard, Dr. Sankaran, Mr. Scarpone, and Mr. Nodarse from the Bergen County Academies. In addition, I'd like to thank Misko Hevery, my mentor when I interned at Google and original author of AngularJS, who taught me more about software engineering in 12 weeks than I had learned in my life leading up to that summer.

—Valeri Karpov

TO QUOTE THE SUCCESSFUL ENTREPRENEUR FELIX DENNIS, "Anyone not busy learning is busy dying." This is a prudent reminder, especially in the constantly evolving field of software engineering, that in order to remain relevant and sustain success we must commit to a lifelong pursuit of knowledge. I would like to thank Professors Tatar and Ribbens from Virginia Tech for enlightening me to this realization. I also want to thank Addy Osmani for helping me discover the importance of intelligent tooling and for inspiring me to contribute to the open source community. Special thanks to my friend and co-author Valeri Karpov for getting me involved with AngularJS during such an early stage.

—Diego Netto

CONTENTS

INTRODUCTION

IT'S AN EXCITING TIME to be a JavaScript developer. Between the meteoric rise of server-side JavaScript's open source community (100,000 packages on the NodeJS package manager as of October 2014—twice as many as in December 2013), the popularity of next-generation client-side frameworks like AngularJS, and the growing number of companies that build web tools based on full-stack JavaScript, JavaScript language skills are in high demand. Modern tools allow you to build sophisticated browser-based clients, highly concurrent servers, and even hybrid native mobile applications using a single language. AngularJS is quickly becoming the leading next-generation client-side web framework, enabling individuals, small teams, and large corporations to build and test phenomenally sophisticated browser-based applications.

WHAT IS ANGULARJS?

Within the rapidly growing JavaScript community, AngularJS burst onto the scene when it released version 1.0 in June 2012. Although a relatively new framework, its powerful features and elegant tools for structuring applications have made it the front-end framework of choice for many developers. AngularJS was originally developed at Google by testing engineer Misko Hevery, who found that existing tools, like jQuery, made it difficult to structure browser user interfaces (UIs) that needed to display large amounts of sophisticated data. Google now has a dedicated team developing and maintaining AngularJS and related tools. AngularJS also powers some active Google applications, ranging from the DoubleClick Digital Marketing Platform to the YouTube app on the PlayStation 3. AngularJS's popularity is growing rapidly: As of October 2014, it powers 143 of the Quantcast Top 10k websites and is rapidly outpacing its closest rivals, KnockoutJS, ReactJS, and EmberJS.

What makes AngularJS so special? One particularly pithy expression borrowed from the `https://angularjs.org/` website describes AngularJS as enabling you to "write less code, go have beer sooner." The heart of AngularJS is a concept called *two-way data binding*, which enables you to bind Hypertext Markup Language (HTML) and cascading style sheets (CSS) to the state of a JavaScript variable. Whenever the variable changes, AngularJS updates all HTML and CSS that references that JavaScript variable. For instance, in the following code:

```
<div ng-show="shouldShow">Hello</div>
```

If the `shouldShow` variable is changed to `false`, AngularJS automatically hides the `div` element for you. There is nothing special about the `shouldShow` variable: AngularJS doesn't require you to wrap your variables in special types; the `shouldShow` variable can be a plain old JavaScript Boolean value.

Although two-way data binding is the basis for what makes AngularJS so useful, it's only the tip of the iceberg. AngularJS provides an elegant framework for organizing your client-side JavaScript in a way to maximize reusability and testability. In addition, AngularJS has a rich set of testing tools, such as Karma, protractor, and ngScenario (see Chapter 9), which are optimized for use with AngularJS. AngularJS's focus on testable structures and rich testing tools makes it a natural choice for mission-critical client-side JavaScript. Not only does it enable you to write sophisticated applications fast, it supplies tools and structure that make testing your application easy. As a matter of fact, Google's DoubleClick team cited AngularJS's "full testing story" as one of its six biggest reasons for porting its digital marketing platform to AngularJS. Here is a brief overview of some of the concepts that make AngularJS special.

Two-Way Data Binding

In many older client-side JavaScript libraries, like jQuery and Backbone, you are expected to manipulate the Document Object Model (DOM) yourself. In other words, if you want to change the HTML contents of a div element, you need to write imperative JavaScript. For example:

```
$('div').html('Hello, world!');
```

AngularJS inverts this paradigm and makes your HTML the definitive source for how your data is displayed. The primary purpose of two-way data binding is to bind an HTML or CSS property (for instance, the HTML contents or background color of a div element) to the value of a JavaScript variable. When the value of the JavaScript variable changes, the HTML or CSS property is updated to match. The opposite is also true: If the user types in an input field, the value of the bound JavaScript variable is updated to match what the user typed. For instance, the following HTML greets whoever's name is typed in the input field. You can find this example in this chapter's sample code as data_binding.html: Simply right-click on the file and open it in your browser—no web server or other dependencies required!

```
<input type="text" ng-model="user" placeholder="Your Name">
<h3>Hello, {{user}}!</h3>
```

No JavaScript is necessary! The ngModel directive and the {{}} shorthand syntax do all the work. There is limited benefit to using AngularJS in this simple example, but, as you'll see when you build a real application in Chapter 1, data binding greatly simplifies your JavaScript. It's not uncommon to see 800 lines of jQuery spaghetti code reduced to 40 lines of clean DOM-independent AngularJS code thanks to data binding.

Scopes in the DOM

DOM scopes are another powerful feature of AngularJS. As you might have guessed, there is no free lunch with data binding; code complexity has to go somewhere. However, AngularJS allows you to create scopes in the DOM that behave similarly to scopes in JavaScript and other programming languages. This permits you to break your HTML and JavaScript into independent and reusable pieces. For instance, here's the same greeting example from earlier, but with two separate scopes: one for greeting in English, the other in Spanish:

```
<div ng-controller="HelloController">
  <input type="text" ng-model="user" placeholder="Your Name">
  <h3>Hello, {{user}}!</h3>
</div>
```

```
<hr>
<div ng-controller="HelloController">
  <input type="text" ng-model="user" placeholder="Su Nombre">
  <h3>Hola, {{user}}!</h3>
</div>

<script type="text/javascript"
        src="angular.js">
</script>
<script type="text/javascript">
  function HelloController($scope) {}
</script>
```

The ngController directive is one way to create a new scope, enabling you to reuse the same code for two different purposes. Chapter 4 includes a thorough overview of two-way data binding and a discussion of internal implementation details.

Directives

Directives are a powerful tool for grouping HTML and JavaScript functionality into one easily reusable bundle. AngularJS has numerous built-in directives, like the ngController and ngModel directives you saw earlier, that enable you to access sophisticated JavaScript functionality from your HTML. You can write your own custom directives as well. In particular, AngularJS allows you to associate HTML with a directive, so you can use directives as a way of reusing HTML as well as a way of tying certain behavior into two-way data binding. Writing custom directives is beyond the scope of this introduction, but Chapter 5 includes a thorough discussion of the subject.

Templates

On top of two-way data binding, AngularJS lets you swap out entire portions of the page based on the state of a JavaScript variable. The ngInclude directive enables you to conditionally include *templates*, pieces of AngularJS-infused HTML, in the page based on the JavaScript state. The following example demonstrates a page with a div that contains different HTML based on the value of the myTemplate variable. You can find this example in templates.html in this chapter's sample code:

```
<div ng-controller="TemplateController">
  <div ng-include="myTemplate">
  </div>
  <br>
  <a ng-click="myTemplate = 'template1';"
     style="cursor: pointer"
     ng-class="{'selected': myTemplate === 'template1' }">
    Display Template 1
  </a>
  <a ng-click="myTemplate = 'template2';"
     style="cursor: pointer"
     ng-class="{'selected': myTemplate === 'template2' }">
    Display Template 2
  </a>
```

```
    </div>

    <script type="text/javascript"
            src="angular.js">
    </script>
    <script type="text/javascript">
      function TemplateController($scope) {
        $scope.myTemplate = 'template1';
      }
    </script>
    <script type="text/ng-template" id="template1">
      <h1>This is Template 1</h1>
    </script>
    <script type="text/ng-template" id="template2">
      <h1>This is Template 2</h1>
    </script>
```

Chapter 6 includes a thorough discussion of AngularJS templates, including how to use them to structure single-page applications.

Testing and Workflow

Providing a framework for writing unit-testable code has been a core AngularJS goal from its first release. AngularJS includes an elegant and sophisticated dependency injector, and all AngularJS *components* (controllers, directives, services, and filters) are constructed using the dependency injector. This ensures that your code's dependencies are easy to stub out as necessary for your tests. Furthermore, the AngularJS team has developed numerous powerful testing tools, such as the Karma test runner and the protractor and ngScenario integration testing frameworks. These bring the sophisticated multibrowser testing infrastructure that was previously only feasible for large companies into the hands of the individual developer.

In addition, AngularJS's architecture and testing tools interface nicely with various open source JavaScript build and workflow tools, such as Gulp and Grunt. With these tools, you can execute your tests seamlessly, tie in tools like code coverage and linting into your test execution, and even scaffold entirely new applications from scratch. Core AngularJS is just a library, but the testing and workflow tools surrounding it make the AngularJS ecosystem as a whole an innovative new paradigm for building browser-based clients. Chapter 9 includes a more detailed discussion of the AngularJS testing ecosystem and the different types of testing strategies you can use for your AngularJS applications.

WHEN NOT TO USE ANGULARJS

Like any library, AngularJS is a perfect fit for some applications and a not-so-good fit for others. In the next section, you learn about several use cases in which AngularJS is a perfect fit. In this section, you learn about a few use cases in which AngularJS is not such a good fit and learn about some of AngularJS's limitations.

Applications Requiring Support for Old Versions of Internet Explorer

One limitation of AngularJS that may be significant for some users is that it doesn't support old versions of Internet Explorer. AngularJS 1.0.x supports Internet Explorer 6 and 7, but the version that you'll be learning about in this book, AngularJS 1.2.x, supports only Internet Explorer 8 and greater. Furthermore, the current experimental versions of AngularJS, 1.3.x, drop support for Internet Explorer 8 entirely. (They only support Internet Explorer 9 and greater.) If your application needs to support Internet Explorer 7, using AngularJS is probably not the right choice.

Applications That Don't Require JavaScript Server I/O

AngularJS is an extremely rich and powerful library, and avid users are often tempted to use it for every application. However, there are many cases in which AngularJS is overkill and adds unnecessary complexity. For instance, if you need to add a button to a page that shows or hides a `div` element whenever a user clicks on it, using AngularJS cannot help you unless you need to persist the state of the `div` in the page's URL or to the server. Similarly, choosing to write your blog in AngularJS is usually a poor decision. Blogs typically display simple data with limited interactivity, so AngularJS is often unnecessary. Also, blogs require good integration with search engines. If you were to write a blog in AngularJS, you would need to do some extra work (see Chapter 6) to make sure search engines could effectively crawl your blog, because search engine crawlers don't execute JavaScript.

WHEN TO USE ANGULARJS

Now that you've learned about a couple of AngularJS's limitations, you'll learn about a few use cases in which AngularJS truly shines.

Internal Data-Intensive Applications

AngularJS is an extremely powerful tool for applications that need to display complex data in a browser UI, such as continuous integration frameworks or product dashboards. Much of the challenge in developing UIs for these applications lies in writing imperative JavaScript to render data correctly every time it changes. Two-way data binding frees you from needing to write this glue code, which results in much slimmer and easier-to-read JavaScript. As you'll see when you write a stock market dashboard in Chapter 1, two-way data binding and directives make it easy to elegantly structure applications that need to display a lot of data.

Mobile Websites

AngularJS has extensive support for most common mobile browsers (Android, Chrome Mobile, iOS Safari). Furthermore, as you'll see in Chapter 6, AngularJS has powerful animation support, and single-page apps enable you to leverage browser caching to minimize your bandwidth usage. This enables you to build mobile web applications that are fast and effectively mimic native applications. In addition, frameworks like Ionic (Chapter 10) enable you to build hybrid mobile applications, applications written in JavaScript but distributed through the Android and iPhone app stores, using AngularJS.

Building a Prototype

One theme that appears numerous times in this book is the idea of two-way data binding creating an effective separation between front-end JavaScript engineering and user interface/user experience (UI/UX) design. Two-way data binding enables the front-end JavaScript engineer to expose an application programming interface (API) that a UI/UX designer can then access in HTML, enabling both the front-end engineer and the designer to work in their preferred environments without stepping on each other's toes. This is particularly useful for building out a prototype browser UI quickly, because you can then effectively parallelize tasks and enable your team to run more smoothly. In addition, AngularJS's rich testing ecosystem enables you to ensure solid test coverage, and thus make sure your prototype doesn't have any obvious bugs when you present it.

HOW TO USE THIS BOOK

Now that you've seen why AngularJS is such a popular library, next up is a brief overview of the contents of this book and how it can take you from writing beginner-level AngularJS to writing professional-level AngularJS.

You can think of this book as a "choose your own adventure" for learning AngularJS. If you are an AngularJS beginner, you will benefit a great deal from reading the book sequentially, as the chapters provide a logical sequence for learning AngularJS from scratch. However, the chapters and their examples are designed to be mostly independent of one another. If you are familiar with AngularJS and are looking to expand your knowledge in one particular area, such as using testing frameworks (Chapter 9), you can simply go to the appropriate chapter and skip the intermediate chapters. Some example code is shared between chapters, but each chapter explains each piece of example code under the assumption that you have never seen it before. Furthermore, some chapters reference information in other chapters, but they always provide a brief overview of the necessary concept. Whether you're just getting started with AngularJS or you're a more advanced user looking to learn about a specific topic, this book allows you to skip right to the most useful information. (However, if you are an AngularJS beginner, you should read Chapter 1 before skipping to other chapters.) Here are some brief highlights of what you can learn in each chapter.

Chapter 1: Building a Simple AngularJS Application

This chapter is geared toward readers who are new to AngularJS. You use AngularJS to build out a stock market dashboard application from scratch and get a high-level overview of the topics covered in subsequent chapters.

Chapter 2: Intelligent Workflow and Build Tools

In this chapter, you learn about the myriad open source tools for scaffolding new AngularJS applications, automating workflow, and including external dependencies. Special emphasis is placed on the popular scaffolding tool Yeoman, which enables you to quickly kick-start new AngularJS applications and provide powerful tools for managing your workflow.

Chapter 3: Architecture

This chapter offers an overview of best practices for structuring AngularJS components, including how to pass data between services, controllers, and directives. In addition, this chapter explores best practices for directory structures in applications of various sizes. Finally, this chapter covers two popular tools for managing file dependencies: RequireJS and Browserify.

Chapter 4: Data Binding

Although AngularJS data binding is elegant and intuitive, intermediate AngularJS developers often benefit from a deeper understanding of how data binding is actually implemented. This chapter explores how AngularJS scopes are structured and the implementation details of the `$digest` loop, so you can avoid common data binding pitfalls. This chapter also includes an overview of filters, including use cases and common mistakes.

Chapter 5: Directives

The first half of this chapter offers a basic working knowledge of how to write your own AngularJS directives and explores various use cases for directives. The second half focuses on designing more advanced directives using tools like transclusion.

Chapter 6: Templates, Location, and Routing

The primary purpose of this chapter is to supply an overview of how to write single-page applications in AngularJS, applications that allow a user to transition between multiple "views" without reloading the page. To build up to creating a single-page application, this chapter provides a detailed overview of AngularJS templates, the template cache, and the `$location` service. This chapter also provides an overview of using CSS3 animations with AngularJS and an example of how to make single-page applications search-engine-friendly using Prerender.

Chapter 7: Services, Factories, and Providers

This chapter provides a thorough description of the different methods of creating a service in AngularJS. You also learn how services work "under the hood" and how to take advantage of services' internal implementation.

Chapter 8: Server Communication

In this chapter, you use basic services and interceptors to create a login system. In addition, you learn how to bootstrap a simple back end using StrongLoop's Loopback API and integrate Facebook login with your client-side AngularJS application and your Loopback API.

Chapter 9: Testing and Debugging AngularJS Applications

This chapter includes a thorough overview of structuring unit tests and DOM integration tests (also known as *halfway tests*) for your AngularJS applications using the popular open source test runner Karma. This chapter also discusses the open source behavior-driven development (BDD) testing frameworks Mocha and Jasmine and explains how to run your tests in SauceLabs's browser cloud.

Chapter 10: Moving On

This chapter contains a brief overview of several popular open source modules that enable AngularJS to do some unexpected things. In particular, you learn how to integrate Twitter Bootstrap components using Angular-UI Bootstrap, how to build hybrid mobile applications with AngularJS and the Ionic framework, and how to integrate two popular open source JavaScript modules, Moment and Mongoose, with AngularJS. You also learn how to use ECMAScript 6 generators with AngularJS's $http service.

HOW TO WORK WITH THIS BOOK'S SAMPLE CODE

Each chapter in this book has its own sample code, available in the Code Downloads section at http://www.wrox.com/go/proangularjs. Each chapter starts with a reminder to visit this URL to download the sample code, so don't worry about bookmarking this exact page. Although each chapter includes code in the text as appropriate, it's best to download each chapter's sample code and try the examples for yourself.

This book's sample code has been designed to have a minimum of outside dependencies. The beginning of each chapter explains any special dependencies required for running its sample code. For many of this book's examples, you only require a modern browser. (The examples were primarily developed with Google Chrome 37 and Mozilla Firefox 32, but Internet Explorer 9 and Safari 6 should be sufficient.) These examples are in the form of .html files that you can open by right-clicking on the file and choosing to open the file in your browser using the file:// protocol. For instance, to view the data_binding.html example from this chapter's sample code, you may navigate to file:///Users/user/Chapter%200/data_binding.html if this chapter's sample code is in the /Users/user/Chapter 0 directory. You may safely assume that you can open any HTML file from this book's sample code in your browser without extra setup unless otherwise specified.

You don't require a special integrated development environment (IDE) for this book's sample code. Text editors like vim and SublimeText should be sufficient for experimenting with the sample code. You can use IDEs like WebStorm if you prefer, but there is limited benefit to using an IDE for this book's sample code.

Many of the concepts covered in this book require a web server to function properly. To make this process as lightweight as possible, this book utilizes NodeJS and the NodeJS package manager npm to start web servers. In addition, many of the tools you'll learn about in this book, like Grunt, Prerender, and Yeoman, are most easily installed through npm. To install NodeJS, you should go to http://nodejs.org/download and follow the instructions for your platform. NodeJS is easy to install and supports virtually every common desktop operating system (including Windows); furthermore, npm is automatically included with NodeJS. Most examples in this book that require NodeJS, however, assume that you are using a bash shell. Linux and OSX users can use their default terminals. On Windows, you should use git bash (http://msysgit.github.io), a bash terminal for Windows, if you want to run the command-line instructions as is. (Keep in mind, NodeJS does not officially support Cygwin, so using Cygwin is not recommended.) Each chapter explains how to install additional dependencies and reminds you to install NodeJS if necessary.

CONVENTIONS

To help you get the most from the text and keep track of what's happening, this book uses a number of conventions.

> **NOTE** *Notes, tips, hints, tricks, and asides to the current discussion are offset like this.*

As for styles in the text:

➤ URLs within the text are presented like so: https://angularjs.org/#!.

➤ Code shows up like this:

```
A monofont type is used for code examples.
```

```
Bold is used to emphasize code that is particularly important in the present
context or to show changes from a previous code snippet.
```

ERRATA

Every effort has been made to ensure that there are no errors in the text or in the code. However, no one is perfect, and mistakes do occur. If you find an error in one of the Wrox books, like a spelling mistake or faulty piece of code, please share your feedback. By sending in errata, you may save another reader hours of frustration; at the same time, you are helping to provide even higher-quality information.

To find the errata page for this book, go to http://www.wrox.com/WileyCDA/ and locate the title using the Search box or one of the title lists. Then, on the Book Search Results page, click the Errata link. On this page you can view all errata that has been submitted for this book and posted by Wrox editors.

> **NOTE** *A complete book list including links to errata is also available at* http://www.wrox.com/WileyCDA/Section/id-105077.html.

If you don't spot "your" error on the Errata page, click the Errata Form link and complete the form to send the error you have found. The information will be checked and, if appropriate, a message will be posted to the book's errata page and the problem corrected in subsequent editions of the book.

P2P.WROX.COM

For author and peer discussion, join the P2P forums at `http://p2p.wrox.com`. The forums are a web-based system for you to post messages relating to Wrox books and related technologies and interact with other readers and technology users. The forums offer a subscription feature to e-mail you topics of interest of your choosing when new posts are made to the forums. Wrox authors, editors, other industry experts, and your fellow readers are present on these forums.

At `http://p2p.wrox.com`, you will find a number of different forums that will help you not only as you read this book, but as you develop your own applications. To join the forums, just follow these steps:

1. Go to `http://p2p.wrox.com` and click the Register link.

2. Read the terms of use and click Agree.

3. Complete the required information to join as well as any optional information you want to provide, and click Submit.

4. You will receive an e-mail with information describing how to verify your account and complete the joining process.

> **NOTE** *You can read messages in the forums without joining P2P but in order to post your own messages, you must join.*

Once you join, you can post new messages and respond to messages that other users post. You can read messages at any time on the web. If you would like to have new messages from a particular forum e-mailed to you, click the Subscribe to this Forum icon by the forum name in the forum listing.

For more information about how to use the Wrox P2P, be sure to read the P2P FAQs for answers to questions about how the forum software works as well as many common questions specific to P2P and Wrox books. To read the FAQs, click the FAQ link on any P2P page.

PROFESSIONAL

AngularJS

1

Building a Simple AngularJS Application

WHAT YOU WILL LEARN IN THIS CHAPTER:

➤ Creating a new AngularJS application from scratch

➤ Creating custom controllers, directives, and services

➤ Communicating with an external API server

➤ Storing data client-side using HTML5 LocalStorage

➤ Creating a simple animation with ngAnimate

➤ Packaging your application for distribution and deployment using GitHub Pages

WROX.COM CODE DOWNLOADS FOR THIS CHAPTER

You can find the wrox.com code downloads for this chapter at `http://www.wrox.com/go/proangularjs` on the Download Code tab. For added clarity, the code downloads contain an individual directory for each step of the application building guide. The `README.md` file located in the root directory of the companion code contains additional information for properly utilizing the code for each step of the guide. Those who prefer to use GitHub can find the repository for this application, which includes Git tags for each step of the guide and detailed documentation, by visiting `http://github.com/diegonetto/stock-dog`.

WHAT YOU ARE BUILDING

The best way to learn AngularJS is to jump directly into a real-world, hands-on application that leverages nearly all key components of the framework. Over the course of this chapter, you will build StockDog, a real-time stock watchlist monitoring and management application. For the unfamiliar, a watchlist in this context is simply an arbitrary grouping of desired stocks that are to be tracked for analytical purposes. The Yahoo Finance API (application programming interface) will be utilized to fetch real-time stock quote information from within the client. The application will not include a dynamic back end, so all information will be fetched from the Yahoo Finance API directly or, in the case of company ticker symbols, be contained within a static JSON (JavaScript Object Notation) file. By the end of this chapter, users of your application will be able to do the following:

➤ Create custom-named watchlists with descriptions

➤ Add stocks from the NYSE, NASDAQ, and AMEX exchanges

➤ Monitor stock price changes in real time

➤ Visualize portfolio performance of watchlists using charts

StockDog will consist of two main views that can be accessed via the application's navigation bar. The dashboard view will serve as the landing page for StockDog, allowing users to create new watchlists and monitor portfolio performance in real time. The four key performance metrics displayed in this view will be Total Market Value, Total Day Change, Market Value by Watchlist (pie chart), and Day Change by Watchlist (bar graph). A sample dashboard view containing three watchlists is shown in Figure 1-1.

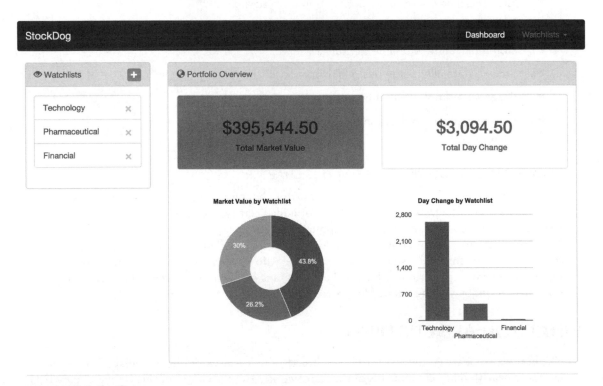

FIGURE 1-1

Each watchlist created in StockDog has its own watchlist view containing an interactive table of stock price information as well as a few basic calculations that assist in monitoring an equity position. Here, users of your application can add new stocks to the selected watchlist, monitor stock price changes in real time (during market hours), and perform in-line editing of the number of shares owned. A sample watchlist view tracking seven stocks is shown in Figure 1-2.

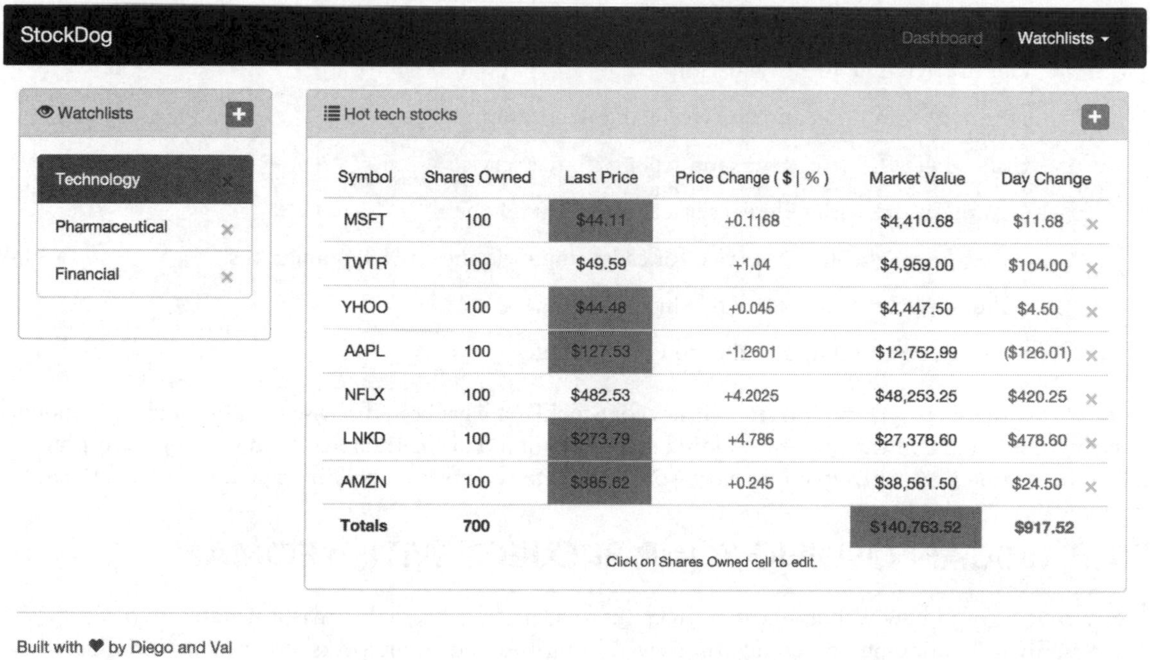

Symbol	Shares Owned	Last Price	Price Change ($ | %)	Market Value	Day Change	
MSFT	100	$44.11	+0.1168	$4,410.68	$11.68	✕
TWTR	100	$49.59	+1.04	$4,959.00	$104.00	✕
YHOO	100	$44.48	+0.045	$4,447.50	$4.50	✕
AAPL	100	$127.53	-1.2601	$12,752.99	($126.01)	✕
NFLX	100	$482.53	+4.2025	$48,253.25	$420.25	✕
LNKD	100	$273.79	+4.786	$27,378.60	$478.60	✕
AMZN	100	$385.62	+0.245	$38,561.50	$24.50	✕
Totals	700			$140,763.52	$917.52	

Click on Shares Owned cell to edit.

Built with ♥ by Diego and Val

FIGURE 1-2

The process of building this application will be described over a series of 12 steps. Each step will focus on developing a key feature of StockDog, with AngularJS components introduced along the way, because they are needed to fulfill requirements defined by the application. Before beginning the construction of StockDog, it is important to establish a high-level overview of what you will be learning.

WHAT YOU WILL LEARN

The step-by-step guide included in this chapter will go beyond basic AngularJS usage. By implementing practical, real-world examples using the main building blocks of this framework, you will be exposed to most of the components provided by AngularJS, which will then be expanded upon in detail in subsequent chapters. It is important to keep this in mind because some of the features required by StockDog will utilize advanced concepts of the framework. In these cases, specific details on how the underlying AngularJS mechanism works will be omitted, but a high-level explanation will always be provided so that you can understand how the component is being utilized in the context of implementing the feature at hand. By the end of this chapter, you will have learned how to do the following:

➤ Structure a multiview single-page application

➤ Create directives, controllers, and services

➤ Configure `$routeProvider` to handle routing between views

➤ Install additional front-end modules

➤ Handle dynamic form validation

➤ Facilitate communication between AngularJS components

➤ Utilize HTML5 `LocalStorage` from within a service

➤ Communicate with external servers using `$http`

➤ Leverage the `$animate` service for cascading style sheet (CSS) animations

➤ Build application assets for production

➤ Deploy your built application to GitHub Pages

Now that the scope and high-level overview for StockDog have been discussed, you should have enough background and context to begin building the application. For those interested in viewing a working demonstration of StockDog immediately, you can find the completed application at `http://stockdog.io`.

STEP 1: SCAFFOLDING YOUR PROJECT WITH YEOMAN

Starting a brand new web application from scratch can be a hassle because it usually involves manually downloading and configuring several libraries and frameworks, creating an intelligent directory structure, and wiring your initial application architecture by hand. However, with major advancements in front-end tooling utilities, this no longer needs to be such a tedious process. Throughout this guide, you will utilize several tools to automate various aspects of your development workflow, but detailed explanations of how these tools work will be saved for discussion in Chapter 2, "Intelligent Workflow and Build Tools." Before getting started with scaffolding your project, you need to verify that you have the following prerequisites installed as part of your development environment:

➤ **Node.js**—`http://nodejs.org/`

➤ **Git**—`http://git-scm.com/downloads`

All the tools used in this chapter were built using Node.js and can be installed from the Node Packaged Modules (NPM) registry using the command-line tool `npm` that is included as part of your Node.js installation. Git is required for one of these tools, so please ensure that you have properly configured both it and Node.js on your system before continuing.

Installing Yeoman

Yeoman is an open source tool with an ecosystem of plug-ins called generators that can be used to scaffold new projects with best practices. It is composed of a robust and opinionated client-side stack that promotes efficient workflows which, coupled with two additional utilities, can help you stay productive and effective as a developer. Following are the tools Yeoman uses to accomplish this task:

➤ **Grunt**—A JavaScript task runner that helps automate repetitive tasks for building and testing your application

➤ **Bower**—A dependency management utility so you no longer have to manually download and manage your front-end scripts

You can find an in-depth discussion of Yeoman, its recommended workflow, and associated tooling in Chapter 2, "Intelligent Workflow and Build Tools." For now, all you need to do to get started is to install Grunt, Bower, and the AngularJS generator by running the following from your command line:

```
npm install -g grunt-cli
npm install -g bower
npm install -g generator-angular@0.9.8
```

> **NOTE** *Specifying the* -g *flag when invoking* npm install *ensures that the desired package will be available globally on your machine. When you're installing* generator-angular, *the official AngularJS generator maintained by the Yeoman team, version 0.9.8 is specified. This should allow you to easily follow along with the rest of the guide, regardless of the current version. For any subsequent projects, it's highly recommended that you update to the latest version. You can do this by simply running* npm install -g generator-angular *once you have completed this chapter.*

Scaffolding Your Project

With all the prerequisite tools installed on your machine, you are ready to get started scaffolding your project. Thankfully, Yeoman makes this process quick and painless. Go ahead and create a new directory named StockDog, and then navigate into it using your command-line application of choice. From within your newly created project directory, run the following from the command line:

```
yo angular StockDog
```

This fires up the AngularJS Yeoman generator, which asks you a few questions regarding how you want to set up your application. The first prompt asks if you want to use Sass with Compass. Although these are both incredibly useful tools for managing your style sheets, their usage is outside the scope of this chapter, so please answer no by typing **n** and then pressing Enter:

```
[?] Would you like to use Sass (with Compass)? (Y/n)
```

The next prompt asks if you want to include Bootstrap, the front-end framework created by Twitter. StockDog makes heavy use of the Hypertext Markup Language (HTML) and CSS assets that

Bootstrap provides, so you need to include this as part of your application. Because the default response to this prompt is yes, as expressed by the capitalized Y, simply pressing the Enter key allows you to continue with Bootstrap included:

```
[?] Would you like to include Bootstrap? (Y/n)
```

The final prompt asks which optional AngularJS modules you want to include in your application. Although you won't necessarily be utilizing all the ones listed in Figure 1-3 for this specific project, it's recommended that you go ahead and include them anyway. You can learn more by visiting https://docs.angularjs.org/api and scrolling down to see what services and directives are made available for each respective module. Simply press the Enter key to continue with all the default modules and have Yeoman begin scaffolding your project, as shown in Figure 1-3.

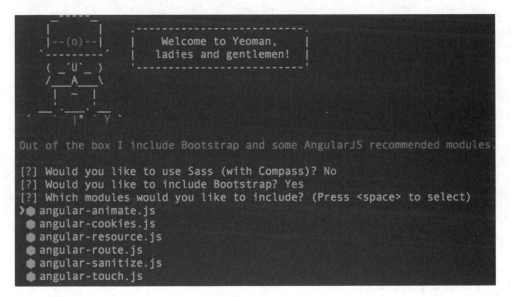

FIGURE 1-3

After pressing Enter on the final prompt and waiting for Yeoman to finish running all the relevant scaffolding tasks, which will take a few brief moments, the foundation for StockDog will be ready for exploration. In the following section, you will take a closer look at the important parts of the directory structure and workflow tasks that Yeoman configured as part of the scaffolding process.

Exploring the Application

Now that your project setup is complete, take a few minutes to explore what the AngularJS Yeoman generator has provided for you. Your project's directory should be structured as follows:

```
StockDog/
├── .bowerrc
├── .editorconfig
├── .gitattributes
```

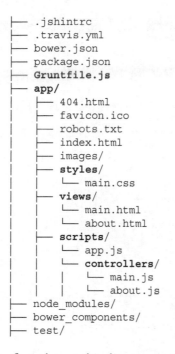

```
├── .jshintrc
├── .travis.yml
├── bower.json
├── package.json
├── Gruntfile.js
├── app/
│   ├── 404.html
│   ├── favicon.ico
│   ├── robots.txt
│   ├── index.html
│   ├── images/
│   ├── styles/
│   │   └── main.css
│   ├── views/
│   │   ├── main.html
│   │   └── about.html
│   ├── scripts/
│   │   └── app.js
│   │   └── controllers/
│   │   │   └── main.js
│   │   │   └── about.js
├── node_modules/
├── bower_components/
├── test/
```

Upon first glance, this directory structure may seem overwhelming, but many of the generated files created by Yeoman are meant to help enforce best practices and can be completely ignored for the remainder of this chapter. The files and directories that you will be focusing on have been bolded for emphasis, so for now you only need to pay attention to those.

> **NOTE** *Depending on how you are viewing your project's directory, your operating system may automatically hide the files prefixed by a dot. These files are meant for configuring various tools such as Git, Bower, and JSHint.*

As you have probably guessed, the bulk of your application is contained inside the app/ directory. Here you can find the main index.html file, which serves as the entry point for your entire application, as well as the styles/, views/, and scripts/ directories, which contain CSS, HTML, and JavaScript files, respectively. Grunfile.js is also of particular interest because it configures several Grunt tasks that support your workflow during the development of StockDog. Go ahead and fire up your terminal application of choice and run the following from the command line:

```
grunt serve
```

This launches the local development server configured by Yeoman during the scaffolding process and opens the current skeleton application within a new tab inside your default browser. At this point, your browser should be pointed at http://localhost:9000/#/ and displaying an application page that looks identical to Figure 1-4.

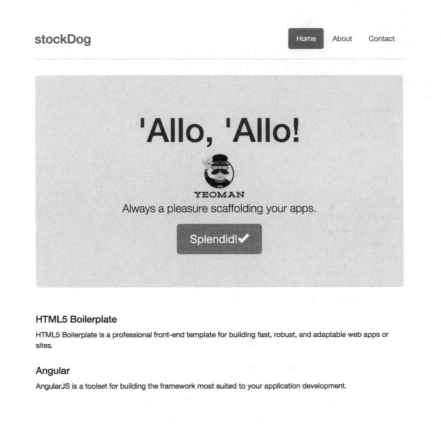

FIGURE 1-4

Congratulations! You have successfully finished scaffolding your project and are almost ready to begin building the first component of the StockDog application. Throughout your development process, be sure to keep the terminal session where you ran the `grunt serve` command open because it is responsible for serving all your application assets for use in your browser. Before moving onto the next section, take a minute to modify the `app/views/main.html` file by removing all its contents. Upon saving your modification, you should notice that your browser tab is refreshed with your changes instantly, which in this case should consist of a mostly empty view. Yeoman set up this automation magic when it configured your `Gruntfile.js` with tasks that watch for modifications in your application's files and refresh your browser accordingly. This functionality alone will prove to be quite helpful as you begin building components of the StockDog application.

Cleaning Up

So far in this chapter, you have seen how to use Yeoman to scaffold a new project from scratch, explored the generated project structure, and gotten a glimpse of how the provided workflow can help you stay productive during development. The last thing you need to do before moving onto the next step of this guide is to delete a few generated files that StockDog won't need and clean up any associated references. Please locate and delete the following files from your project:

```
app/views/main.html
app/views/about.html
```

```
app/scripts/controllers/main.js
app/scripts/controllers/about.js
```

Next, remove the routes Yeoman created by opening the app/scripts/app.js file and deleting the two .when() configurations of the $routeProvider. You can accomplish this by removing the following lines of code:

```
.when('/', {
  templateUrl: 'views/main.html',
  controller: 'MainCtrl'
})
.when('/about', {
  templateUrl: 'views/about.html',
  controller: 'AboutCtrl'
})
```

Finally, remove the references to the previously deleted main.js and about.js controller scripts by deleting the following lines from within the app/index.html file:

```
<script src="scripts/controllers/main.js"></script>
<script src="scripts/controllers/about.js"></script>
```

With these modifications of the generated skeleton application complete, you are now ready to begin building the Watchlist component of StockDog. To access the completed code for this step of the guide in its entirety, please refer to the step-1 directory inside the companion code for this chapter or check out the corresponding tag of the GitHub repository.

STEP 2: CREATING WATCHLISTS

In this section, you will be implementing stock watchlists, the first major component of the StockDog application. As previously mentioned, a watchlist is simply an arbitrary grouping of desired stocks that are to be tracked for analytical purposes. Users of your application will create new watchlists in StockDog by filling out a small form, presented inside a modal, which prompts them for a name and brief description to identify the watchlist. All watchlists registered with the application have their data saved client-side in the browser using HTML5 LocalStorage. Finally, watchlists will be presented by name within a small panel in the user interface. Armed with a high-level understanding of the component's desired functionality, you will now learn how to implement watchlists using AngularJS.

The Application Module

The main entry point for all AngularJS applications is the top-level app module. So what exactly is a module? As mentioned in the official documentation, you can think of a module as a container for the different parts of your application. Although most applications have a main method that instantiates and wires together various components, AngularJS modules declaratively specify how your components should be bootstrapped. Some advantages to this approach are that modules can be loaded asynchronously in any order, and code readability and reusability are enhanced. The main application module is defined by invoking the .module() function, which accepts a name and array of dependencies, located inside the `app/scripts/app.js` file. Make note of the module name, which in this case should be `stockDogApp`, because you will be referencing it shortly. For those who have used RequireJS in the past, this method of declaring module dependencies should look familiar.

Installing Module Dependencies

Currently, the only modules your application depends on should be `ngAnimate`, `ngCookies`, `ngResource`, `ngRoute`, `ngSanitize`, and `ngTouch`, all of which Yeoman installed based on your response to the third prompt of the initial scaffolding process. Later in this section, you will be using the `$modal` service exposed by AngularStrap, a third-party module containing native AngularJS bindings for various components provided by the Bootstrap framework. You can learn more about AngularStrap by visiting its documentation site located at http://mgcrea .github.io/angular-strap/. Because the workflow set up by Yeoman uses Bower for managing front-end scripts, installing AngularStrap is as simple as running the following from your command line:

```
bower install angular-strap#v2.1.0 –save
```

This downloads the AngularStrap library and saves it as a dependency inside your `bower.json` file. If you have left your application server running, which was launched using `grunt serve`, Grunt will have seen the modification to `bower.json` and automatically updated your `index.html` file to reference the CSS and JavaScript files that AngularStrap provides. Not bad for a simple one-line command! Now all that is left is to register the AngularStrap module, which is named `mgcrea .ngStrap`, as a dependency for your `stockDogApp` module by adding it to the array of dependencies, as shown in Listing 1-1.

LISTING 1-1: app/scripts/app.js

```
angular
  .module('stockDogApp', [
    'ngAnimate',
    'ngCookies',
    'ngResource',
    'ngRoute',
    'ngSanitize',
    'ngTouch',
    'mgcrea.ngStrap'
  ]);
```

> **NOTE** *Another commonly used AngularJS companion library that exposes directives for various Bootstrap components is UI Bootstrap, a project that the AngularUI organization maintains. To learn more about UI Bootstrap, please visit the documentation site located at* http://angular-ui.github.io/ bootstrap/.

Bootstrapping the Application

Now that you have seen how to define an application module and register dependencies, the next and final step in bootstrapping StockDog is to reference the `stockDogApp` module from within your HTML. Conveniently enough, Yeoman has already done this for you. Take a look inside your app/ index.html file; on line 19, you should see the following code:

```
<body ng-app="stockDogApp">
```

The `ng-app` attribute that has been attached to the page's `<body>` tag is an AngularJS directive that flags the HTML element, which should be considered the root of your application. Directives will be defined shortly, but for now, the takeaway is that to bootstrap your AngularJS application module, you must add the `ng-app` attribute to your application's HTML. Also worth mentioning is that because ng-app is an element attribute, you have the freedom to move it around and decide whether the entire HTML page or only a portion of it should be treated as the Angular application. With the bootstrapping of your application using the `stockDogApp` module out of the way, you will now be exposed to AngularJS services, another crucial component of the framework.

The Watchlist Service

As defined in the AngularJS documentation, services are substitutable objects that are wired together using dependency injection. Services provide a great way to organize and share encapsulated code across your application. It is worth mentioning that AngularJS services are lazily instantiated singletons, meaning that they are only instantiated when an application component depends on it, with each dependent component receiving a single instance reference generated by the service factory. For the purpose of building out the watchlists functionality for StockDog, you will be creating a custom service that handles reading and writing the watchlists model to HTML5 LocalStorage. To get started, run the following from your command line:

```
yo angular:service Watchlist-Service
```

This uses the AngularJS Yeoman generator's packaged subgenerator for scaffolding out a skeleton service contained within the newly created watchlist-service.js file, which is located inside the app/ scripts/services directory. In addition, Yeoman adds a reference to this newly created script, which can be seen by the addition of the following line of code at the bottom of your app/index.html file:

```
<script src="scripts/services/watchlist-service.js"></script>
```

Now that you have quickly wired up an entry point for your new service, you need to install Lodash, a utility library that offers functional programming helpers for JavaScript, which will be used throughout the remainder of this chapter. Use Bower to install Lodash by running the following from your command line:

```
bower install lodash --save
```

Lodash was initially a fork of the Underscore.js project but has since evolved to become a highly configurable and performant library loaded with a plethora of additional helpers. The WatchlistService implementation, which uses a couple of Lodash methods, is shown in Listing 1-2.

LISTING 1-2: app/scripts/services/watchlist-service.js

```
'use strict';

angular.module('stockDogApp')
  .service('WatchlistService', function WatchlistService() {
    // [1] Helper: Load watchlists from localStorage
    var loadModel = function () {
      var model = {
        watchlists: localStorage['StockDog.watchlists'] ?
          JSON.parse(localStorage['StockDog.watchlists']) : [],
        nextId: localStorage['StockDog.nextId'] ?
          parseInt(localStorage['StockDog.nextId']) : 0
      };
      return model;
    };

    // [2] Helper: Save watchlists to localStorage
    var saveModel = function () {
      localStorage['StockDog.watchlists'] = JSON.stringify(Model.watchlists);
      localStorage['StockDog.nextId'] = Model.nextId;
    };

    // [3] Helper: Use lodash to find a watchlist with given ID
    var findById = function (listId) {
      return _.find(Model.watchlists, function (watchlist) {
        return watchlist.id === parseInt(listId);
      });
    };

    // [4] Return all watchlists or find by given ID
    this.query = function (listId) {
      if (listId) {
        return findById(listId);
      } else {
        return Model.watchlists;
      }
    };

    // [5] Save a new watchlist to watchlists model
    this.save = function (watchlist) {
      watchlist.id = Model.nextId++;
      Model.watchlists.push(watchlist);
      saveModel();
    };

    // [6] Remove given watchlist from watchlists model
    this.remove = function (watchlist) {
      _.remove(Model.watchlists, function (list) {
        return list.id === watchlist.id;
      });
      saveModel();
    };

    // [7] Initialize Model for this singleton service
```

```
    var Model = loadModel();
});
```

The first thing you should notice is the invocation of the `.service()` method on the `stockDogApp` module, which registers this service with the top-level AngularJS application. This allows your service to be referenced elsewhere by injecting `WatchlistService` into the desired component implementation function. The `loadModel()` helper [1] requests the data stored in the browser's LocalStorage using keys that are namespaced under `StockDog` to avoid potential collisions. The `watchlists` value retrieved from `localStorage` is an array, whereas `nextId` is simply an integer used to uniquely identify each watchlist. The ternary operator guarantees that the initial value of both these variables is properly set and correctly parsed. The `saveModel()` helper [2] simply needs to stringify the `watchlists` array before persisting its contents to `localStorage`. Another internal helper function, `findById()` [3], uses Lodash to find a watchlist by a given ID inside the aforementioned array.

With these internal helpers out of the way, you should now notice that the remaining functions are attached directly to the service instance by using the keyword `this`. Although using `this` can be error prone and is not always the best approach, in this case it is quite alright because Angular instantiates a singleton by calling `new` on the function supplied to `.service()`. The service `.query()` function [4] returns all watchlists in the model unless a `listId` is specified. The `.save()` function [5] increments `nextId` and pushes a new watchlist onto the watchlists array before delegating to the `saveModel()` helper. Finally, `.remove()` uses a Lodash method to accomplish the exact opposite [6]. To complete this service, a local `Model` variable is initialized using the `loadModel()` helper. At this point, your `WatchlistService` is ready to be wired up from within an AngularJS directive, which you will be creating in the following section.

> **NOTE** *If up until this point you have left your local development server running, Grunt should be reporting warnings that* `'_'` *is* not defined. *This is because Lodash attaches itself to the global scope via an underscore, but the process in charge of linting your JavaScript files (checking them for errors) is not aware of this fact. Adding* `"_":` false *to the* globals *object located at the bottom of your* .jshintrc *file makes these warnings go away.*

The Watchlist-Panel Directive

By now, you might have already heard about AngularJS directives and how versatile they can be if used correctly. So what exactly is a directive? As defined in the official documentation, *directives* are markers on a Document Object Model (DOM) element (such as an attribute, element name, comment, or CSS class) that tell AngularJS's HTML compiler (`$compile`) to attach a specified behavior to, or even transform, the DOM element and its children. You will take a deeper look at how directives work in Chapter 5, "Directives." For now, all you need to know is that not only can you create your own custom directives, but AngularJS also comes with a set of built-in directives ready for use, like `ng-app`, `ng-view`, and `ng-repeat`, which are all prefixed by `ng`. For the `StockDog` application, all your custom directives are prefixed by `stk` so they are easily identifiable. You can use Yeoman's directive subgenerator to scaffold and wire up a skeleton directive by running the following from your command line:

```
yo angular:directive stk-Watchlist-Panel
```

This creates the `stk-watchlist-panel.js` file inside the `app/scripts/directives` directory and automatically adds a reference to the newly created script inside your `index.html` file. The implementation of this directive is shown in Listing 1-3.

LISTING 1-3: app/scripts/directives/stk-watchlist-panel.js

```javascript
'use strict';

angular.module('stockDogApp')
  // [1] Register directive and inject dependencies
  .directive('stkWatchlistPanel', function ($location, $modal, WatchlistService) {
    return {
      templateUrl: 'views/templates/watchlist-panel.html',
      restrict: 'E',
      scope: {},
      link: function ($scope) {
        // [2] Initialize variables
        $scope.watchlist = {};
        var addListModal = $modal({
          scope: $scope,
          template: 'views/templates/addlist-modal.html',
          show: false
        });

        // [3] Bind model from service to this scope
        $scope.watchlists = WatchlistService.query();

        // [4] Display addlist modal
        $scope.showModal = function () {
          addListModal.$promise.then(addListModal.show);
        };

        // [5] Create a new list from fields in modal
        $scope.createList = function () {
          WatchlistService.save($scope.watchlist);
          addListModal.hide();
          $scope.watchlist = {};
        };

        // [6] Delete desired list and redirect to home
        $scope.deleteList = function (list) {
          WatchlistService.remove(list);
          $location.path('/');
        };
      }
    };
  });
```

The .directive() method handles registering the stkWatchlistPanel directive with the stockDogApp module [1]. This example illustrates the use of Angular's dependency injection mechanism, which is as simple as specifying parameters to the directive's implementation function. Note that the previously created WatchlistService has been injected as a dependency, along with the $location and $modal services, because it will be needed to complete the directive's implementation. The implementation function itself returns an object containing configuration options and a link() function. Inside this function is where the directive's scope variables are initialized [2], which include creating a modal using AngularStrap's $modal service. The .query() method of the WatchlistService is invoked to bind the service's model to the directive's scope [3]. Handler functions are then attached to the $scope and provide functionality for showing the modal [4], creating a new watchlist from the modal's fields [5], and deleting a watchlist [6]. The implementations of these handler functions are straightforward and use the injected services.

The configuration options for the stkWatchlistPanel directive modify its behavior by restricting it for use as an element via restrict: 'E' and isolating its scope so that anything attached to the $scope variable is available only within the context of this directive. The templateUrl option can reference a file that Angular loads and renders into the DOM. For this application, you will be storing templates inside the app/views/templates directory, so go ahead and create that now. The watchlist-panel.html template needed by this directive is shown in Listing 1-4.

LISTING 1-4: app/views/templates/watchlist-panel.html

```html
<div class="panel panel-info">
  <div class="panel-heading">
    <span class="glyphicon glyphicon-eye-open"></span>
    Watchlists
    <!--[1] Invoke showModal() handler on click -->
    <button type="button"
      class="btn btn-success btn-xs pull-right"
      ng-click="showModal()">
      <span class="glyphicon glyphicon-plus"></span>
    </button>
  </div>
  <div class="panel-body">
    <!-- [2] Show help text if no watchlists exist -->
    <div ng-if="!watchlists.length" class="text-center">
      Use <span class="glyphicon glyphicon-plus"></span> to create a list
    </div>
    <div class="list-group">
      <!-- [3] Repeat over each list in watchlists and create link -->
      <a class="list-group-item"
        ng-repeat="list in watchlists track by $index">
        {{list.name}}
        <!-- [4] Delete this list by invoking deleteList() handler -->
        <button type="button" class="close"
          ng-click="deleteList(list)"> &times;
        </button>
      </a>
    </div>
  </div>
</div>
```

> **NOTE** *Upon saving this HTML file, you may have noticed that your browser did not automatically refresh with the changes. That is because the current Grunt workflow is only watching for changes to HTML files in the top-level* app/views *directory. To force Grunt to recursively watch for modifications of any HTML files inside of* app/views, *change the regular expression on line 59 of your* Gruntfile.js *to the following:*
>
>   '<%= yeoman.app %>/**/*.html',

The watchlist-panel.html template makes heavy use of the classes and icons provided by the Bootstrap framework to create a simple, yet polished, interface. The built-in AngularJS ng-click directive is used to invoke the showModal() handler when the plus button is clicked [1]. The ng-if directive conditionally inserts or removes a DOM element based on the evaluation of an expression, which in this case displays instruction text when the watchlists array is empty [2]. To iterate over the watchlists array, ng-repeat is used with the track by $index syntax so that Angular doesn't complain if the array contains identical objects [3]. Worth mentioning is the fact that because ng-repeat is attached to an HTML <a> tag, a unique link is created for each object in the array. The double curly braces, {{ }}, used to reference the current list's name, are called a *binding*, while list.name itself is called an *expression*. The binding tells Angular that it should evaluate the expression and insert the result into the DOM in place of the binding. A binding results in efficient continuous updates whenever the result of the expression evaluation changes. Finally, the deleteList() handler is wired into the interface via another button, connected once again using the ng-click directive [4].

Basic Form Validation

The final step in completing the implementation of the stkWatchlistPanel directive is to build the form that allows users to create new watchlists. If you remember, inside the directive's link() function, the addListModal variable was initialized using the $modal service exposed by the AngularStrap module. The $modal service accepts a template option, which renders the desired HTML inside a Bootstrap modal. Create a new file inside the app/views/templates/ directory named addlist-modal.html. The implementation of this template is shown in Listing 1-5.

LISTING 1-5: app/views/templates/addlist-modal.html

```
<div class="modal" tabindex="-1" role="dialog">
  <div class="modal-dialog">
    <div class="modal-content">
      <div class="modal-header">
        <!-- [1] Invoke $modal.$hide() on click -->
        <button type="button" class="close"
          ng-click="$hide()"> &times;
        </button>
        <h4 class="modal-title">Create New Watchlist</h4>
      </div>
```

```html
<!-- [2] Name this form for validation purposes -->
<form role="form" id="add-list" name="listForm">
  <div class="modal-body">
    <div class="form-group">
      <label for="list-name">Name</label>
      <!-- [3] Bind input to watchlist.name -->
      <input type="text"
        class="form-control"
        id="list-name"
        placeholder="Name this watchlist"
        ng-model="watchlist.name"
        required>
    </div>
    <div class="form-group">
      <label for="list-description">Brief Description</label>
      <!-- [4] Bind input to watchlist.description -->
      <input type="text"
        class="form-control"
        id="list-description"
        maxlength="40"
        placeholder="Describe this watchlist"
        ng-model="watchlist.description"
        required>
    </div>
  </div>
  <div class="modal-footer">
    <!-- [5] Create list on click, but disable if form is invalid -->
    <button type="submit"
      class="btn btn-success"
      ng-click="createList()"
      ng-disabled="!listForm.$valid">Create</button>
    <button type="button"
      class="btn btn-danger"
      ng-click="$hide()">Cancel</button>
  </div>
</form>
    </div>
  </div>
</div>
```

The first thing you should notice with this template is that not only does it reference the handler functions attached to the stkWatchlistPanel directive's scope, it also leverages the $hide() method exposed by the $modal service [1]. Because inputs are required to gather the information necessary to create a new watchlist, an HTML <form> is used [2]. Pay particular attention to the name="listForm" attribute because this is how you reference the form to check its validity. The two <input> tags are augmented with the ng-model directive, which binds the respective input values to the $scope.watchlist variable ([3] & [4]) initialized in the directive's link() function. The HTML required attribute is also used for both inputs because you want to ensure the user specifies both a name and a description before creating a new watchlist. Finally, the directive's createList() handler is invoked when the Create button is clicked, but only when the form is valid. The built-in ng-disabled directive disables or enables the button based on the result of evaluating the !listForm.$valid expression.

Using the Directive

Now that you have completed creating the `stkWatchlistPanel` directive and its associated templates, you will see how easy it is to reference it inside your HTML. Open the `app/index.html` file and insert the following code before the `<div>` tag marked with the `footer` class:

```
<stk-watchlist-panel></stk-watchlist-panel>
```

At this point, you may be wondering why this directive was used as an HTML element tag instead of an attribute. If you remember, the `stkWatchlistPanel` directive was created with the `restrict` configuration property set to `E`, which meant that the directive was to be used as an HTML element. It may also initially seem strange that, although the directive was registered using `camelCase`, it was referenced using `spinal-case` inside the HTML. This is because HTML is case insensitive, so Angular normalizes your directive's name using this convention. With the preceding modification to your `index.html` file saved, Grunt automatically triggers a browser refresh; your application should look identical to the screenshot shown in Figure 1-5.

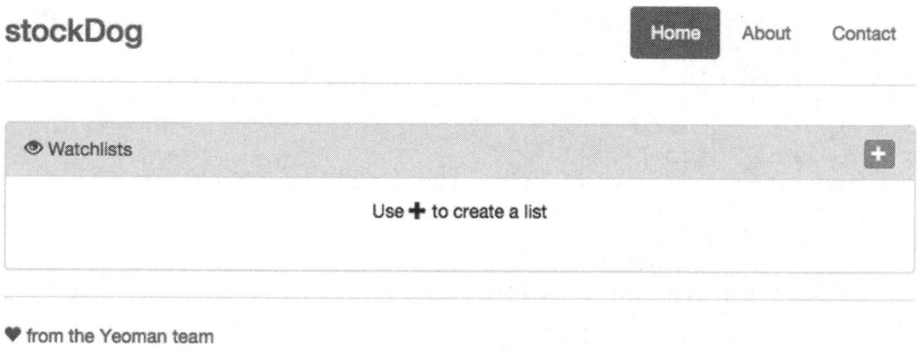

FIGURE 1-5

Clicking the green plus button inside the watchlist panel should launch the Bootstrap modal containing the watchlist creation form, as shown in Figure 1-6.

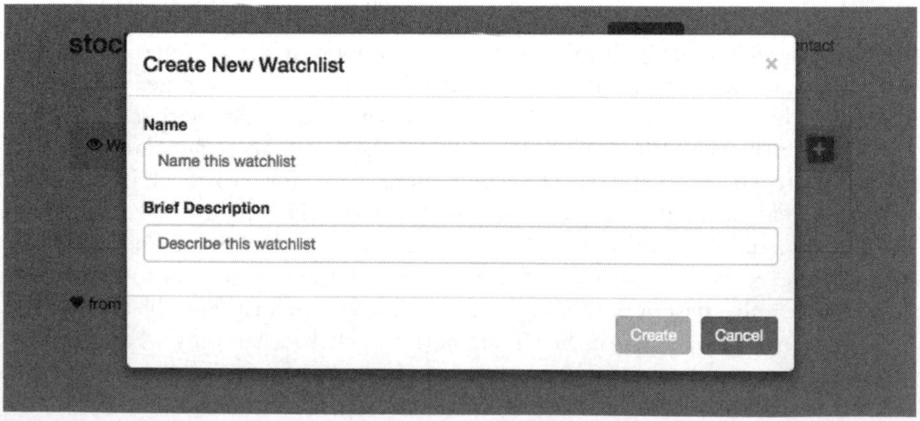

FIGURE 1-6

Congratulations! You have successfully finished implementing the watchlists feature of the StockDog application. In doing so, you have seen how to create an AngularJS service that uses HTML5 LocalStorage as well as a directive that manipulates the DOM and wires together several services. Take a minute to enjoy your handiwork thus far by creating a few watchlists, refreshing your browser to confirm that they were indeed persisted to LocalStorage, and then deleting them from the watchlist panel to ensure that everything is working as expected. If you've gotten stuck at any point during this step, take a moment to examine the completed code by referring to the step-2 directory inside the companion code for this chapter or checking out the corresponding tag of the GitHub repository.

STEP 3: CONFIGURING CLIENT-SIDE ROUTING

Client-side routing is a critical component of any single-page application. Thankfully, AngularJS makes the task of mapping URLs to various front-end views extraordinarily simple. In its current state, StockDog does not contain additional HTML views other than the index.html file, which contains an embedded watchlist panel using the stk-watchlist-panel directive. In this section, you will see how the routing mechanism brings together AngularJS controllers and HTML templates to power the two main views of the StockDog application.

The Angular ngRoute Module

During the initial process of scaffolding the StockDog application, Yeoman asked if you wanted to install any supplemental AngularJS modules. One of these was angular-route, which exposes the ngRoute module that can be listed as a dependency for your application. You can verify that this module has been properly installed for StockDog by looking inside the app/scripts/app.js file and locating the reference to ngRoute inside the array of dependencies for the main stockDogApp module definition, as shown here:

```
angular
  .module('stockDogApp', [
    'ngAnimate',
    'ngCookies',
    'ngResource',
    'ngRoute',     // Include angular-route as dependency
    'ngSanitize',
    'ngTouch',
    'mgcrea.ngStrap'
  ])
```

> **NOTE** *Over the course of developing future AngularJS applications, you will undoubtedly be exposed to, and utilize, several AngularJS modules. The AngularJS team officially maintains some of these modules, like most of the ones seen in the code in the "The Angular ngRoute Module" section, with several others being created by the community. It is imperative that when you install a new module, usually via Bower, you also look at its documentation and properly include the corresponding module reference here as a dependency for your application.*

The ngRoute module exposes the $route service and can be configured using the associated $routeProvider, which allows you to declare how your application's routes map to view templates and controllers. Providers are objects that create instances of services and expose configuration APIs that can be used to control the runtime behavior of a service. You will learn more about providers in a Chapter 7, "Services, Factories, and Providers," but for now, the takeaway is that you can use the $routeProvider to define your application routes and implement deep linking, which allows you to utilize the browser's history navigation and bookmark locations within your application.

Adding New Routes

The process of adding a new route to your application consists of four distinct steps:

1. Define a new controller.
2. Create an HTML view template.
3. Call the $routeProvider.when(path, route) method.
4. Include a <script> tag reference inside index.html if the new controller resides within its own JavaScript file.

The fourth step is only required if your project's architecture mirrors that of the StockDog application, where each new AngularJS component resides within its own JavaScript file. Although these four steps are simple enough on their own, when working on large applications with many routes, views, and controllers, it can become a tedious process. Thankfully, the AngularJS Yeoman generator contains a subgenerator that can be used to entirely automate this four-step process. Go ahead and run the following commands from your terminal to scaffold out the AngularJS controllers, HTML templates, and $routeProvider configurations for the dashboard and watchlist views of the StockDog application:

```
yo angular:route dashboard
yo angular:route watchlist --uri=watchlist/:listId
```

With these two simple commands, you have instructed Yeoman to create the dashboard.js and watchlist.js files inside the app/scripts/controllers/ directory. These files define the DashboardCtrl and WatchlistCtrl, respectively, as well as the dashboard.html and watchlist .html views inside the app/views/ directory. Because Yeoman created two new JavaScript files for the desired route controllers, it also took the liberty of inserting the two required <script> tag references at the bottom of your index.html file. You may have noticed that the second command invoked the route subgenerator with a --uri flag. This instructs Yeoman to use an explicitly defined path when configuring the $routeProvider, which in this case was required because each watchlist created within StockDog will have its own unique view, generated from the listId, which will be passed as a route parameter. Looking inside app/scripts/app.js, you should see the following $routeProvider.when() configurations that Yeoman set up:

```
.when('/dashboard', {
  templateUrl: 'views/dashboard.html',
  controller: 'DashboardCtrl'
})
.when('/watchlist/:listId', {
```

```
    templateUrl: 'views/watchlist.html',
    controller: 'WatchlistCtrl'
})
```

Before continuing onto the next section, take a moment to update the path used in the `$routeProvider.otherwise()` function located at the bottom of this file. The `redirectTo` property currently points to `'/'`, but in this case you will want to modify it to point to `'/dashboard'` because that is the main page of the StockDog application.

Using the Routes

With all the required steps accomplished for adding new client-side routes and wiring together the skeleton dashboard and watchlist views, you can now begin linking together the pages within StockDog using the configured routes. Open the `stkwatchlistpanel.js` file containing the directive that renders out the watchlist panel, and inject the AngularJS `$routeParams` service as a dependency alongside the current `$location`, `$modal`, and `WatchlistService` dependencies. The call to `.directive()` should now look something like this:

```
.directive('stkWatchlistPanel',
    function ($location, $modal, $routeParams, WatchlistService) {
```

Next, you will be adding a new `$scope` variable that will keep track of the current watchlist being displayed, as well as a `gotoList()` function that will send users to the desired watchlist view. You can accomplish this by adding the following code to the directive's implementation:

```
$scope.currentList = $routeParams.listId;
$scope.gotoList = function (listId) {
    $location.path('watchlist/' + listId);
};
```

Once again, the `$location` service is used to route the user to the desired watchlist view, which includes the `listId`. At this point, you might be asking yourself where this `listId` that is passed into the `gotoList()` function is coming from. If you remember, when you first created the `watchlist-panel.html` template view, you used the built-in `ng-repeat` directive to iterate over all the watchlists fetched from the `WatchlistService`. To wire this function into the directive's template, you need to add the `ng-click` directive to the `<a>` tag, which contains a call to the `gotoList()` function that will be evaluated whenever the DOM element is clicked. Because the `stkWatchlistPanel` is used on both the main dashboard and individual watchlist views, you should also go ahead and add an `ng-class` directive to the same element, which can be used to add the `active` class from Bootstrap to the `<a>` tag for the list that the user is currently viewing. The modifications to the `watchlist-panel.html` file located inside the `app/view/templates/` directory are shown here:

```
<a class="list-group-item"
    ng-class="{ active: currentList == list.id }"
    ng-repeat="list in watchlists track by $index"
    ng-click="gotoList(list.id)">
```

Notice that the newly defined `currentList` variable that was attached to the `$scope` is used to evaluate whether the `active` class should be present on the element. In the next section, you

will be laying the foundation structure for the dashboard and watchlist views. Because the
<stk-watchlist-panel> element is used within the context of both views, take a moment to
delete its current reference from within the index.html file.

Template Views

At this point, you might be wondering how AngularJS knows to load the dashboard.html and
watchlist.html views specified in the $routeProvider's template option for each configured
route. The key component behind this functionality is the ngView directive, which was included
in the index.html file when you initially scaffolded your project with Yeoman. This directive
requires the ngRoute module to be installed to function and handles inserting the view template
defined by the $route service into the layout template, which in this case is the index.html file. It
is important to note that the route's template is inserted in the exact DOM location where the
<ng-view> element resides.

In its current state, the StockDog application is devoid of any useful functionality, so go ahead
and modify your generated dashboard.html and watchlist.html files to resemble those shown in
Listing 1-6 and Listing 1-7, respectively.

LISTING 1-6: app/views/dashboard.html

```
<div class="row">
  <!-- Left Column -->
  <div class="col-md-3">
    <stk-watchlist-panel></stk-watchlist-panel>
  </div>

  <!-- Right Column -->
  <div class="col-md-9">
    <div class="panel panel-info">
      <div class="panel-heading">
        <span class="glyphicon glyphicon-globe"></span>
        Portfolio Overview
      </div>
      <div class="panel-body">
      </div>
    </div>
  </div>
</div>
```

LISTING 1-7: app/views/watchlist.html

```
<div class="row">
  <!-- Left Column -->
  <div class="col-md-3">
    <stk-watchlist-panel></stk-watchlist-panel>
  </div>

  <!-- Right Column -->
```

```
    <div class="col-md-9">
    </div>
  </div>
```

Both the `dashboard.html` and `watchlist.html` templates use Bootstrap's grid system to create two distinct columns, with the `<stk-watchlist-panel>` being included in the left column of each view. Now that the modifications to both these files are complete, go ahead and navigate to the Dashboard view in your browser by visiting `http://localhost:9000/#/dashboard`. For testing purposes, take a moment to add a new watchlist to the panel and then click on the newly created list item. The `ngClick` directive you added should evaluate the `gotoList()` function of the `stkWatchlistPanel` directive, which will result in your application routing you to a uniquely named view for that watchlist. You should now see something along the lines of `http://localhost:9000/#/watchlist/1` inside your browser's URL bar. Pressing the Back button of your browser should take you back to the main Dashboard view.

Congratulations! You have successfully implemented the client-side routing for both views of the StockDog application. In doing so, you have seen how the `ngRoute` module can be used to implement deep linking inside an AngularJS application, as well as learning how the `ngView` directive can be used to load route templates. If you've gotten stuck at any point during this step, take a moment to examine the completed code by referring to the `step-3` directory inside the companion code for this chapter or checking out the corresponding tag of the GitHub repository.

STEP 4: CREATING A NAVIGATION BAR

With client-side routing out of the way, you can now take a few moments to spruce up the navigation bar of the StockDog application by using native Bootstrap components. In its current state, your application's navigation bar has yet to be modified from what was initially scaffolded for you by the Yeoman generator. In this section, you will replace this default navigation bar with one that is more fluid and allows for appropriate navigation between the two main views of the StockDog application.

Updating the HTML

First, you need to delete a few lines of code from your current `app/index.html` file. Go ahead and open that file and start by deleting the line containing the opening `<body ng-app="stockDogApp">` tag, located around line 19, and only stop right before the HTML comment containing `<!-- build:js(.) scripts/vendor.js -->`, located around line 61. If you have been following along with the example code, you should have deleted around 42 lines from this file.

> **NOTE** *It is critically important that you do not delete the HTML comment containing* `<!-- build:js(.) scripts/vendor.js -->` *because this inline comment is used by the build system, discussed later in this chapter, to optimize the final distributable version of your application.*

Now that you have deleted the necessary lines from your application's `index.html` file, go ahead and insert the markup shown next in place of the lines that were just deleted:

```html
<!-- [1] Load MainCtrl -->
<body ng-app="stockDogApp" ng-controller="MainCtrl">
  <nav class="navbar navbar-inverse" role="navigation" ng-cloak>
    <div class="container-fluid">
      <div class="navbar-header">
        <button type="button" class="navbar-toggle"
          data-toggle="collapse" data-target="#main-nav">
          <span class="icon-bar"></span>
          <span class="icon-bar"></span>
          <span class="icon-bar"></span>
        </button>
        <a class="navbar-brand" href="/">Stock Dog</a>
      </div>

      <!-- Collect the nav links and other content for toggling -->
      <div class="collapse navbar-collapse" id="main-nav">
        <ul class="nav navbar-nav navbar-right">
          <!-- [2] Add active class to necessary item -->
          <li ng-class="{active: activeView === 'dashboard'}">
            <a href="/">Dashboard</a>
          </li>
          <li ng-class="{active: activeView === 'watchlist'}"
            class="dropdown">
            <a class="dropdown-toggle" data-toggle="dropdown">
              Watchlists <b class="caret"></b>
            </a>
            <ul class="dropdown-menu">
              <li ng-if="!watchlists.length" class="dropdown-header">
                No lists found
              </li>
              <!-- [3] Create a unique link for each watchlist -->
              <li ng-repeat="list in watchlists track by $index">
                <a href="/#/watchlist/{{list.id}}">{{list.name}}</a>
              </li>
            </ul>
          </li>
        </ul>
      </div><!-- /.navbar-collapse -->
    </div><!-- /.container-fluid -->
  </nav>

  <!-- Main container -->
  <div class="container-fluid" id="main">
    <div ng-view=""></div>

    <div class="footer">
      <p>Built with <span class="glyphicon glyphicon-heart"></span></p>
    </div>
  </div>
```

The first difference you should notice in this block of HTML is the use of the `ng-controller` directive on the `body` tag [1]. In the previous section, you discovered how the `ngRoute` module could be used to load the desired controllers and views for a specific route. However, in this case, you want to force AngularJS to load the MainCtrl controller because it will be used for logic that should be applied to your application regardless of the current evaluated route. This approach demonstrates a simple way to encapsulate application-wide logic into a single controller.

Another addition to this markup that is worth mentioning is the use of the ng-class directive [2] to add the Bootstrap active class to the navigation menu links, depending on the value of the activeView scope variable. The final AngularJS component used in this markup for the navigation bar is the ng-repeat directive. It is used here [3] to create a unique <li> for each list in the watchlist scope variable. This example shows how nav links can be dynamically generated based on data that an AngularJS controller provides. In its current state, your application should be displaying an error in your browser's console because the MainCtrl has yet to be defined. This issue will be resolved in the next section when you create and implement the MainCtrl.

Creating MainCtrl

You have seen how to use the Yeoman subgenerators to scaffold out new services, directives, and routes. Now you will be following the same process to have Yeoman scaffold out a new AngularJS controller. To accomplish this, go ahead and run the following from your command line:

```
yo angular:controller Main
```

This instructs Yeoman to create a new controller named MainCtrl inside the app/scripts/controllers/main.js file and add the appropriate <script> tag reference to your app/index .html file. Open this newly created file and replace its entire contents with the code shown in Listing 1-8.

LISTING 1-8: app/scripts/controllers/main.js

```
'use strict';

angular.module('stockDogApp')
  .controller('MainCtrl', function ($scope, $location, WatchlistService) {
    // [1] Populate watchlists for dynamic nav links
    $scope.watchlists = WatchlistService.query();

    // [2] Using the $location.path() function as a $watch expression
    $scope.$watch(function () {
      return $location.path();
    }, function (path) {
      if (_.contains(path, 'watchlist')) {
        $scope.activeView = 'watchlist';
      } else {
        $scope.activeView = 'dashboard';
      }
    });
  });
```

The `MainCtrl` uses both the `$location` service, provided by AngularJS, as well as the `WatchlistService`, created earlier in this chapter. The `WatchlistService` is used to populate the `$scope.watchlist` variable [1], which is used in the markup to dynamically create multiple drop-down links for the top-level Watchlists navigation item. For this controller to figure out the current application route, the `$location` service is used in conjunction with the `$scope.watch()` function so that every time the value returned from the `$location.path()` function changes, your callback function can appropriately update the `$scope.activeView` variable (using the `_.contains()` function from Lodash), which is used to add an `active` class to the navigation bar. The `$scope.$watch()` function is covered in more detail later in this book. For now, all you need to know is that it watches the value returned from the first function for changes and invokes the callback specified as its second argument on each change.

Your application's navigation bar should now be fully functional. See Figure 1-7. For testing purposes, go ahead and create a new watchlist (if you haven't already) and then navigate to it by selecting the appropriate link from the Watchlists drop-down in the nav bar. Then click the Dashboard link to return to the initial view of the StockDog application. If you've gotten stuck at any point during this step, take a moment to examine the completed code by referring to the `step-4` directory inside the companion code for this chapter or checking out the corresponding tag of the GitHub repository.

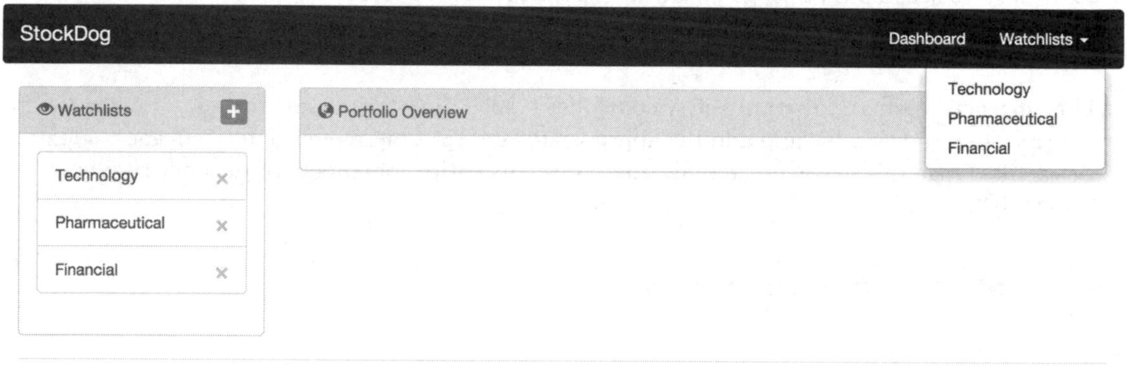

FIGURE 1-7

STEP 5: ADDING STOCKS

The next major piece of functionality that needs to be implemented for StockDog is the ability to add stocks to a watchlist. In a similar fashion to the way users can add a new watchlist to their portfolio, you will be creating a new modal that will be displayed after clicking a specific button on the watchlist view. This modal will allow users to search for companies listed on the NYSE, NASDAQ, and AMEX stock exchanges, and add them, along with a specified number of shares, to part of a desired watchlist. In this section, you will learn how to leverage the various mechanisms provided by AngularJS to accomplish this task.

Creating the CompanyService

The first order of business is to create a new AngularJS service that will be in charge of fetching a list of companies and relevant data for each of the three major exchanges. Normally, this would be accomplished by communicating with a back-end service of some kind, but for the purposes of this application, a JSON file has been created for your perusal. You can find the companies.json file inside the step-5/app/ directory of the associated companion code, as well as inside the app/ directory of the GitHub repo https://github.com/diegonetto/stock-dog. Once you've downloaded the file, go ahead and save it inside the app/ directory of your local project. Next, run the following from your command line to scaffold out and wire up a new AngularJS service:

```
yo angular: service Company-Service
```

This creates a company-service.js file inside your app/scripts/services directory. The implementation for this service is shown in Listing 1-9. Notice that the $resource service, which creates a resource object that facilitates interaction with RESTful server-side data sources and will be covered in detail in a Chapter 8, "Server Communication," is injected as a dependency. The takeaway at this point is that the $resource service is taking care of fetching the companies.json file from your local file system and returning an object that will allow you to query against the provided list of publicly traded companies.

LISTING 1-9: app/scripts/services/company.js

```
'use strict';

angular.module('stockDogApp')
  .service('CompanyService', function CompanyService($resource) {
    return $resource('companies.json');
  });
```

You will be making use of this newly created CompanyService shortly, but before continuing onto the next section, take a moment to open the Gruntfile.js located in your project's root directory and find the src property of the copy task, located around line 300. You will need to add json to the src array so that the companies.json file will be copied into the built distributable when you are preparing your application for production later in this chapter. The modification should leave the first entry of the src array looking like this:

```
'*.{ico,png,txt,json}',
```

Creating the AddStock Modal

With the CompanyService complete, it is time to create a new view that will serve as the modal for allowing your users to add new stocks to the currently selected watchlist. Go ahead and create a new file named addstock-modal.html inside your app/views/templates/ directory. You can see the implementation for this view in Listing 1-10.

LISTING 1-10: app/views/templates/addstock-modal.html

```
<div class="modal" tabindex="-1" role="dialog">
  <div class="modal-dialog">
    <div class="modal-content">
      <div class="modal-header">
        <button type="button" class="close" ng-click="$hide()">&times;</button>
        <h4 class="modal-title">Add New Stock</h4>
      </div>

      <form role="form" id="add-stock" name="stockForm">
        <div class="modal-body">
          <div class="form-group">
            <label for="stock-symbol">Symbol</label>
            // [1] Use ng-options with label syntax and bs-typeahead directive
            <input type="text"
              class="form-control"
              id="stock-symbol"
              placeholder="Stock Symbol"
              ng-model="newStock.company"
              ng-options="company as company.label for company in companies"
              bs-typeahead
              required>
          </div>
          // [2] Only accept numbers for shares owned
          <div class="form-group">
            <label for="stock-shares">Shares Owned</label>
            <input type="number"
              class="form-control"
              id="stock-shares"
              placeholder="# Shares Owned"
              ng-model="newStock.shares"
              required>
          </div>
        </div>
        <div class="modal-footer">
          <button type="submit"
            class="btn btn-success"
            ng-click="addStock()"
            ng-disabled="!stockForm.$valid">Add</button>
          <button type="button"
            class="btn btn-danger"
            ng-click="$hide()">Cancel</button>
        </div>
      </form>

    </div>
  </div>
</div>
```

This should look fairly similar to the previous modal for adding new watchlists to StockDog. The first input [1] uses the bs-typeahead directive from the AngularStrap project, which utilizes the native Angular ng-options directive for providing the data required for the typeahead mechanism to function. The ng-options directive accepts multiple forms of syntax. In this case, you are forcing it to use the `label` property of each company object in the `companies` scope variable, which will be created inside the `WatchlistCtrl` shortly, as the data to be displayed in the typeahead recommendations. The second input [2] simply allows users to specify the number of shares owned of a particular stock.

Updating the WatchlistService

Before continuing on to developing the `WatchlistCtrl` and associated watchlist view, you need to make a few modifications to the existing `WatchlistService`. To abstract the various calculations and interactions between watchlists and their associated stocks, you will be creating two separate objects to be used as models for the required behaviors. Inside the top of the service implementation function of your `watchlist-service.js` file, located inside the `app/scripts/services/` directory, add the following lines of code to create a `StockModel` object with a `save()` function:

```
// Augment Stocks with additional helper functions
var StockModel = {
  save: function () {
    var watchlist = findById(this.listId);
    watchlist.recalculate();
    saveModel();
  }
};
```

Because watchlists are composed of many stocks, you will also need to create a `WatchlistModel` with `addStock()`, `removeStock()`, and `recalculate()` functions, as shown here:

```
// Augment watchlists with additional helper functions
var WatchlistModel = {
  addStock: function (stock) {
    var existingStock = _.find(this.stocks, function (s) {
      return s.company.symbol === stock.company.symbol;
    });
    if (existingStock) {
      existingStock.shares += stock.shares;
    } else {
      _.extend(stock, StockModel);
      this.stocks.push(stock);
    }
    this.recalculate();
    saveModel();
  },
  removeStock: function (stock) {
    _.remove(this.stocks, function (s) {
      return s.company.symbol === stock.company.symbol;
    });
    this.recalculate();
    saveModel();
  },
  recalculate: function () {
    var calcs = _.reduce(this.stocks, function (calcs, stock) {
      calcs.shares += stock.shares;
      calcs.marketValue += stock.marketValue;
      calcs.dayChange += stock.dayChange;
```

```
        return calcs;
      }, { shares: 0, marketValue: 0, dayChange: 0 });

      this.shares = calcs.shares;
      this.marketValue = calcs.marketValue;
      this.dayChange = calcs.dayChange;
    }
  };
```

Finally, the method in which data is serialized and unserialized from `LocalStorage` needs to be modified because you will be extending the two previously created models to create the proper data structure in memory required to power the application. Modify the existing `loadModel()` and `this.save()` functions to look like those shown here:

```
// Helper: Load watchlists from localStorage
var loadModel = function () {
  var model = {
    watchlists: localStorage['StockDog.watchlists'] ?
      JSON.parse(localStorage['StockDog.watchlists']) : [],
    nextId: localStorage['StockDog.nextId'] ?
      parseInt(localStorage['StockDog.nextId']) : 0
  };
  _.each(model.watchlists, function (watchlist) {
    _.extend(watchlist, WatchlistModel);
    _.each(watchlist.stocks, function (stock) {
      _.extend(stock, StockModel);
    });
  });
  return model;
};

// Save a new watchlist to watchlists model
this.save = function (watchlist) {
  watchlist.id = Model.nextId++;
  watchlist.stocks = [];
  _.extend(watchlist, WatchlistModel);
  Model.watchlists.push(watchlist);
  saveModel();
};
```

Implementing WatchlistCtrl

Next, you will be modifying the current `WatchlistCtrl`, which is still an empty skeleton that was created by Yeoman during the scaffolding process. Open up the `watchlist.js` file, located inside the `app/scripts/controllers/` directory, and modify it to look like Listing 1-11.

LISTING 1-11: app/scripts/controllers/watchlist.js

```
'use strict';

angular.module('stockDogApp')
  .controller('WatchlistCtrl', function ($scope, $routeParams, $modal,
                                 WatchlistService, CompanyService) {
```

```
// [1] Initializations
$scope.companies = CompanyService.query();
$scope.watchlist = WatchlistService.query($routeParams.listId);
$scope.stocks = $scope.watchlist.stocks;
$scope.newStock = {};
var addStockModal = $modal({
  scope: $scope,
  template: 'views/templates/addstock-modal.html',
  show: false
});

// [2] Expose showStockModal to view via $scope
$scope.showStockModal = function () {
  addStockModal.$promise.then(addStockModal.show);
};

// [3] Call the WatchlistModel addStock() function and hide the modal
$scope.addStock = function () {
  $scope.watchlist.addStock({
    listId: $routeParams.listId,
    company: $scope.newStock.company,
    shares: $scope.newStock.shares
  });
  addStockModal.hide();
  $scope.newStock = {};
};
});
```

You should notice that $routeParams, $modal, WatchlistService, and CompanyService are all being injected as dependencies. The CompanyService's query() function, provided by the object returned from using the $resource service as previously mentioned, is invoked to populate the companies scope variable, which will be utilized in the watchlist view momentarily. The rest of the code is straightforward, with the WatchlistService being used to initialize the watchlist scope variable, which is in turn used to retrieve the current watchlist variable using the listId passed along in the route parameters [1]. Next, the modal itself is instantiated, and definitions are made for the [2] showStockModal() and [3] addStock() functions.

Modifying the Watchlist View

Because modifications were made to the way watchlists were saved and loaded, take a moment to delete all current watchlists from your application before proceeding with the updates to the watchlist view markup. Once that is complete, go ahead and modify the existing app/views/watchlist.html file to include a Bootstrap panel where the list of stocks will be displayed. As it stands, this file should only contain one row comprised of two columns, with the left column being comprised of the stk-watchlist-panel directive. Modify the right column of this file to match the HTML markup shown in Listing 1-12.

LISTING 1-12: app/views/watchlist.html

```
<div class="row">
  <!-- Left Column -->
```

continues

LISTING 1-12 *(continued)*

```
<div class="col-md-3">
  <stk-watchlist-panel></stk-watchlist-panel>
</div>

<!-- Right Column -->
<div class="col-md-9">
  <div class="panel panel-info">
    <div class="panel-heading">
      <span class="glyphicon glyphicon-list"></span>
      {{watchlist.description}}
      <button type="button"
        class="btn btn-success btn-xs pull-right"
        ng-click="showStockModal()">
      <span class="glyphicon glyphicon-plus"></span>
    </button>
    </div>
    <div class="panel-body table-responsive">
      <div ng-hide="stocks.length" class="jumbotron">
        <h1>Woof.</h1>
        <p>Looks like you haven't added any stocks to this watchlist yet!</p>
        <p>Do so now by clicking the
          <span class="glyphicon glyphicon-plus"></span> located above.
        </p>
      </div>
      <!--[1] loop over all stocks and display company symbols -->
      <p ng-repeat="stock in stocks">{{stock.company.symbol}}</p>
    </div>
  </div>
</div>
</div>
```

By now, you should be comfortable using the ng-click, ng-hide, and ng-repeat directives, the latter of which is currently being used for simply displaying the stock's company ticker symbol. This will be revisited in a later step when it comes time to build the stock table directives.

At this point, you should be able to add new stocks to a selected watchlist by clicking the green plus button in the panel heading, selecting a stock by searching for its company name or ticker symbol, and clicking the desired typeahead recommendation. See Figure 1-8. If your application is not functioning properly, be sure to check your browser's developer tools console for errors, and take a moment to review the code included in this section. You can refer to the step-5 directory inside the companion code for this chapter or check out the corresponding tag of the GitHub repository.

STEP 6: INTEGRATING WITH YAHOO FINANCE

Now that your StockDog application is able to manage manipulating watchlists and stocks, it is time to begin fetching quote information from an external service provider—in this case Yahoo Finance. In this section, you will create a new AngularJS service that will be responsible for making asynchronous HTTP requests to the Yahoo Finance API and updating the in-memory data structure that powers the application.

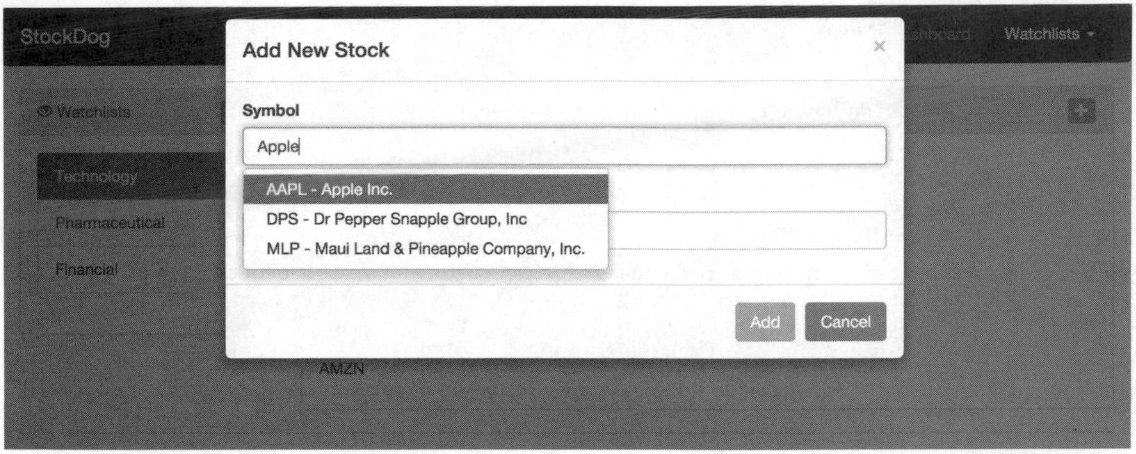

FIGURE 1-8

Creating the QuoteService

To encapsulate the HTTP requests and response parsing into a reusable component, you will be creating a new AngularJS service. Run the following command from your terminal to have Yeoman scaffold your new `QuoteService`:

```
yo angular:service Quote-Service
```

As seen several times in this chapter, this creates a skeleton implementation of, in this case, an AngularJS service named `QuoteService` inside of a newly created `quote-service.js` file located within your `app/scripts/services` directory. You can see the entire implementation for the `QuoteService` in Listing 1-13.

LISTING 1-13: app/scripts/services/quote-service.js

```
'use strict';

angular.module('stockDogApp')
  .service('QuoteService', function ($http, $interval) {
    var stocks = [];
    var BASE = 'http://query.yahooapis.com/v1/public/yql';

    // [1] Handles updating stock model with appropriate data from quote
    var update = function (quotes) {
      console.log(quotes);
      if (quotes.length === stocks.length) {
        _.each(quotes, function (quote, idx) {
          var stock = stocks[idx];
          stock.lastPrice = parseFloat(quote.LastTradePriceOnly);
          stock.change = quote.Change;
          stock.percentChange = quote.ChangeinPercent;
```

continues

LISTING 1-13 *(continued)*

```
          stock.marketValue = stock.shares * stock.lastPrice;
          stock.dayChange = stock.shares * parseFloat(stock.change);
          stock.save();
        });
      }
    };

    // [2] Helper functions for managing which stocks to pull quotes for
    this.register = function (stock) {
      stocks.push(stock);
    };
    this.deregister = function (stock) {
      _.remove(stocks, stock);
    };
    this.clear = function () {
      stocks = [];
    };

    // [3] Main processing function for communicating with Yahoo Finance API
    this.fetch = function () {
      var symbols = _.reduce(stocks, function (symbols, stock) {
        symbols.push(stock.company.symbol);
        return symbols;
      }, []);
      var query = encodeURIComponent('select * from yahoo.finance.quotes ' +
        'where symbol in (\'' + symbols.join(',') + '\')');
      var url = BASE + '?' + 'q=' + query + '&format=json&diagnostics=true' +
        '&env=http://datatables.org/alltables.env';
      $http.jsonp(url + '&callback=JSON_CALLBACK')
        .success(function (data) {
          if (data.query.count) {
            var quotes = data.query.count > 1 ?
              data.query.results.quote : [data.query.results.quote];
            update(quotes);
          }
        })
        .error(function (data) {
          console.log(data);
        });
    };

    // [4] Used to fetch new quote data every 5 seconds
    $interval(this.fetch, 5000);
  });
```

Because the `QuoteService` is in charge of communicating with the Yahoo Finance API, you'll notice that the `$http` service was injected as a dependency. The `$interval` service that was also injected is Angular's wrapper for `window.setInterval`. Internally this service keeps track of an array of stocks for which quote data should be retrieved. The `update()` function [1] handles parsing the response from Yahoo Finance into the required stock model properties. This code also contains helper functions [2] for adding, removing, and clearing the internal array of stocks being tracked. Finally, the fetch() function [3] generates the appropriate Yahoo Finance query URL before invoking the $http service to make an asynchronous request to the desired endpoint. The response from Yahoo is then passed into the update() function for processing as previously described.

Invoking Services from the Console

Because your newly created QuoteService has not been injected and used anywhere in the StockDog application at this time, the easiest way to quickly spot-check this service is by typing a few lines into the console of your browser developer tools. Go ahead and open that now and paste the following lines directly into the browser console:

```
Quote = angular.element(document.body).injector().get('QuoteService')
Watchlist = angular.element(document.body).injector().get('WatchlistService')
Quote.register(Watchlist.query()[0].stocks[0])
```

This grabs a reference to the QuoteService and WatchlistService and then invokes the QuoteService's register() function with the first stock of the first watchlist available. (So make sure you have created at least one watchlist and added at least one stock.) Within five seconds, you should see an array containing a single object. Inspecting that object should show you all the data provided by the Yahoo Finance API for that one particular stock, similar to Figure 1-9.

```
▼ [Object] 🔢
  ▼ 0: Object
      AfterHoursChangeRealtime: "N/A - N/A"
      AnnualizedGain: null
      Ask: "112.87"
      AskRealtime: "112.87"
      AverageDailyVolume: "48785500"
      Bid: "112.80"
      BidRealtime: "112.80"
      BookValue: "19.015"
      Change: "+0.58"
      ChangeFromFiftydayMovingAverage: "+2.263"
      ChangeFromTwoHundreddayMovingAverage: "+8.719"
      ChangeFromYearHigh: "-6.77"
      ChangeFromYearLow: "+42.4729"
      ChangePercentRealtime: "N/A - +0.52%"
      ChangeRealtime: "+0.58"
      Change_PercentChange: "+0.58 - +0.52%"
      ChangeinPercent: "+0.52%"
```

FIGURE 1-9

Now that you have finished creating the QuoteService and verified that it is successfully pulling data from the Yahoo Finance API, you are ready to move onto the next section and display that data in a table on the watchlist view. If your application is not functioning properly, please refer to the step-6 directory inside the companion code for this chapter or check out the corresponding tag of the GitHub repository.

STEP 7: CREATING THE STOCK TABLE

In this section, you will be exposed to a more sophisticated use of AngularJS directives. Specifically, you will see how directives can communicate data between themselves as you build a table for displaying information on a stock's performance.

Creating the StkStockTable Directive

To get started, you will be creating a new directive for the stock table. As you've seen several times, you can do this using the AngularJS Yeoman generator by running the following from your command line:

```
yo angular:directive stk-Stock-Table
```

This creates a `stk-stock-table.js` file inside of `app/scripts/directives` and links the new JavaScript file inside of `index.html`. The implementation of the `stkStockTable` directive is shown in Listing 1-14.

LISTING 1-14: app/scripts/directives/stk-stock-table.js

```
'use strict';

angular.module('stockDogApp')
  .directive('stkStockTable', function () {
    return {
      templateUrl: 'views/templates/stock-table.html',
      restrict: 'E',
      // [1] Isolate scope
      scope: {
        watchlist: '='
      },
      // [2] Create a controller, which serves as an API for this directive
      controller: function ($scope) {
        var rows = [];

        $scope.$watch('showPercent', function (showPercent) {
          if (showPercent) {
            _.each(rows, function (row) {
              row.showPercent = showPercent;
            });
          }
        });

        this.addRow = function (row) {
          rows.push(row);
        };

        this.removeRow = function (row) {
          _.remove(rows, row);
        };
      },

      // [3] Standard link function implementation
```

```
      link: function ($scope) {
        $scope.showPercent = false;
        $scope.removeStock = function (stock) {
          $scope.watchlist.removeStock(stock);
        };
      }
    };
  });
```

The first thing you should notice is that this directive contains an object for its scope property [1]. By isolating the scope of a directive in this way, you can bind an attribute of the directive's DOM element. You will explore this in more detail in Chapter 4, "Data Binding," but for now, know that when you use the stkStockTable directive, you must include an attribute named watchlist and assign it an expression to be evaluated. Also of note in this example is that this directive contains a controller property [2]. This, in a more general sense, is how you expose an API for other directives to use for communication. Because inside the controller property's implementation both the addRow() and removeRow() function are attached to the this object, they will be available for external use. The concept here is that the stkStockTable directive keeps track, internally, of all the rows in the table. This allows it to modify the rows if needed, as is the case, in this example, for toggling the showPercent property of each row's scope. Finally, this directive also includes the link property [3], which is typical for DOM manipulation, and in this case simply initializes the showPercent scope variable and exposes a removeStock() function via the top-level directive scope.

Creating the StkStockRow Directive

Now that the main stkStockTable directive has been created, it's time to create the directive that will be repeated for each table row. Run the following from the command line to create a new stkStockRow directive:

```
yo angular:directive stk-Stock-Row
```

This creates the stk-stock-row.js file inside the app/scripts/directives directory with a skeleton for the stkStockRow directive. The implementation for this directive is shown in Listing 1-15.

LISTING 1-15: app/scripts/directives/stk-stock-row.js

```
'use strict';

angular.module('stockDogApp')
  .directive('stkStockRow', function ($timeout, QuoteService) {
    return {
      // [1] Use as element attribute and require stkStockTable controller
      restrict: 'A',
      require: '^stkStockTable',
      scope: {
        stock: '=',
        isLast: '='
      },
      // [2] The required controller will be made available at the end
```

continues

LISTING 1-15 *(continued)*

```
          link: function ($scope, $element, $attrs, stockTableCtrl) {
            // [3] Create tooltip for stock-row
            $element.tooltip({
              placement: 'left',
              title: $scope.stock.company.name
            });

            // [4] Add this row to the TableCtrl
            stockTableCtrl.addRow($scope);

            // [5] Register this stock with the QuoteService
            QuoteService.register($scope.stock);

            // [6] Deregister company with the QuoteService on $destroy
            $scope.$on('$destroy', function () {
              stockTableCtrl.removeRow($scope);
              QuoteService.deregister($scope.stock);
            });

            // [7] If this is the last 'stock-row', fetch quotes immediately
            if ($scope.isLast) {
              $timeout(QuoteService.fetch);
            }

            // [8] Watch for changes in shares and recalculate fields
            $scope.$watch('stock.shares', function () {
              $scope.stock.marketValue = $scope.stock.shares *
                $scope.stock.lastPrice;
              $scope.stock.dayChange = $scope.stock.shares *
                parseFloat($scope.stock.change);
              $scope.stock.save();
            });
          }
        };
      });
```

For this directive, only $timeout and QuoteService are injected as dependencies. Also, you might have already noticed that the restrict property [1] has been set to A, which means that stkStockRow is meant to be used as an attribute of a DOM element instead of as a DOM element itself as was the case with the previously created directives. You should also make note of the use of the require property. This is how you tell the directive that it needs a specific controller, which in this case was defined inside the stkStockTable directive. The ^ prefix instructs this directive to search for controllers on its parent scopes, which is exactly what you want it to do in this case. The required controller is then available via the last parameter of the link function, as seen in [2]. Because each row has its own tooltip markup, this directive is a great location to put the tooltip initialization code [3]. The rest of the code takes care of registering the $scope for each row using the stkStockTable directive's addRow() function [4], registering the row's stock with the QuoteService on creation [5] and deregistering it when the row is destroyed [6], as well as immediately triggering a QuoteService.fetch() call if the currently created row is the last one in the table [7]. Finally, a $watch() is used to monitor changes to the stock's number of shares so that the appropriate calculations can be made [8].

Creating the Stock Table Template

With both the `stkStockTable` and `stkStockRow` directives now complete, the next order of business is to create a new HTML template view for the stock table. Go ahead and create a new file named `stock-table.html` inside your `app/views/templates/` directory and make it look like the markup shown in Listing 1-16.

LISTING 1-16: app/views/templates/stock-table.html

```html
<table class="table">
  <thead>
    <tr>
      <td>Symbol</td>
      <td>Shares Owned</td>
      <td>Last Price</td>
      <td>Price Change
        <span> (
          <!--[1] Toggle showPercent scope variable on click -->
          <span ng-disabled="showPercent === false">
            <a ng-click="showPercent = !showPercent">$</a>
          </span>|
          <span ng-disabled="showPercent === true">
            <a ng-click="showPercent = !showPercent">%</a>
          </span>)
        </span>
      </td>
      <td>Market Value</td>
      <td>Day Change</td>
    </tr>
  </thead>
  <!-- [2] Only show footer if more than one stock exists -->
  <tfoot ng-show="watchlist.stocks.length > 1">
    <tr>
      <td>Totals</td>
      <td>{{watchlist.shares}}</td>
      <td></td>
      <td></td>
      <td>{{watchlist.marketValue}}</td>
      <td>{{watchlist.dayChange}}</td>
    </tr>
  </tfoot>
  <tbody>
    <!-- [3] Use stk-stock-row to create row for each stock -->
    <tr stk-stock-row
        ng-repeat="stock in watchlist.stocks track by $index"
        stock="stock"
        is-last="$last">
      <td>{{stock.company.symbol}}</td>
      <td>{{stock.shares}}</td>
      <td>{{stock.lastPrice}}</td>
      <td>
        <span ng-hide="showPercent">{{stock.change}}</span>
        <span ng-show="showPercent">{{stock.percentChange}}</span>
```

continues

LISTING 1-16 *(continued)*

```
        </td>
        <td>{{stock.marketValue}}</td>
        <td>{{stock.dayChange}}
          <button type="button" class="close"
            ng-click="removeStock(stock)">x</button>
        </td>
      </tr>
    </tbody>
  </table>
```

Although the markup for `stock-table.html` is not overly complicated, there are a few things worth pointing out. First, inside the `<thead>`, you should notice that the Price Change header cell contains two spans with `ng-click` directives that assign a value to the `showPercent` scope variable [1]. This is the first example using this form of an expression and is a helpful way to accomplish simple tasks, in this case toggling a Boolean without creating a scope function. You should also note the use of `ng-show` to only display the table footer if there is more than one stock in the current watchlist [2] because it contains calculated totals. Finally, although this view template is for the `stkStockTable` directive, under the hood it uses an `ng-repeat` to create `<tr>` elements containing the `stkStockRow` directive [3]. Using external directives inside another directive's template is perfectly acceptable; just take care in not overcomplicating your approach because you may run into situations in which you have to manually compile child directive templates using the `$compile` service.

Updating the Watchlist View

The only remaining task in completing this step is to invoke the `stkStockTable` directive by including it in StockDog's watchlist view. Open your project's `app/views/watchlist.html` file and locate the `<p>` tag containing the `ng-repeat` directive. Instead of simply displaying the stock's company symbol, you want to render the entire interactive table. Replace that entire line with the following code to accomplish this task:

```
<stk-stock-table ng-show="stocks.length" watchlist="watchlist">
```

Congratulations on successfully completing the first pass over the stock table! See Figure 1-10. You might be thinking that it isn't the most beautiful table you've ever created, but don't fret. Over the next three sections, you will be refining it into a more polished product. In the next section, you will see how to make individual cells editable, adding even more interactivity to your table. If your application is not functioning properly, please refer to the `step-7` directory inside the companion code for this chapter or check out the corresponding tag of the GitHub repository.

STEP 8: INLINE FORM EDITING

Now that StockDog has a functioning table that can display information on the various stocks being tracked by a watchlist, the next step is to make the application more interactive by allowing users to edit the number of shares owned for each stock. Because data is being displayed in a table, a common paradigm for editing values is to modify them inline, much like a spreadsheet. In this section, you will see how to create a directive that can be used in conjunction with HTML5's `contenteditable` attribute to accomplish this functionality.

| StockDog | | | | | | Dashboard | Watchlists ▾ |

👁 Watchlists ➕

Technology	✕
Pharmaceutical	✕
Financial	✕

Netflix, Inc.

≡ Hot tech stocks ➕

Symbol	Shares Owned	Last Price	Price Change ($ | %)	Market Value	Day Change	
MSFT	100	44.1	+0.11	4410	11	✕
TWTR	100	49.86	+1.31	4986	131	✕
YHOO	100	44.55	+0.12	4455	12	✕
NFLX	100	485.29	+6.96	48529	696	✕
LNKD	100	273.99	+4.99	27399	499	✕
AMZN	100	386.27	+0.90	38627	90	✕
Totals	600			128406	1439	

FIGURE 1-10

Creating the Contenteditable Directive

Because this new directive will be extending the `contenteditable` attribute's functionality, it must share the same name. Run the following command from your terminal to scaffold out a new AngularJS directive using Yeoman:

```
yo angular:directive contenteditable
```

This creates a new file named `contenteditable.js` inside your `app/scripts/directives/` directory. The `contenteditable` directive is restricted to an attribute and performs sanitization and validation of user-inputted data. You can find the full implementation of this new directive in Listing 1-17.

LISTING 1-17: app/scripts/directives/contenteditable.js

```
'use strict';

var NUMBER_REGEXP = /^\s*(\-|\+)?(\d+|(\d*(\.\d*)))\s*$/;

angular.module('stockDogApp')
  .directive('contenteditable', function ($sce) {
    return {
      restrict: 'A',
      require: 'ngModel', // [1] Get a hold of NgModelController
```

continues

LISTING 1-17: *(continued)*

```
            link: function($scope, $element, $attrs, ngModelCtrl) {
              if(!ngModelCtrl) { return; } // do nothing if no ng-model

              // [2] Specify how UI should be updated
              ngModelCtrl.$render = function() {
                $element.html($sce.getTrustedHtml(ngModelCtrl.$viewValue || ''));
              };

              // [3] Read HTML value, and then write data to the model or reset the view
              var read = function () {
                var value = $element.html();
                if ($attrs.type === 'number' && !NUMBER_REGEXP.test(value)) {
                  ngModelCtrl.$render();
                } else {
                  ngModelCtrl.$setViewValue(value);
                }
              };

              // [4] Add custom parser-based input type (only 'number' supported)
              // This will be applied to the $modelValue
              if ($attrs.type === 'number') {
                ngModelCtrl.$parsers.push(function (value) {
                  return parseFloat(value);
                });
              }

              // [5] Listen for change events to enable binding
              $element.on('blur keyup change', function() {
                $scope.$apply(read);
              });
            }
          };
        });
```

As with the stkStockRow directive, the require property is once again used to grab a handle on an external directive's controller. In this case, ngModel is being required [1] because you want to take advantage of Angular's bidirectional data binding to trigger updates to the rest of the table based on the user's modification. Next, the ngModelCtrl.$render() function is implemented, which is required to inform the ngModel directive how the view should be updated. Here, the Strict Contextual Escaping service $sce is used, which was the only injected dependency, to sanitize user input before updating the view's HTML [2]. A read() function is then defined that inspects the element's current HTML value and, if its type property is set to number, tests to see if the value is a number using a regular expression [3]. In this case, your contenteditable directive is only used for the Shares Owned cell, so only a number type is supported, but you can easily extend this functionality to support other input types and formats. If the current value is not a number, the ngModelCtrl.$render() function is called, which updates the view with the previous value. However, if the user does in fact input a valid number, the directive calls ngModelCtrl.$setViewValue(), which handles invoking $render() with the new value and kicks off the ngModel $parsers pipeline. A custom parser is defined [4] to support number input types. It parses the $viewValue into a number so that ngModel can update the $modelValue, which can then be properly used to recalculate values for the stock table. Finally, the `$element.on()` function is used to listen for the `blur`, `keyup`, and `change` events so that `read()` can be invoked after each modification [5].

Updating the StkStockTable Template

All that is left to do is update the `stock-table.html` file located in the `app/views/templates` directory to utilize this newly created `contenteditable` directive. Find the line containing `<td>{{stock.shares}}</td>` and replace it entirely with the following:

```
<td contenteditable type="number" ng-model="stock.shares"></td>
```

Notice that the `type` attribute is set to `number`, and `ng-model` is used to bind to the shares value of the row's stock object. Because it might not be explicitly clear to your users that you can perform inline edits on the Shares Owned cell, add the following line to the bottom of your `stock-table.html` file:

```
<div class="small text-center">Click on Shares Owned cell to edit.</div>
```

With these two quick modifications complete, take a moment to test out the inline editing functionality, an example of which is shown in Figure 1-11. Attempting to type any characters other than a number into a row's Shares Owned cell immediately resets the value. However, after each successful modification that results in a valid number, the entire stock table is recalculated in real time. If your application is not functioning properly, please refer to the `step-8` directory inside the companion code for this chapter or check out the corresponding tag of the GitHub repository.

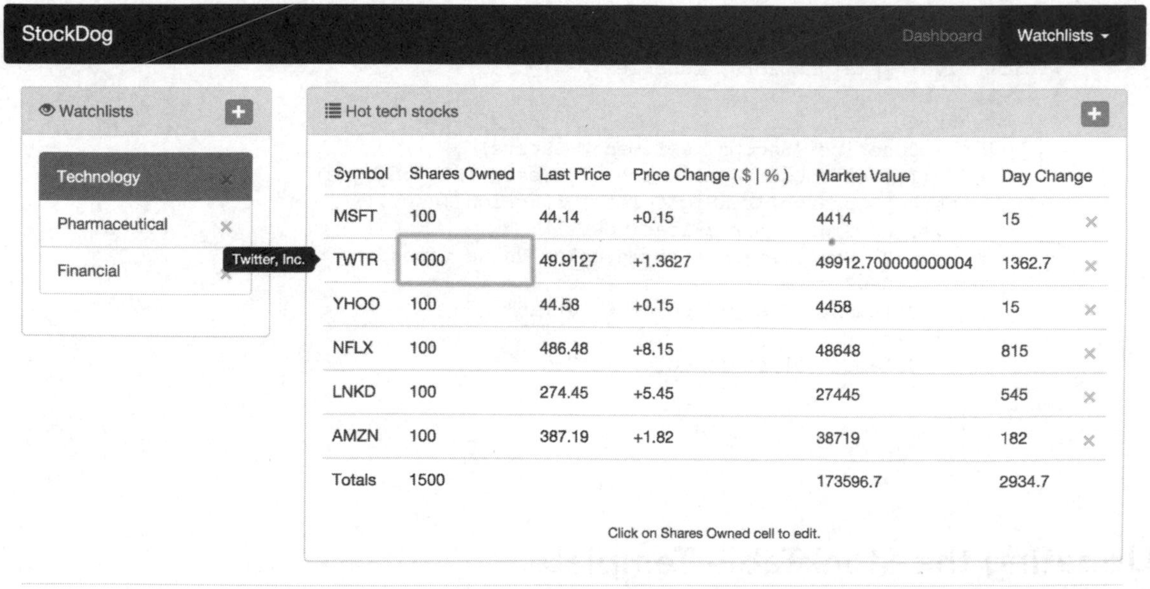

FIGURE 1-11

STEP 9: FORMATTING CURRENCY

At this point, StockDog's watchlist view is fully functional. Watchlists can be created, and stocks can be added, deleted, and edited using the stock table, but the way the data is being displayed isn't ideal. In this section you will be formatting the displayed numbers using Angular's built-in currency filter, in addition to creating a new directive that changes the number's color based on whether it is reflecting a positive or negative change.

Creating the StkSignColor Directive

The first order of business is to create a new stkSignColor directive that you can apply to existing elements to modify their displayed color to be either red or green. Go ahead and run the following command from your terminal to scaffold out this directive:

```
yo angular:directive stk-Sign-Color
```

This creates a new file named stk-sign-color.js inside your app/scripts/directives/ directory. You can see the full implementation of the stkSignColor directive in Listing 1-18. The first thing you may notice is that instead of a $scope.$watch(), an $attrs.$observe() was used to listen to changes in the expression assigned to stkSignColor [1]. Because $observe() is a function of the $attrs object, it can only be used to observe/watch the value change of a DOM attribute, which in this case is exactly what you want. The rest of this directive is incredibly simple because all it has to do is update the $element's style.color property depending on whether the expression's new value is positive or negative [2].

LISTING 1-18: app/scripts/directives/stk-sign-color.js

```javascript
'use strict';

angular.module('stockDogApp')
  .directive('stkSignColor', function () {
    return {
      restrict: 'A',
      link: function ($scope, $element, $attrs) {
        // [1] Use $observe to watch expression for changes
        $attrs.$observe('stkSignColor', function (newVal) {
          var newSign = parseFloat(newVal);
          // [2] Set element's style.color value depending on sign
          if (newSign > 0) {
            $element[0].style.color = 'Green';
          } else {
            $element[0].style.color = 'Red';
          }
        });
      }
    };
  });
```

Updating the StockTable Template

In addition to adding the stkSignColor directive to your stock-table.html template, you need to use Angular's built-in currency filter. Although an in-depth discussion of Angular filters is outside the scope of this chapter, all you need to know to move forward is that a filter formats the value of an expression for display to the user. A filter can be used in view templates, controllers, and services, and it is fairly straightforward to create your own custom filter. You can apply a filter to an expression in a view template using this syntax: `{{ expression | filter }}`. To learn more about what filters are available out of the box, visit the official documentation located at `https://docs.angularjs.org/api/ng/filter`. For this section, you will be using the `currency` filter, with default parameters. The full syntax for the `currency` filter is as follows:

```
{{ currency_expression | currency : symbol : fractionSize}}
```

Because the `symbol` defaults to `$` and the `fractionSize` to the current locale's max fraction size, using the `currency` filter is almost trivial. Go ahead and add `| currency` to the `watchlist.marketValue, watchlist.dayChange, stock.lastPrice, stock.marketValue,` and `stock.dayChange` expression bindings. Then you'll want to add the `stk-sign-color` attribute, with a binding to a value that should be watched for changes, to each `<td>` element that you want to color. In this case, you'll want to color the `watchlist.dayChange` cell in the footer, as well as the Price Change and Day Change columns in the table. Here is an example of applying the `stk-sign-color` directive to the `watchlist.dayChange` row in the footer:

```
<td stk-sign-color="{{watchlist.dayChange}}">
   {{watchlist.dayChange | currency}}
</td>
```

The application of the `stk-sign-color` directive to the remaining two cells is left as an exercise for you, the reader. Once the currency filters and `stk-sign-color` directives are properly in place, your application should look something like Figure 1-12. If you find yourself struggling with applying the directive and `currency` filters in the correct location of the markup, please refer to the `step-9` directory inside the companion code for this chapter or check out the corresponding tag of the GitHub repository.

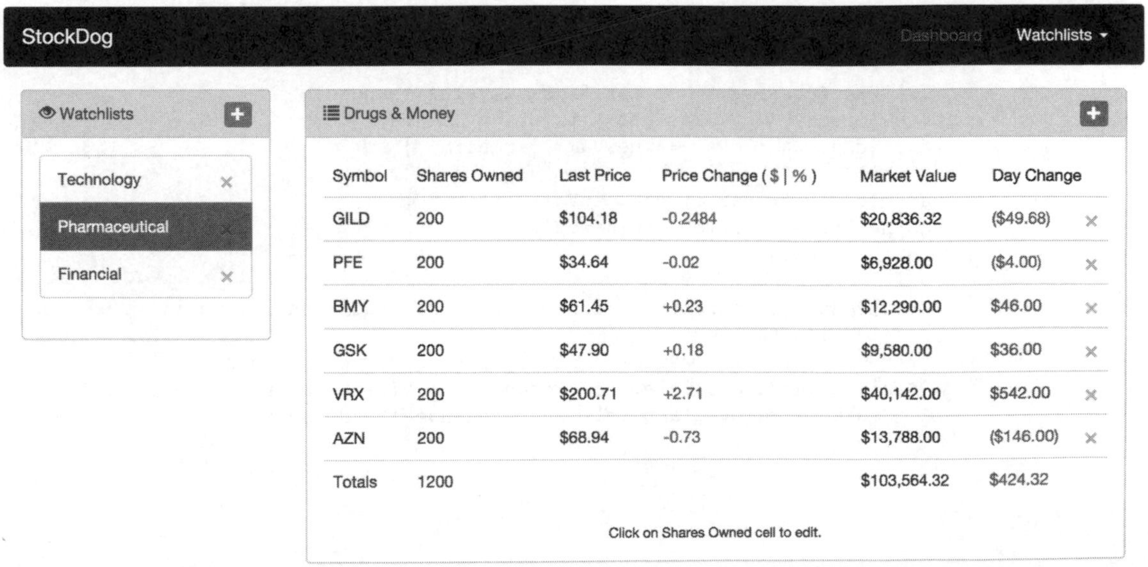

| StockDog | | | | Dashboard | Watchlists ▾ |

Watchlists ⊕

Technology	✕
Pharmaceutical	✕
Financial	✕

Drugs & Money ⊕

Symbol	Shares Owned	Last Price	Price Change ($ | %)	Market Value	Day Change	
GILD	200	$104.18	-0.2484	$20,836.32	($49.68)	✕
PFE	200	$34.64	-0.02	$6,928.00	($4.00)	✕
BMY	200	$61.45	+0.23	$12,290.00	$46.00	✕
GSK	200	$47.90	+0.18	$9,580.00	$36.00	✕
VRX	200	$200.71	+2.71	$40,142.00	$542.00	✕
AZN	200	$68.94	-0.73	$13,788.00	($146.00)	✕
Totals	1200			$103,564.32	$424.32	

Click on Shares Owned cell to edit.

FIGURE 1-12

STEP 10: ANIMATING PRICE CHANGES

In this section, you will learn the basics of how to use Angular's ngAnimate module to perform an animation on StockDog's watchlist view. To visually show your users the price action of a given stock—that is, whether there has been a positive or a negative change in value—a red or green crossfade on the entire cell is performed. Although a complete discussion on creating JavaScript and CSS3 animations with Angular is outside the scope of this chapter, you can find more information by visiting the official documentation at https://docs.angularjs.org/api/ngAnimate.

Creating the StkSignFade Directive

Because the desired result is to crossfade an entire table cell, you need to create another directive that will be used as an attribute so that it can be dropped onto existing elements. To get started, run the following command from your terminal:

```
yo angular:directive stk-Sign-Fade
```

This creates a new stk-sign-fade.js file inside your app/scripts/directives/ directory. Just as with the stkSignColor directive you created in the previous section, this directive will be fairly short and straightforward. You can find the complete implementation of the stkSignFade directive in Listing 1-19.

LISTING 1-19: app/scripts/directives/stk-sign-fade.js

```
'use strict';

angular.module('stockDogApp')
  .directive('stkSignFade', function ($animate) {
    return {
      restrict: 'A',
      link: function ($scope, $element, $attrs) {
        var oldVal = null;
        // [1] Use $observe to be notified on value changes
        $attrs.$observe('stkSignFade', function (newVal) {
          if (oldVal && oldVal == newVal) { return; }

          var oldPrice = parseFloat(oldVal);
          var newPrice = parseFloat(newVal);
          oldVal = newVal;

          // [2] Add the appropriate direction class, and then remove it
          if (oldPrice && newPrice) {
            var direction = newPrice - oldPrice >= 0 ? 'up' : 'down';
            $animate.addClass($element, 'change-' + direction, function() {
              $animate.removeClass($element, 'change-' + direction);
            });
          }
        });
      }
    };
  });
```

The only dependency that was injected into this directive was the $animate service, which is provided by the ngAnimate module. As you saw with the stkSignColor directive, $attrs.$observe() is once gain used to watch for changes to the expression assigned to stkSignFade [1]. A local reference is kept to the oldVal so that on subsequent changes, it can be compared against the newVal and the appropriate direction class can be computed [2]. For this example, the $animate service is used to add, and then quickly remove, the change-up or change-down CSS classes from the directive's element. The $animate service takes an element, class name, and callback function as a parameter, which is used to remove the class after the animation for adding it has been performed. Before attempting to use this directive in the stock-table.html file, you must create a handful of CSS classes using the syntax that Angular requires. Add the following lines of code to the top of your app/styles/main.css file. A few other styles that polish up the stock table's display are also included here:

```css
/* Stock Table Styles */
.table {
  text-align: center;
  margin-bottom: 5px;
}
tfoot {
  font-weight: bold;
}
a {
  cursor: pointer;
}
span[disabled="disabled"] a {
  text-decoration: none;
  color: black;
}
span[disabled="disabled"] {
  pointer-events: none;
}

/* Styles for ngAnimate animations */
.change-up-add {
  transition: background-color linear 1.5s;
  background-color: green;
}
.change-up-add.change-up-add-active {
  background-color: white;
}
.change-down-add {
  transition: background-color linear 1.5s;
  background-color: red;
}
.change-down-add.change-down-add-active {
  background-color: white;
}
```

Angular expects you to define *-add and *-add-active classes for each of your desired animation classes. In the preceding example, change-up-add is applied immediately, which sets the background to green. Then the change-up-add-active class is applied for the duration of the animation. In this case, that sets the background color to white with a 1.5s CSS transition, ultimately creating a crossfade effect from green to white. The same approach is used for change-down-add, which shows a negative price action in red.

Updating the StockTable Template

Now that you have completed the stkSignFade directive and created the appropriate CSS classes expected by the ngAnimate module, it is time to modify your stock-table.html view template. Locate the two lines with <td> elements that are displaying the watchlist.marketValue and stock.lastPrice, and add the stk-sign-fade="{{watchlist.marketValue}}" and stk-sign-fade="{{stock.lastPrice}}" directive to them, respectively.

> **NOTE** *Because the* QuoteService *is updating the* stock.lastPrice *as it fetches data from Yahoo Finance, you may run into a situation in which the market is closed and the price isn't changing, making it difficult to see your new* stkSignFade *directive in action. In this case, modify the* update() *function inside your* quote-service.js *file to randomize the* stock.lastPrice. *You can accomplish this with Lodash by adding* + _.random(-0.5, 0.5) *to the line that parses the* quote.LastTradePriceOnly. *Just don't forget to remove it when you've finished testing!*

Congratulations! You have completely finished StockDog's watchlist view! See Figure 1-13. If you find yourself struggling with getting your animations to properly run, please refer to the step-10 directory inside the companion code for this chapter or check out the corresponding tag of the GitHub repository.

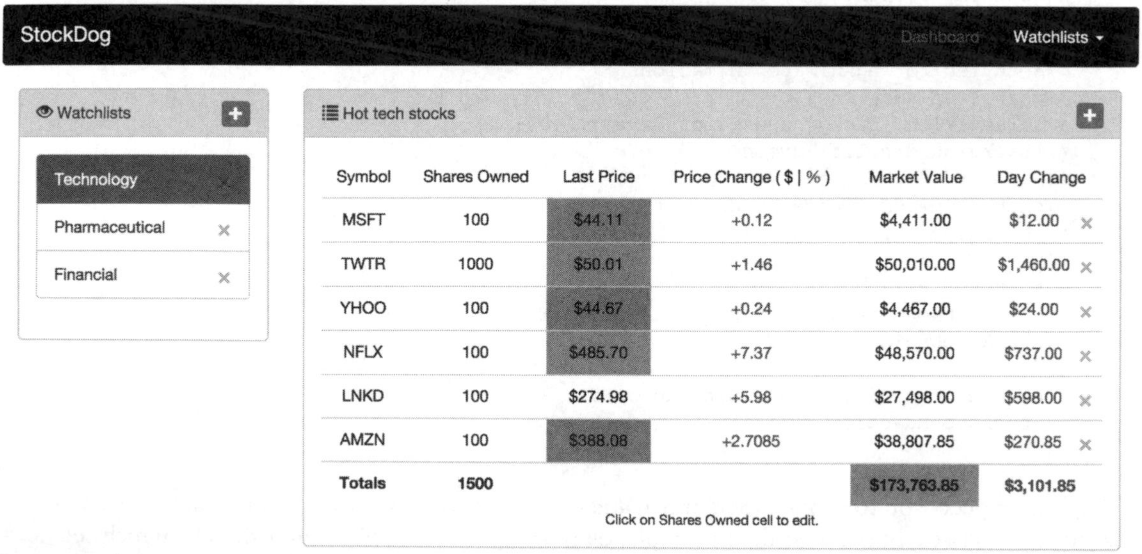

FIGURE 1-13

STEP 11: CREATING THE DASHBOARD

The final outstanding feature that remains to be implemented for the StockDog application is the dashboard view. This view aggregates performance metrics across all created watchlists and reports the analytics in four unique panels. These performance metrics are Total Market Value, Total Day Change, Market Value by Watchlist, and Day Change by Watchlist. Because no dashboard is complete without interactive graphs, you will be taking advantage of the Google Charts library to render two distinct charts.

Updating the Dashboard Controller

To use the Google Charts library from within your AngularJS application, you need to wrap and expose its functionality via directives. For the sake of simplicity, you will be using a preexisting library that has done just that, whose documentation can be found here: `https://github.com/bouil/angular-google-chart`. To get started with the `angular-google-chart` library, run the following command from your terminal to install it using Bower:

```
bower install angular-google-chart –save
```

This downloads and installs the library. It also lists it as a project dependency inside your `bower.json` file. Once that is complete, you must register this library's module with your AngularJS application by updating your `stockDogApp` module dependencies. You can do this by adding `googlechart` to the end of the dependencies array found in your `app/scripts/app.js` file, in the same manner in which the AngularStrap library was registered back in Listing 1-1 of Step 2 earlier in this chapter. Once that is complete, open the `dashboard.js` file located in your `app/scripts/controllers/` directory and replace its contents with the final implementation shown in Listing 1-20.

LISTING 1-20: app/scripts/controllers/dashboard.js

```
'use strict';

angular.module('stockDogApp')
  .controller('DashboardCtrl', function ($scope, WatchlistService, QuoteService) {
    // [1] Initializations
    var unregisterHandlers = [];
    $scope.watchlists = WatchlistService.query();
    $scope.cssStyle = 'height:300px;';
    var formatters = {
      number: [
        {
          columnNum: 1,
          prefix: '$'
        }
      ]
    };

    // [2] Helper: Update chart objects
    var updateCharts = function () {
      // Donut chart
```

continues

LISTING 1-20 *(continued)*

```javascript
      var donutChart = {
        type: 'PieChart',
        displayed: true,
        data: [['Watchlist', 'Market Value']],
        options: {
          title: 'Market Value by Watchlist',
          legend: 'none',
          pieHole: 0.4
        },
        formatters: formatters
      };
      // Column chart
      var columnChart = {
        type: 'ColumnChart',
        displayed: true,
        data: [['Watchlist', 'Change', { role: 'style' }]],
        options: {
          title: 'Day Change by Watchlist',
          legend: 'none',
          animation: {
            duration: 1500,
            easing: 'linear'
          }
        },
        formatters: formatters
      };

      // [3] Push data onto both chart objects
      _.each($scope.watchlists, function (watchlist) {
        donutChart.data.push([watchlist.name, watchlist.marketValue]);
        columnChart.data.push([watchlist.name, watchlist.dayChange,
          watchlist.dayChange < 0 ? 'Red' : 'Green']);
      });
      $scope.donutChart = donutChart;
      $scope.columnChart = columnChart;
    };

    // [4] Helper function for resetting controller state
    var reset = function () {
      // [5] Clear QuoteService before registering new stocks
      QuoteService.clear();
      _.each($scope.watchlists, function (watchlist) {
        _.each(watchlist.stocks, function (stock) {
          QuoteService.register(stock);
        });
      });

      // [6] Unregister existing $watch listeners before creating new ones
      _.each(unregisterHandlers, function(unregister) {
        unregister();
      });
      _.each($scope.watchlists, function (watchlist) {
```

```
          var unregister = $scope.$watch(function () {
            return watchlist.marketValue;
          }, function () {
            recalculate();
          });
          unregisterHandlers.push(unregister);
        });
      };

      // [7] Compute the new total MarketValue and DayChange
      var recalculate = function () {
        $scope.marketValue = 0;
        $scope.dayChange = 0;
        _.each($scope.watchlists, function (watchlist) {
          $scope.marketValue += watchlist.marketValue ?
            watchlist.marketValue : 0;
          $scope.dayChange += watchlist.dayChange ?
            watchlist.dayChange : 0;
        });
        updateCharts();
      };

      // [8] Watch for changes to watchlists.
      $scope.$watch('watchlists.length', function () {
        reset();
      });
    });
```

For the implementation of this DashboardCtrl, both WatchlistService and QuoteService are injected as dependencies. Next, some initializations are made to populate the $scope .watchlists variable using the WatchlistService, with chart style and formatting options also being defined [1]. An updateCharts() function is then created [2] that sets up both a donutChart and a columnChart. The required properties and available configuration options for these objects are defined by the Google Chart library documentation, which can be found here https://developers.google.com/chart/. This function also handles looping over each watchlist being tracked by StockDog and adding the appropriate data onto the respective chart object [3] before attaching both chart structures to the controller's $scope. A reset() function [4] is then defined that is used to clear the controller's state. This function clears all tracked stocks from the QuoteService before registering each stock for each existing watchlist [5]. It then unregisters all existing $watch listeners, whose references are stored in a local array, before creating new $watch targets on each watchlist's marketValue [6]. This is used to invoke the recalculate() function [7], which handles computing new aggregate market value and day change metrics each time a watchlist's computed value changes.

Each time recalculate is invoked, a call to updateCharts() is made so that the existing charts can be redrawn by the Google Chart library with the newest data. Finally, a $watch target is set on the watchlists.length property so that when a watchlist is created or deleted, the reset() function can be triggered to appropriately rebuild the entire controller's state [8]. It's worth mentioning that the watchlists.length expression is used instead of the entire watchlists object because deep-watching large data structures can seriously degrade your application's performance.

Updating the Dashboard View

Now that the `DashboardCtrl` implementation is complete, the next order of business is to update StockDog's dashboard view to render the new data and chart objects that have been created. As it stands, the `app/views/dashboard.html` file only contains a reference to the `stkWatchlistPanel` directive and an empty Portfolio Overview panel. You can find the missing markup for this panel in the completed dashboard view, shown in Listing 1-21.

LISTING 1-21: app/views/dashboard.html

```
<div class="row">
  <!-- Left Column -->
  <div class="col-md-3">
    <stk-watchlist-panel></stk-watchlist-panel>
  </div>

  <!-- Right Column -->
  <div class="col-md-9">
    <div class="panel panel-info">
      <div class="panel-heading">
        <span class="glyphicon glyphicon-globe"></span>
        Portfolio Overview
      </div>
      <div class="panel-body">
        <!-- [1] Display some helpful text to guide new users -->
        <div ng-hide="watchlists.length && watchlists[0].stocks.length"
          class="jumbotron">
          <h1>Unleash the hounds!</h1>
          <p>
            StockDog, your personal investment watchdog, is ready
            to be set loose on the financial markets!
          </p>
          <p>Create a watchlist and add some stocks to begin monitoring.</p>
        </div>

        <div ng-show="watchlists.length && watchlists[0].stocks.length">
          <!-- Top Row -->
          <div class="row">
            <!-- Left Column -->
            <div class="col-md-6">
              <!-- [2] Use sign-fade directive on wrapper element -->
              <div stk-sign-fade="{{marketValue}}" class="well">
                <h2>{{marketValue | currency}}</h2>
                <h5>Total Market Value</h5>
              </div>
            </div>

            <!-- Right Column -->
            <div class="col-md-6">
              <!-- [3] Use sign-color directive on wrapper element -->
              <div class="well" stk-sign-color="{{dayChange}}">
                <h2>{{dayChange | currency}}</h2>
                <h5>Total Day Change</h5>
              </div>
```

```
          </div>
        </div>
        <!-- [4] Use google-chart directive and reference chart objects -->
        <div class="row">
          <!-- Left Column -->
          <div class="col-md-6">
            <div google-chart chart="donutChart" style="{{cssStyle}}"></div>
          </div>

          <!-- Right Column -->
          <div class="col-md-6">
            <div google-chart chart="columnChart" style="{{cssStyle}}"></div>
          </div>
        </div>
      </div>
    </div>
  </div>
</div>
```

The new markup inside the panel-body starts by including some helpful text to guide new users when they first open StockDog and have yet to create any watchlists [1]. You should also notice that both columns of the top row contain references to the stkSignFade [2] and stkSignColor [3] directives, but the directives have been applied to a wrapper element—in this case, Bootstrap wells. Finally, the googleChart directive, exposed by the previously installed angular-google-chart library, is used in both columns of the bottom row, with the chart objects created in the DashboardCtrl being used as the value for each respective element's chart attribute [4]. To polish up the completed dashboard view, the only remaining modification you'll need to make is to add the following CSS to the top of your app/styles/main.css file:

```
/* Dashboard View Styles */
.well {
  background-color: white;
  text-align: center;
}
```

Congratulations! If you have successfully made it through the entirety of this section, you have finally finished building the entire StockDog application! See Figure 1-14. Take a moment to appreciate your hard work and play around with the application by creating several new watchlists, adding new stocks, and monitoring your portfolio's performance from the dashboard view. For the completed application source code, please refer to the step-11 directory inside the companion code for this chapter or check out the corresponding tag of the GitHub repository.

PRODUCTION DEPLOYMENT

Now that you have finished building StockDog, the time has come to unleash the hounds and package the distributable application before deploying it to the Internet so that your users around the world can better manage their stock portfolios. Although an in-depth discussion of production deployment and all the associated intricacies is outside the scope of this section, there are a few simple tasks that can be accomplished to get your application ready for the masses.

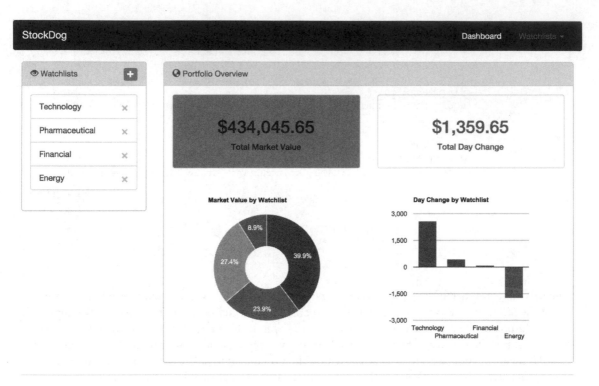

FIGURE 1-14

Because your application was developed using the AngularJS Yeoman generator, your project already includes a sophisticated build system. You will learn more about how this system works in the Chapter 3, "Architecture," but for now, just run the following command from your terminal to run the build system:

```
grunt build
```

This concatenates, obfuscates, and minifies all of StockDog's source files and creates a new `dist/` directory in your project's root folder with the optimized assets. The `dist/` directory contains everything needed for users to run your application, so deployment is as simple as uploading this folder to your hosting service of choice. However, for the purpose of this section, you will be deploying StockDog to GitHub Pages, a hosting service provided free of charge for GitHub-based projects. If you haven't already uploaded your project to GitHub, take a few minutes to do so, consulting `https://help.github.com/articles/adding-an-existing-project-to-github-using-the-command-line/` if you need any further assistance.

Once your project has been uploaded to GitHub, open your `.gitignore` file and remove the line containing `dist`. Out of the box, Yeoman has set up your project to follow best practices by ignoring files generated by the automated build task. However, because you will be hosting your `dist/` directory on GitHub, it must be committed as part of your project. Go ahead and add the dist/ directory to your repository, commit, and then push it upstream. Now you are ready to deploy your application to GitHub using the git subtree command. Run the following command from your terminal to create a new gh-pages branch for your project consisting of all the files residing inside your dist/ directory:

```
git subtree push --prefix dist origin gh-pages
```

Once that is complete, your application will be publicly available at http(s)://<username> .github.io/<projectname>. For example, you can find the StockDog application running at http://diegonetto.github.io/stock-dog. One caveat to this approach is that your Dashboard and Watchlist links must be prefixed with your <projectname> because of the nature of the GitHub Pages URL. Another approach is to set up a custom URL for your project by uploading a new CNAME file to your dist/ directory that contains your custom domain. This is how http:// www.stockdog.io/ has been set up to point to http://diegonetto.github.io/stock-dog. After uploading your CNAME file and redeploying your site using the git subtree command shown earlier, all that is left is to modify the www CNAME record (assuming you want to use the www subdomain) of your DNS provider to point to username.github.io. If you have successfully followed these steps, congratulations! Your application should be live and ready to share with the rest of the world.

> **NOTE** *GitHub recommends using a subdomain and not an apex domain when configuring custom URLs for hosted project pages. If you wish to use your apex domain (*http://stockdog.io *in the above example) for your deployed application, the best way to accomplish this is to use the* www *subdomain CNAME DNS entry with your provider as described and then enable domain forwarding from your apex domain to your* www *URL. In this case,* http:// stockdog.io *has been set up to forward to* http://www.stockdog.io.

CONCLUSION

The journey through this chapter has exposed you to a real-world application of AngularJS by building StockDog, an application that leverages nearly all-key components of the framework. From scaffolding a starter project using the Yeoman AngularJS generator to deploying your application using GitHub Pages, this step-by-step guide should have given you the confidence and instant gratification to inspire a deeper dive into this elegant framework. Along the way, you learned how to structure a multiview single-page application; created several controllers, directives, and services; installed additional front-end modules; handled dynamic form validation; communicated with an external API; and brought your application to life with a simple animation. In the following chapters of this book, you will explore in detail how the various components of the AngularJS framework function and be exposed to various tools, services, and technologies that can be used to create robust, reliable, and maintainable projects for professional consumption.

2

Intelligent Workflow and Build Tools

WHAT YOU WILL LEARN IN THIS CHAPTER:

- ➤ Managing front-end dependencies using Bower
- ➤ Automating development tasks using Grunt/Gulp
- ➤ Scaffolding a new project using Yeoman
- ➤ Using workflow best practices to enhance productivity

WROX.COM CODE DOWNLOADS FOR THIS CHAPTER

You can find the wrox.com code downloads for this chapter at http://www.wrox.com/go/proangularjs on the Download Code tab.

WHAT CAN TOOLING DO FOR ME?

Two words: optimization and automation. Because time is a key factor in productivity, automating repetitive tasks can help you stay effective as a developer. In this chapter, you learn about a few open source tools that can increase the speed at which you develop, debug, test, and distribute your application. By expanding the don't repeat yourself (DRY) philosophy to apply to your workflow process, you can focus more of your energy on doing what you love: building elegant, air-tight code. After discovering how to intelligently apply modern techniques to augment your workflow, you will have established a strong foundation to support building a sample application that allows a deeper exploration of AngularJS.

> **NOTE** *All the tools you will be exploring in this chapter require Node.js to be installed on your machine. For more information, visit* `http://www.nodejs.org` *and follow the installation instructions for your platform.*

WHAT IS BOWER?

Created by Twitter, Bower is a "package manager for the web" that provides an elegant, unopinionated solution to the problem of front-end package management. Distributed as a Node.js command-line tool, Bower helps you manage your front-end JavaScript dependencies by providing package-agnostic mechanisms for searching, installing, and updating your third-party assets.

Getting Started with Bower

Bower's management facilities operate over Git, with SVN support starting from version 1.3.X, for fetching and installing packages, so make sure you have it installed on your system. Mac users should already have Git available on their machines. For Windows users, it's recommended that you download Git Bash (`http://git-scm.com/downloads`).

To begin using Bower, install it globally using the Node Package Manager (npm) utility that is shipped with Node.js. Fire up your terminal application of choice and run this:

```
npm install -g bower
```

This makes the `bower` utility available for use via the command line. Go ahead and run `bower help` to see a list of supported commands before you take a closer look at how you can use a few of these commands to manage your front-end dependencies.

Searching for Packages

Bower maintains a registry containing a plethora of JavaScript libraries that can be easily searched via the `bower search [<package>]` command or by visiting `http://bower.io/search/`. From the command line, run the following:

```
bower search angular
```

This lists all the AngularJS libraries that are available via Bower. Because anyone is able to create and publish new packages to the registry, chances are that you can manage most, if not all, of your third-party dependencies using Bower.

Installing Packages

Installing packages with Bower is as easy as running `bower install <package>`. Because Bower aims at being package agnostic, `<package>` can be a name that maps to a registered Bower package, a public or private Git or Subversion repository, a local directory, or even a uniform resource locator (URL) to a file. For a full list of supported `<package>` variants, visit `http://bower.io/`. Now you'll get started with an example by creating a new directory and then installing the latest stable version of AngularJS by running the following:

```
bower install angular
```

Notice that Bower created a local directory called `bower_components` where it downloaded and installed the AngularJS library. Before continuing with this simple application, you'll look at how to lock down your dependencies by keeping track of their versions.

> **NOTE** *If you would like to change the location where Bower installs your packages, create a* `.bowerrc` *file and set the directory property as shown here:*
>
> ```
> {
>     "directory": "app/bower_components"
> }
> ```
>
> *For a full listing of all possible configuration properties supported by Bower, visit* `http://bower.io/#configuration`.

Versioning Dependencies

To keep better track of your third-party dependencies, you can create a `bower.json` file that contains the name and versions of your required libraries. This works much the same way as Node's `package.json` file and Ruby's `Gemfile`. Since Bower uses the Node.js semantic versioning system (`http://semver.org`), you can create complex ranges when specifying project dependencies as described by the documentation site located at `https://github.com/npm/node-semver`. Bower comes with an interactive command that includes prompts for generating a default file. Simply run the following command in your project's root directory:

```
bower init
```

Now that you have a basic `bower.json` file, you can add AngularJS as a dependency and update your file (`--save`, `-S`) with the latest version (`--force-latest`, `-F`) using a single command:

```
bower install -SF angular
```

> **NOTE** *Bower can install a specified version using the* `<package>#<version>` *syntax. For a listing of all available versions for a given package, run* `bower info <package>`. *If you would like to see more package installation options, use the command* `bower help install`.

If checking in third-party libraries is undesirable, your version control system can track this file, and all the listed dependencies can be subsequently installed by simply running `bower install`. Although it's a matter of preference, it's suggested that you follow the best practice advice listed on the Bower homepage: "If you aren't authoring a package that is intended to be consumed by others (e.g., you're building a web app), you should always check installed packages into source control."

WHAT IS GRUNT?

Grunt is a task runner that helps automate repetitive jobs such as linting, compiling, minification, testing, documentation, and deployment. It is the JavaScript alternative to Rake, Cake, Make, and Ant. Packaged as a Node.js command-line tool and supported by a vibrant ecosystem of plug-ins, Grunt can enhance your workflow by automating most of that mundane work, allowing you to focus on building your application.

Getting Started with Grunt

The first thing you need to start automating your workflow with Grunt is to install the command-line tools globally on your machine. To make the `grunt` utility available for use, run the following from your command line:

```
npm install –g grunt-cli
```

Next, you need a few sample files to experiment with. Using your favorite editor, create the `index .html` shown in Listing 2-1. To keep your application assets organized in a centralized location, go ahead and put them inside a new directory called `app/`.

LISTING 2-1: app/index.html

```
<!DOCTYPE html>
<html ng-app="Workflow">
  <head>
    <link rel="stylesheet" href="main.css">
  </head>

  <body ng-controller="ToolsCtrl">
    <h1>Workflow tools from this chapter:</h1>

    <ul>
      <li ng-repeat="tool in tools">{{tool}}</li>
    </ul>

    <script src="bower_components/angular/angular.js"></script>
    <script src="app.js"></script>
  </body>
</html>
```

> **NOTE** *In an earlier aside, it was mentioned that you could use a* .bowerrc
> *file to set the directory where Bower installs module files. For the purpose
> of your Grunt workflow example, go ahead and create a* .bowerrc *file and
> set the* directory *property to install Bower modules inside your new* app/
> *directory:*
>
> ```
> {
>     "directory": "app/bower_components"
> }
> ```
>
> *The* bower_components/ *directory inside your project root can now be deleted.
> Rerun* bower install *so that a new* bower_components/ *directory is created
> inside of* app/.

To keep your example interesting, create the Less stylesheet shown below in Listing 2-2,
although you could just as easily have chosen to use Sass, another cascading style sheet (CSS)
preprocessor.

LISTING 2-2: app/main.less

```
html,
body {
  h1 {
    color: SteelBlue;
  }
}
```

Finally, you need to create a basic AngularJS application like the one shown below in Listing 2-3,
with a single controller so you can display the list of tools covered in this chapter on the index.html
page.

LISTING 2-3: app/app.js

```
'use strict';

angular.module('Workflow', [])

.controller('ToolsCtrl', function($scope) {
  $scope.tools = [
    'Bower',
    'Grunt',
    'Yeoman'
  ];
});
```

The last thing you need to do for your project is create a `package.json` file that can hold a list of your development dependencies. You can do this interactively from the command line by running the following command inside your project's root directory:

```
npm init
```

Simply follow the prompts, and you'll be set up with a basic package file. Now that you have a few basic assets, you're ready to install some plug-ins and begin constructing your first `Gruntfile.js` to enhance your development workflow.

Installing Plug-Ins

With your current setup, you would have to manually compile your Less file into `main.css` and reopen `index.html` in your browser anytime a file was modified. That doesn't seem like such a terrible task for a simple application like this one, but as it becomes more complex, this manual work would quickly become tedious. To automate this entire process, you need to use a few plug-ins. Run the following from your command line to install the plug-ins as development dependencies for your project:

```
npm install --save-dev grunt
npm install --save-dev load-grunt-tasks
npm install --save-dev grunt-contrib-connect
npm install --save-dev grunt-contrib-jshint
npm install --save-dev grunt-contrib-less
npm install --save-dev grunt-contrib-watch
```

If you look inside your `package.json` file, it should now contain all your installed Grunt plug-ins inside the `devDependencies` property.

> **NOTE** *The Grunt core developers officially maintain plug-ins containing* `contrib` *in their name.*

Directory Structure

Before creating your first Gruntfile, take a minute to look at your current directory structure and ensure that you're not missing any application files, Grunt plug-ins, and Bower dependencies. If you've been following along, your file system should be structured as follows:

```
root-folder/
├── package.json
├── bower.json
├── .bowerrc
├── app/
│   ├── index.html
│   ├── main.less
```

```
|      ├── app.js
|      ├── bower_components/
|      |      └── angular/
├── node_modules/
|      ├── grunt/
|      ├── grunt-contrib-connect/
|      ├── grunt-contrib-jshint/
|      ├── grunt-contrib-less/
|      ├── grunt-contrib-watch/
|      ├── load-grunt-tasks/
```

The Grunt plug-ins you just installed are located inside your node_modules/ folder. You used the .bowerrc file to configure Bower so it would install the Angular.js module assets inside your app/ directory. If your directory structure doesn't quite match, take a second to review this "Getting Started with Grunt" section. You will be using the directory structure just detailed when configuring your first Gruntfile.

The Gruntfile

The Gruntfile.js file belongs in the root directory of your project as a sibling of the package .json file and should be committed with the rest of your source code. Take a look at the various components of a Gruntfile by creating one from scratch starting from a simple skeleton in Listing 2-4.

LISTING 2-4: Skeleton Gruntfile.js

```
// [1] Wrapper function
module.exports = function(grunt) {

  // [2] Project and task configuration
  grunt.initConfig({
    pkg: grunt.file.readJSON('package.json')
  });

  // [3] Load all plug-in tasks automatically
  require('load-grunt-tasks')(grunt);

  // [4] Default task
  grunt.registerTask('default', []);

};
```

The four main parts of a Gruntfile are annotated with comments inside of Listing 2-4. All of your Grunt code must reside inside of [1], the wrapper function. Both the project and task configuration properties are passed into [2], the grunt.initConfig() method. To configure the tasks provided by your installed plug-ins, you must explicitly ask Grunt to load each one [3]. Finally, you can register custom tasks [4] that can run a combination of predefined tasks. The default task is executed when you run grunt from the command line.

> **NOTE** *The* `load-grunt-tasks` *plug-in you installed takes care of loading all the tasks for each Grunt plug-in defined in your* `package.json` *file. Without it, you would have to load plug-ins manually, as follows:*
>
> ```
> grunt.loadNpmTasks('grunt-contrib-connect');
> ```
>
> *Using this plug-in saves you a few lines of code, especially as the number of plug-ins your Gruntfile depends on increases.*

Configuring Tasks and Targets

Now that you have a skeleton Gruntfile and understand its basic structure, you can begin configuring Grunt tasks and targets. Whenever a task is run, Grunt looks for its configuration under a property of the same name. Tasks can have multiple targets, each with its own configuration options. In this section, you configure the tasks made available to you by each of the four specific plug-ins you installed earlier, examining how they come together to automate a simple workflow.

The Connect Task

The `grunt-contrib-connect` plug-in you installed as a development dependency exposes the `connect` task that can be configured inside your Gruntfile. This plug-in allows you to spin up a lightweight Node.js server as part of your workflow to handle serving your application's assets. Modify your Gruntfile by adding the following inside the `grunt` `.initConfig` method:

```
// Configuring the 'connect' task from 'grunt-contrib-connect'
connect: {
  //[1] Task options, overrides built-in defaults
  options: {
    port: 9000,
    open: true,
    livereload: 35729,
    hostname: 'localhost'
  },
  //[2] Arbitrarily named target
  development: {
    // Target options, overrides task options
    options: {
      middleware: function(connect) {
        return [
          connect.static('app')
        ];
      }
    }
  }
}
```

Configuring a Grunt plug-in is as easy as adding a new property matching the name of your plug-in to the JavaScript object passed into `grunt.initConfig()`. Inside each task configuration, you can specify an options object [1] that can be used to override built-in defaults used by the plug-in. In this case, you set the server to run on `http://localhost:9000/`, inject the livereload script tag into your page while running a separate `connect-livereload` server on port 35729, and request that a new tab be opened in your default browser during runtime.

> **NOTE** *Connect is a middleware framework for Node.js created by Sencha Labs that has a rich selection of both bundled and third-party plug-ins (`http://www.senchalabs.org/connect/`).*
>
> *In addition to leveraging the Connect framework to serve your files, the `grunt-contrib-connect` plug-in you installed uses a middleware plug-in called `connect-livereload` to inject a `<script>` tag onto your page during the server response. This is the first step in setting up livereload, which enables your web page to update in real time, without manual intervention, as you make modifications to your application's assets. The next step will be discussed in a later section when configuration of the `grunt-contrib-watch` plug-in is covered.*

The next thing you do is configure a new arbitrarily named target for the `connect` task [2]. Because your application files reside inside the `app/` directory, you need to tell your `development` target to serve static assets from that location. You accomplish this by setting the `middleware` property of the target's `options` object to return a call to `connect.static('app')`, wrapped in an array as seen earlier. Although not shown in this example, it is important to take note that target-level options override task-level options.

Now that you have finished configuring your `connect` task and `development` target with a few appropriate options, you can launch your local development server and open your application in a new browser tab by running the following from the command line:

```
grunt connect:development:keepalive
```

The syntax for executing Grunt tasks from the command line follows the `taskName:targetName:args` pattern you see here. You can specify multiple arguments, but you must separate them with a colon. To keep your connect server running indefinitely, you pass in the `keepalive` argument to the `connect` task. For a full list of supported configuration options and arguments, visit the documentation site located at `https://github.com/gruntjs/grunt-contrib-connect`.

The Less Task

Now that you have a lightweight web server for your static assets, take a look at what it takes to set up a compilation task for your Less files. If you have been following along, you should have noticed that the only styles you have are defined in `main.less`. However, because `index.html` references `main.css`, which does not yet exist, no styles are being applied to your application. Normally, you would need the Less command-line compiler to be installed and invoke it each time you make a modification, as shown here:

```
npm install -g less
lessc app/main.less > app/main.css
```

However, the `grunt-contrib-less` plug-in you installed earlier exposes a `less` task that allows you to configure and automate the compilation process. Modify your Gruntfile by adding the following lines after the `connect` task configuration:

```
// Configuring the 'less' task from 'grunt-contrib-less'
less: {
  development: {
    files: {
      'app/main.css': 'app/main.less'
    }
  }
}
```

Here you specify the transformation of `main.less` into `main.css` inside the `files` property of the `development` target for the `less` task. To trigger this task, follow the pattern described earlier and run the following from the command line:

```
grunt less
```

This should have created the `main.css` file inside your `app/` directory. Although you now have a properly configured Less compilation task, you still need to run `grunt less` each time you make a modification to the `main.less` file. In an upcoming section, you will learn how to automate this task using the `grunt-contrib-watch` plug-in. For a complete list of the available configuration options for the `less` task, visit the plug-in documentation page at `https://github.com/gruntjs/grunt-contrib-less`.

The JSHint Task

JSHint is an open source static code analysis tool that detects errors and potential problems in your JavaScript code and helps enforce coding conventions. This process of static analysis is often referred to as *linting* and should be considered an integral part of any workflow and build system. The `grunt-contrib-jshint` plug-in you installed exposes a configurable `jshint` task that can be automated as part of your Grunt workflow system. Take a look at how you can lint your JavaScript files by adding the following code after the `less` task in your Gruntfile:

```
// Configuring the 'jshint' task from 'grunt-contrib-jshint'
jshint: {
  options: {
    jshintrc: '.jshintrc'
  },
  all: [
    'Gruntfile.js',
    'app/*.js'
  ]
}
```

Here you configure the `jshint` task with a task-level option to look for a `.jshintrc`, which allows you to customize JSHint, and one target called `all` in which you specify the JavaScript files you want to lint. In addition to explicitly referencing each file, regular expressions are supported. Listing 2-5 shows a sample `.jshintrc` file with commonly used preferences that should serve as a helpful starting point. For a detailed list of all supported configuration options and associated documentation, visit `http://www.jshint.com/docs/options/`.

LISTING 2-5: .jshintrc

```
{
    "node": true,
    "browser": true,
    "esnext": true,
    "bitwise": true,
    "camelcase": true,
    "curly": true,
    "eqeqeq": true,
    "immed": true,
    "indent": 2,
    "latedef": true,
    "newcap": true,
    "noarg": true,
    "quotmark": "single",
    "undef": true,
    "unused": true,
    "strict": true,
    "trailing": true,
    "smarttabs": true
}
```

Now that you have configured your project's linting settings using a `.jshintrc` file, go ahead and trigger the Grunt `jshint` task and look at the output:

```
$ grunt jshint
Running "jshint:all" (jshint) task

    Gruntfile.js
        5 |   grunt.initConfig({
                 ^ Missing "use strict" statement.
    app/app.js
        3 |angular.module('Workflow', [])
             ^ 'angular' is not defined.

>> 2 errors in 2 files
Warning: Task "jshint:all" failed. Use --force to continue.

Aborted due to warnings.
```

Here you see JSHint reporting two errors in both of your JavaScript files. The first can be easily fixed by adding `'use strict';` to the top of your Gruntfile. To fix the second error, update your `.jshintrc` file to include the configuration option `"predef": ["angular"]` so that JSHint recognizes `angular` as a globally defined variable. Rerun the `jshint` task from the command line to verify that both of your JavaScript files are lint free. For a complete list of the available configuration options for the `jshint` task, visit the plug-in documentation page at `https://github.com/gruntjs/grunt-contrib-jshint`.

> **NOTE** *Strict Mode is a feature in ECMAScript 5 that allows you to place a program or function in a strict operating context that prevents certain actions from being taken and throws more exceptions. Check* `http://caniuse.com/#feat=use-strict` *for a detailed list of current browser support for Strict Mode. More information about Strict Mode can be found on page 235 of the ES5 specification located here:* `http://www.ecma-international.org/publications/files/ECMA-ST/Ecma-262.pdf.`

The Watch Task

The `grunt-contrib-watch` plug-in exposes a `watch` task that can be easily configured to run predefined tasks whenever watched file patterns are added, changed, or deleted. This allows you to automate execution of your other tasks and provides the final step in setting up livereload integration as part of your workflow, initially discussed during configuration of the `connect` task. Bring all the tasks you've created up to this point together by adding the following code to your Gruntfile after the `jshint` task:

```
// Configuring the 'watch' task from 'grunt-contrib-watch'
watch: {
  options: {
    livereload: '<%= connect.options.livereload %>',
  },
  js: {
    files: ['app/*.js'],
    tasks: ['jshint']
  },
  styles: {
    files: ['app/*.less'],
    tasks: ['less']
  },
  html: {
    files: ['app/*.html']
  }
}
```

Notice that here you use the task-level `option` property so that all subsequently configured targets have livereload enabled. You then proceed to create a new target for each set of files you want to watch for modifications. Inside the `js` and `styles` targets, you specify two options: an array of file pattern, and an array of tasks to be executed when the watched files are modified. The `html` target doesn't specify any task to be run because you're not, for the time being, doing anything with Hypertext Markup Language (HTML) files as part of your workflow other than serving them. Running `grunt watch` from the command line and then modifying a JavaScript or Less file should now automatically trigger the `jshint` and `less` tasks, respectively. For a complete list of the available configuration options for the `watch` task, visit the plug-in documentation page at `https://github.com/gruntjs/grunt-contrib-watch`.

The Default Task

Although running the `watch` task on its own is helpful, to finish setting up your simple workflow, you need to have the connect server running so that livereload can work correctly. To do this, you have to register a new alias task with Grunt by invoking the `grunt.registerTask()` function. This method takes a `taskName` and `taskList` as arguments, where `taskList` must be an array of tasks to run in the order specified. Modify the default task registered at the bottom of your Gruntfile to look like this:

```
// Default Task
grunt.registerTask('default', ['connect:development', 'watch']);
```

After you have ended your previously running `watch` task using Ctrl+C, launch the `default` task by running the following on the command line:

```
grunt
```

This should start the connect server and open an instance of your application inside a new browser tab. Go ahead and modify the `index.html` file by adding `<p>Hello Grunt</p>` after the opening `<body>` tag. Grunt should see this change after the file is saved and notify the livereload server to send a message asking the client for this file to be reloaded. Presto! No need to click the Refresh button in your browser after every modification. Try changing the color of `<h1>` elements inside your `main.less` file from `SteelBlue` to `Red`. Watch Grunt compile it into a `main.css` file and have livereload automatically update your DOM. Finally, add `'Gulp'` to the `$scope.tools` array inside `app.js` and watch Grunt lint it using JSHint and update your browser tab with this quick addition.

Creating a Custom Task

You've seen how to use the simple configuration options provided by a handful of plug-ins that can easily be used to automate several common workflow tasks. However, if you want to create a custom task that does not rely on a preexisting plug-in, you are free to do so because Grunt runs using Node.js. You can easily plug any JavaScript code you want to write into your current workflow, as shown in the next snippet that showcases a few helpful mechanisms provided by Grunt to assist in creating custom tasks:

```
// Custom task
grunt.registerTask('myTask', 'My custom task', function(one, two) {
  // Force task to run in async mode and save handle for completion callback
  var done = this.async();

  setTimeout(function() {
    // [1] Access task name and arguments
    grunt.log.writeln(this.name, one, two);

    // [2] Fail if properties don't exist
```

```
grunt.config.requires('connect.options.livereload');

// [3] Access configuration properties
grunt.log.writeln('The livereload port is '
  + grunt.config('connect.options.livereload'));

// Succeed asynchronously
done();

// [4] Run other tasks
grunt.task.run('default');
  }.bind(this), 1000);
});
```

This example registers a task named `myTask` with Grunt that accepts two arguments and includes a custom description. To demonstrate a task that runs in asynchronous mode, `this.async()` is invoked, and the rest of the code is executed inside a call to `setTimeout()`, with `done()` being called to succeed asynchronously. Here, helper functions are used to access the task name and arguments [1], fail if a specific configuration property is not present [2], and access Grunt configuration options that have been previously defined [3]. Instructing custom tasks to run other workflow tasks is also possible, as shown in [4]. You can invoke this custom task with colon-separated arguments, as mentioned earlier in this chapter. The invocation and output of this task are shown here:

```
$ grunt myTask:Hello:World
Running "myTask:Hello:World" (myTask) task
myTask Hello World
The livereload port is 35729

Running "connect:development" (connect) task
Started connect web server on http://localhost:9000

Running "watch" task
Waiting...
```

> **NOTE** *Notice how the* `grunt.log.writeln()` *helper function was used to print out multiple variables. Grunt provides several helper functions, one of which is* `grunt.log.error()`, *which if invoked with a message halts the execution of any subsequent tasks. The only way to force Grunt to execute remaining tasks after an error occurs is to specify the* `--force` *flag when running* `grunt` *from the command line.*

Now that you have seen how to register custom tasks and leverage a few of the built-in helper functions, the only limitation to what you can accomplish with Grunt will be based on what can be coded in JavaScript, so the sky is the limit! Listing 2-6 shows the completed Gruntfile that automates all the workflow tasks that have been configured in this section, as well as the custom task described earlier. In the next section, you create a similar workflow using Gulp.js, another popular open source JavaScript build system designed with different philosophical principals.

LISTING 2-6: Completed Gruntfile.js

```javascript
'use strict';

// Wrapper function
module.exports = function(grunt) {

  // Project and task configuration
  grunt.initConfig({
    pkg: grunt.file.readJSON('package.json'),

    // Configuring the 'connect' task from 'grunt-contrib-connect'
    connect: {
      // Task options, overrides built-in defaults
      options: {
        port: 9000,
        open: true,
        livereload: 35729,
        hostname: 'localhost'
      },
      // Arbitrarily named target
      development: {
        // Target options, overrides task options
        options: {
          middleware: function(connect) {
            return [
              connect.static('app')
            ];
          }
        }
      }
    },

    // Configuring the 'less' task from 'grunt-contrib-less'
    less: {
      development: {
        files: {
          'app/main.css': 'app/main.less'
        }
      }
    },

    // Configuring the 'jshint' task from 'grunt-contrib-jshint'
    jshint: {
      options: {
        jshintrc: '.jshintrc'
      },
      all: [
        'Gruntfile.js',
        'app/*.js'
      ]
```

continues

LISTING 2-6 *(continued)*

```javascript
    },

    // Configuring the 'watch' task from 'grunt-contrib-watch'
    watch: {
      options: {
        livereload: '<%= connect.options.livereload %>',
      },
      js: {
        files: ['app/*.js'],
        tasks: ['jshint']
      },
      styles: {
        files: ['app/*.less'],
        tasks: ['less']
      },
      html: {
        files: ['app/*.html']
      }
    }
  });

  // Load your desired plug-ins, which provide specific tasks
  require('load-grunt-tasks')(grunt);

  // Default task
  grunt.registerTask('default', ['connect:development', 'watch']);

  // Custom task
  grunt.registerTask('myTask', 'My custom task', function(one, two) {
    // Force task to run in async mode and save handle for completion callback
    var done = this.async();

    setTimeout(function() {
      // Access task name and arguments
      grunt.log.writeln(this.name, one, two);

      // Fail if properties don't exist
      grunt.config.requires('connect.options.livereload');

      // Access configuration properties
      grunt.log.writeln('The livereload port is '
        + grunt.config('connect.options.livereload'));

      // Succeed asynchronously
      done();

      // Run other tasks
      grunt.task.run('default');
    }.bind(this), 1000);
  });

};
```

WHAT IS GULP?

Gulp is another popular workflow automation tool that offers a streaming build system using Node .js streams and favors code-over-configuration. This approach simplifies management of complex tasks by eliminating the need for large configuration files. Similar to Grunt, Gulp provides a command-line tool that is invoked to run tasks created by a growing community of plug-ins, as well as custom tasks developed using JavaScript.

Getting Started with Gulp

The first thing you need to do to start experimenting with Gulp and its elegantly simple application programming interface (API) is install the command-line tool globally on your machine. To be able to access the gulp utility, run the following from the command line:

```
npm install -g gulp
```

Installing Plug-Ins

In this section, you create the same workflow built earlier in this chapter using Grunt, but using Gulp's ecosystem of plug-ins. Now that you have Gulp installed globally, go ahead and install the necessary plug-ins and modules needed to accomplish this task by running the following from your command line:

```
npm install --save-dev gulp
npm install --save-dev gulp-load-plugins
npm install --save-dev gulp-livereload
npm install --save-dev gulp-less
npm install --save-dev gulp-jshint
npm install --save-dev jshint-stylish
npm install --save-dev opn
npm install --save-dev connect
npm install --save-dev connect-livereload
```

Verify that the plug-ins listed in the preceding code have been added as development dependencies by opening your package.json file and checking the devDependencies property. With all the required plug-ins successfully installed, the next step is to create your first Gulpfile.

The Gulpfile

The Gulpfile.js file, analogous to the Gruntfile.js that you created earlier in this chapter, belongs in the root directory of your project as a sibling of the package.json file. It should be committed with the rest of your source code. Listing 2-7 contains a skeleton Gulpfile.js that you will build upon by configuring various tasks in the following sections.

LISTING 2-7: Skeleton Gulpfile.js

```
// [1] Require gulp
var gulp = require('gulp');

// [2] Load plug-ins
var $ = require('gulp-load-plugins')();

// [3] Default task - run with 'gulp'
gulp.task('default', [], function () {
});
```

As shown in the listing, the skeleton Gulpfile consists of [1] requiring the Gulp library, [2] loading all plug-ins listed in your package.json file, and [3] registering a specific task. As with Grunt, the default Gulp task will be executed when you run gulp from the command line. Because Gulp extols the principle of convention over configuration, you should notice that there is no Gulp equivalent of Grunt's initConfig(). Now that you have seen the three main parts of a Gulpfile, you can jump right into programming your first Gulp task.

> **NOTE** *The* gulp-load-plugins *module you installed takes care of loading the Gulp plug-ins listed in your* package.json *file by requiring each one and namespacing them, after stripping the* gulp- *prefix, under the assigned variable. Without this useful module, you have to require each plug-in manually, as follows:*
>
> ```
> var jshint = require('gulp-jshint');
> ```
>
> *Notice that this is different in function from the Grunt* load-grunt-tasks *counterpart because in this case you are requiring a handle to the plug-in module directly instead of loading configurable tasks.*

Creating Tasks

The anatomy of a Gulp task follows the form gulp.task(name[, deps], fn) which consists of a name, a list of optional dependencies in array form, and a callback function that performs the desired operations. The name is used to invoke the task directly from the command line, and the optional dependencies array can contain a list of task names that should be executed and completed before your task function will run. In this section, you will leverage each of the installed Gulp plug-ins and Node.js modules to create an automated workflow for serving your application's assets, compiling Less stylesheets, and linting JavaScript files.

The Connect Task

You might have noticed that not all the modules installed were Gulp-specific plug-ins. Because Gulp takes a more programmatic approach to automating developer workflow, it is often simple enough to directly use a Node.js module to perform the operations of your task. The connect task you are about to implement does just that. Modify your Gulpfile by adding the following code somewhere after loading the Gulp plug-ins:

```
// 'connect' task for starting web server
gulp.task('connect', function () {
  var connect = require('connect');
  var app = connect()
    .use(require('connect-livereload')({ port: 35729 }))
    .use(connect.static('app'))
    .use(connect.directory('app'));

  require('http').createServer(app)
    .listen(9000)
    .on('listening', function () {
      console.log('Started connect web server on http://localhost:9000');
    });
});
```

When you configured this task using Grunt, the grunt-contrib-connect plug-in used the connect and connect-livereload Node.js modules under the hood and exposed configuration options accordingly. Following Gulp's philosophy of convention over configuration, the preceding code interacts directly with these two modules to implement the desired task functionality. A new Connect server is instantiated with three middleware plug-ins via the .use() function. These handles inject the livereload snippet into outgoing requests, serve static assets from within the app directory, and make the directory itself explorable. Finally, Node's built-in http module is used to create a new server set to listen on port 9000 using the Connect application instance. With the implementation of the connect task finalized, go ahead and run the following from the command line:

```
gulp connect
```

Opening your browser to http://localhost:9000/ should bring up the simple application created earlier in this chapter. Although this simple Connect application instance should be enough to satisfy most of your workflow automation needs, you can find a full list of all bundled Connect middleware plug-ins by visiting the documentation site at http://www.senchalabs.org/connect/.

The Less Task

Next up is creating the less task that allows Gulp to compile your Less files into CSS. Because you should have already installed the gulp-less plug-in, the actual implementation of the less task will be straightforward. Add the following code to your Gulpfile after the implementation of the connect task:

```
// 'less' task for compiling styles
gulp.task('less', function () {
  return gulp.src('app/*.less')
    .pipe($.less({ paths: 'app' }))
    .pipe(gulp.dest('app'));
});
```

The first thing this task does is invoke `gulp.src()`, which accepts a glob and returns a file structure stream that can be piped to other plug-ins. *Globbing* is a concept that allows matching files using shell patterns and regular expressions. The Node.js `Stream.pipe()` function is then called to direct the file stream to the `gulp-less` plug-in, which was namespaced under the `$` variable, with the desired `app/` directory specified as a path. At this point, the output stream contains the compiled CSS, and `gulp.dest()`, which accepts a path, is invoked to write the stream to a file. When you're using `gulp.dest()`, folders that do not exist are created automatically. Because the `gulp-less` plug-in maintains folder structure and handles renaming the output file, the path specified is used as a directory. Invoke the completed `less` task by running the following from the command line:

```
gulp less
```

This compiles any Less files inside your `app/` directory into their respective CSS. Worth mentioning is the fact that because `Less` is a Node.js module as well as a command-line tool, it exposes an API for programmatic usage within code. This means that your Gulp `less` task could technically have been implemented directly using the module, but the `gulp-less` plug-in does most of the work for you, making it simpler to get started. You can find a complete list of the available usages for `gulp-less` by visiting the plug-in documentation page at `https://github.com/plus3network/gulp-less`.

NOTE *You may have noticed that the* `less` *task created in this section contains a return statement. By definition, a Gulp task can be made asynchronous if its implementation function accepts a callback, returns a stream, or returns a promise. As the functionality of your build system expands, it becomes increasingly important to leverage Node's asynchronous capabilities. Because both* `ulp.src()` *and* `Stream.pipe()` *return chainable streams, the* `less` *task's implementation function fits one of the three criteria required to instruct Gulp to run this task in asynchronous mode. Accepting a callback can be implemented like this:*

```
gulp.task('taskName', function(done) {
  // Do some work and fail asynchronously
  done(err);
});
```

You can return a promise using the popular q *library, as shown here:*

```
var Q = require('q');

gulp.task('taskName', function() {
  var deferred = Q.defer();
  // Do async work
  setTimeout(function() {
    deferred.resolve();
  }, 1);
  return deferred.promise;
});
```

The JSHint Task

Because linting JavaScript files is an important part of any serious front-end build system, you will be using the `gulp-jshint` plug-in that should have been installed earlier to add this functionality to your Gulp workflow. Go ahead and implement the `jshint` task by adding the following code after the `less` task in your Gulpfile:

```
// 'jshint' task for linting JS files
gulp.task('jshint', function () {
  return gulp.src('app/*.js')
    .pipe($.jshint())
    .pipe($.jshint.reporter(require('jshint-stylish')));
});
```

Here, the `app/*.js` glob pattern is passed to `gulp.src()` so that all JavaScript files inside your `app/` directory are read and represented as a stream that can piped to the `gulp-jshint` plug-in, which is accessed via `$.jshint()`. Notice that there is no need to write the output to disk, so in this case using `gulp.dest()` is unnecessary. It is also worth mentioning that, because this task implementation function returns a Node.js stream, Gulp lints your JavaScript files asynchronously. Run the following from your command line to invoke the completed `jshint` task:

```
gulp jshint
```

At this point, the output from the linting process should display no errors. To demonstrate a linting error, remove the `'use strict';` line from your app/app.js file and rerun the `jshint` task. You should notice that the output is formatted differently than when `grunt jshint` is invoked. This is because JSHint was set up to use the `jshint-stylish` reporter, installed earlier in this section, instead of the built-in default. Replace the line where the reporter is registered with the following:

```
.pipe($.jshint.reporter('default'));
```

Rerunning the Gulp `jshint` task should now produce different results. As you can see, JSHint reporters manipulate the way errors are formatted. In this case, the `jshint-stylish` reporter breaks the error message into multiple lines and colorizes parts of it for easier readability. You can find information on creating custom reporters to suit your individual needs at `http://jshint .com/docs/reporters/`. Before continuing onto the implementation of the `watch` task, be sure to revert your changes to the app/app.js file and `jshint` task accordingly. For a detailed list of all supported invocations of the `gulp-jshint` plug-in, visit `https://github.com/spenceralger/ gulp-jshint`.

The Watch Task

Whereas with Grunt you had to install and configure the `grunt-contrib-watch` plug-in, Gulp has file-watching capabilities directly built into its API via the `gulp.watch()` function. To automate the previously defined tasks using watch functionality, you need to add the following lines of code to your Gulpfile after the `jshint` task:

```
// 'watch' task for responding to file modifications
gulp.task('watch', function () {
  // Start a livereload server on default port 35729
```

```
    $.livereload.listen();

    // Watch for changes and notify LR server
    gulp.watch([
      'app/*.html',
      'app/*.css',
      'app/*.js'
    ]).on('change', function (file) {
      $.livereload.changed(file.path);
    });

    // Run gulp tasks on specified file changes
    gulp.watch('app/*.js', ['jshint']);
    gulp.watch('app/*.less', ['less']);
  });
```

The first thing the `watch` task does is fire up a livereload server on the default port using the previously installed `gulp-livereload` plug-in. After that, a call to `gulp.watch()` is made with an array of file glob patterns that should be monitored for modifications. Because `gulp.watch()` returns a Node.js EventEmitter that emits `change` events, the `EventEmitter.on()` function is called in chain so that the livereload server can be notified of subsequent file modifications. This is done by invoking the plug-in's `changed()` function with the path to the modified file. At this point, the `watch` task has been set up to monitor HTML, CSS, and JavaScript files for changes and is able to communicate with the livereload server so that updates can automatically be propagated to all connected browsers. However, to leverage the previously defined `jshint` and `less` tasks, two additional calls to `gulp.watch()` need to be made that instruct Gulp to run these tasks when your JavaScript and Less files are changed. Running `gulp watch` from the command line and then modifying a JavaScript or Less file should now automatically trigger the `jshint` and `less` tasks, respectively. For a complete list of the available Gulp API functions, visit the documentation page at `https://github.com/gulpjs/gulp/blob/master/docs/API.md`.

The Default Task

As was the case with the Grunt workflow you set up previously in this chapter, you need to configure the default Gulp task to run both the `connect` and the `watch` tasks to achieve a more automated solution. To accomplish this, modify the `default` task located at the bottom of your Gulpfile to match the code shown here:

```
// Default task - run with 'gulp'
gulp.task('default', ['connect', 'watch'], function () {
  require('opn')('http://localhost:9000');
});
```

Notice that this invocation of `gulp.task()` uses the optional array of task dependencies that are executed and completed before the task implementation function is run. After the `connect` and `watch` tasks are executed, the previously installed `opn` library is used to open this example application in your default browser. In the case of Grunt, this functionality was handled by a configurable option of the `grunt-contrib-connect` plug-in. If you previously ran `gulp watch`, ensure that it has been terminated before launching the `default` task by running the following on the command line:

```
gulp
```

As with Grunt, this should launch the connect server, initiate file-watching functionality, and open an instance of your application inside a new browser tab. To verify that your Gulp workflow is working as intended, go ahead and make a few modifications to the index.html, app.js, and main .less files inside your app/ directory. Gulp should now be linting your JavaScript files, compiling your Less files into CSS, and serving all your application assets with livereload capability. Revert your changes to these files before proceeding onto the next section.

Arguments and Asynchronous Behavior

The last example in the Grunt section covered creating a custom task that accepted arguments and utilized a few built-in helper functions. Because, in the case of Gulp, the entire Gulpfile consists of custom tasks, in this section you will re-create myTask using two libraries that assist in parsing command-line options and facilitate asynchronous programming. Install the required modules by running the following on the command line:

```
npm install --save-dev nopt
npm install --save-dev q
```

The nopt module is a well-maintained argument-parsing library, whereas the q module is a tool for making and composing asynchronous promises in JavaScript. Two other popular option-parsing libraries are minimist and yargs. The async module is also worth mentioning, because it is one of the most depended upon Node modules on the NPM registry and provides straightforward, powerful utility functions for working with asynchronous JavaScript. To see how to use these libraries within the context of a Gulp task, add var nopt = require('nopt'); to the top of your Gulpfile below the other require statements, and then add the following code to the bottom of the file:

```
// [1] Set up parsing of CLI arguments
var knownOpts = {
  'one': String,
  'two': String
};
var shorthands = {
  'o': ['--one', 'Hello'],
  't': ['--two', 'World']
};
var options = nopt(knownOpts, shorthands);

// Custom task
gulp.task('myTask', function () {
  var deferred = Q.defer();

  setTimeout(function() {
    // [2] Fail if CLI arguments don't exist
    if (!options.one || !options.two) {
      deferred.reject('Error: Please specify the --one and --two flags.');
    } else {
      // [3] Access CLI arguments
      console.log(options.one + ' ' + options.two);

      // [4] Succeed asynchronously
```

```
        deferred.resolve();
      }
    }, 1000);

    return deferred.promise;
});
```

> **NOTE** *Promises are an asynchronous programming abstraction that uninvert the "inversion of control" pattern associated with passing callback functions around as arguments. Instead of accepting a callback, the* `myTask` *implementation function returns a promise, which Gulp is designed to handle to support asynchronous behavior. Although more detailed discussion of promises is outside the scope of this chapter, it is worth mentioning that the* `q` *module is Promises/A+ compliant. For a detailed explanation of the Promises/A+ open standard, visit the specification page at* `http://promises-aplus.github.io/promises-spec/`.

Before the implementation of `myTask`, the `nopt` module is configured to explicitly parse two command-line options and their associated shorthand flags [1]. Shorthand definitions can specify default values for each option flag, which is the case in this example. Inside the task implementation function, a new deferred object is created, and its `.reject()` function is called with an error message if the desired command-line flags are not present [2]. Running `gulp mytask` results in an error and causes Gulp to display this failure message in the terminal. The command-line options are made available as object properties after being parsed by `nopt` and can be accessed as shown in [3]. Finally, `myTask` succeeds asynchronously if the deferred object's `.resolve()` function is invoked [4]. Running any of the following from the command line results in valid executions of this task:

```
gulp myTask --one Hello --two World
gulp myTask -o --two Gulp
gulp myTask -ot
```

Because Gulp tasks do not accept command-line arguments as function parameters directly, you should now be comfortable using a parsing library to augment your tasks as necessary. At this point, you have finished using Gulp to re-create the automated workflow that was initially introduced using Grunt. Listing 2-8 shows the completed Gulpfile that provides identical functionality to the Gruntfile created earlier in this chapter. In the next section, you will find a brief discussion on utilizing the Make command-line tool to automate common JavaScript build-related tasks.

LISTING 2-8: Completed Gulpfile.js

```
'use strict';

var gulp = require('gulp');
var nopt = require('nopt');
```

```
var Q = require('q');

// Load plug-ins
var $ = require('gulp-load-plugins')();

// Set up parsing of CLI arguments
var knownOpts = {
  'one': String,
  'two': String
};
var shorthands = {
  'o': ['--one', 'Hello'],
  't': ['--two', 'World']
};
var options = nopt(knownOpts, shorthands);

// 'connect' task for starting web server
gulp.task('connect', function () {
  var connect = require('connect');
  var app = connect()
    .use(require('connect-livereload')({ port: 35729 }))
    .use(connect.static('app'))
    .use(connect.directory('app'));

  require('http').createServer(app)
    .listen(9000)
    .on('listening', function () {
      console.log('Started connect web server on http://localhost:9000');
    });
});

// 'less' task for compiling styles
gulp.task('less', function () {
  return gulp.src('app/*.less')
    .pipe($.less({ paths: 'app' }))
    .pipe(gulp.dest('app'));
});

// 'jshint' task for linting JS files
gulp.task('jshint', function () {
  return gulp.src('app/*.js')
    .pipe($.jshint())
    .pipe($.jshint.reporter(require('jshint-stylish')));
});

// 'watch' task for responding to file modifications
gulp.task('watch', function () {
  // Start a livereload server on default port 35729
  $.livereload.listen();

  // Watch for changes and notify LR server
  gulp.watch([
    'app/*.html',
    'app/*.css',
```

continues

LISTING 2-8 *(continued)*

```
    'app/*.js'
  ]).on('change', function (file) {
    $.livereload.changed(file.path);
  });

  // Run gulp tasks on specified file changes
  gulp.watch('app/*.js', ['jshint']);
  gulp.watch('app/*.less', ['less']);
});

// Default task - run with 'gulp'
gulp.task('default', ['connect', 'watch'], function () {
  require('opn')('http://localhost:9000');
});

// Custom task
gulp.task('myTask', function () {
  var deferred = Q.defer();

  setTimeout(function() {
    // Fail if CLI arguments don't exist
    if (!options.one || !options.two) {
      deferred.reject('Error: Please specify the --one and --two flags.');
    } else {
      // Access CLI arguments
      console.log(options.one + ' ' + options.two);

      // Succeed asynchronously
      deferred.resolve();
    }
  }, 1000);

  return deferred.promise;
});
```

Gulp, Grunt, and Make

As you have seen, Grunt and Gulp are exceedingly sophisticated and powerful workflow automation tools. Although both are exceedingly popular in the JavaScript open source community, somewhat surprisingly, a number of popular modules use an automation tool from the 1970s: Make. If you have experience programming in C, you likely have used Make for automating your compilation process. This section explores how to use Make to automate common workflow tasks while developing projects using JavaScript. It also discusses when it might be appropriate to utilize one tool versus another.

Automation Using Make

Make has a number of sophisticated features for compiling and linking C code, but in the JavaScript community, Make is primarily used to create aliases for commonly used shell scripts. In addition,

Make allows you to define variables for paths to commonly used programs, enabling you to create more readable commands. Make usually comes preinstalled on Linux-like systems, including Mac OSX. Before proceeding, verify that you have Make installed by running the `make` command from your terminal. You should get output that looks like this:

```
make: *** No targets specified and no makefile found.  Stop.
```

As with Grunt and Gulp, the rules you define for Make should be contained in a file named `Makefile`, which should exist in your project's root directory. When you run the `make` command, it tries to parse the Makefile in your current working directory. Listing 2-9 contains a simple Makefile that handles compiling your Less assets.

LISTING 2-9: Makefile

```
LESSC = node_modules/less/bin/lessc

less:
$(LESSC) app/main.less > app/main.css
```

For this example to work, you need to have the Less compiler available as part of your project, which can be accomplished by running `npm install less`. Now you can compile your Less assets by running the following from your command line:

```
make less
```

This Makefile defines a new rule, `less`, so that the `make` command knows to run the corresponding shell script when you run `make less`. Furthermore, Make can expand macros; for example, the `$(LESSC)` shown earlier is a macro that is expanded into `node_modules/less/bin/lessc` before Make executes the shell script. This removes the need to install NPM modules globally via `npm install less -g`, which might be advantageous in certain development environment configurations.

The most apt comparison of Make versus Grunt and Gulp is that Make is roughly equivalent to Gulp, but rules are written in your shell scripting language instead of creating tasks using JavaScript. Although shell scripts can be simple and elegant, they are not as platform independent as Node.js scripts, and there is no decent way to define which external programs your Makefile requires.

To illustrate this point, consider the exercise of introducing functionality similar to the `gulp watch` task you defined earlier in this chapter: Run the `make less` command every time the `main.less` file changes. Because the `lessc` program currently doesn't allow you to watch a file, your Makefile is responsible for handling that. Unfortunately, watching a file for modifications is a classic example of something that does not map well to standard shell commands. One approach may be using the `watch` command; however, this command is not available by default on OSX. You can also implement this using a `while` loop, but that's generally a bad idea. Maintaining and testing shell scripts is notoriously difficult, and writing logic into bash scripts can quickly spiral out of control. That being said, some utilities can watch files built in. For example, the JavaScript unit-testing framework Mocha has a `-w` command-line flag that instructs the utility to watch files for modifications. In this case, writing a `watch` rule is simple; all you need to do is run Mocha with the -w command-line flag.

When to Use Make

So when should you use Make over Gulp or Grunt? The general rule of thumb is to keep things as simple as possible for you and your team. If the only requirement is the ability to run your test suite or minify a JavaScript file with an easy-to-type command, Make is sufficient and can provide a simpler alternative than using Gulp or Grunt. Make is an excellent choice depending on how comfortable and familiar you are with shell scripting, if your build process relies on many existing shell scripts, and depending on your development environment. However, once you need more sophisticated capabilities, such as watching files or conditional logic, Gulp or Grunt would likely serve you better.

When to Use Grunt

Because Grunt is highly configurable, chances are high that the community has already created a plug-in for most tasks you might want to accomplish as far as workflow automation and build systems are concerned. This means that a sophisticated Gruntfile can be created with little to no coding simply by configuring the task and targets for each installed plug-in. This lends itself to teams that include designers who want Less/Sass compilation and livereload functionality to be part of their workflow but don't necessarily specialize in JavaScript programming. Designers and developers who prefer configuration to programming using Node.js streams and don't wish to mess with shell scripting should choose to use Grunt for their workflow needs.

When to Use Gulp

By adopting the convention over configuration philosophy, Gulp lends itself well to more seasoned developers and programmers who are comfortable enough using asynchronous Node.js streams. Although the open source community has been constantly expanding the selection of plug-ins, Gulp makes it just as easy to write tasks that utilize the underlying plug-in libraries directly, thereby reducing the number of dependencies for your workflow and build system. This, coupled with Gulp's use of Node.js streams, can help keep your build system fast, lightweight, and easy to manage. Developers who require a sophisticated workflow automation tool and have adopted the convention over configuration philosophy should opt to use Gulp over Grunt and Make.

So far in this chapter you have learned how to automate identical workflows using Grunt and Gulp and discovered how to use Make in the context of JavaScript for shell-heavy projects or those with simpler automation requirements. What is left is a discussion on explicit build system automation. In the next section, you build on your knowledge of Grunt and Gulp by exploring a new tool that can scaffold out complex build pipeline tasks that support concatenation, minification, obfuscation, and test harness execution.

WHAT IS YEOMAN?

Yeoman is an open source scaffolding tool that helps you kick-start new projects with sensible defaults, enforcing best practices and utilizing tools that help you stay productive while developing modern web applications. Yeoman accomplishes this by supporting an ecosystem of generators, which are plug-ins that can be run with the yo command to scaffold complete projects or useful parts. For those familiar with Ruby on Rails development, this process is analogous to the rails generate command. Projects generated with the Yeoman command-line tool are supported by a robust and opinionated client-side stack, composed of tools and frameworks that can help you quickly build beautiful web applications.

The promoted "Yeoman workflow" builds on the success and lessons learned from several open-source communities, so you can rest assured that your development stack is as intelligent as possible. The Yeoman workflow is composed of a scaffolding tool (yo), the build tools (grunt and gulp), and the package managers (bower and npm). Yeoman leverages these tools to remove the hassle associated with manually setting up a new project, improving your development productivity and satisfaction by allowing you to focus on building your application right out of the box.

Getting Started with Yeoman

For you to begin scaffolding projects with Yeoman, a generator must be installed first. For the purpose of this chapter, you will be exploring the official AngularJS generator that is maintained by the Yeoman team, but a full list of both official and community-maintained generators is located at http://yeoman.io/generators/. To get started with this generator, simply run the following from the command line:

```
npm install –g generator-angular@0.9.8
```

Scaffolding a New Project

The project scaffolding process is simple for all Yeoman generators. Simply create a new directory, navigate into it using your command line, and then run the appropriate yo command for the desired generator. Typically, this is the name of the generator following the generator- prefix. Because for this chapter you have installed the AngularJS generator, the following command kicks off the new project scaffolding process:

```
yo angular
```

At this point, most generators display a few prompts that allow you to configure how Yeoman scaffolds your new project. As is the case with generator-angular, the first few prompts ask if you would like to include Sass, Twitter's Bootstrap framework, and a few commonly used AngularJS modules. For the purpose of this section, go ahead and press Enter during each prompt so that Yeoman can finish generating the necessary files and installing the required dependencies to support the promoted workflow. Because the AngularJS generator uses Grunt for automating all workflow and build system tasks, the following section briefly discusses each plug-in and associated task as it appears in your newly generated Gruntfile.js.

Exploring Plug-Ins and Tasks

As previously mentioned, Yeoman promotes best practices by setting you up with an opinionated workflow that can improve developer productivity and satisfaction. The promoted workflow is made possible by meticulously configuring one of the build system tools (Grunt or Gulp) with a set of tasks that handle automating local development, testing, and production packaging. Over time, the opinions behind the generated workflow tasks might change. However, the goal of this section is to help you become familiar with the various opinions made by the Yeoman team so that you can decide for yourself what best fits your future needs for any given project. Let the plug-ins described next serve as examples for the types of tasks that can be accomplished by leveraging an intelligent workflow for building modern web applications.

> **NOTE** *Due to the length of the generated* `Gruntfile.js` *that is discussed in this section, the configuration code for each task has been intentionally omitted. However, if you want to follow along without explicitly generating a new project, the* `yeoman/` *directory located inside the companion code for this chapter contains the full project as scaffolded by the AngularJS generator. Be sure to first run* `npm install && bower install` *from the command line within that directory before attempting to execute workflow tasks.*

load-grunt-tasks

As previously mentioned in the section on Grunt earlier in this chapter, this plug-in takes care of loading all the Grunt tasks exposed by the various plug-ins required for this workflow, which are located inside the `devDependencies` object of your `package.json` file. The reference occurs on Line 13, and you can view the documentation for this plug-in at `https://github.com/sindresorhus/load-grunt-tasks`.

time-grunt

The `time-grunt` plug-in does not expose a task but instead displays the elapsed execution time for all Grunt tasks on the command line using a cleanly formatted layout. This is especially helpful when debugging poorly configured tasks or attempting to optimize areas of your build system. You can find the documentation for this plug-in at `https://github.com/sindresorhus/time-grunt`.

grunt-newer

This plug-in is used in conjunction with tasks that perform file manipulations requiring `src` and `dest` configuration properties. It exposes the `newer` task, which doesn't require special configuration but can be prefixed onto the invocation of other tasks to reduce the number of file manipulation operations performed by your build system. For example, you can use this plug-in with the JSHint linter like so: `newer:jshint:all`. All source files are linted when this task is first run, but after that only files that have been modified are run through the linter. You can find the full documentation for this plug-in at `https://github.com/tschaub/grunt-newer`.

grunt-contrib-watch

This plug-in exposes the `watch` task, which monitors specified files for modifications before running the desired tasks. Its configuration has been discussed already, with the only difference this time around being a few new targets: `bower`, `jsTest`, `compass`, and `gruntfile`. These new targets handle rewiring front-end dependencies, rerunning unit tests, compiling Sass into CSS, and restarting the build system, respectively. For more information, please visit `https://github.com/gruntjs/grunt-contrib-watch`.

grunt-contrib-connect

Also discussed in a previous section, this plug-in exposes the `connect` task, which spins up a Hypertext Transfer Protocol (HTTP) server used to serve local assets. The task configuration for this `Gruntfile.js` contains additional targets for serving unit tests (`test`) and previewing production-built assets (`dist`). The full documentation for this plug-in, which is maintained by the Grunt core team, is located at `https://github.com/gruntjs/grunt-contrib-connect`.

grunt-contrib-jshint

As configured earlier in this chapter, this plug-in exposes the `jshint` task that runs JavaScript files through the JSHint linting utility. This time around, the task configuration contains an additional target specifically for linting the associated JavaScript unit test files. For further documentation on the `grunt-contrib-jshint` plug-in, please visit `https://github.com/gruntjs/grunt-contrib-jshint`.

grunt-contrib-clean

This plug-in exposes a `clean` task that is useful for removing undesired files and directories. If you look at the configuration for this task, you'll notice that it has been set up to remove the `.tmp/` and `dist/` directories. Yeoman uses the `.tmp/` directory for storing files that need to be processed by multiple tasks (such as for uglification and concatenation) and builds out your packaged application to the `dist/` directory. Because both of these directories are auto-generated, best practices dictate having a way to clean out both of them between builds. For more information, visit `https://github.com/gruntjs/grunt-contrib-clean`.

> **NOTE** *You may by now have noticed the presence of* `<%= yeoman.app %>` *and* `<%= yeoman.dist %>` *inside the task configuration blocks for the* `Gruntfile.js` *created by* `generator-angular`*. These templates are used by Yeoman to allow you to configure your project's directory structure as you see fit. Located at the top of the* `Gruntfile.js`*, you will find an* `appConfig` *object that contains the values Yeoman will use to render against the templates referenced throughout the various task configurations.*

grunt-autoprefixer

Autoprefixer is a standalone tool that parses CSS and adds vendor-prefixed CSS properties using the Can I Use (`http://caniuse.com/`) database. This plug-in exposes the `autoprefixer` Grunt task, which allows you to configure the way autoprefixer works for your project. By default, Yeoman sets the `browsers` property of the task-level `options` object to `last 1 version`. If your project needs to support older browsers, be sure to modify this setting. A detailed explanation of all available

options for the `grunt-autoprefixer` plug-in is documented at https://github.com/nDmitry/
grunt-autoprefixer.

grunt-wiredep

Wiredep is a standalone tool that wires dependencies into your source code. This plug-in exposes the
`wiredep` Grunt task, which allows you to inject Bower packages directly into your source code as part
of your Grunt workflow. Yeoman has configured this task to look at your main `index.html` file, which
wiredep parses for comments that tell it where to inject dependencies. Thankfully, Yeoman has already
added the necessary comments as well. For JavaScript dependencies, `bower:js` is used, whereas CSS
dependencies can be injected using `bower:css`. Both of these comment blocks must be closed with an
`endbower` comment, and nothing should be inserted between these comment blocks, because wiredep
overwrites those sections with dependencies as defined in your `bower.json` file. For a complete list of
supported options, please visit https://github.com/stephenplusplus/grunt-wiredep.

grunt-contrib-compass

This plug-in exposes the `compass` Grunt task, which configures the way the standalone tool
Compass is integrated into your workflow. Compass is an open source authoring framework
that compiles your Sass files into CSS. This plug-in requires that you have Ruby, Sass, and
Compass installed on your machine to function. Yeoman has set up the `compass` task to look
for Sass files in the `styles/` directory of your designated application root. If you want to change
this behavior, simply modify the appropriate configuration options for this task. For in-depth
documentation, please visit the plug-in's repository located at https://github.com/gruntjs/
grunt-contrib-compass.

grunt-filerev

This plug-in exposes the `filerev` task, which provides configuration options that support
integrating static asset revisioning through file content hashing as part of your workflow. This is a
good practice to follow when deploying your application into a production environment because
you have better control over how your assets are cached. When new builds are generated, your
optimized application files are postfixed with a different hash, allowing your cachebusting strategy
to take effect. By default, Yeoman has configured this task to revision all your scripts, styles, images,
and fonts. For more information, please visit https://github.com/yeoman/grunt-filerev.

grunt-usemin

This plug-in replaces references from nonoptimized scripts, style sheets, and other assets to their
optimized version within a set of HTML files (or any templates/views). To accomplish this, the
useminPrepare and usemin tasks are exposed for configuration inside your Gruntfile.js.
Remember how the `filerev` task creates revisioned copies of your assets? Well, the grunt-usemin
plug-in allows you to add configuration blocks (similar to those used by wiredep) so that you
can specify how the revisioned and optimized versions of your assets should be replaced in your
source code. If you look inside your `index.html` file, you should notice that the `bower:js` block
that wiredep uses is wrapped with a comment containing `build:js(.) scripts/vendor.js`. This
instructs usemin to create a single `vendor.js` file from any of the JavaScript files contained within

this comment block (in this case your Bower dependencies), which is closed by an `endbuild` comment. You can see a similar usemin comment block at the bottom of your `index.html` file; it is used to compile a single `scripts.js` for all your application's custom JavaScript files.

The `useminPrepare` task updates the Grunt configuration to apply a transformation flow to the files wrapped in the appropriate comment build blocks. By default, usemin configures the `concat` and `uglify` tasks, exposed by the `grunt-contrib-concat` and `grunt-contrib-uglify` plug-ins, respectively. These two tasks take care of combining all your JavaScript files, as defined by the usemin build blocks, and obfuscating the result by running it through UglifyJS. Yeoman has gone ahead and added the `cssmin` task from the `grunt-contrib-cssmin` plug-in as part flow as well, which handles compressing your CSS files.

The `usemin` task replaces all the blocks with a single "summary" line, pointing to a file created by the transformation flow. It then looks for references to assets and replaces them with their revved versions, which were created by the `filerev` task. The result of using the `grunt-usemin` plug-in is that your workflow is now enhanced with the ability to concatenate, obfuscate, minify, and revision your source files. It is worth mentioning that, if so desired, you can manually configure the `concat`, `uglify`, and `cssmin` tasks. This plug-in simply makes it easier to manage your transformation flow by configuring those tasks for you based on the comment build blocks inside the `index.html` file. For more information, including examples of additional transformation flows, visit the plug-in documentation at `https://github.com/yeoman/grunt-usemin`.

grunt-contrib-imagemin

This plug-in exposes the `imagemin` task, which allows you to compress your application's images using the gifsicle (for GIFs), jpegtran (for JPEGs), optipng (for PNGs), and svgo (for SVGs) image optimizers. The optimizers are bundled with the plug-in, so you don't have to worry about installing them on your machine. Yeoman configures the `imagemin` task to look for images in the `images/` directory of your application root, but you can modify this as desired. For a complete list of the compression options available for this plug-in, visit the documentation at `https://github.com/gruntjs/grunt-contrib-imagemin`.

grunt-svgmin

Although you can technically use the `grunt-contrib-imagemin` plug-in for compressing SVGs, Yeoman also includes the `grunt-svgmin` plug-in by default, which offers finer control in the scalable vector graphics (SVG) compression process through the exposed `svgmin` Grunt task. This plug-in also uses the svgo optimizer and can be helpful when handling more complex SVG images. You can find a list of all available compression options at `https://github.com/sindresorhus/grunt-svgmin`.

grunt-contrib-htmlmin

This plug-in uses the `html-minifier` open source tool, a highly configurable, well-tested, JavaScript based minifier, to compress your HTML files. The minifier can be configured via Grunt using the exposed `htmlmin` task, which Yeoman has set up for you with a few default options enabled (`collapseWhitespace`, `removeOptionalTags`, and so on). To learn more about how to pass configuration options to the bundled `html-minifier` via Grunt, look at the documentation located at `https://github.com/gruntjs/grunt-contrib-htmlmin`.

grunt-ng-annotate

This plug-in is based on the `ng-annotate` command-line tool, which can add, remove, and rebuild AngularJS dependency injection annotations. By default, the `ngAnnotate` task tries to make your AngularJS code safe for minification by automatically using the "long form" for dependency injection. If this is your first time coming across AngularJS annotations, here is an example of what your code usually looks like without annotations:

```
angular.module("MyApp").controller("MyCtrl", function($scope, $timeout) {
});
```

Due to the nature of how AngularJS handles dependency injection, the preceding code cannot be safely minified without breaking your application. Instead, the following "long form" must be used so that your application properly holds up after undergoing the minification process:

```
angular.module("MyApp").controller("MyCtrl", ["$scope", "$timeout",
function($scope, $timeout) {
}]);
```

Although you can surely use this long form manually, it does become tedious and error prone to enforce as your codebase grows. Yeoman saves you this hassle by automatically using the `grunt-ng-annotate` plug-in to convert your code to this form before running it through the `uglify` task (configured by usemin), thereby ensuring that your application does not break when compressed for production. You can find more information and usage examples for the `ngAnnotate` task at `https://github.com/mzgol/grunt-ng-annotate`.

grunt-google-cdn

This plug-in exposes the `cdnify` task, which allows you to replace local JavaScript references to resources hosted on the Google Content Delivery Network (CDN). Depending on your production environment, it may be advantageous to lower the bandwidth required by your server to deliver the application by allowing Google's servers to deliver some of your vendor JavaScript files (such as the AngularJS library itself). If this doesn't sound like something you need for your production setup, you can easily remove this task, as described in the "Modifications" section located later in this chapter. For more information, please visit the plug-in documentation located at `https://github.com/btford/grunt-google-cdn`.

grunt-contrib-copy

This plug-in exposes the configurable `copy` task, which allows for easily copying files and folders defined from within your Grunt workflow. In this case, Yeoman has configured the task to copy assets needed for production to the `dist/` directory and styles to be autoprefixed into the `.tmp/` directory. You can find more information about the `copy` task at `https://github.com/gruntjs/grunt-contrib-copy`.

grunt-concurrent

This plug-in exposes the `concurrent` task, which is mainly used for build optimization purposes. Running slow tasks like Coffee and Sass concurrently can improve your build time significantly.

Yeoman uses this task for precisely that, with the addition of running the image optimization tasks concurrently when building your application for production. The `concurrent` task is also useful if you need to run multiple blocking tasks like `nodemon` and `watch` at once. For more information, visit `https://github.com/sindresorhus/grunt-concurrent`.

grunt-karma

The AngularJS Yeoman generator uses the `generator-karma` generator to scaffold out a skeleton `karma.conf.js` file inside your `test/` directory. For the unfamiliar, Karma is an open source JavaScript test runner created by the AngularJS team. Out of the box, this generator allows you to run your Karma tests traditionally using the binary located inside the `node_modules/karma/bin/` directory, but if you want to invoke your test harness via Grunt, you must also install the `grunt-karma` plug-in by running the following from your command line:

```
npm install --save-dev grunt-karma
```

This allows you to properly invoke the alias task for testing your application, described in the following section. For more information on the `grunt-karma` plug-in, please visit the official documentation located at `https://github.com/karma-runner/grunt-karma`.

Alias Tasks and Workflow

Although you are able to run each of the exposed plug-in tasks mentioned earlier directly from your command line, where the promoted Yeoman workflow really stands out is with the alias tasks that bring everything together. The four main workflow tasks are located at the bottom of the generated `Gruntfile.js` and are described next.

serve

The `grunt serve` task functions similarly to the one you created earlier in this chapter. Running this task cleans any temporary files, wires your Bower dependencies, runs the Sass compiler, autoprefixes your CSS, launches the livereload server, and finally watches your application files for modifications. A key difference from the version you created earlier, however, is that Yeoman set up this task to accept an additional argument. If you run `grunt serve:dist`, Grunt first builds your application for production before launching a connect server that is pointed at the `dist/` directory so you can preview your compressed application.

test

The `grunt test` command is an alias that spins up a connect server pointed at your unit test files before invoking the `karma` task that runs your test harness in `singleRun` mode. Because the `package.json` file created by Yeoman sets the `test` property of the `scripts` object to run `grunt test`, you can also invoke your entire test harness by simply running `npm test` from the command line. It is worth mentioning that the generated `test/karma.conf.js` file is initially configured to run your test harness using PhantomJS, a headless WebKit browser. For help configuring Karma, visit the documentation page at `http://karma-runner.github.io/0.8/config/configuration-file.html`.

build

The `grunt build` alias task that Yeoman configures handles compressing your AngularJS application and preparing it for a production environment. The task starts by cleaning temporary files and then wires your Bower dependencies, prepares usemin, concurrently runs Sass and the image optimizers, autoprefixes your CSS, concatenates your JavaScript, copies application assets to `dist/`, replaces script references with CDN versions, minifies your CSS, minifies your scripts, revisions your assets, and finally minifies your HTML. Although there are many tasks being invoked as part of the process, the ultimate output of the `grunt build` task is a standalone `dist/` directory that can be deployed to your server of choice and is ready for production.

default

As mentioned earlier in this chapter, the default alias task is triggered when `grunt` is run from the command line with no specified task arguments. In this case, Yeoman has set up the default task to lint your JavaScript files, before testing and building your application production. You can easily modify this command to fit your particular needs, but do take care when modifying the `build` task, because the order in which tasks are invoked matters.

Modifications

The workflow generated by Yeoman is designed to be both modular and scalable. Although the generators are opinionated, the decision on which tasks to include or exclude is left entirely to you. If you want to remove a task from the workflow, simply delete it from the configured `Gruntfile.js` (or `Gulpfile.js`) and uninstall the associated plug-in from your project. For example, if you want to remove the `cdnify` task exposed by the `grunt-google-cdn` plug-in, run the following from the command line to uninstall it from your project:

```
npm uninstall grunt-google-cdn --save-dev
```

This removes the plug-in from the `node_modules/` folder and updates your `package.json` so that the plug-in no longer appears as a development dependency. When removing tasks from your workflow, pay particular attention to task dependencies. If the deleted task is referenced inside the configuration block of other tasks, your task runner throws an error during execution. To avoid workflow errors, be sure to remove all references to tasks you decide to delete after the initial scaffolding process.

Subgenerators

Some Yeoman generators also come packaged with one or more subgenerators, which you can use to scaffold helpful parts of a project after creation. For example, the AngularJS generator you installed comes packaged with additional subgenerators that can be invoked as follows:

➤ **controller**—`yo angular:controller user`

➤ **directive**—`yo angular:directive myDirective`

➤ **filter**—`yo angular:filter myFilter`

➤ **route**—`yo angular:route myroute`

> ➤ **service**—yo angular:service myService

> ➤ **decorator**—yo angular:decorator serviceName

> ➤ **view**—yo angular:view user

These subgenerators scaffold new AngularJS components for your application by creating new files (or updating existing ones), creating accompanying unit test skeletons (when appropriate), and wiring up the generated files into index.html. This means that invoking one of the preceding commands while your workflow system is running triggers the appropriate watch targets as expected, allowing you to seamlessly add new components to your application without slowing down your workflow. For more information on the official AngularJS generator and its packaged subgenerators, please visit the official documentation page located at https://github.com/yeoman/generator-angular.

Popular Generators

The purpose of this section was to explore the workflow and automated build system promoted by Yeoman in the context of developing AngularJS applications. It therefore made sense to focus on the official Yeoman generator, but other popular AngularJS generators are worth briefly mentioning.

angular-fullstack

This Yeoman generator is a fork of the official AngularJS generator, and as such contains all the same functionality. However, it modifies the directory structure of your scaffolded application to also include an Express server. For those interested in experimenting with the MongoDB, Express, Angular, and Node (MEAN) stack, this generator is a fantastic place to start. Install it by running the following from your command line:

```
npm install -g generator-angular-fullstack
```

Create a new project directory, navigate into it, and run yo angular-fullstack to create a new application. For more information, visit https://github.com/DaftMonk/generator-angular-fullstack.

jhipster

For the full-stack developers who prefer to write their back-end services using Java yet desire to utilize many of the open source utilities targeted at creating beautiful front-end applications, this Yeoman generator is worth looking into. It can be used to quickly create a Spring Boot (http://projects.spring.io/spring-boot/) project that incorporates an AngularJS single-page application along with the promoted Yeoman workflow. Install it by running the following from the command line:

```
npm install -g generator-jhipster
```

Create a new project directory, navigate into it, and run yo jhipster to create a new application. For more information, visit http://jhipster.github.io/.

ionic

This Yeoman generator helps front-end developers get started with building hybrid mobile applications using the IonicFramework, a beautiful, open source framework for developing mobile applications with HTML5. In addition to incorporating the promoted Yeoman workflow discussed in this chapter, it prescribes best practices for managing Cordova-based projects through the intelligent use of Cordova hooks. Install it by running the following from the command line:

```
npm install -g generator-ionic
```

Create a new project directory, navigate into it, and run `yo ionic` to create a new application. For more information, visit `https://github.com/diegonetto/generator-ionic`.

CONCLUSION

Over the course of this chapter, you have learned how to manage front-end dependencies using Bower, how to automate development tasks using Grunt and Gulp, how to scaffold new projects using Yeoman, and how to enhance your productivity and satisfaction during development by subscribing to a few workflow best practices. Regardless of whether you choose to use these tools and practices going forward in your future AngularJS projects or not, you have been exposed to the current state of modern front-end application development tooling. Picking the right tool for the job can be a tough decision to make when starting a new project, but through the examples of this chapter, it should be clear that the optimization and automation of mundane, repetitive tasks can help you stay effective in the constantly shifting world of front-end web application development.

3

Architecture

WHAT YOU WILL LEARN IN THIS CHAPTER:

➤ Communication between AngularJS components

➤ Structuring infinite scrolling with AngularJS

➤ Running A/B tests with AngularJS modules

➤ Structuring application files based on project size

➤ Organizing your application with a module loader

➤ Best practices for structuring user authentication

WROX.COM CODE DOWNLOADS FOR THIS CHAPTER

You can find the wrox.com code downloads for this chapter at `http://www.wrox.com/go/ proangularjs` on the Download Code tab.

WHY IS ARCHITECTURE IMPORTANT?

Readability and maintainability are two fundamental requirements when working on any project. Attempting to contribute to a poorly organized and architected application can be extremely frustrating and severely affect developer productivity. Spending a bit of time upfront thinking about how an application's files and JavaScript modules will be organized can save time and money later down the line, especially on larger projects with many contributing developers. In this chapter, you learn various techniques for organizing the many components provided by AngularJS, using best practices and conventions reinforced by the community. You are exposed to various techniques for communicating data between AngularJS components effectively, so you can make intelligent decisions when designing the architecture for your next application.

This chapter is broken up into five sections. In the first section, you get a high-level overview of the primary components of AngularJS code: controllers, services, and directives. The second section discusses AngularJS modules and the reason for the mysterious `angular.module()` calls you may have seen in previous chapters. In the third section, you learn about several different paradigms for arranging AngularJS files. The fourth section covers two popular open source tools for aggregating and loading your various AngularJS components: RequireJS and Browserify. The fifth and final section ties all these components together and discusses the concepts from the previous four sections in the context of creating a general user authentication mechanism.

CONTROLLERS, SERVICES, AND DIRECTIVES

The majority of AngularJS code you will write is contained in one of three components: controllers, services, or directives. Each of these components has its own unique properties. Effective AngularJS code takes advantage of the differences between these components. In this section, you get a high-level overview of the differences between these components and how they fit together. In addition, you learn how to share data between different components.

At a high level, the three components are related as follows. Services are responsible for fetching and storing data from remote servers. Controllers build on top of services to provide data and functionality to AngularJS's scope hierarchy. Directives build on top of controllers and services to interface with Document Object Model (DOM) elements directly.

> **NOTE** *This section offers a cursory overview of controllers, services, and directives, focusing on the trade-offs of using each of the three components in the context of writing AngularJS applications. If you are interested in learning about directives and services in more detail, Chapter 5, "Directives," features a more detailed guide to writing custom directives, and Chapter 7, "Services, Factories, and Providers," discusses design patterns for services.*

Controllers

Controllers are the AngularJS component responsible for exposing JavaScript data and functions to your Hypertext Markup Language (HTML). Typically, controllers are instantiated from your HTML using the `ng-controller` directive:

```
<div ng-controller="MyController"></div>
```

> **NOTE** *One key recurring theme in this book is the idea that controllers are responsible for exposing an application programming interface (API) to your HTML. Directives like* ngClick *and* ngBind *then interact with this API to create your page's user experience.*

Controllers are instantiated using AngularJS's dependency injector, a tool that inspects the controller's parameters and constructs them as necessary. Because services are registered with the dependency injector, a controller can utilize any number of services. However, controllers are *not* registered with the dependency injector, so controllers and services cannot list controllers as dependencies. For instance, you can create a service called `myService` and then list it as a dependency of the `MyController` controller:

```
var m = angular.module('myModule');

m.factory('myService', function() {
  return { answer: 42 };
});

m.controller('MyController', function(myService) {
  // Utilize myService
});
```

However, you cannot create another controller or service that lists `MyController` as a dependency:

```
var m = angular.module('myModule');

m.controller('MyController', function() {
});

m.factory('myService2', function(MyController) {
  // Error: MyController not registered with
  // dependency injector
});

m.controller('MyOtherController', function(MyController) {
  // Error: MyController not registered with
  // dependency injector
});
```

There are two other unique properties of controllers relative to services that are worth mentioning. First, each instance of the `ng-controller` directive creates a new instance of the controller (that is, calls the controller function). This is in stark contrast to services; a service is instantiated at most once, and the instance is shared between all controllers, services, and directives that depend on that service.

Second, in addition to the services registered through the AngularJS dependency injector, controllers can list objects called locals as dependencies. A *local* is a context-specific object registered with the dependency injector for that specific instance of the controller. The most common example of a local is the `$scope` object, which virtually every controller utilizes to fulfill its core purpose of exposing JavaScript functions and data to HTML. As far as the controller is concerned, listing a local as a dependency is no different from listing a service as a dependency:

```
m.controller('MyController', function($scope) {
  $scope.data = { answer: 42 };
});
```

However, a service *cannot* list a local as a dependency. The following code will cause an error:

```
m.factory('myService', function($scope) {
  // Error: $scope not registered with
  // dependency injector
});
```

This is why controllers are AngularJS's primary tool for exposing JavaScript data and functions to HTML: Controllers have access to `$scope`, whereas services do not. However, there is nothing to stop a controller from listing a service as a dependency and adding that service to its scope:

```
m.factory('myService', function() {
  return { answer: 42 };
});

m.controller('MyController', function($scope, myService) {
  // Enable accessing myService from the scope
  $scope.myService = myService;
});
```

Now that you understand the basic purpose and unique properties of controllers, you will learn how to share data between controllers. This task is a common source of confusion among AngularJS beginners and a common discussion topic on question and answer forums like Stack Overflow. AngularJS provides numerous methods for inter-controller communication. This section covers three such methods: scope inheritance, broadcasting events through `$scope`, and services.

Scope Inheritance

The first inter-controller communication method you learn about takes advantage of AngularJS's ability to nest scopes. Chapter 4, "Data Binding," covers scopes and scope inheritance in more detail. However, for the purposes of this section, it suffices to know that each instance of the `ng-controller` directive creates a new scope, and nested instances of the `ng-controller` directive create nested scopes:

```
<div  ng-controller="MyController"
      ng-init="answer = 42;">
  <h1>This is the parent scope</h1>
  <div  ng-controller="MyController">
    <h2>This scope inherits from the parent scope</h2>
    This prints '42': {{ answer }}
  </div>
</div>
```

This means that child scopes have access to variables and functions declared in each of their ancestor scopes. This is true both in the HTML, as shown earlier, and in controllers. For instance, with the following HTML:

```
<div ng-controller="Controller1">
  <div ng-controller="Controller2">
    This prints '42': {{ answer }}
  </div>
</div>
```

you can actually access the $scope.answer variable in the Controller2 controller:

```
m.controller('Controller1', function($scope) {
  $scope.answer = 42;
});

m.controller('Controller2', function($scope) {
  // Prints '42' if $scope is a descendant of
  // a scope that Controller1 operated on
  console.log($scope.answer);
});
```

This may seem trivial, but you have successfully shared data between two completely separate controllers. This approach, however, suffers from a limitation: now Controller2 has an implicit dependency on Controller1. Specifically, now Controller2 needs to be extra careful that it behaves properly with or without Controller1, or you need to be extra careful that you never use Controller2 without Controller1. Furthermore, you can imagine more complex examples in which Controller1 loads the answer variable from a remote server: How do you communicate any errors that may occur to Controller2? This practice can easily lead to buggy and brittle code. Although the scope inheritance approach is reasonable for simple use cases, it is typically the wrong choice for sharing data that's loaded from the server. Thankfully, subsequent approaches enable you to communicate errors as well as data in a clean way.

Event Transmission

AngularJS scopes contain an implementation of the pervasive event emitter design pattern. This design pattern allows objects to $emit() named events that then trigger listener functions registered using the $on() function. For instance:

```
$scope.$on('error', function(error) {
  console.log('An error occurred: ' + error);
});

$scope.$emit('error', 'Could not connect to server');
```

In the preceding example, the code emits an error event, which then triggers the handler registered with the .$on('error') function call. The power of the event emitter paradigm lies in the fact that there can be any number of listeners for a given event, and these listeners can be registered in any function that has access to the $scope variable. In other words, the $emit() call is completely decoupled from the listeners. There may be zero, one, or many listeners registered to the error event, but that does not affect the syntax of the $emit() call.

AngularJS scopes have two added layers of indirection on top of the conventional event emitter design pattern. First, the $emit() call bubbles up the scope hierarchy, so listeners registered with $on() on ancestor scopes will be triggered. For instance, with the following HTML:

```
<div ng-controller="Controller1">
  <div ng-controller="Controller2">
  </div>
</div>
```

Controller2 is able to $emit() events that trigger listeners registered on Controller1's scope:

```
<div ng-controller="Controller1">
  <div ng-controller="Controller2">
  </div>
</div>

m.controller('Controller1', function($scope) {
  // This will catch the 'ping' event emitted by
  // Controller2's scope when Controller2's scope
  // is a child of $scope
  $scope.$on('ping', function() {
    console.log('pong');
  });
});

m.controller('Controller2', function($scope) {
  $scope.$emit('ping');
});
```

Furthermore, scopes have a $broadcast() function, which behaves a lot like the $emit() function, except that the event propagates to descendant scopes instead of ancestor scopes. In other words, using the $broadcast() function, Controller1 can trigger listeners registered on Controller2's scope, whereas the $emit() function propagates events in the opposite direction. For instance:

```
m.controller('Controller1', function($scope) {
  $scope.$broadcast('ping');
});

m.controller('Controller2', function($scope) {
  // This will catch the 'ping' event broadcasted by
  // Controller1's scope when Controller1's scope
  // is an ancestor of $scope
  $scope.$on('ping', function() {
    console.log('pong');
  });
});
```

The technical details of event emitters are relatively straightforward, but using them effectively is a more subtle challenge. Event emitters are a powerful tool because they add a layer of indirection on top of function calls; the code that emits the event isn't aware of what functions are registered as listeners. However, this also makes code that relies heavily on event emitters difficult to understand, so event emitters are best used sparingly. In the case of transmitting data between controllers, however, they are an excellent tool.

One example that demonstrates scope event emitters being the right tool for the job is handling infinite scrolling, a user experience (UX) design pattern in which scrolling to the bottom of the page causes more data to load. There are numerous directives in the open source community to handle infinite scrolling, but using directives for infinite scrolling is a case of trying to fit a square peg into a round hole. Infinite scrolling is triggered by events that are global to the page (user scrolling to the bottom of the page or user resizing the page). Thus, a directive that enables infinite scroll doesn't interact directly with the DOM element that it is attached to. Infinite scrolling is better implemented as an event on the page's root scope, represented by the $rootScope service, and propagated down to the descendant scopes via the $broadcast() function. Here is an example of how you might implement infinite scrolling using scope event emitters:

```
app.run(function($rootScope) {
  var lastCheck = 0;
  var INTERVAL_TO_CHECK = 500; // Only check every half second

  var check = function() {
    if (Date.now() - lastCheck < INTERVAL_TO_CHECK) {
      return;
    }

    lastCheck = Date.now();

    if ($(window).scrollTop() >=
        $(document).height() - $(window).height() - 50) {
      $rootScope.$broadcast('SCROLL_TO_BOTTOM');
    }
  }

  setTimeout(function() {
    check();
  }, 0);
  $(window).on('scroll', check);
  $(window).on('resize', check);
});
```

The preceding module broadcasts an event called SCROLL_TO_BOTTOM whenever the user reaches near the bottom of the page. The event emitter approach is such a good fit here because there are multiple possible causes for a SCROLL_TO_BOTTOM event, and multiple controllers may want to do something when this event is emitted. This sort of many-to-many relationship between events and event handlers is precisely where the event emitter paradigm shines. In addition, this approach decouples the logic for triggering the event and the event handlers, so you can abstract the complexity for detecting the conditions for the SCROLL_TO_BOTTOM event behind a $on() call. This is convenient for testing because your test code can trigger the SCROLL_TO_BOTTOM event without having to run in an actual browser.

> **NOTE** *You may have noticed that the previous code uses jQuery, where the $ function in the $(window) lines is defined. It uses jQuery for its reliable abstraction layer for window and document scroll offsets that work across a variety of browsers. AngularJS does not provide this functionality, so AngularJS developers often utilize jQuery for its convenience wrappers around browser-level events. In fact, jQuery and AngularJS are arguably more complementary libraries than competing libraries.*

You can find an example of utilizing this infinite scroll code in the `infinite_scroll_emitter` `.html` file in this chapter's sample code. What follows is a controller that utilizes the infinite scroll event:

```
app.controller('InfiniteScrollController', function($scope) {
  $scope.images = [];
  var CYCLE_IMAGES = [
    // ...
  ];

  $scope.$on('SCROLL_TO_BOTTOM', function() {
    for (var i = 0; i < 3; ++i) {
      $scope.images.push({
        url: CYCLE_IMAGES[$scope.images.length % CYCLE_IMAGES.length]
      });
    }
    $scope.$apply();
  });
});
```

This controller adds several images to `$scope.images` whenever it receives the SCROLL_TO_BOTTOM event. You can now utilize this infinite scrolling code in the `infinite_scroll_emitter.html` file using the following HTML:

```
<div ng-controller="InfiniteScrollController">
  <div ng-repeat="image in images">
    <img ng-src="{{image.url}}">
  </div>
</div>
```

As you can see, the SCROLL_TO_BOTTOM event abstracts out all the complexity of computing whether the user has scrolled to the bottom of the page. This enables your AngularJS controllers to define infinite scrolling behavior with a layer of abstraction between the controllers and the infinite scrolling trigger. The scope event emitter paradigm thus allows you to transmit data between controllers or between run blocks and controllers. However, although the event emitter paradigm works well for infinite scrolling, it doesn't work well for all cases in which you want to transmit data between controllers. The primary difficulty is determining which controller should be responsible for generating an event. For some common use cases, such as loading data from a server, it isn't necessarily clear which controller should be responsible for querying the server and generating an event. In use cases involving loading data from a server, typically the next paradigm that you learn about is the best choice.

The ModelService Paradigm

The event emitter paradigm works well for transmitting results of user interaction between controllers. However, controllers also often need to share data loaded from the server. For instance, multiple controllers on a page often need to have access to the currently logged-in user, which is data that needs to be loaded from the server. Services are a perfect tool for exposing data loaded from the server because services are *singletons*, in the sense that a service is instantiated at most once, and that instance is shared between all controllers and services that rely on the service. Note that the notion of singleton here is marginally different from the commonly used singleton design pattern. Services are still accessed through the AngularJS dependency injector, rather than through global state. You learn more about services and the notion of services as singletons in Chapter 7. For the purposes of this section, however, it is sufficient to understand that all controllers share the same instance of a service.

The following example demonstrates using userService to wrap an asynchronous loading of the currently logged-in user. To avoid having to set up a server, you use a $timeout call instead of a real $http call to simulate an actual Hypertext Transfer Protocol (HTTP) request. If you were to use the $http service instead of $timeout, the service implementation would change slightly, but the controller code or HTML would not change at all. What follows is the sample code, which you can find in the user_service.html file in this chapter's sample code:

```html
<div ng-controller="FirstController">
  <h1>{{user.name}}</h1>
</div>
<div ng-controller="SecondController">
  <input type="text" ng-model="user.name">
</div>

<script type="text/javascript" src="angular.js">
</script>
<script type="text/javascript">
  var app = angular.module('app', []);

  app.factory('userService', function($timeout) {
    var user = {};
    $timeout(function() {
      user.name = 'Username';
    }, 500);

    return user;
  });

  app.controller('FirstController', function($scope, userService) {
    $scope.user = userService;
  });

  app.controller('SecondController', function($scope, userService) {
    $scope.user = userService;
  });
</script>
```

There are two key concepts in the preceding example. First is that, once again, there is one instance of userService shared between both FirstController and SecondController. Thus, when the text field is modified in the scope of SecondController, the header in the scope of FirstController is reflected to update the changes, despite the fact that these two scopes are completely independent. Second, the asynchronous code in userService triggers changes in the scopes of FirstController and SecondController. Under the hood, the $timeout service (and the

$http service as well) calls $apply() on the page's root scope, which is why userService doesn't need to emit an event when it loads the user data. This enables you to simply write controllers that utilize userService as if userService pulled data synchronously. Combined, these two concepts make services an ideal tool for abstracting out the results of asynchronous HTTP calls. In the next section, you learn some more sophisticated techniques to transmit data between different services as well as between services and controllers.

Services

Services are objects that are wired together by AngularJS's dependency injector outside the scope hierarchy. Controllers typically list multiple services as dependencies, but services cannot list controllers as dependencies. As mentioned in the previous section, services are singletons in the sense that each service is instantiated only once. This makes services ideal for storing data that is loaded from or persisted to the server.

In the previous section, you learned about several approaches to communicate between different controllers. The last approach relied on the fact that services are singletons. Communication between services is fundamentally different from communication between controllers because services don't have access to a scope, and your HTML can't instantiate a service without help from a controller. However, there are several handy approaches to enable services to communicate with each other.

Services Depending on Other Services

The most basic tool for communicating between services is that one service can list other services as dependencies. This approach is admittedly fairly trivial, but it does illustrate one key point about services and scopes. To demonstrate this key point, suppose you had a service called profileService that depended on userService. Suppose the primary purpose of profileService is to provide an API for enabling controllers to modify the data provided by userService and save the changes to the server. Following are the contents of the profile_service.html file in this chapter's sample code:

```html
<div ng-controller="ProfileController">
  <input type="text" ng-model="profile.user.name">
  <h2 ng-show="!profile.isValid()">
    Username required
  </h2>
</div>

<script type="text/javascript" src="angular.js">
</script>
<script type="text/javascript">
  var app = angular.module('app', []);

  app.factory('userService', function($timeout) {
    var user = {};
    $timeout(function() {
      user.name = 'Username';
    }, 500);

    return user;
```

```
        });

        app.factory('profileService', function(userService) {
          var ret = {
            user: userService,
            isValid: function() {
              return ret.user && ret.user.name;
            }
          };

          return ret;
        });

        app.controller('ProfileController', function($scope, profileService) {
          $scope.profile = profileService;
        });
      </script>
```

This code correctly updates the visibility of the Username required error message based on the value of the isValid() function, despite the fact that the profileService function has no code to handle changes to the data in the underlying userService. Despite the fact that services are outside the scope hierarchy, they can still trigger scope updates using services like $timeout and $http that trigger an update on the page's root scope, as represented by the $rootScope service. Thus, you can build services on top of other services without having to have these services interact at all because the AngularJS scope hierarchy can tie all this together in the controllers. Chapter 4 covers more about the particulars of AngularJS scopes. However, for the purposes of high-level code organization, it suffices to understand that updates to the root scope propagate down to all scopes on the page.

In the next section, you learn how to use event emitters with services. Although the AngularJS scope hierarchy can handle the case in which a change in a service needs to propagate up to a controller, it isn't necessarily the right choice for propagating a change in a service to another service. As shown in the profileService example, you can often get away with not propagating changes between services and rely on the scope hierarchy to tie it all together. However, as you see next, sometimes it's helpful to have services transmit events to enable true inter-service communication.

The *event-emitter* Module

The scope event emitter paradigm you learned about in the section on inter-controller communication is not limited to AngularJS scopes. Event emitters are pervasive in the JavaScript community, precisely because they are an elegant and lightweight way of propagating data from one object to another. In particular, NodeJS's core includes a robust event emitter framework, which the NodeJS community ported into a standalone event-emitter module. There are numerous other JavaScript modules that provide event emitter functionality, but the event-emitter module includes only a robust event emitter and nothing else. The event-emitter module is thus useful both for minimizing code bloat and for instructional purposes.

The event-emitter module works similarly to the scope event emitters you worked with in the previous section. There are three key differences. First, the event-emitter module is scope-independent, so it is ideal for use in services that don't have access to scopes. Second, the functions you interact with are named .on() and .emit(). These correspond to .$on() and .$emit() on

AngularJS scopes. Third, there is no function corresponding to `$broadcast()` because the event-emitter module does not include support for event propagation between emitters. Although the lack of event propagation may seem limiting, this module actually turns out to be an excellent fit for services due to the singleton nature of services.

A good example of a service that would benefit from event emitters is the `userService` example you saw previously. When `userService` is instantiated, it needs to do an asynchronous HTTP request to load data about the currently logged-in user from the server. Furthermore, if your page is expected to be long-lived (for instance, a single page app or a real-time dashboard), you may want to rerequest data from the server every hour in case the user's session has timed out. To complicate things even more, numerous services and controllers rely on `userService`, and the underlying HTTP request can fail. How will `userService` propagate new data (as well as any errors) asynchronously to the services that rely on it? Event emitters provide an elegant solution to this design challenge.

You can find the following example in the `user_service_emitter.html` file in this chapter's sample code. For your convenience, the `event-emitter` module has been packaged with this chapter's sample code as `event-emitter.js` and included in `user_service_emitter.html`:

```
<script type="text/javascript" src="angular.js">
</script>
<script type="text/javascript" src="event-emitter.js">
</script>
<script type="text/javascript">
  var app = angular.module('app', []);

  app.factory('userService', function($timeout, $window) {
    var emitter = $window.emitter();

    var user = {};
    $timeout(function() {
      // Simulate an HTTP error
      user.emit('error', 'Could not connect to server');
    }, 2000);

    ['on', 'once', 'emit'].forEach(function(fn) {
      user[fn] = function() {
        emitter[fn].apply(emitter, arguments);
      };
    });

    return user;
  });

  app.factory('profileService', function(userService) {
    var ret = {
      user: userService,
      isValid: function() {
        return ret.user && ret.user.name;
      }
    };

    userService.on('error', function(error) {
      ret.error = 'This is a sample error message ' +
```

```
        'that would tell the user that you can\'t ' +
        'connect to the server';
    });

    return ret;
  });

  app.controller('ProfileController', function($scope, profileService) {
    $scope.profile = profileService;
  });
</script>
```

In the preceding code, `userService` emits an `error` event that `profileService` listens for and uses to display a message. Once again, this event doesn't necessarily need to be propagated up to the controller because `$timeout` notifies the scope hierarchy that something has changed. However, the event emitter enables `profileService` to be notified of errors in `userService` and handle them appropriately. Thus, if you need to communicate between two services, event emitters are usually the best choice.

> **NOTE** *You may have noticed that this chapter's sample code includes an* `event-emitter-index.js` *file in addition to* `event-emitter.js`*. This is because, under the hood, the* `event-emitter` *module is a NodeJS module compiled for the browser using Browserify. The purpose of the* `event-emitter-index.js` *file is to expose the event emitter functionality to the global* `window` *object. You will learn more about Browserify in the section "Module Loaders."*

Directives

A *directive* is a rule for how the DOM should interact with JavaScript variables. In other words, directives are AngularJS's abstraction around DOM interactions. For instance, the `ngClick` directive defines a rule that says, "When this element is clicked, evaluate this code snippet." You will learn a lot more about directives in Chapter 5, but for the purposes of this section, just think of directives as rules for DOM interaction. Directives may have an associated controller, but controllers and services cannot list directives as dependencies.

> **NOTE** *Directives should be the* only *place where your code interacts with DOM elements (with the possible exception of the global* `window` *element). A surefire sign of bad AngularJS code is calling* `document.getElementById()` *in a controller.*

Because directives are tied into scoping, inter-directive communication behaves quite similarly to inter-controller communication. As a matter of fact, custom directives often have their own controllers, so you can use the familiar design patterns from the earlier "Controllers" section on inter-controller communication. However, directives have an additional feature for inter-directive communication that you'll learn about next.

Exposing API Using Controllers

Earlier in this section, you learned that, because of scope inheritance, a controller can access variables defined in its ancestor scopes. This enables a controller to access the internal state of other controllers so long as the other controller is tied to an ancestor scope of the first controller. Unfortunately, the scope inheritance approach was limited because there was no good way to enforce that one controller could only be defined in a descendant scope of another controller. Directives, on the other hand, have a mechanism to ensure that a directive's scope must always be a descendant of another directive's scope.

The StockDog application that you saw in Chapter 1, "Building a Simple AngularJS Application," includes an example of this functionality. The StockDog application has two directives—stockTable and stockRow—that are meant to be used together. Specifically, a stockTable contains numerous instances of the stockRow directive. Following is the definition of the stockRow directive:

```
angular.module('stockDogApp')
  .directive('stockTable', function () {
    return {
      templateUrl: 'views/templates/stock-table.html',
      restrict: 'E',
      scope: {
        watchlist: '='
      },
      controller: function ($scope) {
        // ...
      }
    }
  });
```

The stockTable directive's controller exposes some functionality in its controller. To ensure the stockRow directive is only declared within a stockTable directive, you can use the require directive option as shown here:

```
angular.module('stockDogApp')
  .directive('stockRow', function ($timeout, QuoteService) {
    return {
      restrict: 'A',
      require: '^stockTable',
      scope: {
        stock: '=',
        isLast: '='
      },
      link: function ($scope, $element, $attrs, stockTableCtrl) {
        // ...
      }
    };
  });
```

The require directive option mandates that the stockRow directive's scope must be a descendant of a stockTable directive's scope. Furthermore, you can access the instantiated stockTable directive's controller as the fourth parameter to the link function. (Chapter 5 covers the link function in more detail.) If you have two directives that need to be used together, the `require` directive option is the right tool for the job.

Conclusion

In this section, you learned about the conceptual differences between directives, services, and controllers and how you can share state between different components. Each component has properties that make it uniquely suited for certain tasks: services for loading data from and persisting data to the server, controllers for exposing an API to directives, and directives for managing DOM interactions. In the next section, you will learn about *modules*, AngularJS's high-level organizational tool for bundling related components into a single reusable group.

ORGANIZING YOUR CODE WITH MODULES

You may have noticed that all the sample code in this book includes a call to the `angular.module()` function. Modules are AngularJS's highest level organizational unit. A module is effectively a map from a string to a set of controllers, services, filters, and directives. Because modules provide such a high level of abstraction, small AngularJS codebases typically use only one module. However, as your codebase grows and matures, you may find yourself needing to break your code into separate modules to optimize readability and reusability.

The most powerful feature of modules is that they can list other modules as dependencies, which enables you to include components from another module in your module. For instance:

```
// 'MyModule' depends on 'OtherModule' and thus includes
// all services, directives, controllers, and other
// components defined in 'OtherModule'.
var myModule = angular.module('MyModule', ['OtherModule']);
```

A word of warning: you may expect AngularJS to handle loading the contents of `OtherModule` for you. That is not the case. The preceding code does not work unless you include JavaScript code that creates `OtherModule` with a call to the `angular.module()` function.

The ability to list modules as dependencies of other modules allows you to easily swap out large chunks of your AngularJS code without having to remove files from your codebase. This is useful for testing, experimenting with new features, and UX testing (for instance, A/B tests). To provide a more concrete example of how you can utilize modules, you must develop a simple A/B test for a page's registration flow using AngularJS modules.

> **NOTE** *An A/B test (or "split test") is an experiment in which a visitor randomly sees one of two slightly different variants of your website. A basic example is randomly showing visitors one of two different promotional images on your homepage and tracking to see which one gets more users to sign up. A/B testing is popular because it offers an evidence-based approach to incrementally improving your website's user experience.*

There are numerous popular A/B testing frameworks, such as Optimizely, but they are primarily designed to work with static websites as opposed to rich AJAX-based content. Furthermore, these A/B testing frameworks fail to take advantage of AngularJS modules, which allow you to easily replace large sections of functionality. In this example, you will be using a developer-friendly analytics framework called KeenIO, which provides a REST API for sending arbitrary JSON objects and then querying the results. KeenIO requires signing up for an account on keen.io to get an API key. KeenIO is free for up to 50,000 requests per month, which should be more than sufficient for the purposes of this sample chapter. Furthermore, you can replace KeenIO with your analytics framework of choice in this example if you believe another tool fits your needs better. This section primarily focuses on the concepts necessary to run A/B tests with modules. The integration with KeenIO is minimal. Most other analytics frameworks should be able to provide similar functionality, but KeenIO is used in this example because of its generous free tier and straightforward data model.

Integrating KeenIO with AngularJS is simple. KeenIO has a software development kit (SDK) for browser-side JavaScript that you can include with a script tag as shown here.

```
<script src="https://d26b395fwzu5fz.cloudfront.net/3.1.0/keen.min.js"
        type="text/javascript">
</script>
```

Once you have included KeenIO's JavaScript SDK, you should create a KeenIO client in your page's global scope:

```
var keenClient = new Keen({
  projectId: '<Your KeenIO project ID>',
  writeKey: '<Your KeenIO write key>'
});
```

Don't forget to set the projectId and writeKey fields to your project's KeenIO project ID and write key, respectively. Once you have set up the keenClient variable, you're ready to start building out the AngularJS code for your A/B test.

A/B tests are so easy with AngularJS modules because you can easily replace one module with another, so long as they provide compatible controllers, directives, and services. In this A/B testing example (the complete source code for this example is available in this chapter's sample code in the a_b_test_example.html file), you create four modules. Two of these modules are slightly different implementations of a simple registration flow, and one of these modules is selected at random when the page loads.

The first module you write is simple. It defines a single value that represents the KeenIO collection name the results are stored in. A KeenIO *collection* is simply a logical storage unit for related events. In other words, if you were to run other A/B tests, you would want to put those results into a separate collection so you could easily distinguish data from different tests. Following is the source code for the module that defines the KeenIO collection name you use:

```
var abTest = angular.module('abTestRegistration', []);
abTest.value('abTestCollection', 'registration_AB_test_20141112');
```

In the preceding code, you defined a service called abTestCollection that's simply a string representing the collection name. The reason for this module is so the two registration variants that you test can utilize the same collection. What follows are the two registration variants that are the subjects of your A/B test: registrationA and registrationB:

```
var registrationModuleA = angular.module('registrationA',
  ['abTestRegistration']);

registrationModuleA.controller('RegistrationController',
  function($scope, $window, $timeout, abTestCollection) {
    keenClient.addEvent(abTestCollection, {
      type: 'view',
      variant: 'A'
    });

    $scope.useTemplate = '/registration/a';

    $scope.submit = function() {
      $timeout(function() {
        $scope.registered = true;
        keenClient.addEvent(abTestCollection, {
          type: 'registered',
          variant: 'A'
        });
      }, 1000);
    };
  });

var registrationModuleB = angular.module('registrationB',
  ['abTestRegistration']);

registrationModuleB.controller('RegistrationController',
  function($scope, $window, $timeout, abTestCollection) {
    keenClient.addEvent(abTestCollection, {
      type: 'view',
      variant: 'B'
    });
    $scope.useTemplate = '/registration/b';

    $scope.submit = function() {
      $scope.inProgress = true;
      $timeout(function() {
        $scope.inProgress = false;
        $scope.registered = true;
        keenClient.addEvent(abTestCollection, {
          type: 'registered',
          variant: 'B'
        });
      }, 1000);
    };
  });
```

The registrationA and registrationB modules both define a single controller: RegistrationController. Each module's controller tracks two different events: a view event when the controller is loaded, and a registered event when a user successfully registers. However, each module has a slightly different version of RegistrationController. There are three key differences.

First, when `registrationA` sends an event to KeenIO, it sets the `variant` field to `'A'`, whereas the `registrationB` module sets it to `'B'`. This enables you to categorize which events occurred on which variant when you analyze the results of your experiment. Second, the `registrationB` module sets an `inProgress` variable to `true`. This represents one of the UX changes whose effectiveness the A/B test measures. Specifically, the `registrationB` module shows a `loading` message to communicate to the user that the page successfully processed the user's registration request. The UX experiment aims to determine whether this site can increase its registration rate by reducing the number of users who exit the page while the registration process is happening because they think the page is broken.

Finally, the `registrationA` module sets a `useTemplate` variable to `'/registration/a'`, whereas the `registrationB` module sets it to `'/registration/b'`. The reason for this may not be immediately clear without looking at the corresponding HTML for the page, shown here:

```
<body>
  <div ng-controller="RegistrationController" ng-include="useTemplate">
  </div>
</body>
```

The `ngInclude` directive, which you learn about in much greater detail in Chapter 6, "Templates, Location, and Routing," includes the HTML from the template named '/registration/a' or '/registration/b' (depending on which variant is showing) in the `div` element shown previously. As you can see, AngularJS's template functionality is another handy tool for A/B testing: You can conditionally display different pieces of HTML depending on which variant you're showing, without changing any code. Following are the two templates representing the two variants in the A/B test:

```
<script type="text/ng-template" id="/registration/a">
  <h1>Registration Variant A</h1>
  <h3>Please Enter Your Email:</h3>
  <input type="text" ng-model="email">
  <br>
  <input type="button" ng-click="submit()" value="Submit">
  <h4 ng-show="registered">
    Thanks for Registering!
  </h4>
</script>

<script type="text/ng-template" id="/registration/b">
  <h1>Registration Variant B</h1>
  <input type="text" ng-model="email" placeholder="Email">
  <br>
  <input type="button" ng-click="submit()" value="Register">
  <h4 ng-show="inProgress">
    Registering...
  </h4>
  <h4 ng-show="registered">
    Thanks for Registering!
  </h4>
</script>
```

Once you have the preceding templates, all you need to do is tie everything together with a fourth module that selects either the `registrationA` or `registrationB` module at random. The next code chooses one of these variants based on the output of the `Math.random()` function:

```
var myModule = angular.module('myApp',
        [(Math.random() >= 0.5 ? 'registrationB' : 'registrationA')]);
```

Now when you open the `a_b_test_example.html` file, you should see either variant A or variant B. You can then try registering a few times and querying back the results of your A/B test using KeenIO's REST API. For instance, to ask KeenIO how many users have registered using variant A, you can visit the following uniform resource locator (URL) in your browser:

```
https://api.keen.io/3.0/projects/<project_id>/queries/
count?event_collection=registration_AB_test_20141112&api_key=
<your_api_key>&filters=<your_filters>
```

You need to include your project ID, API key, and uniform resource identifier (URI)-encoded JSON filters of choice in the preceding URL. Specifically, to get the number of users who registered through variant A, your filters should be a URI-encoded version of the following JSON:

```
[
  {
    "property_name":"type",
    "operator":"eq",
    "property_value":"registered"
  },
  {
    "property_name":"variant",
    "operator":"eq",
    "property_value":"a"
  }
]
```

Congratulations! You have just run a basic A/B test using AngularJS modules. Modules may seem like an unnecessary feature at first, but as your codebase grows, they become indispensible. In particular, the ability to seamlessly replace broad swaths of your codebase during module configuration makes A/B testing simple.

DIRECTORY STRUCTURE

The simplest way to improve your application's architecture is to break your code down into files and arrange these files in a sensible manner. Sample applications often keep all controllers, services, and directives in a single file to make the content easier to absorb; however, production applications typically have too many components to reasonably keep them in a single file.

The AngularJS team at Google has its own set of recommendations for structuring AngularJS applications. In this section, you investigate various directory-structuring paradigms for different app sizes, all of which borrow heavily from the AngularJS team's recommendations.

Before you dive in to directory structure, it is important to consider AngularJS file-naming conventions. Google's "Best Practice Recommendations for Angular App Structure" document recommends naming files on a per-component basis using hyphen-delimited names. For instance, `FooController` would be defined in a file named `foo-controller.js`, and unit tests for `FooController` would be in a file named `foo-controller_test.js`. The reason for these conventions is Google's internal inter-language file-naming specification.

In general, it is not necessary (or recommended) to follow these naming practices outside of Google. In practice, AngularJS controllers usually have Pascal case names (for instance, `FooBarController`), and services usually have camel case names (for instance, `fooBarService`). Directives must have camel case names (for instance, `fooBarDirective`) because AngularJS converts camel case directive names to hyphen case (for instance, `foo-bar-directive`) for use in HTML. Thus, using hyphen-delimited file names simply adds an additional level of indirection between what a variable is named and the file it's defined in. You may choose to follow the hyphen-delimited filename convention because it is a well-accepted language-independent practice. However, you may also choose to make the filename match the component name as closely as possible. For instance, if `FooController` has its own file, the file should be named `FooController.js`. Similarly, unit tests for `FooController` should be in a file named `FooController.test.js`. Either convention is reasonable. Both approaches are used in this section. What is most important, though, is to pick an approach and use it consistently throughout your application.

However, as you will see in this section, you don't necessarily need a separate file for each component. Larger applications typically find it necessary to have a separate file for each component; having several controllers that are hundreds of lines long in a single file is poor organization. But if you're developing a prototype and your controllers are 5–10 lines of code, defining separate files can slow you down. As a general rule of thumb, components that you think are nontrivial should have their own files. For instance, controllers will typically have their own files, but even large applications often keep a single file for common one-line filters. In this section, you learn about directory structuring guidelines for various project sizes (small, medium, and large) and thus gain a framework for allowing your codebase to grow gracefully.

Small Projects

One possible directory structuring approach for small applications, prototypes, and starter projects is having one file for controllers, one for services, and one for directives. A good example is the Ionic framework "tabs" starter project (Ionic is a tool for developing hybrid mobile applications that you'll learn about in Chapter 10, "Moving On") available at `https://github.com/driftyco/ionic-starter-tabs`. This project stores its AngularJS files in a `js` directory, with a single `app.js` file that contains a module definition and application-level configuration logic, including any single-page app routing. The controller file, `controllers.js`, and the services file, `services.js`, contain their own module definitions, which the `app.js` file assembles into a single module for use in the HTML. The AngularJS files are isolated in this `js` directory, leaving the top-level directory for HTML and directories for images.

For your convenience, this chapter's sample code has a `small_project` directory that contains a project structured according to these guidelines. The project is trivial from a code perspective but serves as a concrete example of how such a project would be structured. This project contains a `js` directory, which contains `app.js`, `services.js`, `controllers.js`, and `directives.js`. The `app.js` file is responsible for bootstrapping the application:

```
angular.
  module('foo', ['foo.controllers', 'foo.services', 'foo.directives']).
  config(function($rootScopeProvider) {
    // Configuration logic goes here
  });
```

Each of the `services.js`, `controllers.js`, and `directives.js` files contains a separate module: `foo.services`, `foo.controllers`, and `foo.directives`, respectively. Each file is responsible for defining every component of its class; for instance, `controllers.js` defines all the controllers for this app:

```
angular.
  module('foo.controllers', []).
  controller('FooController', function($scope) {
    // Use $scope
  });
```

This project structure is good for small projects, like the Ionic framework starter project, which is meant to be a starting point to build more sophisticated apps. Because AngularJS does so much work under the hood, you can build prototypes and even production applications that easily fit within this project structure without breaking the rule of thumb you learned about earlier. However, production projects typically outgrow this project structure fairly quickly because controllers and services rapidly grow in complexity. Controllers and services that start out as trivial usually start to encompass additional business logic. As your project begins to hit the stage where your components are too large to fit into a single file without taking a readability hit, you will want to consider breaking your code into a paradigm closer to the "Medium Projects" guidelines you will learn about next.

Medium Projects

Medium-sized projects can be structured by having a separate directory for controllers, directives, and services. Each controller, directive, and service can then have its own file, or several small components can share a file. A good example of such a project is the Stock Dog application that you saw in Chapter 1, available at `github.com/diegonetto/stock-dog`. In addition, this chapter's sample code includes a `medium_project` directory that has a skeleton project structured using this paradigm. Once again, this app is bootstrapped in the `js/app.js` file:

```
angular.
  module('foo', ['foo.controllers', 'foo.services', 'foo.directives']).
  config(function($rootScopeProvider) {
    // Configuration logic goes here
  });
```

This application now includes separate directories for the `foo.controllers` and `foo.directives` modules, but the `foo.services` module is still defined in a single file. That is, `services.js` is the same as in the previous example:

```
angular.
  module('foo.services', []).
  factory('fooService', function() {
    // Empty service
    return {};
  });
```

However, directives and controllers now have their own directories. The `controllers/module.js` file is responsible for declaring the `foo.controllers` module:

```
angular.module('foo.controllers', []);
```

The `controllers` directory also contains a file that defines `FooController`, `controllers/FooController.js`:

```
angular.
  module('foo.controllers').
  controller('FooController', function($scope) {
    // Use $scope
  });
```

Finally, the foo module declared in `js/app.js` is used in the `index.html` file to bootstrap the web page:

```
<html ng-app="foo">
  <head>
    <title></title>
  </head>

  <body>
    <div ng-controller="FooController">
    </div>

    <script type="text/javascript" src="../angular.js"></script>
    <script type="text/javascript" src="js/controllers/module.js"></script>
    <script type="text/javascript" src="js/controllers/FooController.js">
    </script>
    <script type="text/javascript" src="js/services.js"></script>
    <script type="text/javascript" src="js/directives/module.js"></script>
    <script type="text/javascript" src="js/directives/fooDirective.js">
    </script>
    <script type="text/javascript" src="js/app.js"></script>
  </body>
</html>
```

This paradigm is a natural extension of the small project directory structure. This application has a single file for services, but it has directories for controllers and directives to illustrate the key point that when your small app begins to grow too large for the small project paradigm, you can easily start separating components into separate files under a new directory. For instance, if you have two controllers that have become nontrivial, you can create a `controllers` directory with a separate file for each controller without changing the rest of the directory structure.

The medium project paradigm is sufficient for many apps. However, mature applications sometimes outgrow this paradigm as well: You may have too many controllers to reasonably keep in one folder and thus want to further separate your project to keep the various components of your project manageable. If your project hits this stage, you should consider breaking up your code in a paradigm similar to the "Large Projects" guidelines you learn about next.

Large Projects

Large projects benefit from grouping their AngularJS components by functionality. For instance, if you have a large AngularJS app, you may want to have a separate directory (or *functionality group*) called `registration` that contains `controllers`, `services`, and `directives` directories that contain components unique to the app's registration flow. Each of these separate directories should be independent of each other; a controller in the `registration` directory should not depend on a service in the `dashboard` directory, for instance. Components that are common between multiple functionality groups can reside in a `shared` directory. Each of the functionality groups can contain either a single file or a directory for its controllers, directives, and services depending on your needs. In other words, each functionality group is organized as if it were its own separate project, except for potential dependencies on the `shared` module. To provide a more concrete example, this chapter's sample code includes a directory called `large_project` that demonstrates this directory-structuring paradigm.

In the `large_project` directory, there are two functional groups: `js/dashboard` and `js/registration`. In addition, there's a `js/shared` directory that contains common filters and services. The `dashboard` group contains a module definition and a single file that defines all its controllers:

```
angular.module('foo.dashboard',
  ['foo.dashboard.controllers', 'foo.shared']);
```

The `registration` group is a bit more sophisticated and contains a directory of controllers as well as a file for all its directives. Here is the module definition for `foo.registration`:

```
angular.module(
  'foo.registration',
  [
    'foo.registration.directives',
    'foo.registration.controllers',
    'foo.shared'
  ]);
```

Like the "Medium Project" guidelines, this directory-structuring paradigm grows organically from the directory structuring guidelines for smaller projects. To start transitioning a "Medium Project" into a "Large Project," you can create a directory for a functional group and move all the controllers, directives, and services for that functional group into this directory. In addition, you may have to create the `shared` directory as well so you can store any services of the functional group as well as the code that's still arranged according to the "Medium Project" guidelines. This is so the functional group doesn't have to depend on modules that are still arranged according to the "Medium Project" guidelines, which would break the rule that functional groups should be independent of each other.

Now that you have learned about some of the different methods for organizing your AngularJS code into files, you learn about two open source tools for addressing the problem of loading modules. In the "Large Projects" paradigm, for instance, the index.html file is complex because it needs to load all the project's JavaScript files using a carefully ordered list of script tags:

```html
<html ng-app="foo">
  <head>
    <title></title>
  </head>

  <body>
    <div ng-controller="FooController">
    </div>

    <script type="text/javascript" src="../angular.js">
    </script>
    <script type="text/javascript" src="js/shared/filters.js">
    </script>
    <script type="text/javascript" src="js/shared/services.js">
    </script>
    <script type="text/javascript" src="js/shared/module.js">
    </script>
    <script type="text/javascript" src="js/registration/controllers/module.js">
    </script>
    <script type="text/javascript"
            src="js/registration/controllers/FooController.js">
    </script>
    <script type="text/javascript" src="js/registration/directives.js">
    </script>
    <script type="text/javascript" src="js/registration/module.js">
    </script>
    <script type="text/javascript" src="js/dashboard/controllers.js">
    </script>
    <script type="text/javascript" src="js/dashboard/module.js">
    </script>
    <script type="text/javascript" src="js/app.js">
    </script>
  </body>
</html>
```

As the number of files in your application grows, so does the number of script tags you need to include in your HTML. This wasn't much of a problem for small projects, but by the time you started using the "Large Project" directory structure, the fact that your JavaScript files needed to be included using script tags in a particular order made your HTML pretty cumbersome. In larger applications, it's easy to introduce difficult-to-trace bugs by forgetting the order that your script tags are in or forgetting to include a particular file. In programming languages like C or Python, each code file is responsible for declaring its dependencies and the compiler (in the case of C) or the language runtime (in the case of Python) is responsible for providing these dependencies to the file. Several open source tools allow you to take advantage of this paradigm in JavaScript so you don't have to explicitly list your files using script tags. Although it is certainly possible to build large AngularJS applications by explicitly listing every file using script tags (AngularJS engineer Brian Ford once famously wrote that he "[hasn't] seen any instance where RequireJS was beneficial in practice"), you may find it more convenient to use module loaders, tools that resolve dependencies declared in your JavaScript so you don't have to rely on `script` tags. In the next section, you learn about how to use RequireJS and Browserify, two different module loading tools that make JavaScript dependencies less error-prone with AngularJS.

MODULE LOADERS

One difficulty that you may encounter as your application grows is finding the right solution for including all JavaScript dependencies in a page. The fundamental difficulty with browser-side JavaScript dependencies is that you need to load your JavaScript in HTML by listing all your JavaScript `script` tags in a particular order. For small applications, the fact that dependencies are included in one file and used in another file is unwieldy. For large applications, managing JavaScript via `script` tags is exceptionally tedious and error-prone: As your codebase grows larger and larger, you are going to have to rearrange `script` tags on numerous pages just to make sure your code doesn't break! As you might have guessed, there are several open source tools that address the issue of browser-side JavaScript dependencies. RequireJS is a popular tool for this task that you learn about in this section. In addition, you learn about the common NodeJS-to-browser compiler Browserify, which offers a novel approach to browser-side JavaScript dependencies.

RequireJS

RequireJS is a framework for asynchronously loading JavaScript files. Instead of explicitly listing all your files with `script` tags in your HTML, each JavaScript file lists the JavaScript files it depends on. RequireJS then resolves these dependencies by loading all the file's dependencies and then loading the actual file. In addition, JavaScript files are loaded *asynchronously*—that is, the browser will start rendering the page while waiting for the JavaScript files that RequireJS loads. This is ideal for performance because asynchronous loading allows the browser to do useful work while waiting for the JavaScript rather than blocking.

In the following example, you use RequireJS to structure the `small_project` directory from the previous section, "Directory Structure." This example demonstrates the high-level principles of using RequireJS with AngularJS. You can find this example in the `small_project_require` directory in this chapter's sample code. The `small_project_require` directory is almost identical to the `small_project` you worked with previously, but with three significant changes. First, the `js` directory now includes a file called `require.js`, which, unsurprisingly, is the file that defines the RequireJS API. Second, to illustrate how you can work with nested dependencies in RequireJS, the `foo.controllers` module now depends on the `foo.services` module, and `FooController` now depends on `fooService`. The new code for the `foo.controllers` module, which is in the `small_project_require/js/controllers.js` file, is next:

```
require(
  ['js/services.js'],
  function() {
    angular.
      module('foo.controllers', ['foo.services']).
        controller('FooController', function(fooService) {
```

```
        // Use fooService
      });
  });
```

RequireJS's syntax is straightforward. The `require()` function takes two parameters: a list of files and a function. RequireJS loads and executes the files listed exactly once before executing the function; therefore, in the preceding code `foo.controllers` can depend on `foo.services` without having to worry about the order of `script` tags in HTML.

Configuring RequireJS is similarly straightforward. To initialize RequireJS, you simply need to give it a map of module names to URL so that RequireJS knows where to look for files. In the case of the `small_project_require` project, this map is a trivial identity map. For instance, `'js/services .js'` maps to `'js/services.js'`. In applications in which you are loading JavaScript from a remote server, you may want to create a nontrivial mapping, but the identity map is sufficient for this example. What follows is the new `app.js` file, which is now responsible for bootstrapping RequireJS as well as the main AngularJS module:

```
var paths = [
  'js/controllers.js',
  'js/services.js',
  'js/directives.js'
];

var requireConfigPaths = {};
for (var i = 0; i < paths.length; ++i) {
  requireConfigPaths[paths[i]] = paths[i];
}

require.config({
  paths: requireConfigPaths
});

require(
  paths,
  function() {
    angular.
      module(
        'foo',
        [
          'foo.controllers',
          'foo.services',
          'foo.directives'
        ]).
      config(function($rootScopeProvider) {
        // Configuration logic goes here
      });

    angular.bootstrap(document, ['foo']);
  });
```

As in the preceding example, bootstrapping RequireJS requires calling the `require.config()` function, passing in a configuration object that includes the map of paths. Then you can call `require()` to load all the files necessary to declare the AngularJS module `foo`.

You may be wondering about the reason for the angular.bootstrap() call in the preceding code. There is one significant difficulty in integrating AngularJS and RequireJS: Because the JavaScript files are loaded asynchronously, you can't use the familiar ng-app syntax to initialize your application. When AngularJS attempts to load the module specified in the ng-app directive, RequireJS may not have loaded the module yet. Thankfully, the ng-app directive is a thin wrapper around the angular.bootstrap() function, so you can simply call the angular.bootstrap() function to initialize your application when RequireJS is finished loading files.

Now that you have integrated RequireJS into your AngularJS code, the small_project_require/ index.html file can be concise. Once again, note that the html tag that follows does not have an ng-app directive because you need to manually initialize your application using the angular .bootstrap() function when RequireJS is finished loading files:

```html
<html>
  <head>
    <title></title>
  </head>

  <body>
    <div ng-controller="FooController">
    </div>

    <script type="text/javascript" src="../angular.js">
    </script>
    <script data-main="js/app.js" src="js/require.js">
    </script>
  </body>
</html>
```

Note that, in the preceding code, you use only two script tags. You can further reduce it to one script tag by using RequireJS to load AngularJS. As your project grows to utilize the "Medium Project" directory structuring guidelines or even the "Large Project" directory structuring guidelines, you will still only need two script tags. Instead, you will have a call to require() in each file that explicitly lists the files this file depends on.

As you can see, RequireJS is an excellent tool for loading JavaScript dependencies in a more robust manner than listing script tags. In addition, asynchronous loading can be good for performance. However, asynchronous loading is not a popular paradigm outside of RequireJS precisely for performance reasons: No matter how small your JavaScript file is, you incur a significant minimum performance overhead loading any individual JavaScript file. Outside of RequireJS, many JavaScript projects concatenate their JavaScript—that is, they combine all their JavaScript files into a single file and then serve that file to the browser. This minimizes the number of JavaScript files you need to load, which is a better choice for some applications than asynchronous loading. RequireJS is useful for applications that have large JavaScript resources that don't need to be present when the page loads. However, in many AngularJS applications, the size of AngularJS dwarfs the size of the application code. The next tool you'll learn about, Browserify, supplies an alternative approach to module loading that's more conducive to the concatenation approach than RequireJS.

Browserify

If you are familiar with server-side JavaScript, you may be surprised to see Browserify in a list of module loaders. Browserify is not designed to be a module loader in the same sense as RequireJS, but it provides an effective solution to browser-side module loading as a by-product of its primary purpose: compiling NodeJS-style JavaScript into a browser-friendly form. NodeJS is a popular server-side JavaScript runtime that has numerous elegant features, including file-level scoping and a global function called `require()` for importing external dependencies. In this section, you learn the fundamentals of the NodeJS `require()` function and how you can utilize Browserify to take advantage of NodeJS's more structured approach to dependency management in your AngularJS applications.

Note that, for the purposes of this section, you need to have NodeJS installed. If you have not done so, please navigate to `http://www.nodejs.org/downloads` and follow the instructions for your platform of choice.

Although NodeJS does implement the JavaScript language standard, NodeJS's runtime is fundamentally different from a browser's runtime. In particular, the global objects `document` and `window` that you may have seen in browser-side JavaScript do not exist in the NodeJS runtime. Furthermore, NodeJS enforces file-level scoping: By default, a variable declared with `var` in the top-level scope of a file is not visible in other files. For instance, if you had two JavaScript files, `foo.js` and `bar.js`, and `foo.js` contained the following code:

```
var x = 1;
```

if `bar.js` were to include `foo.js` via the `require()` function, `bar.js` would not be able to access the value of the x variable:

```
require('./foo.js');

console.log(x); // undefined
```

To export functions and objects from a NodeJS file, you need to explicitly attach them to the `module.exports` (or `exports` as a shorthand) object. For instance, if `foo.js` contained the following code:

```
exports.x = 1;
```

then `bar.js` could access the value of the x variable like this:

```
var foo = require('./foo.js');

console.log(foo.x); // 1
```

There are two important details to note about the `require()` function in the preceding examples. First, the return value of `require()` is the `module.exports` object from the required file. Second, the path passed to the `require()` function must be relative to the file that calls the `require()` function (only if the path isn't in the `node_modules` directory that you'll learn about shortly). In other words, if a third file in a separate directory calls `require()` on `bar.js`, `bar.js` can still call `require('./foo.js')` successfully.

NodeJS also allows you to include external dependencies in a `node_modules` directory and `require()` them without a relative path. Specifically, if you call `require('foo')` in a file and there is no file or directory named foo or foo.js in that file's directory, NodeJS walks up your directory tree looking for a directory named node_modules. If NodeJS finds a node_modules directory, it looks for a file or directory named foo in the node_modules directory. This approach may seem unwieldy if you are used to programming languages in which a file includes the need to be relative to the project's root directory. NodeJS's approach has its merits, however. For instance, NodeJS code's directory structure is often considerably easier to refactor because individual directories don't necessarily have to be aware of their place in their directory structure.

Now that you understand the high-level concepts of the require() function, you're going to write some NodeJS-style AngularJS code and use Browserify to compile this code into a browser-friendly format. You can install Browserify by navigating to the root directory of this chapter's sample code and running the npm install command. Note that, to do this, you need to have NodeJS and npm installed. If you have not done so yet, please install NodeJS from http://nodejs.org/download. Running the npm install command downloads Browserify into the node_modules/browserify directory under the root directory of this chapter's sample code. You can utilize Browserify in NodeJS itself, but the easiest way to get started with Browserify is to use it as a command-line utility. For instance, consider these two simple NodeJS files that you can find in this chapter's sample code, browserify_module.js and browserify_controller.js. First, here is browserify_controller.js:

```
module.exports = function($scope) {
  $scope.answer = 42;
};
```

Here is browserify_module.js:

```
if (typeof window !== 'undefined' && window.angular) {
  var myModule = angular.module('MyModule', []);
  myModule.controller('BrowserifyController',
    require('./browserify_controller.js'));
}
```

Naturally, since this code uses require() and module.exports, it doesn't work in the browser. This is where the Browserify command-line utility comes in. To generate a browser-friendly file called browserify_output.js from the preceding files, you can run the following command:

```
./node_modules/browserify/bin/cmd.js \
  -o ./browserify_output.js ./browserify_module.js
```

For your convenience, the Makefile in this chapter's sample code provides a convenient shorthand for the preceding command: make browserify. Once you run this command, you should have a file called browserify_output.js in this chapter's sample code directory that looks something like this:

```
(function e(t,n,r){/*...*/({1:[function(require,module,exports){
module.exports = function($scope) {
  $scope.answer = 42;
};

},{}],2:[function(require,module,exports){
```

```
if (typeof window !== 'undefined' && window.angular) {
  var myModule = angular.module('MyModule', []);
  myModule.controller('BrowserifyController',
    require('./browserify_controller.js'));
}

},{"./browserify_controller.js":1}]},{},[2]);
```

The `browserify_output.js` file looks a little difficult to read, but it's valid JavaScript that can run in the browser. For example, consider the `browserify_example.html` file in this chapter's sample code:

```html
<body>
  <div ng-controller="BrowserifyController">
    <h1>The answer is {{answer}}</h1>
  </div>

  <script type="text/javascript" src="angular.js"></script>
  <script type="text/javascript" src="browserify_output.js"></script>
</body>
```

In the preceding code, you can utilize the `BrowserifyController` that you declared in `browserify_controller.js` and included in `MyModule` in `browserify_module.js`. Once you have compiled the `browserify_output.js` file, you can use the components and modules you declared using NodeJS's `require()` function in the same way as you would if you had written conventional browser-side JavaScript.

The key advantage of writing your browser-side JavaScript in NodeJS-style is that NodeJS's `require()` function can serve a similar purpose as RequireJS. Specifically, the `require()` function allows you to include external JavaScript files from your JavaScript, rather than relying on `script` tags.

However, Browserify has one key difference from RequireJS: Browserify outputs a single file, which you're expected to include in your page using a `script` tag. Browserify has no client-side mechanism for loading external JavaScript; it's a purely compile-time tool that concatenates all your JavaScript into one browser-friendly file. Conversely, RequireJS operates in the browser and loads extra JavaScript as necessary using HTTP. Thus, Browserify isn't as good as RequireJS for ensuring that you only load the JavaScript that you need because you have to use Browserify to compile a separate JavaScript file for each page.

This disadvantage, however, can be a big advantage in certain cases. Often, AngularJS apps compiled with Browserify simply compile all their browser-side JavaScript into a single file, minify it, and ask the browser to cache the file. Once the file is cached, subsequent page loads are much faster because there's no need to load additional JavaScript. The trade-off is that the initial page load is slower. In fact, many AngularJS applications prefer to concatenate all their JavaScript into a single file because even requesting a small JavaScript file incurs overhead due to network latency. As a side effect of compiling NodeJS JavaScript, Browserify provides concatenation as well.

> **NOTE** *Browserify works by parsing your code and doing some rudimentary static analysis to resolve calls to the* `require()` *function. In particular, if you call* `require('./foo.js')`, *Browserify includes the* `./foo.js` *file in the output. However, because Browserify only does static analysis, it cannot resolve* `require()` *calls that pass a variable as a parameter. For instance,* `var x = './foo.js' && require(x)` *works normally in NodeJS, but Browserify does not attempt to resolve the value of* x. *Thus, if you choose to use Browserify, you should only pass hard-coded strings to* `require()` *calls.*

The other primary advantage to using Browserify is the ability to use the NodeJS package manager, npm. If your server-side code is also written in NodeJS, you can use only one package manager throughout your codebase. Even if your server-side code is not written in NodeJS, npm is typically more elegant and easy to use than client-side JavaScript package managers like Bower. In addition, the npm central repository offers you access to more than 100,000 packages as of 2014, making it the largest package ecosystem in the world. With Browserify, you can take advantage of these packages in your browser-side JavaScript. For instance, earlier in this chapter you used a module called `event-emitter` to broadcast events between services. Actually, this module was originally written for NodeJS and distributed via npm. The `event-emitter.js` file you used in this chapter was compiled with Browserify so you could access it in your browser-side JavaScript.

> **NOTE** *You don't have to use Browserify to compile the entirety of your client-side JavaScript. As with the* `event-emitter.js` *file you used earlier, you can use Browserify to compile certain npm modules for use in the browser and include the files using* `script` *tags. Browserify, along with similar tools like OneJS and Webmake, is often used to compile NodeJS JavaScript modules into files that can be included into browser JavaScript using* `script` *tags. For instance, Mongoose, a NodeJS schema validation tool that you'll learn about in Chapter 10, has a browser component that's compiled with Browserify.*

Now that you understand Browserify's role in compiling NodeJS modules for the browser, you'll see how to use the `event-emitter` module in your Browserify-compiled AngularJS app. In this chapter's sample code, you'll see that the `event-emitter` module is listed as a dependency in the `package.json` file:

```
"dependencies": {
  "browserify": "6.3.2",
  "event-emitter": "0.3.1"
}
```

The package.json file is where npm looks for dependencies to install when you run npm install. When you run npm install, you'll find that npm created an event-emitter directory in the node_modules directory. You can then use require() to include the event-emitter module in your AngularJS app:

```
var emitter = require('event-emitter');

if (typeof window !== 'undefined' && window.angular) {
  var myModule = angular.module('MyModule', []);
  myModule.controller('BrowserifyController',
    function($scope) {
      $scope.emitter = emitter();

      $scope.numPings = 0;
      $scope.emitter.on('ping', function() {
        ++$scope.numPings;
      });
    });
}
```

You can then compile this file into a single browser-friendly file called browserify_emitter_output.js using the Browserify command-line tool:

```
./node_modules/browserify/bin/cmd.js -o ./browserify_emitter_output.js \
  ./browserify_emitter_module.js
```

Once you've compiled the browserify_emitter_output.js file, you can include it using a script tag and utilize the event emitter you attached to the BrowserifyController scope:

```
<body>
  <div ng-controller="BrowserifyController">
    <h1 ng-click="emitter.emit('ping')">
      You've Clicked This {{numPings}} Times
    </h1>
  </div>

  <script type="text/javascript" src="angular.js"></script>
  <script type="text/javascript" src="browserify_emitter_output.js">
  </script>
</body>
```

As you can see, Browserify allows you to leverage the power of NodeJS's require() function and the rich npm ecosystem in your AngularJS applications. Browserify is a very different solution to the module loading problem than RequireJS. Browserify is a purely compile-time tool, so it may load unnecessary modules, but it does load all your dependencies into one file. Depending on your use case, this may be an advantage. One further difficulty of using Browserify is that your AngularJS application will not run in the browser unless it's compiled through Browserify, which makes debugging more difficult. Whether these difficulties are offset by Browserify's significant benefits depends on your development team's skill sets and whether your server code is written in NodeJS.

BEST PRACTICES FOR STRUCTURING USER AUTHENTICATION

This section ties together the concepts you learned in this chapter and distills them into some best practices for structuring AngularJS login/logout functionality. Every application is different, but virtually every application has some notion of user authentication. This section uses user authentication as a case study on how to organize your code using modules, services, controllers, and directives.

Services: Loading from and Storing Data to the Server

Because a service is instantiated at most once, services are ideal for loading information about the currently logged-in user. This means the service can query the server for data when it's instantiated, and any controller or service can use that data without having to query the server again. To take advantage of this, you will implement a service called userService that will be responsible for periodically asking the server about the user's information. To avoid the overhead of creating a REST API, you'll use $timeout to simulate an asynchronous HTTP call. What follows is an implementation of userService that uses $timeout. You can find this code in authentication_example.html:

```
app.factory('userService', function($timeout) {
  var user = {
    loggedIn: false
  };

  user.loadFromServer = function() {
    $timeout(function() {
      user.loggedIn = true;
      user.name = 'Username';
    }, 500);
  };

  user.login = function(username, password) {
    $timeout(function() {
      user.loggedIn = true;
      user.name = username;
    }, 500);
  };

  user.logout = function() {
    user.loggedIn = false;
    user.name = undefined;
  };

  user.loadFromServer();
  return user;
});
```

The preceding implementation of userService implements the core functionality around user authentication: logging in, logging out, and loading data about the current user. Because userService is instantiated exactly once, loadFromServer() is called once when the service is instantiated, and logout() clears the user data for all controllers, services, and directives.

Controllers: Exposing an API to HTML

Typically, you want to create a top-level controller attached to either the page's `body` tag or an all-encompassing `div` tag that exposes the data `userService` loads from the server, as well as the `logout()` and `login()` functions. This enables your HTML to access this functionality without having to make every controller rely on `userService`. This implementation of `userService` is an excellent candidate to be exposed in a top-level `AppController` because it is typically accessed in HTML more than in controllers. In other words, other controllers typically don't call the `logout()` function directly. Instead, the `logout()` function is likely called through directives like `ngClick`. Here is the implementation of the top-level `AppController`:

```
app.controller('AppController', function($scope, userService) {
  $scope.user = userService;
});
```

This controller exposes the `userService` functionality throughout the page's HTML. Once again, recall that the core purpose of controllers is to expose JavaScript data and functions to directives so that directives can bind DOM interactions to this API and create a user experience. What follows is a basic example of utilizing the API that `AppController` provides using built-in directives:

```
<body ng-controller="AppController">
  <div ng-show="user.loggedIn">
    <h1>{{user.name}}</h1>
    <input   type="button"
             ng-click="user.logout()"
             value="Log Out">
  </div>
  <div ng-show="!user.loggedIn">
    <input   type="button"
             ng-click="user.login('Username')"
             value="Log In">
  </div>
</body>
```

Directives: Interfacing with the DOM

You will learn about writing custom directives in more detail in Chapter 5. For the purposes of architecting an authentication system, however, you will primarily focus on using directives to create reusable HTML components. Reusable HTML components are just a small subset of the more general purpose of directives: tying DOM interactions to the API that controllers provide. Next, you'll use directives to build up a reusable `login` directive that you can utilize throughout your application:

```
app.directive('login', function() {
  return {
    restrict: 'E',
    scope: true,
    template: 'Username: <input type="text" ng-model="username">' +
      '<br>' +
      'Password: <input type="password" ng-model="password">' +
```

```
        '<br>' +
        '<input type="button" ng-click="login()" value="Log In">',
      controller: function($scope, userService) {
        $scope.login = function() {
          userService.login($scope.username, $scope.password);
        };
      }
    }
  });
```

You can then utilize the `login` directive in your HTML as shown here:

```
<div ng-show="user.loggedIn">
  <h1>{{user.name}}</h1>
  <input   type="button"
           ng-click="user.logout()"
           value="Log Out">
</div>
<div ng-show="!user.loggedIn">
  <login></login>
</div>
```

Building reusable components using directives is an important best practice and one of the most common use cases for directives.

CONCLUSION

In this chapter, you learned about best practices for organizing AngularJS code and structuring your applications. In particular, you discovered the differences between services, controllers, and directives and the use cases that each component is uniquely suited for. You read about using modules to organize components into related groups and how to use modules to set up A/B tests. You learned directory-structuring paradigms for projects of various sizes. Finally, you read about two module loaders, which some AngularJS applications use to make including JavaScript dependencies a less error-prone process.

4

Data Binding

WHAT YOU WILL LEARN IN THIS CHAPTER:

➤ How to create and use data bindings

➤ Best practices for performance with data bindings

➤ How to tie filters into data binding

WROX.COM CODE DOWNLOADS FOR THIS CHAPTER

You can find the wrox.com code downloads for this chapter at http://www.wrox.com/go/proangularjs on the Download Code tab.

WHAT IS DATA BINDING?

Data binding is the feature that's at the heart of all AngularJS functionality. In Chapter 2, "Intelligent Workflow and Build Systems," you saw some basic data binding using the {{ }} symbol.

At a high level, *data binding* is the ability to tie two JavaScript values together. When the first variable changes, the second is updated to reflect the changes to the first. The most common use case of data binding is to tie your user interface (UI), which is often called a *view*, to a set of UI-independent values, which are often referred to as your *model*. Your model will consist of simple strings, numbers, and other primitive JavaScript types. Using data binding, your view defines how to render the model.

> **NOTE** *You may have heard the terms model and view before in the context of the well-known pattern known as Model-View-Controller (MVC). You can think of data binding as being a general replacement for the C in MVC. AngularJS has been referred to as a client-side Model-View-ViewManager (MVVM) or Model-View-Whatever (MVW) framework for this exact reason. Yes, Model-View-Whatever is actually a technical term.*

Data binding allows you to tie your view to your model directly from your Hypertext Markup Language (HTML) using directives, which you will learn more about in Chapter 5. To better understand the power of data binding, you'll take a look at a simple case: a page that says "Hello" to the user based on the name the user enters into a text box. Here's an example of how this works in jQuery, a popular lightweight JavaScript library:

```html
<input type="text" id="username">
<div>
    Hello,
    <span id="display_username">
    </span>
</div>

<script type="application/javascript">
    $(document).ready(function() {
        $('#username').on('keyup', function() {
            $('#display_username').html($('#username').val());
        });
    });
</script>
```

This may look familiar to you if you have experience with UI development. Assigning an event handler for a specific event on a specific UI element is a standard paradigm in most common UI toolkits, whether Android, iOS, Swing, or jQuery. However, AngularJS data binding inverts this paradigm and enables you to instead define these handlers within the HTML in a declarative fashion:

```html
<div ng-controller="HelloController">
    <input type="text" id="username" ng-model="username">
    <div>
        Hello,
        <span id="display_username">
            {{ username }}
        </span>
    </div>
</div>

<script type="text/javascript">
    function HelloController($scope) {
        $scope.username = "";
    }
</script>
```

The {{ }} symbol around the preceding username variable is an example of one-way data binding. This symbol is convenient shorthand for the following:

```
<span id="display_username" ng-bind="username"></span>
```

The attribute ngBind is a directive telling AngularJS that this span has a one-way binding to the username variable. In other words, ngBind tells AngularJS that every time the value of username changes, the contents of the span should update to reflect the new value of username. AngularJS's data binding takes care of this bookkeeping for you; all you have to worry about is making sure that username has the correct value.

The attribute ngModel is a directive that creates a two-way data binding between the input field and the variable username. In other words, when the value of the input field changes because the user typed something, the value of username changes to reflect the new value of the input field. In addition, when the value of the username variable changes, the value of the input field changes to reflect the new value of username. You can try this out for yourself in the following example, in which you'll add a button to the previous example to clear the username variable:

```
<div ng-controller="HelloController">
    <input type="text" id="username" ng-model="username">
    <button ng-click="clear()">
      Clear Username
    </button>
    <div>
        Hello,
        <span id="display_username">
            {{ username }}
        </span>
    </div>
</div>

<script type="text/javascript">
    function HelloController($scope) {
        $scope.username = "";

        $scope.clear = function() {
          $scope.username = "";
        };
    }
</script>
```

If you're paying attention, you'll notice that a new type of directive was used in the preceding code: ngClick. You can embed JavaScript click handlers in your HTML using the onClick attribute, so why do you need a special directive? The full answer to this question requires a deeper dive into the internals of directives, which you'll explore in detail in Chapter 5, "Directives." However, at a high level, you should use ngClick to attach a click handler instead of onClick because ngClick ties into two powerful and integral pieces of AngularJS: scopes and the $digest loop. Both of these concepts are explored in much detail over the next couple of sections.

In the two previous examples, you saw that ngClick interacts with data binding in a very different way from ngBind. In general, directives fall into three classes in terms of their interaction with data binding: 1) directives that only handle displaying data via a one-way binding such as `ngBind`, 2) directives that wrap event handlers like `ngClick`, and 3) directives that do two-way data binding such as `ngModel`. At a high level, these types of directives differ in terms of how they interact with the JavaScript data in your scopes. The first class of directive is called a *render-only directive*. Directives of this type specify rules for how data is displayed but do not modify data. The second class of directive is an *event handler wrapper*. Directives of this type do not render data, but they may modify it. The third and final class of directives, *two-way directives*, both render and modify data. Note that these definitions aren't actually part of the AngularJS codebase. They are presented here simply as a tool to help classify directives into more easily comprehensible chunks.

DIRECTIVE CLASS	DOES IT RENDER DATA?	DOES IT MODIFY DATA?	EXAMPLES OF BUILT-IN DIRECTIVES IN THIS CLASS
Render-only	Yes	No	`ngBind`, `ngBindHtml`, `ngRepeat`, `ngShow`, `ngHide`
Event handler wrapper	No	Maybe	`ngClick`, `ngMouseenter`, `ngDblclick`
Two-way	Yes	Yes	`ngModel`

Hopefully, now you have a better idea of why data binding is magical. Before you really dig into the nitty-gritty of how data binding works and how to use it effectively, you'll take a step back and learn what the advantages of data binding are.

WHAT DATA BINDING CAN DO FOR YOU

There are three primary advantages to data binding over using event handlers directly. First, your model and your controller logic are completely independent of your UI. In the previous code, you can add another UI element that is tied to the variable `username`, or you can create another element that shows if `username` is defined, all without changing the controller code. Your controller code can load data and provide an application programming interface (API) to the HTML for data manipulation and handle loading and saving the data, while all decisions for the way the data is presented in the UI can be in your HTML and cascading style sheets (CSS).

The clean separation between view and controller provided by AngularJS is valuable in a single-person project, but just wait until you see what it can do for you in an interdisciplinary team setting. On a product team, you probably have at least one person who is focused on the user interface/user experience (UI/UX). In other words, you probably have a developer or developers who are responsible for getting the data (also known as the *model*) from the server to the browser, and a designer or designers who are responsible for how this data is presented to a user.

Without AngularJS, the glue between the model and the view is a gray area. In practice, this ends up being where developers and designers step on each other's toes. A classic nightmare scenario occurs when the designer goes through and tweaks all the CSS classes, but then the glue code often needs to be updated to make sure it is creating elements with the proper CSS classes. Even with a strong MVC framework like BackboneJS, separating code and design is near impossible. At some point you have to have a designer tweaking JavaScript or a developer deciding how data is rendered.

With data binding, your design guru doesn't have to code JavaScript, and your developer doesn't have to tweak HTML. Instead, in an ideal world, these two interact through a well-defined API, with the developer writing JavaScript functions and exposing variables in the controller, and the designer tying into these using directives like ngClick from their HTML.

Also, data binding allows you to write more code in a declarative language like HTML, and less code in a more imperative language like JavaScript. Generally speaking, *imperative* programming involves providing a computer with exact instructions for how to execute a task. In contrast, *declarative* programming allows you to specify what you would like to happen, while allowing the computer to optimize the details of how it should be done. Or, in other words, in an imperative language you deal with verbs, whereas in a declarative language, like HTML, you write only nouns. The precise technical definitions of imperative and declarative programming are more complicated and subject to debate, but suffice it to say that declarative programming syntax makes high-level concepts, like visual rendering of data, much simpler.

Declarative languages tend to be terser and more conducive to UI/UX development because, fundamentally, a UI is built of objects that have potential actions associated with them. This means that rather than writing code to explicitly construct UI objects, you simply define how you want the objects to be structured and let the browser handle the rendering specifics. Just imagine the mess if you had to build up your entire page's structure using jQuery! Developers who have used the Java Swing package will recall the frustration of having to build up a full structure of frames and buttons from within Java code—no wonder Swing UIs are infamous for looking terrible!

With AngularJS data binding, your HTML not only defines the UI structure, but your UX structure as well. Because the UX (the decisions about the concrete actions your user can take) is defined in your HTML, there is no need for messy event handler-binding code, which is overly verbose and pollutes the global scope.

Lastly, AngularJS scoping provides a neat framework for organizing your code. The ng-controller directive creates a new instance of HelloController each time, so your UI can reuse the controller in different places without making changes to the JavaScript. For example, perhaps you want HelloController to greet different users in different languages:

```
<div ng-controller="HelloController">
    English:
    <input type="text" ng-model="username">
    <div ng-click="clear()">
      Clear Username
    </div>

    <div>
        Hello,
        <span>
            {{ username }}
        </span>
    </div>
```

```
        </div>
    </div>

    <br>
    <br>

    <div ng-controller="HelloController">
        Spanish:
        <input type="text" ng-model="username">
        <div ng-click="clear()">
          Clear Username
        </div>

        <div>
            Hola,
            <span>
                {{ username }}
            </span>
        </div>
    </div>

    <script type="text/javascript">
        function HelloController($scope) {
            $scope.username = "";

            $scope.clear = function() {
              $scope.username = "";
            };
        }
    </script>
```

When you run the preceding code, you notice that the two `username` variables are independent of one another. You can type **Jack** in the first one and **Juan** in the other, and the corresponding `div` elements will say `Hello, Jack` and `Hola, Juan`. This is a result of AngularJS creating a new scope every time you use the `ng-controller` directive. Each of the `div` elements with `HelloController` attached has its own instance of `HelloController` and thus its own `username` variable. Scopes are an extraordinarily powerful tool in AngularJS, and they play an integral role in how data binding is used. Because of this, it's worth looking closer at what scopes are and what they do.

SCOPING OUT ANGULARJS SCOPES

One extremely powerful AngularJS feature is the introduction of scopes into the Document Object Model (DOM). A *scope* is an execution context for AngularJS expressions. An *expression* is a string containing JavaScript code that's meant to be evaluated by AngularJS. For example, the values of the `ngClick` and `ngModel` attributes, as well as the contents of the {{ }} symbol, are expressions. Under the hood, AngularJS parses these expressions and evaluates them against the associated scope. A key point to remember is that expressions are very different from the code that's in your controllers: AngularJS handles parsing and evaluating expressions in its own way, whereas controller code runs directly against your browser. Code that works in an expression may not work in a controller and vice versa.

In the previous section, you saw that the ng-controller directive creates a new scope that expressions attached to directives can access. Much like in JavaScript, scopes play an invaluable role in making code more modular and more easily reusable. For example, you saw that, with the power of scopes, you had two independent HelloController instances on the same page. In addition, the ngClick, ngModel, and ngBind expressions nested under the ng-controller directive each had access to the correct instance.

Most other JavaScript libraries provide only a thin wrapper around built-in HTML event handlers like onClick. These have a fatal flaw: A function, called in an in-HTML event handler, must be visible from the global scope of the page, commonly referred to as the *window*. A dependence on global state makes your code more difficult to manage. For example, maybe you had written the HelloController example using onClick and global state. If you wanted to add another language, say French, you would have to add a separate instance of HelloController to the window. You would have to make sure that this new instance didn't overwrite any global state that other elements depend on. In addition, you'd have to have the DOM know which instance of HelloController to access, which is way too much work for a simple task.

With scopes in the DOM, however, using in-HTML event handlers becomes much more viable. You may have noticed that the first parameter passed into a controller is $scope, which corresponds to the scope created by the ng-controller directive. You can then augment this scope with variables and functions from the controller. Note that these functions are accessible only from $scope and children of $scope. AngularJS creates a root scope for every page, and all scopes created, whether by ng-controller or other directives, are children of the root scope. There aren't many cases for dealing with the root scope directly, but just in case you need to, know that you can access the root scope via dependency injection in your controllers as $rootScope.

Scope Inheritance

DOM scopes in AngularJS behave much like scopes in the JavaScript language itself. In JavaScript, keyword-like functions like for and if create *child scopes*, which allow you to define variables local to that scope using the var keyword.

Unsurprisingly, the AngularJS equivalents, ngRepeat and ngIf, create scopes in the DOM. Scopes inherit from their parents using prototype-based inheritance and keep a pointer to their parent scope in their $parent field, so scopes can access variables from their parent scope. In the DOM, you can access the full scope chain:

```html
<div ng-controller="LanguagesController">
    <div ng-repeat="language in languages" ng-controller="HelloController">
        {{ language.name }}:
        <input type="text" id="username" ng-model="username">
        <div>
            {{ greet(language, username) }}
        </div>
    </div>
</div>

<script type="text/javascript">
```

```
            function LanguagesController($scope) {
                $scope.languages = [
                    { name : "English", greeting : "Hello, " },
                    { name : "Spanish", greeting : "Hola, "}
                ];

                $scope.greet = function(language, name) {
                    return language.greeting + " " + name;
                };
            }

            function HelloController($scope) {
                $scope.username = "";
            }
        </script>
```

Scopes are powerful tools, and, if you learned anything from *Spiderman*, it's that with great power comes great responsibility. One of the most common ways to shoot yourself in the foot with AngularJS is by forgetting that, although you can read variables from parent scopes, AngularJS won't let you assign a value to a parent scope. This mistake is most easily illustrated with what seems like a perfectly innocuous example. Perhaps you wanted to bind both the English and the Spanish username inputs from the previous example to a single variable. You might try moving the username variable into LanguagesController like this:

```
        <div ng-controller="LanguagesController">
            <div ng-repeat="language in languages" ng-controller="HelloController">
                {{ language.name }}:
                <input type="text" id="username" ng-model="username">
                <div>
                    {{ greet(language, username) }}
                </div>
            </div>
        </div>

        <script type="text/javascript">
            function LanguagesController($scope) {
                $scope.languages = [
                    { name : "English", greeting : "Hello, " },
                    { name : "Spanish", greeting : "Hola, "}
                ];

                $scope.greet = function(language, name) {
                    return language.greeting + " " + name;
                };

                $scope.username = "Juan";
            }

            function HelloController($scope) {
            }
        </script>
```

However, when you try to run this code, you see that when you enter **John** into the English input, the Spanish input won't change. What will really blow your mind is that both inputs will say Juan initially. What's wrong here? Well, even though ngModel can read from the value of username from its parent scope, it can only assign to its current scope. Thus, when you change the English input, the ngModel directive creates a new username variable within the scope defined by its copy of HelloController!

To get around this issue, you can use the ngChange directive and the fact that you can call functions from the parent scope. The ngChange directive evaluates the attached expression every time the value of the corresponding input changes, so you can use it to call a function on LanguagesController every time the username changes:

```html
<div ng-controller="LanguagesController">
    <div ng-repeat="language in languages" ng-controller="HelloController">
        {{ language.name }}:
        <input   type="text"
                 ng-model="username"
                 ng-change="updateUsername(username)">
        <div>
            {{ greet(language, username) }}
        </div>
    </div>
</div>

<script type="text/javascript">
    function LanguagesController($scope) {
        $scope.languages = [
            { name : "English", greeting : "Hello, " },
            { name : "Spanish", greeting : "Hola, "}
        ];

        $scope.greet = function(language, name) {
            return language.greeting + " " + name;
        };

        $scope.username = "Juan";

        $scope.updateUsername = function(username) {
            $scope.username = username;
        }
    }

    function HelloController($scope) {
    }
</script>
```

AngularJS also allows you to disable scope inheritance. A scope can be marked as an *isolate*, which means that it does not inherit from its parent. You'll learn more about isolate scopes when you dive into directives in Chapter 5.

Another common way of shooting yourself in the foot with scopes is failing to remember that functions on the global window object cannot be accessed from within AngularJS expressions. For example, the encodeURIComponent function escapes string values for use in URLs. Virtually every JavaScript program that communicates with a server uses encodeURIComponent. This function is attached to window and can be accessed as window.encodeURIComponent. To illustrate this, here's a common mistake that virtually everyone makes when starting out with AngularJS:

```
{{ encodeURIComponent(username) }}
```

When you try this, you'll notice that your AngularJS error handler is triggered and that the span in the UI is empty. This is because expressions are strictly limited to variables in the current scope and its ancestors: No global state or functions are allowed. As a matter of fact, AngularJS describes itself as "lethally allergic to global state" in its online documentation. Whether this is a bug or a feature is for you to decide for yourself. Either way, the lack of window access from expressions has been with AngularJS since the first public release and is unlikely to change in the near future.

However, the encodeURIComponent function is accessible from within a controller. If you recall the difference between code in expressions and code in controllers (that the latter is parsed and evaluated by AngularJS, whereas the browser's interpreter directly evaluates the former), this shouldn't be a surprise. Because their code runs directly against the browser, controllers can access the window object. One way to get the encodeURIComponent function into your expressions is to attach the function to the scope in a controller:

```
$scope.encodeURIComponent = window.encodeURIComponent;
```

However, this approach is frustrating if you find yourself having to attach encodeURIComponent to the scope in every controller you write. Don't worry; there is a good AngularJS way to make encodeURIComponent accessible from within expressions. You'll explore this solution in the final section of this chapter, "Filters and Data-Binding Gotchas."

In addition to storing data, scopes have three important functions that are fundamental to the way data binding works. Make a note; you will see these functions mentioned time and time again in this book. These functions are called $watch, $apply, and $digest.

$watch

$watch makes up one side of two-way data binding: it enables you to set a callback function to be called whenever the value of a given expression changes. The callback function is often referred to as a *watcher*. A simple usage of $watch is to update a firstName and lastName variable every time the user changes his name:

```
$scope.$watch('name', function(value) {
  var firstSpace = (value || "").indexOf(' ');
  if (firstSpace == -1) {
    $scope.firstName = value;
    $scope.lastName = "";
  } else {
    $scope.firstName = value.substr(0, firstSpace);
    $scope.lastName = value.substr(firstSpace + 1);
  }
});
```

Internally, $watch is a trivial function. Each scope maintains a list of watchers, called $scope.$$watchers. $watch simply adds a new watcher, which includes some internal bookkeeping to keep track of the last computed value of the expression.

$apply

$apply makes up the other half of two-way data binding: It informs AngularJS that something has changed and the values of $watch expressions should be recomputed. You usually won't have to call $apply yourself, because AngularJS's built-in directives (such as ngClick) and services (such as $timeout) call $apply for you.

You're most likely to run into $apply in the context of custom event handlers. When an event occurs, such as a user clicking a button, or an outstanding HTTP request has completed, AngularJS needs to be informed that the model may have changed. Directives like ngClick and ngDblclick call $apply internally for this reason.

Another example is if you were to implement your own simple replacement to AngularJS's $http service. You would use $apply after you'd made whatever changes to the scope you needed, to make sure AngularJS was aware that the model may have changed. For instance, perhaps you wanted to use jQuery's $.get function instead of AngularJS' $http service to ask the OpenWeatherMap API for the current weather in New York City:

```
<div ng-controller="HttpController">
    <input type="submit" value="Stuck? Click Here!" ng-click="">
    <br>
    {{ weather }}
</div>
<script type="text/javascript">
    function HttpController($scope) {
        var weatherUrl =
            "http://api.openweathermap.org/data/2.5/weather" +
            "?q=NewYork,NY";
        $scope.weather = "Loading...";

        $scope.getNYCWeather = function() {
            $.get(weatherUrl, function(data) {
                $scope.weather = data;
                $scope.$apply();
            });
        }

        setTimeout(function() {
            $scope.getNYCWeather();
        }, 0);
    }
</script>
```

Try an experiment: commenting out the preceding $apply call. You will see that the view will not be updated when the HTTP request returns. However, it will be updated if you click the "Stuck? Click Here!" button because the ng-click directive calls $apply, even though the expression is empty.

$digest

$digest is the magic glue function that ties together $watch and $apply. You would be hard-pressed to find an example where you need to interface with $digest directly rather than through $watch and $apply. However, due to this function's unique place at the core of data binding, its internals merit a more detailed discussion.

At a high level, $digest evaluates all the $watch expressions in a scope, as well as the scope's children, and fires the watcher callback on any that have changed. This process may seem simple, but there's a subtle difficulty: A watcher can change the scope, which in turn means that there may be other watchers that need to be informed of changes. Thus, $digest actually occurs in a loop that conceptually looks like the following pseudocode:

```
var dirty = true;
var iterations = 0;
while (dirty && iterations++ < TIMES_TO_LOOP) {
  dirty = false;
  for (var i = 0; i < scope.watchers.length(); ++i) {
    var currentValue = scope.watchers[i].get();
    if (currentValue != scope.watchers[i].oldValue) {
      dirty = true;
      scope.watchers[i].callback(currentValue, scope.watchers[i].oldValue);
      scope.watchers[i].oldValue = currentValue;
    }
  }
}
```

One important note: the TIMES_TO_LOOP constraint exists to prevent AngularJS from getting stuck in an infinite loop in $digest. If your code causes the dirty flag to be set to true after every iteration, this loop could run forever and completely freeze the browser. Right now, AngularJS sets TIMES_TO_LOOP (which AngularJS calls TTL for short) to 10. If the loop executes more than TTL times, AngularJS throws a 10 $digest iterations reached. Aborting! error. This may seem like a small limit, but in practice seeing more than 3 or 4 $digest iterations is rare unless you have an infinite loop.

If you find yourself needing to change the TTL value for some reason, AngularJS allows you to change this value on a per-module basis using the $rootScope service and the digestTtl function. To set the TTL to 15, for example, you can use the following code when declaring your top-level app module:

```
var app = angular.module('MyApp', [], function($rootScopeProvider) {
    $rootScopeProvider.digestTtl(15);
});
```

Performance Considerations

You may think that AngularJS's *dirty checking* approach using $digest is ridiculously inefficient compared to attaching event handlers to the DOM. In reality, dirty checking is usually efficient enough, and the advantages in terms of correctness and predictability outweigh the performance impact most of the time. In this section, you learn how to minimize this performance impact and make sure your application looks snappy to your user.

First and foremost, before you dive into the performance internals of dirty checking, remember the wise words of legendary Stanford computer science professor Donald Knuth: "Premature optimization is the root of all evil ("Structured Programming with Go To Statements", *ACM* journal, 1974)." You should first make sure your application works as advertised before you start to optimize its performance.

When you do start considering performance, you shouldn't be asking how to make your app fast; you should be asking how to make your app fast enough for what it needs to do. In the end, if you never ship a functioning version of your app to users, it doesn't matter how efficient the half-finished prototype was. AngularJS was built precisely to address the problem of being able to put together a sophisticated and easily testable browser-based client quickly and easily. Many developers find benchmark comparisons between AngularJS and vanilla jQuery code to be moot, because they simply wouldn't be able to replicate their existing AngularJS functionality in jQuery within a reasonable amount of time.

Next, there are two important guidelines to remember when thinking about AngularJS performance. First, the AngularJS team informally recommends that you have less than 2,000 watchers on a single page. Consider the 2,000 watcher guideline when designing your app, and remember that essentially every directive in your UI creates at least one watcher. Remember that the `$digest` loop checks every watcher, and if you're watching many complex variables, this loop can become a bottleneck.

The second important guideline to remember is that AngularJS performance issues almost always come down to not using `ngRepeat` wisely. You might have guessed that creating 2,000 directives in a page without some sort of looping construct would be nearly impossible. The `ngRepeat` directive is the looping construct that opens up the possibility to create directives in a loop. The `ngRepeat` directive can thus create additional watchers: If you have an expression within an `ngRepeat`, you've created an extra watcher for each element within your array! Furthermore, `ngRepeat` usually watches an array, which is an expensive comparison for very large arrays.

An ngRepeat Gone Wrong

You'll create a simple benchmark to demonstrate what happens when you stress `ngRepeat`. The following code creates 10,000 `div` elements in your browser, displaying the numbers 0–9999. The jQuery code looks like this:

```
<script src="https://code.jquery.com/jquery-1.10.2.min.js">
</script>
<script type="application/javascript">
    $(document).ready(function() {

        var arrayPusher = {};

        arrayPusher.value = [];
        arrayPusher.get = function() {
            return arrayPusher.value;
        };
        arrayPusher.set = function(v) {
            var start = Date.now();
            arrayPusher.value = [];
            $('#container').empty();
            for (var i = 0; i < v.length; ++i) {
                arrayPusher.value.push(v[i]);
                $('#container').append('<div>' + v[i] + '</div>');
            }

            console.log("Time in MS: " + (Date.now() - start));
        };

        var arr = [];
```

```
        for (var i = 0; i < 10000; ++i) {
            arr.push(i);
        }

        arrayPusher.set(arr);
    });
</script>
```

The AngularJS code for doing this is considerably simpler. The reason for the setTimeout call is to make sure that you're not calling $digest within another $digest loop. AngularJS executes a $digest after the controller initialization is done. The setTimeout call makes sure that the only dirty watchers are those on the array itself when the $digest call happens:

```
<script type="application/javascript">
    function ArrayPushController($scope) {
        $scope.arr = [];

        $scope.push = function(v) {
            setTimeout(function() {
                var start = Date.now();
                $scope.arr = v;
                $scope.$digest();
                console.log("Time in MS: " + (Date.now() - start));
            }, 500);
        };

        $scope.newArr = [];
        for (var i = 0; i < 10000; ++i) {
            $scope.newArr.push(i);
        }
    }
</script>
<div ng-controller="ArrayPushController" ng-init="push(newArr)">
    <div ng-repeat="x in arr">
        {{ x }}
    </div>
</div>
```

When you run the preceding code, your console tells you that the AngularJS code is considerably slower. In Google Chrome, you'll likely see that the AngularJS code takes somewhere in the neighborhood of 1,500 milliseconds, whereas the jQuery code takes about 500 milliseconds. Keep in mind, these numbers come from an N=1 experiment and are only here to illustrate relative performance.

First, think about how many scopes and how many watchers you have in the AngularJS example. You might think that the only watcher is created by ngRepeat on the value of arr. However, there are actually 10,000 other watchers on the page. The ngRepeat directive creates a new scope for every element in the array, so the scope defined by the preceding ngController directive has one watcher and 10,000 child scopes, each with its own single watcher.

How does this execute within AngularJS? The $digest loop executes twice. The first iteration is the most expensive, because that's where AngularJS creates the 10,000 scopes and then attaches watchers on the value of x to each of them. The second iteration happens because the last iteration changed the value of x within each of the child scopes. If you break down these two, the first loop takes roughly 1,300 milliseconds of the 1,500, and the second takes 200 milliseconds.

How can you improve this performance? A common pattern for speeding up AngularJS on large lists is to get rid of the 10,000 watchers on the child scopes. At a high level, ngBind works by assigning a watcher to the contents of {{ }} and telling the browser to change the contents of the DOM element each time the watcher fires. Thus, each time the contents of arr change, AngularJS needs two $digest iterations. It also needs to create and destroy these one-watcher scopes.

How much overhead can you save by avoiding the creation of these watchers? A more thorough answer to this question requires a deep dive into how directives work; you will explore the answer in Chapter 5. In the meantime, you can do a simple experiment by replacing the {{ x }} expression in the preceding code with a static value, such as:

```
<div ng-controller="ArrayPushController" ng-init="push(newArr)">
    <div ng-repeat="x in arr">
        1
    </div>
</div>
```

The results are pretty significant. AngularJS executes the preceding code in about 800 milliseconds and executes only one $digest loop!

The one-time binding approach may seem like a significant handicap to the two-way data binding functionality. However, this approach works well in practice. If your application is doing an ngRepeat over a very long list, this portion of your application most likely gives users a list of items and the ability to click on one to view more details. This pattern is often referred to as the *master-detail design pattern*, a master list of items in which clicking on one brings up a detail view.

The master-detail pattern usually displays static information in the master list. Suppose your application is a list of upcoming events: You don't want people browsing events to be able to change the title of any given event! In cases like this, setting a watcher on the event title is a waste because the user should not be able to modify the title anyway.

Filters and Data-Binding Gotchas

Filters are an underrated AngularJS feature, and one that ties in closely with data binding and expressions. Filters are chainable functions that are accessible from any AngularJS expression. They are usually used for last-second data post-processing before the data is rendered. Filters tie in to data binding in a one-way manner, so you can use filters with directives like ngBind and ngClick, but not directives like ngModel. You'll recall from the introduction to this chapter that directives fall into three classes; only the first two classes of directives can be used with a filter. An important note to remember is that a filter does not change the underlying value of the JavaScript variable.

Filters are invoked using the | symbol, and additional parameters are delimited by : symbols after the filter name. A simple example of a filter is the built-in limitTo filter, which takes a string and returns a string that is limited to a certain number of characters:

```
{{ '123456789' | limitTo:9 }} => "123456789"
{{ '123456789' | limitTo:4 }} => "1234"
```

There are three common use cases for filters. You'll learn about each of them by example next. Each example also illustrates a common mistake that people make with both data binding in general and filters in particular, so hopefully after this section you'll really be a data binding pro.

Use Case 1: Rules for Converting Objects to Strings

When you're building a UI, inevitably you'll find yourself converting objects to strings. For example, perhaps you have a user object with a first name and a last name. You may find yourself writing the user's name like this:

```
{{ user.name.first }} {{ user.name.last }}
```

As a one-off, this approach works well. However, when this pattern starts popping up in multiple places, you start violating a key programming tenant: *don't repeat yourself*, commonly abbreviated DRY. What happens when your code is littered with these statements, but, later, you decide that you would really only prefer to have the last letter of the last name. Or, what if you decide that you have to limit the total length of the name to 40 characters? Find-and-replace approaches can work, but they're the wrong approach because they're messy and error-prone.

As an aside, you could attach a function to the `user.name` object called `user.name.toString()` that handles converting the object to a string. Those of you who come from an object-oriented language like Java or C++ might think this is the right approach in JavaScript. Although this approach is certainly possible in JavaScript, it usually doesn't make sense in the context of web development using AngularJS. Because JavaScript is not strongly typed, the type-checking benefits of a strict object-oriented approach aren't realized in JavaScript. Furthermore, because JSON APIs are often deeply nested, attempts to do strict object-oriented programming (or OOP for short) with JavaScript end up with a lot of repetitive code that looks like this:

```
var group = new Group(jsonData.group);
for (var i = 0; i < group.members.length; ++i) {
  group.members[i] = new User(group.members[i]);
}
```

Code like this fails to take advantage of the terse expressiveness that comes from JavaScript's functional features. Although this type of approach certainly works, it's not optimal given the language's feature set.

Filters provide a way to expose this string conversion functionality to AngularJS expressions in a way that retains the unit-test-friendly structure that AngularJS is known for. Here's a simple filter that handles your username use case:

```
angular.
  module('filters').
  filter('displayName', function() {
    return function(name) {
      return name.first + " " + name.last;
    }
  });
```

Not surprisingly, filters are attached to an AngularJS module with a given name, which you can then use to access the filter from an expression. For example, to utilize this filter, you would do this:

```
{{ user.name | displayName }}
```

Now the watcher for this expression knows to pass the value of user.name through the preceding function when evaluating the expression. Note that the filter is defined using the common *function-that-returns-a-function* pattern that you often see in AngularJS. The returned function is the function that actually does the work. The returned function receives the piped value as its first parameter and any parameters delimited by : as subsequent parameters. The outer function is a factory and can tie in to AngularJS dependency injection. Although filters should usually be lightweight functions that have no dependencies, a filter can ask for any service in the associated module. For example, your filter can get the $http service, as in the example that follows. However, using the $http service in a filter is generally a bad idea because the code sends an HTTP request every time the expression is executed:

```
angular.
    module('filters').
    filter('displayName', function($http) {
        return function(name) {
            $http.post('/api/log', name).success(function() {});
            return name.first + " " + name.last;
        }
    });
```

Another slick feature of filters is that they can be piped together. Those of you familiar with the bash shell will recognize the | symbol as a tool for piping input from one program to another. AngularJS uses the | symbol for filters because filters can be piped together in a similar way. For example, maybe you want to limit usernames to 40 characters in a certain part of your UI because of design considerations. You can achieve this quite elegantly by piping the output from the preceding displayName filter into AngularJS's built-in limitTo filter like so:

```
{{ user.name | displayName | limitTo:40 }}
```

But imagine that you want to limit all displayName outputs to be at most 40 characters. You can do this fairly simply by making the displayName filter return a substring if the string is too long, but there's an alternative approach that demonstrates another common use case of filters. The filters associated with the current module are accessible via dependency injection as the $filter service. By pulling this service into the displayName filter, you can reuse the limitTo filter and win a prize for keeping your code more DRY than the Sahara Desert:

```
angular.
    module('filters').
    filter('displayName', function($filter) {
        return function(name) {
            return $filter('limitTo')(name.first + " " + name.last, 40);
        }
    });
```

A good example of a built-in AngularJS filter that fits this use case is the date filter. The date filter provides some sophisticated functionality for converting a date or date-like object into a string. Another advantage of using a filter rather than creating a new object is that the date filter can be passed a date object, an appropriately formatted string, or a numeric timestamp, and AngularJS handles it correctly.

The second argument to the date filter specifies the format used for outputting the date. Conceptually, the date filter is similar to the strptime function in C and C++, but it uses a completely different syntax. The following table illustrates the most commonly used formatting elements for the date filter.

ELEMENT	OUTPUT	EXAMPLE
yyyy	4-digit year	`{{"2009-02-03"	date:"yyyy"}} => "2009"`
yy	Last two digits of year, padded	`{{"2009-02-03"	date:"yy"}} => "09"`
MMMM	Full month name, January–December	`{{"2009-02-03"	date:"MMMM yy"}} => "February 09"`
MMM	Short month name, Jan–Dec	`{{"2009-02-03"	date:"MMM yyyy"}} => "Feb 2009"`
MM	Padded numeric month, 01–12	`{{"2009-02-03"	date:"MM/yyyy"}} => "02/2009"`
M	Unpadded numeric month, 1–12	`{{"2009-02-03"	date:"M/yyyy"}} => "2/2009"`
dd	Padded day of month, 01–31	`{{"2009-02-03"	date:"MMM dd"}} => "Feb 03"`
d	Unpadded day of month, 1–31	`{{"2009-02-03"	date:"MMM d"}} => "Feb 3"`
EEEE	Day of week, Sunday–Saturday	`{{"2009-02-03"	date:"EEEE, MMM d"}} => "Tuesday, Feb 3"`
EEE	Short day of week, Sun–Sat	`{{"2009-02-03"	date:"EEE, MMM d"}} => "Tue, Feb 3"`
HH	Hour of day, padded, 00–23	`{{"2009-02-03T08:00:00"	date:"HH"}} => "08"`
H	Hour of day, unpadded, 0–23	`{{"2009-02-03T08:00:00"	date:"H"}} => "8"`
hh	Hour of day, a.m./p.m., padded, 01–12	`{{"2009-02-03T14:00:00"	date:"hh"}} => "02"`
h	Hour of day, a.m./p.m., unpadded, 1–12	`{{"2009-02-03T14:00:00"	date:"h"}} => "2"`

mm	Minutes, padded, 00–59	`{{"2009-02-03T14:00:00"	date:"h:mm"}} => "2:00"`
m	Minutes, unpadded, 0–59	`{{"2009-02-03T14:00:00"	date:"h:m"}} => "2:0"`
ss	Seconds, padded, 00–59	`{{"2009-02-03T14:00:59"	date:"h:mm:ss"}} => "2:00:59"`
s	Seconds, unpadded, 0–59	`{{"2009-02-03T14:00:09"	date:"m:s"}} => "0:9"`
a	a.m./p.m.	`{{"2009-02-03T14:00:00"	date:"h:mm a"}} => "2:00 pm"`

In addition to providing you with a host of options for custom date formatting, the `date` filter provides a few handy shortcuts for common date formats. A few of the most commonly used ones are listed here.

SHORTCUT	FORMAT EQUIVALENT	EXAMPLE
medium	MMM d, y h:mm:ss a	`{{"2009-02-03T14:00:09"	date:"medium"}} => "Feb 3, 2009 2:00:09 pm"`
short	M/d/yy h:mm a	`{{"2009-02-03T14:00:09"	date:"short"}} => "2/3/09 2:00 pm"`
fullDate	EEEE, MMMM d, y	`{{"2009-02-03T14:00:09"	date:"fullDate"}} => "Tuesday, February 3, 2009"`
mediumTime	h:mm:ss a	`{{"2009-02-03T14:00:09"	date:"mediumTime"}} => "2:00:09 pm"`

Pitfall

AngularJS's `ngBind` directive, which underlies the common {{ }} shorthand, escapes HTML in the expression's output. This is a basic defense against cross-site scripting attacks. What does this mean for you? Well, one application of using filters to format strings is the process of *linkifying* your text, such as converting all instances of `http://www.angularjs.com` in your text to links using the HTML a tag. When you run the following code, you see that you don't get the links you want, but you do get text with escaped HTML tags:

```
<div>
    <h1>Using ngBind</h1>
    <span ng-bind="'Go to http://www.google.com to search' | linkify">
    </span>
</div>

<script type="text/javascript">
    module.filter('linkify', function() {
        return function(str) {
```

```
        return str.replace(/(http:\/\/\S+)/ig, function(match) {
            return "<a href='" + match + "'>" + match + "</a>";
        });
    };
});
</script>
```

The way to get around this is fairly simple. There is a separate directive called ngBindHtml that behaves almost identically to ngBind, except that it doesn't escape reasonably safe HTML tags. In other words, ngBindHtml doesn't escape tags such as a or div, but it escapes potentially dangerous tags like script and style. Older, stable versions of AngularJS before version 1.2.0 did not have ngBindHtml. However, those versions did have an ngBindHtmlUnsafe directive, which does not do any escaping. You should not use ngBindHtmlUnsafe unless you are sure there's no way a malicious user could inject script tags into the ngBindHtmlUnsafe expression.

Use Case 2: Wrappers for Global Functions

Remember the difficulty caused by the fact that functions that are attached to the global window object (like encodeURIComponent) are not accessible from AngularJS expressions by default? Filters are the preferred solution for making such functions accessible from your expressions. For example, here's a filter that wraps the encodeURIComponent function:

```
filter('encodeUri', function() {
    return function(x) {
        return encodeURIComponent(x);
    };
});
```

Congratulations! You can now use encodeURIComponent expressions within your module! The key difference is that, like controllers, the filter function code runs directly against the browser instead of being evaluated internally against the scope. This new filter is pretty useful with the ngHref directive. Maybe you want to do an ngRepeat over the products in your catalog and include a link to each product. That code would look like this:

```
<div ng-repeat="product in products">
    <a ng-href="/product/{{product.name | encodeUri}}">
        {{ product.name }}
    </a>
</div>
```

There are a few other window functions that you may want to attach to filters, such as isNaN and decodeURIComponent. Thankfully, there probably aren't that many global functions that you want to use in expressions, so you'll only have to create a few filters with this use case.

Pitfall

Another pitfall that AngularJS rookies often run into is trying to use the ternary operator in expressions. Unfortunately, expressions like these aren't going to work, because the expressions parser doesn't understand the ternary operator:

```
{{ request.done ? "Done" : "In Progress" }}
```

There are several alternatives to this tragically flawed approach. You can use the `ngIf` directive as an approximation. However, note that there's no corresponding `ngElse` directive, so this approach isn't as terse as the ternary operator. If you're using an old version of AngularJS, keep in mind that `ngIf` was introduced in version 1.1.5. In this case, the following approach will work about as well if you use `ngShow` in place of `ngIf`, and `ngShow` has been in AngularJS since the beginning:

```
<div ng-if="request.done">
  Done
</div>
<div ng-if="!request.done">
  In Progress
</div>
```

However, you can achieve this more tersely using filters. Once again, recall that filter function code is executed against the browser rather than evaluated by AngularJS. If you find yourself needing to use functionality that's available in JavaScript but not in expressions, generally a filter is the right approach. As you might have guessed, you can write a filter that wraps the ternary operator like the filter you wrote to wrap the `encodeURIComponent` function:

```
<div ng-controller="RequestsController">
    <div ng-repeat="request in requests">
        {{ request.done | conditional:'Done':'In Progress' }}
    </div>
</div>

<script type="text/javascript">
    function RequestsController($scope) {
        $scope.requests = [];
        for (var i = 0; i < 50; ++i) {
            $scope.requests.push({ done : (i % 3 == 0) });
        }
    }

    module.filter('conditional', function() {
        return function(b, t, f) {
            return b ? t : f;
        };
    });
</script>
```

When you run the preceding code, the browser displays `Done` every third line and `In Progress` otherwise, as expected. In addition, you can use this `conditional` filter in expressions passed to directives. The `conditional` filter is particularly useful in combination with the `ngHref` directive. For example, you can modify the preceding HTML to have a conditional link:

```
<div ng-controller="RequestsController">
    <div ng-repeat="request in requests">
        <a ng-href="{{request.done | conditional:'/history':'/request'}}">
            {{ request.done | conditional:'Done':'In Progress' }}
        </a>
    </div>
</div>
```

```
    </div>

    <script type="text/javascript">
        function RequestsController($scope) {
            $scope.requests = [];
            for (var i = 0; i < 50; ++i) {
                $scope.requests.push({ done : (i % 3 == 0) });
            }
        }

        module.filter('conditional', function() {
            return function(b, t, f) {
                return b ? t : f;
            };
        });
    </script>
```

The preceding code now has a link to /history on every third line and /request otherwise. Of course, these URLs link to nonexistent pages, but the usefulness of the conditional filter for generating dynamic URLs should be clear regardless.

Use Case 3: Manipulating Arrays

As you might have guessed from their name, filters are useful for filtering, sorting, and manipulating arrays. AngularJS has two filters that operate exclusively on arrays: the confusingly named filter filter, which searches arrays, and the orderBy filter, which sorts them. The limitTo filter, which works on arrays as well as strings, manipulates an array to fit a maximum length. Filters are chainable and can be used within the ngRepeat directive, so you may see all three of these filters used in concert.

Perhaps you have a list of requests, and each request has three fields: a done flag, a name, and the amount of time the request has been outstanding. If you want to display the 10 longest outstanding requests that haven't been done yet, you could use a combination of the filter, orderBy, and limitTo filters with the ngRepeat directive like this:

```
    <div ng-controller="RequestsController">
        <div ng-repeat="request in requests |
            filter:{'done':false} | orderBy:'-time' |
            limitTo:10">
            {{ request.name }}
        </div>
    </div>

    <script type="text/javascript">
        function RequestsController($scope) {
            $scope.requests = [];
            for (var i = 0; i < 50; ++i) {
                $scope.requests.push({
                    done : (i % 3 == 0),
                    name : "" + i,
                    time : (i - 25) * (i - 25)
                });
```

```
            }
        }
    </script>
```

In the preceding code, the second argument to the `filter` filter specifies that `filter` should only return requests that are not done. The second argument to `orderBy`, `-time`, specifies that the requests should be sorted by the `time` field in descending order—that is, the largest value of `time` first. Finally, the argument to `limitTo` tells AngularJS to display at most 10 results.

Another interesting array-related problem that you can solve with a filter is partially hard-coding the order of an array. Perhaps you're writing the checkout portion of your shopping cart application. The checkout page has a drop-down for your user to select which country she wants her purchase shipped to. Because most of your customers are in the United States, you want to list United States first in your drop-down, but you want the rest of the list to be in alphabetical order. You'll write a filter that places USA first in the list. This is not a particularly difficult task normally, but filters provide a framework for writing this code in an elegant and easily reusable way so that you don't drown in small hacks:

```
<div ng-controller="CountriesController">
    <select ng-model="country"
            ng-options="country.name for country in countries |
                orderBy:'name' | hardcodeFirst:'name':'USA'">
    </select>
    <br>
    {{ country.name }}
</div>

<script type="text/javascript">
    function CountriesController($scope) {
        $scope.countries = [
            { name : "Germany" },
            { name : "Australia" },
            { name : "Norway" },
            { name : "USA" },
            { name : "Sweden" },
            { name : "Austria" }
        ];
    }

    module.filter('hardcodeFirst', function() {
        return function(arr, field, val) {
            var first = null;
            for (var i = 0; i < arr.length; ++i) {
                if (arr[i][field] == val) {
                    first = i;
                    break;
                }
            }

            if (!first) {
                return arr;
            }

            var firstEl = arr[first];
```

```
                    arr.splice(first, 0);
                    arr.unshift(firstEl);

                    return arr;
                };
            });
        </script>
```

The `hardcodeFirst` filter is a bit complex, but its result is simple enough: It finds the first element in the array where the value of `field` is equal to `val`, removes that value from the array, and inserts it at the beginning of the array. You can see that this filter is reasonably general, and the framework of filters provides an elegant way to reuse this code wherever you need to.

Pitfall

Recall that the `$digest` loop continues so long as an expression continues to evaluate to something different, as defined by the `angular.equals` function. Writing a simple expression that triggers an infinite `$digest` loop is not trivial. However, filters make shooting yourself in the foot considerably easier with the `ngRepeat` directive. For example, perhaps you had the list of countries in the previous example as an array of plain strings. To convert this array of strings into an array of objects with a `name` attribute, you might think that you can use a filter:

```
<div ng-controller="CountriesController">
    <div ng-repeat="country in countries | lift:'name'">
        {{ country.name }}
    </div>
</div>

<script type="text/javascript">
    function CountriesController($scope) {
        $scope.countries = [
            "Germany",
            "Australia",
            "Norway",
            "USA",
            "Sweden",
            "Austria"
        ];
    }

    module.filter('lift', function() {
        return function(arr, field) {
            var ret = [];
            for (var i = 0; i < arr.length; ++i) {
                var newEl = {};
                newEl[field] = arr[i];
                ret.push(newEl);
            }

            return ret;
        }
    });
</script>
```

But if you run this, you get an infinite $digest loop in the console output! What gives? Well, the dirty (pun intended) secret is that AngularJS doesn't always use angular.equals to check for equality. There is an alternative $watchCollection function on scopes that only does a shallow equality check. That is, the $watchCollection function determines that two arrays are different if they have different lengths or if one of the elements of the array is not equal to another using the === operator. Note that, in JavaScript, the === operator only returns true if the two objects being compared have the same memory address. The $watchCollection function is rarely used in practice, and you're unlikely to see it outside of the AngularJS internals.

However, in a somewhat questionable decision to improve performance, ngRepeat uses the $watchCollection function to watch the value on the right side of in. Because the lift filter is creating an array of new objects every time, $watchCollection thinks that it's getting a different array every time! Try replacing the ngRepeat block with a simple string rendering of the filter result, such as {{ countries | lift:'name' }}. You'll see that you no longer get an infinite $digest loop, because the dirty check for expressions uses angular.equals except for ngRepeat.

The difference between $watchCollection and $watch is a pretty subtle pitfall. The best way to avoid running into it is to avoid creating new objects in your filters, especially if you intend to use that filter to operate on an array that you will ngRepeat over. If you find yourself needing to perform an operation similar to what the lift filter does, you should not rely on a filter. You should perform this operation in your controller code or in a separate service.

CONCLUSION

In this chapter, you learned the "how" and the "why" of data binding. You explored the internals of data binding and the implementation details of AngularJS's $digest loop, including best practices for how to optimize this loop. In learning about the internals of the $digest loop, you saw several common pitfalls and how to avoid them. Now, if you run into a 10 $digest iterations reached .Aborting! error message, you'll have a better idea of what's going wrong. In addition, you learned how AngularJS data binding can allow you to achieve a cleaner separation between frontend JavaScript and UI/UX decisions, enabling more effective teamwork.

5

Directives

WHAT YOU WILL LEARN IN THIS CHAPTER:

➤ What directives are and why they are so powerful

➤ The three classes of basic directives

➤ Directive objects and directive composition

➤ Scope manipulation with directives

➤ How to use transclude and compile

WROX.COM CODE DOWNLOADS FOR THIS CHAPTER

You can find the wrox.com code downloads for this chapter at http://www.wrox.com/go/proangularjs on the Download Code tab.

WHAT IS A DIRECTIVE?

You may have noticed that the word *directive* has been used to describe AngularJS-specific HTML attributes, such as ngClick and ngBind. Directives are integral to how data binding works in practice: Scopes allow you to watch variables for changes using $watch and trigger a digest loop with $apply, but how can you use these functions to update your user interface (UI)? Directives provide an abstraction for precisely this purpose.

The built-in directives you've already seen, like ngClick, are just the tip of the iceberg. In this chapter, you'll not only dive in to the internals of how built-in directives work, you'll also learn to write your own sophisticated directives.

Understanding Directives

Fundamentally, a *directive* is a rule for defining how your UI interacts with data binding. In other words, a directive defines how the associated element interacts with its corresponding scope. You'll experiment with this by writing a simple directive: your own implementation of the built-in ngClick directive. Fundamentally, the ngClick directive needs to execute the JavaScript code provided in the Document Object Model (DOM) attribute against the associated element's scope whenever the element is clicked. Although this may seem tricky, AngularJS tracks which scope an element belongs to for you, and executing code against a scope is easy. All you have to do is provide the glue between the element and the scope.

The key idea behind the interaction of data binding and directives is that your Hypertext Markup Language (HTML) should define your user interface/user experience (UI/UX) decisions, and your JavaScript should provide an application programming interface (API) for your HTML. In other words, your controllers should provide an API by attaching functions and variables to a scope, and your HTML defines how the API should be used to create your page's user experience. This idea is a significant paradigm shift from how JavaScript is written in many other frameworks, where HTML provides a basic structure that JavaScript is responsible for modifying. Another characterization of this distinction is that, in AngularJS, your HTML is a client of your JavaScript, whereas in jQuery, your JavaScript is a client of your HTML.

In addition to the filter, controller, and service functions you've already seen, an AngularJS module also has a directive function that allows you to attach a directive to a module. You can use this function in several different ways, but the simplest way is to pass the name of the directive in camel case and a factory function that returns the *link function*. The *factory function*, the function that returns the link function, is tied in to dependency injection and enables you to use services like $filter in your directives. The link function is invoked on each element you attach the directive to. This function takes the DOM element, its associated scope, and a map of the element's attributes. Here's the actual code that creates the myNgClick directive:

```
var module = angular.
    module('MyApp', []);

module.directive('myNgClick', function() {
    return function(scope, element, attributes) {
        element.click(function() {
            scope.$eval(attributes.myNgClick);
            scope.$apply();
        });
    };
});
```

Note that, in HTML, you access this directive using the hyphenated version of the directive name, which is my-ng-click in this case. For example:

```
<div my-ng-click="counter = counter + 1">
    Increment Counter
</div>
```

AngularJS internally converts my-ng-click (hyphenated) into myNgClick (camel case) for use in your JavaScript code for readability. Generally, camel case is accepted as the correct convention for naming variables in JavaScript. However, generally cascading style sheets (CSS) and HTML are written with hyphen-delimited names; AngularJS makes this conversion for you so you can use the appropriate naming convention in the appropriate context.

> **NOTE** *An* attribute *is a string name/value pair associated with a DOM element in HTML. For instance, in the following HTML code*
>
> ```
> 
> ```
>
> *the* div *element has two attributes, named* style *and* my-ng-click, *with values* "width:100px" *and* "counter = counter + 1", *respectively.*

Congratulations! You've essentially implemented ngClick as it exists in AngularJS 1.0.8! Seriously, this is the exact code in the AngularJS codebase:

```
forEach(
  'click dblclick mousedown mouseup mouseover mouseout mousemove mouseenter
mouseleave submit'.split(' '),
  function(name) {
    var directiveName = directiveNormalize('ng-' + name);
    ngEventDirectives[directiveName] = ['$parse', function($parse) {
      return function(scope, element, attr) {
        var fn = $parse(attr[directiveName]);
        element.bind(lowercase(name), function(event) {
          scope.$apply(function() {
            fn(scope, {$event:event});
          });
        });
      };
    }];
  }
);
```

Now you've taken your first step to being a directives pro. In the next section, you'll take the next steps to directives mastery.

An 80/20 Understanding of Directives

Directives have a really rich feature set, and it's easy to fall down a rabbit hole when learning about them. However, I've found that directives follow the Pareto distribution: The vast majority of the directives that you will write with AngularJS use only a small percentage of the features and design patterns available. The three classes of directives defined in Chapter 4 each correspond to a simple design pattern. Mastery of these design patterns will provide you with a solid basis for writing the majority of directives you'll need to write.

These three classes of directives are:

➤ **Render-only directives**—These directives render data from the scope but do not modify data.

➤ **Event handler wrappers**—These directives wrap event handlers to interface with data binding, such as ngClick. These directives do not render data.

➤ **Two-way directives**—These directives both render and modify data.

Note that these classes of directives are not actually part of the AngularJS codebase, and these are not classes in the object-oriented programming sense. You do *not* declare a new object of render-only directive type. These classes are only a helpful means of breaking the subject of directives into more manageable chunks.

Now that you know the three classes of simple directive, you'll learn the design pattern for writing directives of each class. These classes may seem limited, but they cover a wide array of different use cases. To illustrate this, you'll build an image carousel composed of custom directives from each of the different classes. A *carousel* is a common UI element that cycles through a collection of images in a slideshow.

Writing Your Own Render-Only Directive

The first type of directive that you'll write is a render-only directive. These directives follow a simple design pattern: They watch a variable and update a DOM element to reflect the change in the variable. This design pattern is flexible, and numerous built-in directives, like ngBind and ngClass, use this pattern.

The render-only directive you'll write in this section is going to be the basis for your carousel: a myBackgroundImage directive that binds the background image of an HTML div element to a variable in a scope. This directive watches the provided expression and updates the associated HTML div element's background-image CSS property. Without further ado, here's what your myBackgroundImage directive will look like:

```
var module = angular.
    module('MyApp', []);

module.directive('myBackgroundImage', function() {
    return function(scope, element, attributes) {
        scope.$watch(attributes.myBackgroundImage, function(newVal, oldVal) {
            element.css('background-image', 'url(' + newVal + ')');
        });
    };
});
```

This simple seven-line directive may not look like much at first, but because of data binding, it is very powerful. With data binding, this directive allows you to bind a JavaScript variable to any element's background image. This will be important for building a carousel, because the carousel has to cycle through a collection of images. The most basic usage of this directive is to display a static image—in this case, the Google logo:

```
<body ng-init="image = 'http://upload.wikimedia.org/wikipedia/commons/a/aa/
    Logo_Google_2013_Official.svg';">
    <div style="height: 180px; width: 840px; border: 1px solid red" my-background-
image="image">
    </div>
</body>
```

Furthermore, the *watch and update* pattern, assigning the scope to watch a variable and update a CSS property when the value changes, is something you will see frequently when writing directives. Render-only directives are essentially defined by this pattern. A classic example of a render-only directive is ngBind, better known as the directive underlying the { { } } shorthand. Following is

AngularJS 1.0.8's definition of `ngBind`. You'll notice that this directive relies on the same watch and update pattern that you used to write the `myBackgroundImage` directive.

```
var ngBindDirective = ngDirective(function(scope, element, attr) {
  element.addClass('ng-binding').data('$binding', attr.ngBind);
  scope.$watch(attr.ngBind, function ngBindWatchAction(value) {
    element.text(value == undefined ? '' : value);
  });
});
```

In addition to built-in directives like `ngClass` and `ngBind`, you can write an incredible variety of powerful directives using this simple design pattern. Common use cases range from the mundane, such as implementing a directive that renders input field placeholders in old versions of Internet Explorer, to the flashy, such as a directive that displays a list of items on a Google Map.

AngularJS does a lot of magic under the hood with data binding and directives. To demystify how directives work, take a look at how the `myBackgroundImage` directive would be implemented using jQuery, a popular lightweight JavaScript library that doesn't have anything analogous to AngularJS's data binding. Although the following example doesn't support data binding, it does provide a high-level overview of how AngularJS processes directives. Similar to the following code, AngularJS runs the link function on every element that has the hyphenated version of the directive name:

```
<!DOCTYPE html>
<html>
<head>
    <title>jQuery directive</title>
    <script src="https://ajax.googleapis.com/ajax/libs/jquery/1.10.2/jquery.min.js">
    </script>
    <script type="application/javascript">
        var image = 'http://upload.wikimedia.org/wikipedia/commons/c/ca/' +
          'AngularJS_logo.svg';

        $(document).ready(function() {
            $('div[my-background-image]').each(function(i, el) {
                $(el).css({
                    'background-image': 'url(' + eval($(el).attr('my-background-image'))
+')',
                });
            });
        });
    </script>
</head>

<body>
    <div my-background-image="image" style="width: 700px; height: 180px"></div>
</body>

</html>
```

AngularJS directives have two key advantages over the preceding jQuery faux directive pattern. First, the `myBackgroundImage` directive ties in to data binding. Once you have defined the link function, your JavaScript code no longer has to directly modify the element CSS; all you need to do is assign a new image URL to the variable, and all elements that are watching that variable have their background image updated automatically.

Second, the faux directive is inherently tied to the global scope. In other words, for the faux directive to work properly, the variable specified in the my-background-image attribute must be visible from the JavaScript scope that contains the eval function call. In other words, unless you change the faux directive code, the image variable must be in the global scope. Polluting the global scope is a shortsighted decision that prevents effective code reuse and should be avoided. Thankfully, AngularJS creates an HTML scoping structure independent of JavaScript scopes, so it is unnecessary to have the variable referenced in the directive's my-background-image attribute in the global scope.

Congratulations! You've written your first render-only directive and gotten a taste of how directives make writing sophisticated UI code easier. Next, you'll dive in to writing an event handler directive and explore the idea of AngularJS scopes as APIs in greater detail.

Writing Your Own Event Handler Directive

At a high level, event handler directives enable DOM events to tie in to data binding by calling the $apply function. This should sound familiar, because this is exactly how you wrote your first directive in this section: the myNgClick directive. Recall the definition of the myNgClick directive:

```
module.directive('myNgClick', function() {
    return function(scope, element, attributes) {
        element.click(function() {
            scope.$eval(attributes.myNgClick);
            scope.$apply();
        });
    };
});
```

The myNgClick directive is a standard event handler directive, the second simple directive design pattern you'll learn about. Event handler directives typically register a conventional non-AngularJS event handler that performs some action on the scope, followed by an $apply call.

Don't underestimate the importance of calling $apply! Forgetting to call $apply in an event handler is an easy mistake to make when you're getting started with directives, because all the built-in event handler directives, such as ngClick, make the call for you. However, because the event handler callback (the function passed to element.click() earlier) is called asynchronously, data binding doesn't know when to trigger the $digest loop unless you explicitly call $apply. To drive this point home, try removing the $apply call in the myNgClick directive and pulling up the page in your browser:

```
module.directive('myNgClick', function() {
    return function(scope, element, attributes) {
        element.click(function() {
            scope.$eval(attributes.myNgClick);
            console.log('Counter is ' + scope.counter);
        });
    };
});
```

In your console, you'll see that the counter variable is being incremented, but the div that's supposed to display the counter will stay at 0 forever!

Now that you understand the fundamentals of writing an event handler directive, you'll write a much more interesting set of event handler directives. Specifically, you'll write two directives that are indispensible for mobile development with AngularJS: `ngSwipeLeft` and `ngSwipeRight`. These directives, along with `myBackgroundImage`, allow you to create a rudimentary swipe-enabled carousel.

For computing what constitutes a swipe, you will use a popular multi-touch event library for JavaScript called HammerJS. In practice, you will most often see event handler directives tie existing event-generating libraries into data binding. Similarly, in this example, you'll write directives to tie HammerJS' swipe event generators into data binding. Here are the three directives that you'll tie together to make a carousel, utilizing the render-only and event handler design patterns:

```
module.directive('myBackgroundImage', function() {
    return function(scope, element, attributes) {
        scope.$watch(attributes.myBackgroundImage, function(newVal, oldVal) {
            element.css('background-image', 'url(' + newVal + ')');
        });
    };
});

module.directive('ngSwipeLeft', function() {
    return function(scope, element, attributes) {
        Hammer(element).on('swipeleft', function() {
            scope.$eval(attributes.ngSwipeLeft);
            scope.$apply();
        });
    };
});

module.directive('ngSwipeRight', function() {
    return function(scope, element, attributes) {
        Hammer(element).on('swiperight', function() {
            scope.$eval(attributes.ngSwipeRight);
            scope.$apply();
        });
    };
});
```

The new `ngSwipeLeft` and `ngSwipeRight` directives are textbook event handler directives. The particular syntax for a HammerJS event handler notwithstanding, these directives are essentially identical to the `myNgClick` directive. The event handler design pattern is flexible, and there are countless directives that you can write that require only minor additions to the design pattern. Some other directives that you may write using this design pattern include a submit button directive with custom validation, a directive wrapper around the Google Places autocomplete, and a directive that gives an input field an orange border when the user is nearing a character limit.

To tie these directives together and provide data, you need to create a controller that defines the list of images in the carousel and helper functions that will be sent to `ngSwipeLeft` and `ngSwipeRight`. The controller looks like this:

```
function CarouselController($scope) {
    $scope.images = [
        "http://upload.wikimedia.org/wikipedia/commons/c/ca/AngularJS_logo.svg",
```

```
                     "http://upload.wikimedia.org/wikipedia/commons/a/aa/" +
                       "Logo_Google_2013_Official.svg",
                     "http://upload.wikimedia.org/wikipedia/en/9/9e/JQuery_logo.svg"
               ];

               $scope.currentIndex = 0;

               $scope.next = function() {
                   $scope.currentIndex =
                       ($scope.currentIndex + 1) % $scope.images.length;
               };

               $scope.previous = function() {
                   $scope.currentIndex = $scope.currentIndex == 0 ?
                       $scope.images.length - 1 :
                       $scope.currentIndex - 1;
               };
           }
```

The next and previous functions are convenience functions that are called by ngSwipeLeft and ngSwipeRight, respectively. Now that you've created CarouselController, the HTML to create a swipe-enabled carousel that cycles through the AngularJS logo, Google logo, and jQuery logo is simple. Note that you can trigger swipe left and swipe right events on a desktop browser by clicking and quickly dragging left or right, respectively:

```
<body ng-controller="CarouselController">
    <div    my-background-image="images[currentIndex]"
            ng-swipe-left="next()"
            ng-swipe-right="previous()"
            style="height: 120px; width: 600px; border: 1px solid red">
    </div>
    <h1>Image index: {{currentIndex}}</h1>
</body>
```

Recall the idea of scopes and controllers as an API for your HTML. The three directives use the variables and functions that CarouselController attaches to its corresponding scope to define the concrete user experience. If your design guru were to decide that users should only be allowed to swipe left, the changes would be limited to the HTML. A more realistic example would be adding buttons to cycle left and right. This requires no changes to the controller's API—only a minor addition to the UI/UX decisions defined in your HTML:

```
<body ng-controller="CarouselController">
    <div    my-background-image="images[currentIndex]"
            ng-swipe-left="next()"
            ng-swipe-right="previous()"
            style="height: 120px; width: 600px; border: 1px solid red">
    </div>
    <h2 ng-click="previous()">Previous</h2>
    <h2 ng-click="next()">Next</h2>
    <h1>Image index: {{currentIndex}}</h1>
</body>
```

This paradigm creates a powerful decoupling effect that is indispensible in a team environment. A common point of friction in web development is multiple developers working on the same code in different contexts. For example, while you're refactoring your interactions with your server's REST API, your designer is trying to add functionality to a new button. In the old JavaScript paradigm, this code would most likely be in the same JavaScript file, which means you would have two developers modifying the same code. AngularJS data binding and the idea of scopes as an API for your HTML help eliminate this point of friction by creating a clean and well-defined separation of concerns between developers and designers.

Now that you've explored the particulars and applications of basic event handler directives, you're going to take a look at the last basic directive design pattern. The final design pattern is a combination of the previous two that assists in managing the state of a given variable.

Writing Your Own Two-Way Directive

The third and final design pattern that you'll learn about in this section is a two-way directive. This design pattern utilizes both the render-only design pattern and the event handler design pattern to create a directive that controls the state of a variable. Specifically, you'll implement a toggle button directive that will be used to enable and disable automatic cycling of the image every 2 seconds.

This toggle button directive should both accurately reflect the state of the underlying JavaScript variable and be able to toggle the state of the JavaScript variable when the button is clicked. The former calls for a render-only directive, the latter for an event handler directive. Without further ado, here's the code with the two directive design patterns combined, along with the modified CarouselController:

```
module.directive('toggleButton', function() {
    return function(scope, element, attributes) {
        // watch and update
        scope.$watch(attributes.toggleButton, function(v) {
            element.val(!v ? 'Disable' : 'Enable');
        });

        // event handler
        element.click(function() {
            scope[attributes.toggleButton] =
                !scope[attributes.toggleButton];
            scope.$apply();
        });
    };
});

function CarouselController($scope) {
    $scope.images = [
        "http://upload.wikimedia.org/wikipedia/commons/c/ca/AngularJS_logo.svg",
        "http://upload.wikimedia.org/wikipedia/commons/a/aa/" +
          "Logo_Google_2013_Official.svg",
        "http://upload.wikimedia.org/wikipedia/en/9/9e/JQuery_logo.svg"
    ];

    $scope.currentIndex = 0;

    $scope.next = function() {
        $scope.currentIndex =
```

```
                    ($scope.currentIndex + 1) % $scope.images.length;
        };

        $scope.previous = function() {
            $scope.currentIndex = $scope.currentIndex == 0 ?
                $scope.images.length - 1 :
                $scope.currentIndex - 1;
        };

        $scope.disabled = false;

        setInterval(function() {
            if ($scope.disabled) {
                return;
            }
            $scope.next();
            $scope.$apply();
        }, 2000);
    }
```

You can then access the `toggleButton` directive from HTML like this:

```
<input type="button" toggle-button="disabled">
```

There are several other useful directives that you can build using the simple combination of a
render-only directive and an event handler directive. For example, you can build a YouTube-style
rating directive that allows a user to click on the third star to give something a three-star rating.
Many AngularJS projects choose to implement their own date picker directive, which is another
textbook application of this design pattern.

You may have guessed that breaking up the `toggleButton` directive into two separate directives is
pretty straightforward. Indeed, you can achieve the same functionality using the built-in directives
`ngBind` and `ngClick`:

```
<input  type="button"
        ng-click="disabled = !disabled;"
        value="{{ { true : 'Enable', false : 'Disable' }[disabled] }}">
```

So which way is correct? Either method works, but the correct choice depends on your use case.
AngularJS makes it easy to build directives on top of other directives in myriad ways, which you'll
explore in greater detail in the next section. However, as is often the case in software development,
there is a trade-off between reusability and customizability.

In the two different implementations of `toggleButton`, the latter implementation, using the
built-in directives `ngBind` and `ngClick`, makes it easy to make changes to how that one individual
`toggleButton` behaves, but reusing it requires copying/pasting some nontrivial code. The former
implementation—using one integrated `toggleButton` directive, is easy to reuse but makes it difficult
to change the behavior of a single `toggleButton`. Generally speaking, the integrated directive is
usually the right choice when the `toggleButton` functionality is going to be used in multiple parts of
your codebase. The separate directives approach, however, is usually more advantageous when you
need a greater degree of customization. As you'll see in the subsequent sections, directives provide
you with a significant degree of control as to how much you want to bundle directives together.

Beyond the Simple Design Patterns

Now that you've gone through the three most basic directive design patterns, you know the proverbial 20 percent of the features that you need to get 80 percent of the benefit of directives. Of course, these numbers are not exact, but the design patterns you've learned so far will allow you to write some sophisticated directives and have a basic grasp of how many directives in the open source community are implemented. However, what you've seen so far is just the beginning. In the next section, you learn about the sophisticated features AngularJS provides for reusing code and constructing directives from a combination of other directives.

A DEEPER UNDERSTANDING OF DIRECTIVES

If you've seen directives before, you may have seen them implemented using a different syntax that does return a link function. Indeed, the factory function, which up until now you used only to return a single function, can return a rich configuration object that enables you to tweak more under-the-hood parameters. The link function that you used in the previous section can be set using the `link` setting in the configuration object. For example, here is the `myBackgroundImage` directive using the configuration object syntax:

```
module.directive('myBackgroundImage', function() {
    return {
        link: function(scope, element, attributes) {
            scope.$watch(attributes.myBackgroundImage, function(newVal) {
                element.css('background-image', 'url(' + newVal + ')');
            });
        }
    };
});
```

What other options can you tweak in the configuration object? You'll get to see several more configuration object settings in practice in the next few sections. In particular, in the next section you'll explore three common directive settings—`template`, `templateURL`, and `controller`—in the context of combining the carousel you constructed in the previous section into a single directive.

Directive Composition Using Templates

Directives have a couple of powerful composition features: the ability to associate a controller and an HTML template, which may contain other directives, with a directive. By default, AngularJS inserts the contents of the HTML template as a child of the DOM element associated with the directive. It also attaches a controller. The general idea is to enable combining a sophisticated directive structure into one directive in a way that doesn't rely on the implementation details of the underlying directives. In this section, you explore this idea by composing the `myBackgroundImage`, `ngSwipeLeft`, `ngSwipeRight`, and `toggleButton` directives into a single `imageCarousel` directive. Here's the implementation of the `imageCarousel` directive:

```
module.directive('imageCarousel', function() {
    return {
        template:
```

```
                  '<div  my-background-image="images[currentIndex]"' +
                  '       ng-swipe-left="next()"' +
                  '       ng-swipe-right="previous()"' +
                  '       style="height: 120px; width: 600px; border: 1px solid red">' +
                  '</div>' +
                  '<input type="button" toggle-button="disabled">' +
                  '<h1>Image index: {{currentIndex}}</h1>',
            controller : CarouselController,
            link : function(scope, element, attributes) {
                scope.$watch(attributes.imageCarousel, function(v) {
                    scope.images = v;
                });
            }
        }
    });
```

In addition to running the link function on every element that has the directive attribute, this directive inserts the HTML specified in the template setting as a child of every element with the directive attribute. In addition, this directive runs CarouselController on the scope that the template HTML will be in. In the next section, you learn that directives can create their own scope, so the template HTML may be in a child scope. However, in this case, CarouselController runs on the same scope that the directive is in.

Note that the link function for the imageCarousel directive uses the watch and update render-only directive design pattern. However, underlying the simple link function, the template has an ecosystem of directives interacting with the images variable in different ways. Through the magic of scopes, these directives can access the images variable, which is in turn bound to the value of the imageCarousel attribute of the element associated with the directive. For example, you can use this directive by writing a simple controller that defines the images that will be in the carousel:

```
function BodyController($scope) {
    $scope.defaultImages = [
        ANGULARJS_LOGO_URL,
        GOOGLE_LOGO_URL,
        JQUERY_LOGO_URL
    ];
}
```

With this controller in place, you can set up the imageCarousel directive using the following simple HTML:

```
<body ng-controller="BodyController">
    <div image-carousel="defaultImages"></div>
</body>
```

As an alternative to the template setting, you can also use templateURL. The templateURL setting tells AngularJS to make an HTTP GET request to the specified templateURL and use the contents of the server response as the directive's template. In practice, using templateURL is generally preferred because of cleaner separation of concerns and easier template reuse; however, there is a performance cost. The performance overhead from templateURL is limited by the fact that AngularJS only sends one request to templateURL, even if multiple directives use the same templateURL. However, because template doesn't make any HTTP requests, it incurs less performance overhead.

Now you've bundled the `imageCarousel` directive into one isolated directive. This powerful code reuse pattern makes directives popular among designers because it provides a sophisticated way to organize complex UI structures. Much like the way developers write functions to abstract away implementation details, designers can use directives to build high-level components that are easier to reuse and reason about. For example, as a developer you would prefer having a single function called `readFile` instead of writing code to manipulate the hard drive directly. A designer can derive similar benefits from being able to say, "This `div` should have the standard carousel capabilities" instead of building the structure every time out of `div` elements and event handlers.

There are two weaknesses to the `imageCarousel` directive as implemented. The first one is an unfortunate limitation to AngularJS: There is no way to change the directive's template without modifying the directive's code. This limitation is not significant if your directive is internal to your project; however, if you're maintaining an open source AngularJS carousel like the AngularUI team, this is a significant problem. In the AngularUI case, the inability to customize templates would prevent clients of the AngularUI module from tweaking the AngularUI carousel's look and feel without changing its code. This is why, as of version 0.10, AngularUI distributes two different files: one with a template specified for every directive, and one with no templates specified for any directives.

The second weakness becomes clearer when you try to use two directives with two different sets of images:

```
<body ng-controller="BodyController">
    <div image-carousel="defaultImages"></div>
    <div image-carousel="otherImages"></div>
</body>
```

Both carousels only show the Google logo. What gives? The problem is that the `imageCarousel` directive doesn't have its own scope, so the second `imageCarousel` directive clobbers the first's `images` variable. Luckily, AngularJS provides some deep functionality around directive scopes, which you explore in the next section.

Creating Separate Scopes for Directives

As you saw in the previous section, directives can manage their own internal state. But, to do so effectively, such a directive needs its own scope to provide encapsulation for its internal state. Luckily, AngularJS provides several powerful settings in the directive object for creating a new scope for your directive.

Your directive object can specify a `scope` setting that can be used in one of three ways:

- ➤ `{ scope: true }` creates a new scope for each instance of the directive.
- ➤ `{ scope: {} }` creates a new *isolate* scope for each instance of the directive.
- ➤ `{ scope: false }` is the default. With this setting, no scope is created for the directive.

The third way is exactly how you have used directives up to this point. However, as you saw when multiple carousels in the same scope clobbered each other's internal state, sophisticated directives typically need to have their own scope. The first two ways provide two different mechanisms to give your directive its own scope. The first and second ways are often a source of confusion. The difference is that the second option creates an *isolate* scope for each instance of the directive. Recall that an isolate scope doesn't inherit from its parent scope, so the directive `template` in an isolate scope can't access any variables outside the directive's scope. Although the second way sounds limiting, it has numerous powerful features that require careful discussion. But first, you can use the second way to enable proper encapsulation for the `imageCarousel` directive's internal state.

> **NOTE** *To avoid confusion, for the rest of this chapter, the scope that a directive's declaration is in will be referred to as the isolate scope's parent scope. Although an isolate scope doesn't have a parent in the same sense that a non-isolate scope does, there are numerous benefits of thinking of an isolate scope in the context of a scope hierarchy. In particular, the fact that an isolate scope is still part of the scope hierarchy is key to understanding transclusion—the last subject covered in this chapter. Please remember that, even though an isolated scope doesn't inherit from its parent, it still has a parent.*

The First Way of Using the scope Setting

The code for the first way of using the `scope` setting looks something like this:

```
module.directive('imageCarousel', function() {
    return {
        template:
            '<div  my-background-image="images[currentIndex]"' +
            '       ng-swipe-left="next()"' +
            '       ng-swipe-right="previous()"' +
            '       style="height: 120px; width: 600px; border: 1px solid red">' +
            '</div>' +
            '<input type="button" toggle-button="disabled">' +
            '<h1>Image index: {{currentIndex}}</h1>',
        controller : CarouselController,
        scope : true,
        link : function(scope, element, attributes) {
            scope.$parent.$watch(attributes.imageCarousel, function(v) {
                scope.images = v;
            });
        }
    }
});
```

There are two key differences between this `imageCarousel` directive's implementation and the original implementation. The most obvious difference is that you used the `scope` setting to create a new scope for each instance of the directive. The second difference is that this new implementation calls $watch on the parent scope—that is, scope.$parent.$watch() instead of scope.$watch(). The reason for this change is subtle, and you might not notice it because the code will still work with scope.$watch().

The problem is that the $watch() function watches a given value in the given scope by name. Therefore, if attributes.imageCarousel happens to specify a variable name that exists in the directive's scope, the directive does not watch the right variable. For example, if attributes

.imageCarousel had the value images, scope.$watch() would watch the directive scope's images variable. Using scope.$parent.$watch() ameliorates this particular problem by making sure your directive doesn't occlude the client code's variables.

Typically, directive authors choose to use the scope setting in the second way. As you'll see, one of the primary advantages of isolate scopes is that they eliminate the possibility of variable occlusion.

The Second Way of Using the scope Setting

Recall that the second way of using the scope setting, specifying a JavaScript object (possibly empty, that is, { }), creates a new scope for the directive that does not have a parent scope. Thus, the scope.$parent.$watch() pattern from the previous section does not work, because the directive's scope is outside the page's scope hierarchy. If you're worried that this means your directives will not have a way to access variables in the page's scope, don't worry—AngularJS provides a slick way to pull outside variables into the isolate scope. Here's an example of how this works:

```
module.directive('imageCarousel', function() {
    return {
        template:
            '<div  my-background-image="images[currentIndex]"' +
            '       ng-swipe-left="next()"' +
            '       ng-swipe-right="previous()"' +
            '       style="height: 120px; width: 600px; border: 1px solid red">' +
            '</div>' +
            '<input type="button" toggle-button="disabled">' +
            '<h1>Image index: {{currentIndex}}</h1>',
        controller : CarouselController,
        scope : {
            images : '=imageCarousel'
        }
    }
});
```

The =imageCarousel syntax in the scope setting is a handy shortcut for the scope.$parent.$watch() call you did in the previous section. In the scope setting, = tells AngularJS that the images variable should be bound to the variable specified in the imageCarousel attribute, with the understanding that the imageCarousel attribute should be evaluated in the directive's parent scope. You will see this shortcut used extensively in AngularJS directive code, so make sure you remember its semantics. In particular, make sure you remember that, in the scope setting, the object keys are the variables in the scope, and the object values refer to the HTML attribute that the scope variable should be bound to.

But doesn't this shortcut defeat the point of having an isolate scope? Actually, if you want a strict isolate scope, where there is no data binding between the isolate scope and the page's scope structure, you can use an empty object { } for the scope setting. However, the use cases for strict isolate scopes are somewhat limited, because such a directive must be entirely self-contained. Such directives are often called *components* and will be discussed later in this chapter.

The = shortcut for isolate scopes serves two primary functions. First, writing =imageCarousel is far more concise than writing out the full scope.$parent.$watch() call. Second, the fact that the scope is marked as isolate ensures that the directive's template doesn't access any variables outside the directive except for as explicitly specified in the `scope` setting. This makes your directives easier to understand and use, because your client is guaranteed that your directive only interacts with the outside world through the `scope` setting. The isolate scope also serves as a preventive measure against silly mistakes. For example, try to spot the bug in the following code:

```
module.directive('imageCarousel', function() {
    return {
        template:
            '<div  my-background-image="defaultImages[currentIndex]"' +
            '      ng-swipe-left="next()"' +
            '      ng-swipe-right="previous()"' +
            '      style="height: 120px; width: 600px; border: 1px solid red">' +
            '</div>' +
            '<input type="button" toggle-button="disabled">' +
            '<h1>Image index: {{currentIndex}}</h1>',
        controller : CarouselController,
        scope : true,
        link : function(scope, element, attributes) {
            scope.$parent.$watch(attributes.imageCarousel, function(v) {
                scope.images = v;
            });
        }
    }
});
```

The `myBackgroundImage` directive in the template uses the `defaultImages` variable, which is defined in the parent scope. This approach may work in some cases, but relying on the existence of a variable in a parent scope is bad practice for writing directives. Recall that directives are meant to serve as an in-HTML API to your JavaScript, and separate controllers define separate APIs. A directive that relies on a variable in a parent scope effectively makes the directive's API dependent on a separate API in such a way that the client is responsible for the separate API. In other words, directives are excellent because they allow you to define abstractions around HTML to prevent you from rewriting the same 15 lines every time you want a carousel. Don't make clients of your directives have to read that HTML when they want to figure out how to use your directive.

Your dive into directives with isolated scopes wouldn't be complete without a discussion of the other shortcuts AngularJS provides for the `scope` setting: `@` and `&`. The distinction between these three shortcuts is often a source of confusion when you're just getting started with AngularJS. First, note that `=` is a shortcut for two-way data binding. In the `=imageCarousel` implementation, if you were to modify the `images` variable in the directive's scope, this change would also affect whatever variable in the parent scope the `images` variable is bound to, such as `defaultImages`.

In addition, the `=` shortcut binds the value of the `images` variable to another variable. This behavior, although slick, doesn't allow you to bind the `images` variable to the value of an AngularJS expression. A simple yet common use case for expressions in directive attributes would be a title for your `imageCarousel` directive. Suppose you want to enable users of your directive to specify a custom title for their carousel. This simple task becomes a lot more complex when you decide you want users to be able to use expressions in their title. For example, you want to display the value of the following expression as the title of your carousel:

```
There are {{defaultImages.length}} images
```

The @ shortcut exists to provide a one-way render-only binding to an expression provided in an element's attribute. In other words, the @ shortcut enables users of your `imageCarousel` directive to bind the carousel's title to the above expression by adding a `carouselTitle` attribute in their HTML. Here's how the code for the title-enabled `imageCarousel` directive looks:

```
module.directive('imageCarousel', function() {
    return {
        template:
            '<h1>Title: {{carouselTitle}}</h1>' +
            '<div  my-background-image="images[currentIndex]"' +
            '      ng-swipe-left="next()"' +
            '      ng-swipe-right="previous()"' +
            '      style="height: 120px; width: 600px; border: 1px solid red">' +
            '</div>' +
            '<input type="button" toggle-button="disabled">',
        controller : CarouselController,
        scope : {
            images : '=imageCarousel',
            carouselTitle : '@'
        }
    }
});
```

> **NOTE** *The* `carouselTitle: '@'` *setting is equivalent to* `carouselTitle: '@carouselTitle'`. *AngularJS assumes that the attribute name is the same as the scope variable name if no attribute name is specified. For example,* `images: '='` *binds the* `images` *variable to the variable specified in the* `images` *attribute.*

Using this directive, users of your directive can bind the carousel's title to an expression of their choosing. For example:

```
<div    image-carousel="defaultImages"
        carousel-title="There are {{defaultImages.length}} images">
</div>
<div    image-carousel="otherImages"
        carousel-title="I have {{otherImages.length}} images">
</div>
```

Note that, because `carouselTitle` is a variable in the directive's scope, there is nothing stopping you from assigning to it and overwriting the user's expression. However, because the @ shortcut only provides a one-way binding, any changes you make to `carouselTitle` in the directive's scope do not affect variables outside the directive's scope.

The final shortcut, &, is essentially the inverse of the @ shortcut. At a high level, the & shortcut attaches a function variable to the scope that performs an $eval on the value of the corresponding attribute in the directive's parent scope. If you were not using an isolate scope, the equivalent of the & shortcut would be implemented with the following code in the directive's link function:

```
scope.onChange = function() {
  scope.$parent.$eval(attributes.onChange);
  scope.$parent.$apply();
};
```

The & shortcut is typically used to provide an interface for passing custom events out of the isolate scope. You can use the & shortcut to enable clients of your imageCarousel directive to specify a custom event handler for changes in the rendered image. Specifically, you can allow your imageCarousel directive to evaluate the contents of the onChange attribute every time next() and previous() are called in the directive's controller. In this case, the onChange attribute increments a counter that tracks the total number of times a carousel has changed its image. Here's how the new imageCarousel code will look:

```
module.directive('imageCarousel', function() {
    return {
        template:
            '<h1>Title: {{carouselTitle}}</h1>' +
            '<div  my-background-image="images[currentIndex]"' +
            '         ng-swipe-left="next()"' +
            '         ng-swipe-right="previous()"' +
            '         style="height: 120px; width: 600px; border: 1px solid red">' +
            '</div>' +
            '<input type="button" toggle-button="disabled">',
        controller : CarouselController,
        scope : {
            images : '=imageCarousel',
            carouselTitle : '@',
            onChange : '&'
        }
    }
});
```

Now the scope has an onChange function that serves as a wrapper for an $eval on the onChange attribute. Note that, just like in the carouselTitle setting, the isolated '&' value is equivalent to '&onChange'. The CarouselController can now call this function in its next() and previous() functions. Here's how the new CarouselController implementation looks:

```
function CarouselController($scope) {
    $scope.currentIndex = 0;

    $scope.next = function() {
        var old = $scope.currentIndex;
        $scope.currentIndex =
            ($scope.currentIndex + 1) % $scope.images.length;
        if ($scope.currentIndex != old) {
```

```
                        $scope.onChange();
                    }
                };

                $scope.previous = function() {
                    var old = $scope.currentIndex;
                    $scope.currentIndex = $scope.currentIndex == 0 ?
                        $scope.images.length - 1 :
                        $scope.currentIndex - 1;
                    if ($scope.currentIndex != old) {
                        $scope.onChange();
                    }
                };

                $scope.disabled = false;

                setInterval(function() {
                    if ($scope.disabled) {
                        return;
                    }
                    $scope.next();
                    $scope.$apply();
                }, 2000);
            }
```

Setting the expression that onChange evaluates in your HTML is easy. Remember that the expression in onChange is evaluated against the directive's parent scope. To illustrate this, take a look at the HTML for the imageCarousel with onChange integration:

```
<body ng-controller="BodyController" ng-init="count = 0;">
    <h1>Image has changed {{count}} times</h1>
    <div     image-carousel="defaultImages"
             carousel-title="There are {{defaultImages.length}} images"
             on-change="count = count + 1">
    </div>
    <div     image-carousel="otherImages"
             carousel-title="I have {{otherImages.length}} images"
             on-change="count = count + 1">
    </div>
</body>
```

Note that the count variable is in the page's root scope, but it's being modified from within an isolate scope. This new functionality allows you to define a myriad of complex in-HTML hooks for your directives. Now, finally, you'll see how the scope setting ties in to the central theme of directives as a declarative UI/UX API.

Once again, recall the idea of directives as a JavaScript API for determining high-level UI/UX decisions from HTML. The =, @, and & shortcuts allow you to expand this JavaScript API by allowing you to declaratively add additional parameters. Much like how a web developer would look at a REST API and find the parameters necessary to achieve their desired functionality, a designer can easily inspect the list of scope variables and get a sense of what parameters they can tweak on the directive without diving in to the underlying code. In addition, because your HTML is the one true source of all your UI/UX decisions in AngularJS, these options are tweaked in HTML rather than a JavaScript configuration object.

The restrict and replace Settings

You will see the `restrict` and `replace` settings used heavily in many directive libraries. These settings primarily function as syntactic sugar, making HTML that uses directives more intuitively pleasing. Although these settings don't add much in the way of what you can do with directives, you should never underestimate the benefit of some particularly elegant syntactic sugar.

Many directives, like the `imageCarousel` directive, feel like they should just be DOM elements. There's nothing wrong with creating a `div` with an `imageCarousel` attribute, but wouldn't it be awesome if you could skip the `div` and create an `imageCarousel` tag in your HTML? Turns out, custom HTML tags are just one of the cool functionalities that the `restrict` and `replace` settings enable you to access.

Up to this point, directives were defined purely by HTML attributes. In fact, AngularJS supports four ways of using a directive in HTML:

➤ **By attribute**—`<div image-carousel='images'></div>`

➤ **By CSS class**—`<div class="image-carousel: images;"></div>`

➤ **By comment**—`<!-- directive: image-carousel images -->`

➤ **By element**—`<image-carousel></image-carousel>`

You can specify which of these usages your directive supports using the restrict setting. The `restrict` setting takes a string that lists which of the four usages the directive allows. Each of the four usages is represented by a single character: A usage is allowed if and only if the usage's character is in the `restrict` string. The corresponding characters follow:

➤ **By attribute**—`'A'`

➤ **By CSS class**—`'C'`

➤ **By comment**—`'M'`

➤ **By element**—`'E'`

For example, here is the `imageCarousel` directive using the `restrict: 'E'` setting:

```
module.directive('imageCarousel', function() {
    return {
        restrict: 'E',
        template:
          '<h1>Title: {{carouselTitle}}</h1>' +
          '<div  my-background-image="images[currentIndex]"' +
          '      ng-swipe-left="next()"' +
          '      ng-swipe-right="previous()"' +
          '      style="height: 120px; width: 600px; border: 1px solid red">' +
          '</div>' +
          '<input type="button" toggle-button="disabled">',
        controller : CarouselController,
        scope : {
```

```
                        images : '=',
                        carouselTitle : '@',
                        onChange : '&'
                }
        }
    });
```

Note that the scope's `images` variable is now bound to the element's `images` attribute instead of the `imageCarousel` attribute as before. More often than not, directives do not support both E and A values for `restrict`. This is because, in the case of A, the directive itself is an attribute with an associated value. In the case of E, there is no string associated with the directive itself because the directive is an HTML tag rather than an attribute. Reconciling this difference is usually more trouble than it's worth, so you will likely use either one or the other.

Here's how your associated HTML will look with the HTML-tag-enabled `imageCarousel` directive:

```
<body ng-controller="BodyController" ng-init="count = 0;">
    <h1>Image has changed {{count}} times</h1>
    <image-carousel images="defaultImages"
                    carousel-title="There are {{defaultImages.length}} images"
                    on-change="count = count + 1">
    </image-carousel>
    <image-carousel images="otherImages"
                    carousel-title="I have {{otherImages.length}} images"
                    on-change="count = count + 1">
    </image-carousel>
</body>
```

Although there is no additional functionality, this new `imageCarousel` directive is more elegant syntactically. One limitation worth noting: E style directives won't work as is in Internet Explorer 8 and older. There is an MIT-licensed JavaScript library called "HTML5 Shiv," which you need to include (a copy is packaged with the sample code for this chapter) to use E-style directives in older versions of Internet Explorer.

If you look at the state of the DOM after the page is loaded, you'll see that the `imageCarousel` tag stays in the DOM as the parent of the HTML in the template. Here's what the DOM state looks like in the case of the `imageCarousel`:

```
<image-carousel   images="defaultImages"
                  carousel-title="There are 3 images"
                  on-change="count = count + 1"
                  class="ng-isolate-scope ng-scope">
    <h1 class="ng-binding">
        Title: There are 3 images
    </h1>
    <div    my-background-image="images[currentIndex]"
            ng-swipe-left="next()"
            ng-swipe-right="previous()"
            style="height: 120px; width: 600px; border: 1px solid red;
                   background-image: url(...);">
    </div>
    <input type="button" toggle-button="disabled" value="Disable">
</image-carousel>
```

For most directives, this behavior is sufficient. However, if you have a strong preference against the `imageCarousel` tag being in the DOM, the `replace` setting is for you. The `replace` setting is a Boolean value (`false` by default) that determines whether the template is inserted as a child of the DOM element or replaces the DOM element entirely. Here's how to use the `replace` setting with the `imageCarousel` directive:

```
module.directive('imageCarousel', function() {
    return {
        restrict: 'E',
        replace: true,
        template:
            '<div>' +
            '    <h1>Title: {{carouselTitle}}</h1>' +
            '    <div    my-background-image="images[currentIndex]"' +
            '            ng-swipe-left="next()"' +
            '            ng-swipe-right="previous()"' +
            '            style="height: 120px; width: 600px; '+
            '                    border: 1px solid red">' +
            '    </div>' +
            '    <input type="button" toggle-button="disabled">' +
            '</div>',
        controller : CarouselController,
        scope : {
            images : '=',
            carouselTitle : '@',
            onChange : '&'
        }
    }
});
```

There are two key differences in the `replace: true` implementation as opposed to the previous implementation. The first is the obvious `replace: true` setting. The second is that the HTML template now includes a `div` tag that wraps the `h1`, `div`, and `input` tags. The reason for the new `div` tag becomes clear when you look at the DOM state with this new directive:

```
<div    images="defaultImages"
        carousel-title="There are 3 images"
        on-change="count = count + 1">
    <h1 class="ng-binding">
        Title: There are 3 images
    </h1>
    <div    my-background-image="images[currentIndex]"
            ng-swipe-left="next()"
            ng-swipe-right="previous()"
            style="height: 120px; width: 600px; border: 1px solid red;
                    background-image: url(...);">
    </div>
    <input type="button" toggle-button="disabled" value="Disable">
</div>
```

The `replace: true` setting replaces the `image-carousel` tag with the root element in the directive's HTML template—in this case, the top `div` tag. Note that there must be exactly one root element in the HTML template; otherwise, AngularJS throws an error: `Template must have exactly one root element`.

Moving On

Now that you've learned about how to utilize the basic settings of a directive object, you have enough knowledge to understand most open source directives you'll see. In addition, you've built a fairly flexible image carousel. In the last section of this chapter, you'll dive into the two most complex settings in a directive object: `compile` and `transclude`. You won't see these settings used often, but there are certain use cases where they are indispensable. In the next section, you'll dive into how these settings work by exploring the internals of the `ngRepeat` directive and making a key addition to your `imageCarousel` directive.

CHANGING DIRECTIVE TEMPLATES AT RUNTIME

One limitation you may have noticed with the directives in the previous chapter is that the HTML template is static. This means that the current `imageCarousel` directive is doomed to always have a title. However, using the advanced `compile` and `transclude` settings, you can enable your `imageCarousel` directive's clients to modify the template in sophisticated ways. As you'll see when you explore a simplified implementation of `ngRepeat`, these settings also tie in closely to how the `ngRepeat` directive works.

Transclusion

According to Wikipedia, *transclusion* is the inclusion of a document into another document by reference. The term was coined by Ted Nelson, better known as the inventor of the term *hypertext*, the "HT" in HTTP and HTML. In line with this definition, AngularJS directives' `transclude` setting and its corresponding `ngTransclude` directive exist to reference external HTML code from within your directive's HTML template. In other words, transclusion allows you to parameterize your directive's template, enabling you to modify some HTML in the template based on your needs.

Similar to the `scope` setting, the `transclude` setting can take one of three different values. The `transclude` setting is `false` by default, but you can set it to either `true` or the string `'element'`. If transclusion seems a bit mind warping, don't worry; it's actually fairly simple once you get your hands on a straightforward example.

Using the transclude: true Setting

Here's a basic example of how `transclude: true` works in action. First, here's a simple directive that introduces a person with a specified name:

```
module.directive('ngGreeting', function() {
    return {
        restrict: 'E',
        transclude: true,
        template:
            'Hi, my name is ' +
```

```
                        '<span ng-transclude></span>',
                };
        });
```

Note that the template HTML has an element with an `ng-transclude` attribute. The `ng-transclude` attribute means that the contents of the span will be replaced with the contents of the original HTML element. Here's how the `ngGreeting` directive can be used in HTML:

```
<ng-greeting>
    Val
</ng-greeting>
<br>
<br>
<ng-greeting>
    <b>Val </b>
</ng-greeting>
```

The real magic happens when you take a look at the state of the DOM after AngularJS is done:

```
<ng-greeting>
    Hi, my name is
    <span ng-transclude="">
        <span class="ng-scope">
            Val
        </span>
    </span>
</ng-greeting>
<br>
<br>
<ng-greeting>
    Hi, my name is
    <span ng-transclude="">
        <b class="ng-scope">
            Val
        </b>
    </span>
</ng-greeting>
```

Congratulations! You now have a directive with a parameterized template! AngularJS pulls any HTML you put into the directive element into the directive's template.

However, how does this work with isolate scopes? If `ngGreeting` had an isolate scope, would that mean any HTML you transclude into the `ngGreeting` directive would only be able to access variables in the isolate scope? Here's the `ngGreeting` directive with an isolate scope:

```
module.directive('ngGreeting', function() {
    return {
        restrict: 'E',
        transclude: true,
        scope: {},
        template:
            'Hi, my name is ' +
            '<span ng-transclude></span>',
    };
});
```

Now try using the directive with transcluded HTML that includes a binding to a variable outside the isolate scope:

```
<body ng-init="myName = 'Val';">
    <ng-greeting>
        {{ myName }}
    </ng-greeting>
</body>
```

How does this look in the DOM once the browser is finished rendering? Turns out, AngularJS does the right thing: It allows the transcluded HTML to access the `myName` variable in spite of the fact that the HTML is transcluded into an isolate scope!

```
<body ng-init="myName = 'Val';">
    <ng-greeting class="ng-isolate-scope ng-scope">
        Hi, my name is
        <span ng-transclude="">
            <span class="ng-scope ng-binding">
                Val
            </span>
        </span>
    </ng-greeting>
</body>
```

This may seem like a strange decision given the nature of isolate scopes. In fact, the transcluded HTML is not actually evaluated in the isolate scope; it's evaluated in the isolate scope's parent! To illustrate this, try adding a variable to the isolate scope:

```
module.directive('ngGreeting', function() {
    return {
        restrict: 'E',
        transclude: true,
        scope: {},
        template:
            'Hi, my name is ' +
            '<span ng-transclude></span>',
        link: function(scope) {
            scope.lastName = 'Karpov';
        }
    };
});
```

And now, try to access this scope variable from the transcluded HTML:

```
<body ng-init="myName = 'Val';">
    <ng-greeting>
        {{ myName }} {{ lastName }}
    </ng-greeting>
</body>
```

The `lastName` variable will be undefined in the transcluded HTML, so the output will still be, "Hi, my name is Val." That's because the transcluded HTML is evaluated as if the directive didn't have any scope at all. This decision makes working with directives easier, because you can write your transcluded HTML without worrying about whether the directive has an isolate scope, or any scope for that matter.

Using the transclude: 'element' Setting

The transclude: 'element' setting works almost identically to transclude: true, but with two minor caveats. First, with the transclude: 'element' setting, you're responsible for modifying the DOM in the compile setting (which you'll explore in the next section), unless you specify replace: true. This is a common gotcha when you first start working with the transclude: 'element' setting: if you don't set either compile or replace, your directive won't appear at all!

Also, the transclude: 'element' setting modifies the DOM in a way akin to replace: true. Here's the ngGreeting directive using the transclude: 'element' setting:

```
module.directive('ngGreeting', function() {
    return {
        restrict: 'E',
        transclude: 'element',
        replace: true,
        scope: {},
        template:
            '<div><h1 ng-transclude></h1></div>',
        link: function(scope) {
            scope.lastName = 'Karpov';
        }
    };
});
```

Using the following HTML:

```
<ng-greeting>
    Hi, my name is {{ myName }}
</ng-greeting>
```

The resulting DOM state after the browser is done rendering looks like this:

```
<body ng-init="myName = 'Val';">
    <div>
        <h1 ng-transclude="">
            <ng-greeting class="ng-isolate-scope ng-scope ng-binding">
                Hi, my name is Val
            </ng-greeting>
        </h1>
    </div>
</body>
```

If you had set transclude: true instead, the ng-greeting tag would not be there. Instead, AngularJS would insert a span tag. This behavior is helpful when you want to pull the entire directive-declaring element into the template and avoid wrapping the contents into a span tag. This gives users of your directive more fine-grained control of the HTML within the template.

Now that you've learned how transclusion works, it's time to finish your directives education by learning about the compile setting.

The compile Setting, or compile Versus link

The `compile` function and its relationship with the `link` function is a common source of confusion for AngularJS beginners. For the majority of directives you will write, `compile` is superfluous. There are two major reasons to use the `compile` function. The first is for performance in directives that do heavy DOM manipulation—the most obvious example being `ngRepeat` and similar directives that create multiple DOM elements. The second reason is that the `compile` function can modify the directive's template. The second reason is somewhat limited, however, because the *compile function* is run before the directive's scope is created. Therefore, the compile function does not have access to the directive's scope, so it can't evaluate attributes.

So what is the `compile` function actually useful for? In this section, you explore the benefits and limitations of the compile function by building your own simplified version of the built-in `ngRepeat` directive.

Your simplified `ngRepeat` directive, `ngRepeatOnce`, implements a common AngularJS performance optimization: reducing the number of heavy watchers on the page. Recall that, in Chapter 4, "Data Binding," you saw that the `ngRepeat` directive over a large array can make your page sluggish because each `$apply` call must iterate over the entire array. Your `ngRepeatOnce` directive ameliorates this problem by not calling `$watch` on the underlying array. This directive does not update when users add or remove elements from the underlying array, but it does allow you to handle larger arrays than `ngRepeat`. Although the inability to update when elements are added or removed is limiting, in many cases this functionality is unnecessary.

One key point to remember: You should not rely on setting both the `compile` and `link` functions in a directive object. The compile function is expected to return the link function. If you overwrite the default `compile` setting, the `link` setting is ignored unless you explicitly return the function in the `link` setting. As you'll see in the `ngRepeatOnce` directive, you don't necessarily have to set the `link` function; you can just have the compile function return an anonymous `link` function. Here's how your `ngRepeatOnce` directive will look:

```
module.directive('ngRepeatOnce', function() {
    return {
        restrict: 'A',
        transclude: 'element',
        compile: function(originalEl, attributes, transcludeFn) {
            return function(scope, element, attributes) {
                var loop = attributes.ngRepeatOnce.split(' in ');

                var elementScopeName = loop[0];
                var arr = scope.$eval(loop[1]);

                for (var i = 0; i < arr.length; ++i) {
                    var childScope = scope.$new();
                    childScope['$index'] = i;
                    childScope[elementScopeName] = arr[i];

                    transcludeFn(childScope, function(clone) {
                        originalEl.parent().append(clone);
                    });
                }
```

```
                    }
                }
            }
        });
```

This code may seem a bit intimidating at first, but it's quite simple once you look at it step by step. First, to duplicate the nice `in` looping syntax of `ngRepeat`, you just split the input string by the string `' in '`. The left side is the name that you should assign each array element to in the corresponding child scope, and the right side is the array to loop over. Next, you loop over the array, create a new scope for each element, and call the magic `transcludeFn` function on each new scope. This `transcludeFn` function creates a new DOM element with the scope you provided, and transcludes in the HTML specified by the `transclude` setting. The `transcludeFn` function then fires a callback with the newly created DOM element, which you're responsible for inserting into the DOM in the proper place.

Congratulations! You've implemented a simplified yet useful version of `ngRepeat`! The `compile` function is indispensable for this directive, because the `transcludeFn` function, which the `compile` function provides, allows you to create new DOM elements with correctly transcluded scopes. In fact, without the `compile` function, directives like `ngRepeat` would be incredibly difficult to write. Thanks to `compile` and `transclude`, however, your directives can manipulate the DOM in powerful yet intuitive ways. For instance, the `ngRepeat` directive's implementation is fairly complex and requires an understanding of some of AngularJS's deepest features, yet using the `ngRepeat` directive is incredibly simple and intuitive.

CONCLUSION

If you've made it through this entire chapter, congratulations! You learned all the tools you'll need to write highly sophisticated directives that can make the browser do anything short of singing and dancing. You learned about the three classes of directives you can write using just a link function: render-only directives, like `myBackgroundImage`; event handler directives, like `swipeLeft` and `swipeRight`; and two-way directives, like `toggleButton`. You then learned how to use the directive object and its settings to compose directives together using templates. Finally, you explored the depths of directive sorcery and learned how to parameterize and compose directive templates using `transclude` and `compile`.

All these concepts are tied together by the idea of directives as rules for manipulating the DOM tied in to the UI/UX API specified by your controllers. Fancy tools like templates and transclusion exist to allow you to easily wrap highly customizable bundles of HTML and JavaScript into a bundle that you can access from your HTML and tie in to your controllers and data binding. Directives provide a clean abstraction to reason about an HTML view in a high-level way, so you can reason about carousels and other UI controls rather than low-level `div`s. In addition, tools like the `scope` setting allow you to tie data binding in to your directives, so your directives can integrate with your data binding API in a clean and powerful way.

6

Templates, Location, and Routing

WHAT YOU WILL LEARN IN THIS CHAPTER:

➤ Templating using the ngInclude directive

➤ Performance implications of templating

➤ Using $location to save page state

➤ Routing between different views with ngView

➤ Single-page apps with ngView

➤ Search engine integration for single-page apps

➤ Animating transitions between views

WROX.COM CODE DOWNLOADS FOR THIS CHAPTER

You can find the wrox.com code downloads for this chapter at `http://www.wrox.com/go/proangularjs` on the Download Code tab.

In this chapter, you learn how to use AngularJS's templating system, the `$location` service, and AngularJS's client-side routing system. Using these building blocks, you create a *single-page application* (or SPA for short). The SPA paradigm is about building a fully functional web application that never reloads the page. SPAs offer you incredibly fine-grained control over your site's user experience (UX) by eliminating the ever-painful page reload in favor of loading Hypertext Markup Language (HTML) from the server via JavaScript.

To fully understand how SPAs in AngularJS work, you need to understand how templating, location, and routing work. This chapter is broken into three parts—one for each of these three building blocks. The templating and location sections are mostly independent of each other, so if you want to learn about templating but not the `$location` service or vice versa, feel free to skip to your desired section. However, the third section, about using AngularJS's routing framework to build an SPA, requires you to be familiar with the information from the first two sections.

Over the course of this chapter, you'll build a sample SPA, a catalog of books. The app uses the *master-detail design pattern*, which means there will be two views: a view that displays the master list of books, and a view that displays detailed information on a single book. In AngularJS, the terms *template* and *view* are mostly interchangeable, although the term *view* typically describes a template tied to the ngView directive that you'll learn about in Part III.

This chapter uses a NodeJS Hypertext Transfer Protocol (HTTP) server to serve up HTML content. An HTTP server is necessary because AngularJS loads templates using JavaScript HTTP requests, which don't work right if you just open the HTML file in the browser using file:///. If you have not installed NodeJS yet, please go to http://www.nodejs.org and follow the instructions for your platform of choice. After you have installed NodeJS and run npm install from the root directory of this chapter's sample code, you should be able to start an HTTP server on port 8080 by running node server.js. This server simply serves static files over HTTP, so you should be able to view the file angular.js in your browser by navigating to http://localhost:8080/angular.js.

However, the book catalog app will not load data from a server. You will be using a hard-coded list of books included in the $books service (see books.js in the sample code). Here's what your $books service will look like. It will primarily serve as a stub for a server, enabling you to load a list of books and load a specific book:

```
var booksService = function() {
  var books = [
    {
      _id: 1,
      title: "Les Miserables",
      author: "Victor Hugo",
      image: "//upload.wikimedia.org/wikipedia/commons/6/6c/Jean_Valjean.JPG",
      preview: "In 1815, M. Charles-Francois-Bienvenu Myriel was Bishop..."
    },
    {
      _id: 2,
      title: "The Book of Five Rings",
      author: "Musashi Miyamoto",
      image: "//upload.wikimedia.org/wikipedia/commons/2/20/Musashi_ts_pic.jpg",
      preview: "I have been many years training in the Way of strategy..."
    },
    {
      _id: 3,
      title: "Moby Dick",
      author: "Herman Melville",
      image:  "//upload.wikimedia.org/wikipedia/commons/3/36/" +
              "Moby-Dick_FE_title_page.jpg",
      preview: "Call me Ishmael. Some years ago—never mind how long precisely..."
    },
    {
      _id: 4,
      title: "The Hour of the Dragon",
```

```
          author: "Robert E. Howard",
          image: "//upload.wikimedia.org/wikipedia/en/6/60/Conan_the_Conqueror.jpg",
          preview: "The long tapers flickered, sending the black shadows..."
        },
        {
          _id: 5,
          title: "The Brothers Karamazov",
          author: "Fyodor Dostoyevsky",
          image:  "//upload.wikimedia.org/wikipedia/commons/2/2d/" +
                  "Dostoevsky-Brothers_Karamazov.jpg",
          preview: "Alexey Fyodorovitch Karamazov was the third son..."
        }
    ];

    return {
      getAll: function() {
        return books;
      },
      getById: function(id) {
        for (var i = 0; i < books.length; ++i) {
          if (books[i]._id === id) {
            return books[i];
          }
        }
        return null;
      }
    };
  };
```

For the purposes of this chapter, you'll be using the simple two-function interface shown earlier: getAll() to load all five books, and getById(id) to get a specific book by its identifier _id. Each book contains four properties in addition to its identifier: the title, the author, an image, and a preview featuring the first couple of paragraphs of the book. Now it's time to write your first templates using this new service.

PART I: TEMPLATES

A common difficulty in web development is reusing HTML. You may have certain HTML components that appear in multiple pages. In the past, web developers used server-side templating tools to include pieces of HTML in a page before sending it to the client. AngularJS templates bring the notion of including external HTML into your page to the client side. Although AngularJS's templates are functionally similar to server-side templating tools like Jade and eRuby, AngularJS templates provide additional features and performance benefits.

The most important advantage of client-side HTML templating over server-side templating is the ability to swap out large portions of the current page's HTML without reloading the page. This gives you more fine-grained control over your UX and thus the opportunity to make your UX smoother. For instance, when your user clicks on a link, you can show a nifty loading screen instead of making your user wait on an uninformative blank screen while his requested page is loading.

Using client-side templating, you'll implement the master view, the view that lists all the books, for your book catalog SPA. Although you can implement the master view without using templates, as you'll see, templates offer a wider range of control over how data is rendered.

> **NOTE** *You may be wondering what the difference between a template and a directive is. Directives also provide the ability to include blocks of HTML using the* template *and* templateURL *options. In fact, these* template *and* templateURL *options utilize the same templating framework that you explore in this chapter. The difference is that directives are typically implemented with associated JavaScript code to define user interactions, whereas templates are effectively just HTML strings. However, a directive may have an associated template, and a template's HTML can utilize directives. In this chapter, you'll learn by example where you should use a directive rather than a plain template and vice versa.*

Templating with ngInclude

The ngInclude directive is the simplest way to utilize client-side templating. This directive enables you to replace the associated Document Object Model (DOM) element's inner HTML with a given template's HTML. As you'll see later in this section, one of the biggest advantages of ngInclude is that the template being rendered is tied to two-way data binding, so you can easily render different templates for different pieces of data. Here's a simple example of using the ngInclude directive with ngRepeat to render a list of books, alternating between two different templates. You can find this page in the part_i_ng_include.html file in the sample code:

```html
<div ng-controller="BooksController">
  <div  ng-repeat="book in books"
        ng-include="book.templateUrl">
  </div>
</div>

<script type="text/javascript" src="angular.js"></script>
<script type="text/javascript" src="books.js"></script>
<script type="text/javascript">
  var booksModule = angular.module('booksModule', []);
  booksModule.factory('$books', booksService);

  function BooksController($scope, $books) {
    $scope.books = $books.getAll();

    for (var i = 0; i < $scope.books.length; ++i) {
      $scope.books[i].templateUrl = (i % 2 === 0 ?
        'master_img_left.template.html' :
        'master_img_right.template.html');
    }
  }
</script>
```

> **NOTE** *In this chapter, template files end with* `.template.html` *to distinguish them from full HTML files. Naming template files in a manner that distinguishes them from full HTML files is good practice and ensures that there is no confusion. In many applications, template files are stored in a separate directory from full HTML files for this same reason.*

As in the preceding example, the `ngInclude` directive takes as a parameter an expression that AngularJS evaluates to get the template's uniform resource locator (URL). In that example, each book is given a `templateUrl` property, which the `ngInclude` directive then evaluates to determine which template to load. Templates are loaded *lazily*—that is, the `ngInclude` directive does not load a template until it is asked to. Furthermore, the `ngInclude` directive caches templates by their URL, so a given template is only loaded from the server once.

To use the `ngInclude` directive properly, there are a couple of important details to keep in mind. First of all, because the `ngInclude` directive's template cache is just a plain old JavaScript object (POJO), this cache is destroyed when the page is reloaded. In the case of SPAs, this cache can persist for a long time, so you may need to manually refresh the cache. (You'll learn how to clear the template cache later in the section "The $templateCache Service.") If you are using templates on a standard page, the templates have to be reloaded every time the page is refreshed. However, because templates are loaded by HTTP requests, you can leverage the browser to cache the HTTP responses.

Second, the template cache is global across all instances of the `ngInclude` directive. In other words, if two completely separate instances of the `ngInclude` directive are told to render `foo.template.html`, there is only one request to the server, and both instances of the `ngInclude` directive receive the same data.

Now the question is, what do these `.template.html` files look like? A template file contains standard AngularJS-infused HTML, and the template is included as-is in any element that uses the `ngInclude` directive to include it. Here's what the first template, `master_img_left.template .html`, looks like:

```
<div class="book-preview">
  <div class="book-preview-image">
    <img ng-src="{{ book.image }}">
  </div>
  <div class="book-preview-text">
    <h3>
      {{ book.title }}
    </h3>
    <h4>
      By {{ book.author }}
    </h4>
    <em>
      {{ book.preview | limitTo:140 }}
    </em>
  </div>
  <div style="clear: both">
  </div>
</div>
```

> **NOTE** *Because the* `ngInclude` *directive loads templates using an HTTP request, you can write your templates in server-side templating languages like Jade and eRuby. The only requirement is that the HTTP response contains HTML, so you can write your templates in Jade as long as your server can parse Jade into HTML before responding to the client.*

As you can see, the `master_img_left.template.html` file contains fairly standard AngularJS-infused HTML. You may be wondering what the `book` variable in the preceding expressions refers to. The `book` variable in this template is the book variable defined in the `ngRepeat` in the `part_i_ng_include.html` file. Although the ability to include templates that use external variables is powerful, be careful! There is nothing to prevent you from including the `master_img_left.template.html` template in a scope that doesn't have a `book` variable, or a scope that contains a `book` variable without an image. Make sure your templates use as few outside variables as possible to maximize their reusability and minimize the barrier to entry to understanding them.

There's one more template used in the `part_i_ng_include.html` file: the `master_img_right.template.html` template. Here's the content of that template:

```html
<div class="book-preview">
  <div class="book-preview-text">
    <h3>
      {{ book.title }}
    </h3>
    <h4>
      By {{ book.author }}
    </h4>
    <em>
      {{ book.preview | limitTo:140 }}
    </em>
  </div>
  <div class="book-preview-image">
    <img ng-src="{{ book.image }}">
  </div>
  <div style="clear: both">
  </div>
</div>
```

The difference between this template and the `master_img_left.template.html` template is that the book image is on the right side of the title, rather than on the left. There are numerous other ways of achieving this effect in AngularJS; however, those typically involve conditional logic in your HTML. AngularJS novices often find the concept of being able to include logic in their HTML so exciting that they go overboard and turn their HTML into spaghetti code. Templates are a tool to prune your AngularJS-infused HTML when its complexity grows out of control: If you have a `div` with ten children that have both an `ngClass` and an `ngIf`, you probably should abstract that complexity out behind two or more templates.

ngInclude and Performance

AngularJS's client-side templating offers two performance benefits over conventional server-side templating. First, the HTML template only needs to be loaded once. Thus, if you have a page with a lot of duplicated HTML, you can conserve your scarce bandwidth by using a template to load repeated blocks of HTML. The second benefit is more subtle. Because templates are lazy-loaded, or not loaded until the ngInclude directive needs it, your template HTML loading is deferred until the main page is done loading. This lazy-loading of HTML is particularly useful for templates that display content loaded by an $http call, because there will be no data to display until the $http call has returned anyway.

Of course, lazy-loading is a double-edged sword when it comes to performance. In some cases, lazy-loading gives you a great benefit. However, a classic case that illustrates where lazy-loading performs suboptimally would be a Facebook-style notifications window. On Facebook, whenever users visit their homepages, they can click a button to view their most recent notifications. One way you might implement such a component in AngularJS would be to have a separate template for each type of notification. (You probably want to render a photo notification differently from someone commenting on your wall, for instance.) In addition, you probably want to load the notifications from the server with an HTTP request when the user clicks the Show Notifications button. That means, in the worst case, you would have to do six HTTP requests to load five notifications: one to load the notification data, and five to load five different templates. In other words, using this naïve approach, the notifications would show up more slowly than we would like. Thankfully, you don't have to throw ngInclude out the window if you have a similar situation. You'll learn about an alternative approach to loading templates that ameliorates this difficulty in the next section.

To illustrate how lazy-loading works, take a look at the Network tab in Chrome Developer Tools when loading http://localhost:8080/part_i_ng_include.html. The timeline shows that the templates are loaded after the page HTML is done loading, and then the images included in the templates are loaded.

Including Templates with script Tags

The ngInclude directive's ability to lazy-load templates is powerful, but it's not right for all applications. When lazy-loading isn't the right choice, AngularJS allows you to embed templates into a standard HTML script tag. This enables you to avoid having to do an individual HTTP request to load a particular template, but it requires you to embed the template code in the page itself. Here's how loading templates with the script tag works in practice:

```
<div ng-controller="BooksController">
  <div  ng-repeat="book in books"
        ng-include="book.templateUrl">
  </div>
</div>

<script type="text/javascript" src="angular.js"></script>
<script type="text/javascript" src="books.js"></script>
<script type="text/javascript">
  var booksModule = angular.module('booksModule', []);
```

```
    booksModule.factory('$books', booksService);

    function BooksController($scope, $books) {
      $scope.books = $books.getAll();

      for (var i = 0; i < $scope.books.length; ++i) {
        $scope.books[i].templateUrl = (i % 2 === 0 ?
          'master_img_left.template.html' :
          'master_img_right.template.html');
      }
    }
</script>

<script type="text/ng-template" id="master_img_left.template.html">
  <div class="book-preview">
    <div class="book-preview-image">
      <img ng-src="{{ book.image }}">
    </div>
    <div class="book-preview-text">
      <h3>
        {{ book.title }}
      </h3>
      <h4>
        By {{ book.author }}
      </h4>
      <em>
        {{ book.preview | limitTo:140 }}
      </em>
    </div>
    <div style="clear: both">
    </div>
  </div>
</script>
<script type="text/ng-template" id="master_img_right.template.html">
  <div class="book-preview">
    <div class="book-preview-text">
      <h3>
        {{ book.title }}
      </h3>
      <h4>
        By {{ book.author }}
      </h4>
      <em>
        {{ book.preview | limitTo:140 }}
      </em>
    </div>
    <div class="book-preview-image">
      <img ng-src="{{ book.image }}">
    </div>
    <div style="clear: both">
    </div>
  </div>
</script>
```

In the preceding example, both the `master_img_left.template.html` and `master_img_right` `.template.html` files are loaded as part of the page's HTML. If you take a look at the Chrome Developer Tools Network tab, you'll notice that the `ngInclude` directive doesn't make an HTTP request to load either of these template files. That's because the `$templateCache` service, which you'll learn about in the next section, finds every script tag with `type=text/ng-template` and stores the contents. Each template is then associated with its `id` attribute (which serves the same role the template URL did when you were lazy-loading templates), which `ngInclude` can then reference.

You'll notice that the actual HTML structure wasn't changed. One of the big advantages of templates is a cleaner separation of concerns. Neither the structure of the page nor the templates themselves have to change based on how you load templates. This is convenient because, as you're going to see in this next section, there are a lot of other ways for you to load templates into the template cache.

The $templateCache Service

Over the course of this section on `ngInclude`, you've heard a fair amount about AngularJS's template cache. In practice, you rarely have to interact with the template cache beyond being aware of its existence, but you may find yourself needing to clear the cache or add a template to it manually. For this reason, AngularJS provides an interface to the template cache in the form of the `$templateCache` service. The `$templateCache` service is available through the standard dependency injector, so you can utilize it in any directive, controller, or service.

Probably the most common use case for the `$templateCache` service is loading templates via HTTP request after the page has finished loading. Recall that the two methods you've used to load templates so far were lazy-loading the template via HTTP request the first time it is used, and including the template in your HTML in a `script` tag. With the `$templateCache` service, you're not limited to these two approaches; in fact, you can have fine-grained control over what templates are loaded when. Here's a simple example that loads the `master_img_left.template` `.html` and `master_img_right.template.html` templates on controller initialization using the `$http` and `$templateCache` services. This approach can give you the best of both worlds in terms of performance: You can defer the template loading until after the main page has done rendering, but the templates will likely be done loading by the time the user is able to switch the view. This code is available in this chapter's sample code as `part_i_template_cache.html`:

```
<div ng-controller="BooksController">
    <div  ng-repeat="book in books"
          ng-include="book.templateUrl">
    </div>
</div>

<script type="text/javascript" src="angular.js"></script>
<script type="text/javascript" src="books.js"></script>
<script type="text/javascript">
    var booksModule = angular.module('booksModule', []);
    booksModule.factory('$books', booksService);

    function BooksController($scope, $books, $templateCache, $http) {
      var templates = [
        'master_img_left.template.html',
```

```
                   'master_img_right.template.html'
               ];

               $scope.loadBooks = function() {
                 $scope.books = $books.getAll();

                 for (var i = 0; i < $scope.books.length; ++i) {
                   $scope.books[i].templateUrl = templates[i % 2];
                 }
               };

               var done = 0;
               angular.forEach(templates, function(templateUrl) {
                 $http.get(templateUrl).success(function(data) {
                   $templateCache.put(templateUrl, data);
                   if (++done === templates.length) {
                     $scope.loadBooks();
                   }
                 });
               });
             }
           </script>
```

The $templateCache.put function used in the preceding code allows you to insert a template into the template cache. The $templateCache service also exposes the $templateCache.get function, which allows you to get the template associated with the given ID, and the $templateCache.removeAll function, which removes all templates from the cache. The $templateCache.removeAll function is the standard way to make sure the ngInclude directive reloads your templates from the server. The $templateCache service doesn't have a function to explicitly remove a single template from the cache, but $templateCache.put(id, undefined) works for removing the template with a given ID.

One last important detail to remember about ngInclude and the template cache: If the ngInclude directive is asked to render a template that isn't in the cache, it attempts to load the template via HTTP request and put it back in the cache. However, the ngInclude directive is tied to AngularJS's $digest loop, so it doesn't check the template cache or do any HTTP requests unless the value of the expression it's watching changes. In the case of the master view for your book catalog, to force the ngInclude directive to reload the master_img_left.template.html and master_img_right .template.html templates, you have to call the $templateCache.removeAll function, as well as change each value of book.templateUrl to trigger the ngInclude directive's watcher.

Next Steps: Templates and Data Binding

You may have noticed that the ngInclude directive evaluates an expression to determine which template to render. In fact, the ngInclude directive is tied to two-way data binding. In the master list of books, if a single book's templateUrl member changes, that particular book's div element is rerendered with a different template. You can find an example of how this works in the part_i_template_data_binding.html in this chapter's sample code:

```
<div ng-controller="BooksController">
    <select ng-model="currentOption"
            ng-options="key for (key, value) in options"
            ng-change="currentOption()">
```

```
      </select>
      <div   ng-repeat="book in books"
             ng-include="book.templateUrl">
      </div>
</div>

<script type="text/javascript" src="angular.js"></script>
<script type="text/javascript" src="books.js"></script>
<script type="text/javascript">
  var booksModule = angular.module('booksModule', []);
  booksModule.factory('$books', booksService);

  function BooksController($scope, $books) {
    $scope.books = $books.getAll();

    $scope.setAlternatingTemplates = function() {
      for (var i = 0; i < $scope.books.length; ++i) {
        $scope.books[i].templateUrl = (i % 2 === 0 ?
          'master_img_left.template.html' :
          'master_img_right.template.html');
      }
    };

    $scope.setAllLeft = function() {
      for (var i = 0; i < $scope.books.length; ++i) {
        $scope.books[i].templateUrl = 'master_img_left.template.html';
      }
    };

    $scope.setAllRight = function() {
      for (var i = 0; i < $scope.books.length; ++i) {
        $scope.books[i].templateUrl = 'master_img_right.template.html';
      }
    };

    $scope.options = {
      'Alternating': $scope.setAlternatingTemplates,
      'All Left': $scope.setAllLeft,
      'All Right': $scope.setAllRight
    };
    $scope.currentOption = $scope.options['Alternating'];
    $scope.setAlternatingTemplates();
  }
</script>
```

This page has a drop-down that allows you to set whether to render books using only the master_img_left.template.html template, using only the master_img_right.template.html template, or alternating between the two. Because of AngularJS's data binding, you don't need to do any extra work beyond setting each book's templateUrl property; the ngInclude directive takes care of the rest.

The most common application of dynamically changing templates based on user behavior is an SPA, where the entire content of the page is a single template that can be swapped out. Conveniently, that's precisely what you're going to learn about in Part III of this chapter. However, before you dive into learning about routing and SPAs, you need to learn how to track what view the user is on in the URL. Part of what makes URLs so convenient is that you can copy/paste (or bookmark) a given URL and return to it later. Unfortunately, when you keep the users on the same page and just swap out AngularJS templates, the URL stays the same, and the users can't just paste a URL to return to where they were! In the next section, you'll learn to ameliorate this difficulty using the `$location` service, which the AngularJS routing code that you use in Part III leverages. The `$location` service provides a clean way of tracking JavaScript state in the page's URL without triggering a page reload.

PART II: THE $LOCATION SERVICE

Much like how AngularJS's templating framework allows you to easily transform large blocks of HTML, the `$location` service provides a convenient interface for reading and modifying the current URL without reloading the page. The most common reason to modify the current URL in JavaScript is for *deep linking*: encoding page state, such as the state of a check box or the window's current scroll position, in the URL. As you might have guessed, deep linking is extremely important for SPAs. However, because there are strict rules around what portions of a URL can change without page reload, the `$location` service has several gotchas that you need to be aware of.

> **NOTE** *A common source of confusion related to the* `$location` *service is that there is no way to use* `$location` *to force a page reload. You cannot use the* `$location` *service to redirect your user to an entirely new page.*

What's in a URL?

A URL is a string that you can enter into your browser to load a given file. A common example is `http://www.google.com`, which resolves to the HTML for Google's homepage. URLs can be far more complex than just this simple example, though, and for the purposes of this section, you need to be familiar with the different components of a URL.

A slightly more interesting URL than the preceding trivial example would look more like this: `http://www.google.com/foo?bar=baz#qux`. The three portions of a URL that you need to be familiar with are the *path*, `/foo`; the *query string*, `#?bar=baz#`; and the *hash*, `#qux`. The path and query string communicate to the server the precise resource you're looking for. Changing the path or the query string triggers a page reload in modern browsers. However, the browser does not send the hash portion to the server; thus, you can modify the hash component without triggering a page reload. The hash portion is typically used for deep linking functionality.

Browsers typically consider the first instance of `?` as the start of the query string and the first instance of `#` as the start of the hash portion. This means that the hash portion can contain anything your application desires. In particular, as you'll see later in this section, AngularJS's `$location` service provides an interface for you to construct URLs that look like this: `http://www.google.com/#/foo?bar=baz`. Notice that `/foo?bar=baz` is in the hash portion!

> **NOTE** *The IETF RFC-3986 specification, the definitive specification for the format of a URL, doesn't explicitly specify the format of the query string. The established convention is that the query string should be a list of key/value pairs delimited by an* `&`, *but this isn't mandatory. Technically, the query string can be whatever you want.*

Introducing $location

The $location service is AngularJS's preferred method of manipulating the hash portion of a URL. In particular, the $location service exposes four important functions: url(), path(), search(), and hash(). As you'll see, these functions are somewhat confusingly named given the established URL nomenclature. For example, the path() function doesn't modify the actual URL path portion.

The $location service is designed with routing for SPAs in mind, so these functions are designed to operate on the hash portion of the URL. For example, $location.path('foo') navigates the user to /#/foo (note that the # signifies the start of the hash portion) instead of /foo and does not cause a page reload. In other words, the $location service interacts with a pseudo-URL defined in the URL's hash portion.

For example, assume that your user is on the URL http://google.com/foo?bar=baz#qux. If you were to execute the following functions when your user is at this URL, here is what the browser's address bar would show:

```
// Before: http://google.com/foo?bar=baz#qux
$location.url('/path/to?query-1');
// After: http://google.com/foo?bar=baz#/path/to?query=1

// Before: http://google.com/foo?bar=baz#qux
$location.path('/path/to');
// After: http://google.com/foo?bar=baz#/path/to

// Before: http://google.com/foo?bar=baz#qux
$location.search('query', '1');
// After: http://google.com/foo?bar=baz#/qux?query=1

// Before: http://google.com/foo?bar=baz#qux
$location.hash('fi');
// After: http://google.com/foo?bar=baz#/qux#fi
```

As you can see, the $location service takes full advantage of the fact that the hash portion of the URL can be any string and provides an easy-to-manipulate pseudo-URL in the hash portion. For the purposes of this chapter, to avoid confusion with the actual URL in the browser's address bar, the hash portion URL will be referred to as the *hash pseudo-URL*. The individual portions of the hash pseudo-URL will be referred to by their function name. For instance, the hash pseudo-URL's search portion will be referred to as $location.search, to avoid confusion between the address bar URL's search portion and the hash pseudo-URL's search portion.

One important detail about these four functions associated with the $location service: They are both getters and setters. Invoking the url(), path(), or hash() functions with no parameters will return the current value of the hash pseudo-URL, the pseudo-path, or the pseudo-hash, respectively. Similarly, calling the search() function with no parameters will return a JavaScript object representation of the pseudo-URL's search portion. For example:

```
// URL: http://google.com/foo?bar=baz#qux
$location.url(); // => '/qux'

// URL: http://google.com/foo?bar=baz#qux
```

```
$location.path(); // => '/'

// URL: http://google.com/#/foo/bar?baz=qux
$location.search(); // => '{ "baz": "qux" }'

// URL: http://google.com/#/foo/bar#baz
$location.hash(); // => 'baz'
```

Tracking Page State with $location

The most common use case for modifying the hash portion of the URL is to enable the user to save some intra-page state, such as a JavaScript variable or the user's scroll position. The $location service allows you to do much more with the hash portion of the URL. In this section, you use the $location service to enable users to highlight bits of text from the book preview and track what they've highlighted in the page's URL. This enables your users to bookmark favorite passages or share powerful quotes on social media.

In this section, you write the detail view for the book's catalog SPA—that is, the view that shows detailed information about a single book. In the interest of simplicity and to avoid having to use client-side routing, this page hard-codes the book that's displayed, which in this case is Victor Hugo's novel *Les Miserables*. More interestingly, the page enables users to click to highlight certain pieces of text in the book's preview and store the highlight position in the page's URL. For instance, perhaps while reading the preview, your user is particularly touched by Hugo's adage "That which is said of men often occupies as important a place in their lives, and above all in their destinies, as that which they do." The code that follows highlights the given text and changes the page's URL to part_ii_highlight.html#?highlight=that%2520which%2520is%2520 said... when the user selects the text. This code can be found in this chapter's sample code as part_ii_highlight.html:

```html
<div ng-controller="BookDetailController">
  <div style="float:left; width: 300px; margin: 25px">
    <img ng-src="http://{{ book.image }}" style="width: 300px">
  </div>
  <div style="float: left; width: 600px;">
    <h1>
      {{ book.title }}
    </h1>
    <h3>
      By: {{ book.author }}
    </h3>
    <p  ng-click="getSelection()"
        ng-bind-html-unsafe="book.preview | highlight:selectedText">
    </p>
  </div>
  <div style="clear: both"></div>
</div>

<script type="text/javascript" src="angular.js"></script>
<script type="text/javascript" src="books.js"></script>
<script type="text/javascript">
```

```javascript
var booksModule = angular.module('booksModule', []);
booksModule.factory('$books', booksService);

function BookDetailController($scope, $books, $location) {
  $scope.book = $books.getById(1); // Les Miserables
  $scope.selectedText = $location.search()['highlight'] ?
    decodeURIComponent($location.search()['highlight']) :
    null;

  $scope.getSelection = function() {
    var selected = window.getSelection().toString();
    $location.search('highlight', encodeURIComponent(selected));
    $scope.selectedText = selected;
  };
}

booksModule.filter('highlight', function() {
  return function(input, highlight) {
    if (!highlight) {
      return input;
    }
    return input.replace(highlight,
      '<span class="highlight">' + highlight + '</span>');
  }
});

booksModule.directive('ngBindHtmlUnsafe', function() {
  return function(scope, element, attrs) {
    scope.$watch(attrs.ngBindHtmlUnsafe, function(v) {
      element.html(v);
    });
  }
});
</script>

<style rel="stylesheet">
  .highlight {
    background-color: yellow;
  }
</style>
```

> **NOTE** *You may have noticed that, in this example, the code only searches for a given string when determining what to highlight, rather than actually storing how many characters into the text the quote is. This approach is fairly limited and has numerous bad behaviors. (Try highlighting the word* which *is in the* BookDetailController *in the preceding example.) Implementing a real highlighting system in this manner would be a poor decision. However, the details of implementing such a system would add unnecessary complexity to this example and thus detract from its effectiveness as a tool for learning about the* $location *service.*

The preceding code illustrates the fundamental design pattern for interfacing with the `$location` service. Typically, when using the `$location` service to track JavaScript state in the URL, you will first load the data from the URL immediately after the page loads (that is, when controllers initialize). In this example, the `$scope.selectedText = $location .search()['highlight']` line represents this step. The second part of this design pattern is updating the URL whenever the variable changes, so the URL stays in sync with the JavaScript state. In this example, this step is represented by the `$location .search('highlight', encodeURIComponent(selected));` line.

Typically, for storing JavaScript data, the `$location.search` function is the correct approach, because it gives you the ability to modify named attributes. For example, in the previous code, you stored only a `highlight` attribute. Adding other attributes to store other JavaScript state would be fairly straightforward. However, `$location.url`, `$location.hash`, and `$location.path` only allow you to directly modify a single string, so if you store the `selectedText` variable in one of those portions, you will be stuck with a tricky engineering problem if you need to add additional JavaScript state to the URL.

Once again, it is worth noting that the `$location.search` function doesn't change the actual query portion of the URL (the search portion is another term often used to mean the query portion of the URL); it modifies the query portion of the hash pseudo-URL. Because of this, changes made to the URL with the `$location.search` function do not interfere with server interaction; however, any non-AngularJS functions that parse the query string do not see the changes.

Next Steps: Routing and SPAs

Over the course of Part II, you've primarily used the `$location` service in a minimal capacity to track page state using the `$location.search` function. You haven't really used the `url()`, `path()`, or `hash()` functions. There is a good reason for this: the `$location.search` function is uniquely suited for storing general JavaScript state because it provides the ability to manipulate key-value pairs. The `url()`, `path()`, or `hash()` functions instead manipulate whole portions of the hash pseudo-URL. These functions are designed with a different purpose in mind: providing a URL-like interface for SPAs. If you're not interested in SPAs, you're unlikely to ever need the `url()`, `path()`, or `hash()` functions. Nevertheless, understanding these functions is key to understanding how client-side routing and SPAs work, so keep this in mind for Part III.

PART III: ROUTING

Now that you've learned the basics of how templates work and how to use the `$location` service to manipulate the hash pseudo-URL, you're going to learn how to combine these two concepts to do client-side routing for your book catalog SPA.

At a high level, the term *routing* in web development means mapping the path portion of a URL to a handler for that particular route. In the context of AngularJS, a route is defined by the path portion of the hash pseudo-URL. AngularJS has a provider called `$routeProvider` that enables you to declaratively define a mapping from hash pseudo-paths to handlers. In AngularJS, a route handler is typically an object that defines the template URL that should be rendered and the controller for the template.

NOTE *Typically, in server-side routing frameworks, a route is defined by the combination of a path and an HTTP verb (GET, POST, PUT, or DELETE). However, because AngularJS handles routing on the client side and thus doesn't receive HTTP requests, the HTTP verb component doesn't necessarily make sense. That is why AngularJS routing only uses the (hash pseudo-URL) path. If you're used to server-side routing with frameworks like Ruby on Rails or Express, be cognizant of this distinction.*

AngularJS's routing framework is not included in the core `angular.js` file; it's instead packaged as a separate file called `angular-routes.js`. You can download the `angular-routes.js` file for your preferred version of AngularJS on `http://code.angularjs.org`. For your convenience, the version of the `angular-routes.js` file corresponding to AngularJS 1.2.16 has been packaged with the sample code for this chapter. This file contains a module called `ngRoute` that contains all the services and directives you need to build your SPA.

Under the hood, the `ngRoute` module manages the interaction between the `$location` service and the rendered view—that is, when `$location.path()` has a certain value, the `ngRoute` module renders the template you specified for that particular value. This functionality forms the core of your basic SPA. The general idea behind an SPA in AngularJS is that your links modify the hash portion of the URL rather than linking to a new page. The `ngRoute` module then handles interacting with the `$location` service and making sure the correct view is rendered based on the value of `$location.path()`.

The SPA paradigm offers numerous advantages. In addition to giving you more fine-grained control over UX, SPAs provide a clean separation between client and server, as well as between data and display. The server behind an SPA doesn't need to handle templating and routing; it only needs to provide a REST API and static HTML files representing the AngularJS templates. The client JavaScript and HTML can thus be entirely responsible for how data is displayed, and the server can focus on providing an API for manipulating the data. In addition, because AngularJS templates are static HTML, they can be cached by the browser, leading to reduced bandwidth usage and better performance. You can explore these advantages in more detail when building out your SPA.

The most significant limitation of SPAs is search engine optimization. Search engines like Google use programs called *crawlers* to explore your site and report information about your pages to the search engine. These crawlers, however, are designed to analyze static HTML only; they don't actually execute JavaScript. This means that your SPA won't be crawl-able by Google! Thankfully, there are tools for dealing with this limitation that you'll learn about toward the end of this chapter.

NOTE *In AngularJS 1.2, the* `ngRoute` *module is not packaged with AngularJS by default. It is included in a file called* `angular-route.js`; *you can download the version corresponding to your preferred version of AngularJS on* `code.angularjs.org`. *For your convenience, the* `ngRoute` *module for AngularJS 1.2.16 has been packaged with the sample code for this section. If you are using AngularJS 1.0.x, you don't need this extra file, because* `ngRoute` *is packaged with AngularJS.*

Using the ngRoute Module

The ngRoute module's fundamentals are most easily learned by example. Using the ngRoute module, you're going to build a book catalog SPA with two views: a master view and a detail view. Conveniently, these two views are identical to the master view that you wrote in Part I and the detail view that you wrote in Part II. The following code represents the full JavaScript for the SPA and can be found in this chapter's sample code as part_iii.html. Most of this code should look familiar from Part I and Part II, but take careful note of how these three new AngularJS components are used: the ngView directive, the $routeProvider provider, and the $routeParams service.

```
<div ng-view="true">
</div>

<script type="text/javascript" src="angular.js"></script>
<script type="text/javascript" src="angular-route.js"></script>
<script type="text/javascript" src="books.js"></script>
<script type="text/javascript">
  var booksModule = angular.module('booksModule', ['ngRoute']);
  booksModule.factory('$books', booksService);

  booksModule.config(function($routeProvider) {
    $routeProvider.
      when('/', {
        templateUrl: 'part_iii_master.template.html',
        controller: BooksController
      }).
      when('/book/:id', {
        templateUrl: 'part_iii_detail.template.html',
        controller: BookDetailController,
        reloadOnSearch: false
      });
  });

  function BooksController($scope, $books) {
    $scope.books = $books.getAll();

    for (var i = 0; i < $scope.books.length; ++i) {
      $scope.books[i].templateUrl = (i % 2 === 0 ?
        'master_img_left.template.html' :
        'master_img_right.template.html');
    }
  }

  function BookDetailController($scope, $books, $location,
    $routeParams) {
    $scope.book = $books.getById(parseInt($routeParams.id, 10));
    $scope.selectedText = $location.search()['highlight'] ?
      decodeURIComponent($location.search()['highlight']) :
      null;
    $scope.getSelection = function() {
      var selected = window.getSelection().toString();
      if (selected) {
        $location.search('highlight', encodeURIComponent(selected));
```

```
        }
        $scope.selectedText = selected;
      };
    }
  </script>
```

There isn't a lot of new code here, but the small amount of new code does a significant amount of work. The first component—the ngView directive—performs the relatively straightforward task of informing ngRoute which div should contain the template for the current route. The ngView directive itself isn't particularly complex. In AngularJS, you'll typically create a div with the ngView directive attached and never touch it again. You'll briefly touch on the ngView directive again when you learn about animations in the last section of Part III. However, now you're going to take a deep dive into the particulars of the two other new components in the preceding code: the $routeProvider provider and the $routeParams service.

The $routeProvider Provider

The previous section introduced a new provider, $routeProvider, that's worth exploring in more detail. This component is the canonical tool for configuring client-side routing, so you see it in virtually every AngularJS SPA. The $routeProvider provider must be configured in a *configuration block*—that is, in a function passed to a module's config() function. You can configure the $routeProvider provider using the chainable when() function, which creates mappings between routes and handler objects. Recall the use of the $routeProvider provider in part_iii.html:

```
booksModule.config(function($routeProvider) {
  $routeProvider.
    when('/', {
      templateUrl: 'part_iii_master.template.html',
      controller: BooksController
    }).
    when('/book/:id', {
      templateUrl: 'part_iii_detail.template.html',
      controller: BookDetailController,
      reloadOnSearch: false
    });
});
```

Handler objects have several configurable parameters, but the ones that you'll see most often are template, templateUrl, and controller. If you worked through Chapter 5, "Directives," these parameters will look familiar because they behave identically to the corresponding directive object settings. The template parameter enables you to write the template HTML inline. The templateUrl parameter allows you to specify which template the ngRoute module renders by its template cache ID, much like how the ngInclude directive that you used in Part I did.

The controller parameter tells the ngRoute module to wrap the given template with a particular controller. One important detail about the controller parameter that isn't highlighted in the previous example is that the controller parameter can take a string as well as a function. In part_iii.html, the controller parameter is always set to a function variable—namely, BookController or BookDetailController. However, if you declare controllers using the `module.controller()` syntax, you can reference the controller by its name in the `controller` parameter. For instance, if you declared `BookDetailController` like this:

```
booksModule.controller('DetailController', function($scope, $books,
  $location, $routeParams) {
  $scope.book = $books.getById(parseInt($routeParams.id, 10));
  $scope.selectedText = $location.search()['highlight'] ?
    decodeURIComponent($location.search()['highlight']) :
    null;

  $scope.getSelection = function() {
    var selected = window.getSelection().toString();
    if (selected) {
      $location.search('highlight', encodeURIComponent(selected));
    }
    $scope.selectedText = selected;
  };
});
```

you could then declare your route configuration like this:

```
booksModule.config(function($routeProvider) {
  $routeProvider.
    when('/', {
      templateUrl: 'part_iii_master.template.html',
      controller: BooksController
    }).
    when('/book/:id', {
      templateUrl: 'part_iii_detail.template.html',
      controller: 'DetailController',
      reloadOnSearch: false
    });
});
```

In the preceding example, the string passed to the `controller` parameter must match the controller's name—that is, the first parameter you passed in to `module.controller()`.

> **NOTE** *You may have noticed that the previous example sets a* `reloadOnSearch` *option in the handler for the* `/book/:id` *route. This highlights a minor detail related to the interaction between* `$location` *and* `ngRoute`. *By default, the* `ngRoute` *module emulates conventional server-side routing; thus, it "reloads" the view every time* `$location.path` *or* `$location.search` *changes by default. When AngularJS reloads a view, it destroys the old* `$scope`, *creates a new one, and executes the controller function again. Thus, if you modify* `$location.search` *in controller initialization and you've included the* `ngRoute` *module without setting the* `reloadOnSearch` *option to* `false`, *AngularJS gets stuck in an infinite loop of creating and destroying scopes. There are three ways you can avoid this problem. You can either set the* `reloadOnSearch` *option to* `false` *for that route, store your JavaScript state in* `$location.hash` *(changes to* `$location.hash` *never cause* `ngRoute` *to change the view), or avoid using the* `ngRoute` *module.*

Another important concept in the use of `$routeProvider` in `part_iii.html` is the notion of *route parameters*. The `ngRoute` module allows route strings to contain parameterizable components denoted by a `:` sign. A typical usage is the `/book/:id` route: if the user navigates to `#/book/3`, `#/book/42`, or `#/book/foo`, the handler for the `/book/:id` route is used. However, the handler has access to the (string) value of whatever value was in the part of the URL denoted by the `:id`. In the previous examples, the handler would have access to an `id` parameter (typically using the `$routeParams` service that you'll learn about in the next section) that would be equal to `'3'`, `'42'`, or `'foo'`, respectively. If you are familiar with routing in MVC frameworks like Ruby on Rails or Express, route parameters in AngularJS are essentially identical.

> **NOTE** *Recall that a* provider *is a function that acts as a recipe for creating AngularJS services. The* `$routeProvider` *provider is atypical in that the service it provides,* `$route`, *is less useful than the provider itself. The* `$route` *service exposes data about the current route (including the route parameters), but to use it, you need to use the* `$routeProvider` *provider to define the routing structure for this app. As you can see in* `part_iii.html`, *you can fairly easily write an SPA without using the* `$route` *service.*

The $routeParams Service

The `$routeParams` service provides a POJO that contains the current route's route parameters and `$location.search` values. In case of a collision, for instance, if a user were to navigate to `#/book/foo?id=bar` on `part_iii.html`, the route parameter would take precedence over the `$location.search` value. That is, in the `#/book/foo?id=bar` example, `$routeParams.id` would equal `'foo'` rather than `'bar'`.

> **NOTE** *In most cases, the properties of* `$routeParams` *stay constant throughout the life cycle of your controllers, because the controller and scope are destroyed when the view changes. However, if you set the previously mentioned* `reloadOnSearch` *option to* `false` *in your route handler, the keys and values of* `$routeParams` *may change without your controller being reinstantiated.*

Navigation in Your SPA

You may have noticed that you haven't seen the source code yet for the master template `part_iii_master.html` and the detail template `part_iii_detail.html`. That's because they are virtually identical to the HTML code from Part I's code (`part_i_ng_include.html`) and Part II's code (`part_ii_highlight.html`). For the sake of completeness, here is `part_iii_master.html`:

```
<div  ng-repeat="book in books"
      ng-include="book.templateUrl">
</div>
```

The templates that are included using `ngInclude` are essentially identical to the
`master_img_template.left.html` and `master_img_template.right.html` templates you saw in
Part I. Here is the slightly modified `master_img_template.left.html` template:

```
<div class="book-preview">
  <div class="book-preview-image">
    <img ng-src="{{ book.image }}">
  </div>
  <div class="book-preview-text">
    <h3>
      <a ng-href="#/book/{{book._id}}">
        {{ book.title }}
      </a>
    </h3>
    <h4>
      By {{ book.author }}
    </h4>
    <em>
      {{ book.preview | limitTo:140 }}
    </em>
  </div>
  <div style="clear: both">
  </div>
</div>
```

And `part_iii_detail.html`:

```
<h3 style="cursor: pointer">
  <a ng-href="#/">
    Back to Master List
  </a>
</h3>
<div style="float:left; width: 300px; margin: 25px">
  <img ng-src="{{ book.image }}" style="width: 300px">
</div>
<div style="float: left; width: 600px;">
  <h1>
    {{ book.title }}
  </h1>
  <h3>
    By: {{ book.author }}
  </h3>
  <p  ng-click="getSelection()"
      ng-bind-html-unsafe="book.preview | highlight:selectedText">
  </p>
</div>
<div style="clear: both"></div>
```

As you can see, the `master_img_template.left.html` template and the `part_iii_detail.html`
template have been modified to include some links for easier browsing. These links, however, use
the `ngHref` directive and only modify the hash portion of the URL. For instance, notice that, in the
`part_iii_detail.html` template, the link to return to the master view navigates the user to #/

rather than /. To integrate properly with the ngRoute module, the URLs that you link to with the a tag must start with #/.

As you may already know, AngularJS can properly evaluate expressions in an a tag's href attribute. The ngHref directive is not strictly necessary to get AngularJS to evaluate expressions, but it does have two advantages over the a tag. First, the ngHref directive doesn't change the href attribute if your expression is broken, so your user isn't redirected to a garbage URL if you have a bug in your expression. The second reason is to prevent search engine crawlers from crawling AngularJS links. Typical search engine crawlers don't evaluate JavaScript. They instead just parse the page's HTML and find where all the href attributes link to, which, in the context of AngularJS, may be a URL that contains a lot of variable names wrapped in {{}}. Thankfully, there are tools out there to enable search engines to crawl your AngularJS website. You'll learn about one such tool in the next few sections.

Search Engines and SPAs

Search engine crawlers don't actually run your page's JavaScript, so if you're building an SPA, you have a potential problem: Google can't crawl your site. Of course, this may be an advantage. For instance, if your application is internal to your company or requires you to be logged in before showing any meaningful functionality, you might not want search engines to crawl your site anyway. However, if you want to write a forward-facing SPA and it is crucial to your business plan that you show up at the top of Google search results, don't worry; you will learn a strategy in this section for making sure your SPA is search engine friendly.

First, a word of warning: In this section, you'll be doing some server-side work. There is simply no way to properly interface with a typical search engine crawler without a functioning web server, so you'll have to write about six lines of server-side JavaScript in NodeJS. If you are looking to integrate AngularJS with a different server framework, don't worry; you can adapt the approach you'll learn in this section to work with Ruby on Rails, PHP's Zend framework, Nginx, and most other web server tools out there.

Furthermore, this section requires you to write very little code (a few lines of server-side JavaScript, one line of HTML, and two lines of AngularJS JavaScript), but this code will be fairly dense and perform a lot of sophisticated operations under the hood. Specifically, in every other section of this book, you've written only client-side JavaScript, whereas in this section the meat of the work will consist of setting up two servers on your machine. However, don't be intimidated; so long as you're reasonably familiar with a Linux-style terminal, you should be able to set up a crawler-friendly SPA.

Setting Up Prerender on the Server

The approach you'll be learning about in this section relies on a service called Prerender (http://www.prerender.io). At a high level, Prerender crawls your website using PhantomJS, an open-source headless browser with a JavaScript API. Because PhantomJS is a full-fledged browser, it actually runs your AngularJS app in virtually the same way Google Chrome would. When a crawler identifies a page as an SPA, it asks the server for a crawler-friendly prerendered version of the page—essentially a plain HTML version of the SPA. Prerender has plug-ins and guides for many server frameworks (you can find these guides on Prerender's website at `http://www.prerender.io`), but in this chapter, you'll be using its NodeJS plug-in.

> **NOTE** *Prerender has a paid option, but for the purposes of this chapter, you don't have to sign up for an account with Prerender. Prerender's code is open source, and in this section you'll be creating your own locally-hosted version of Prerender's crawling service. Although using Prerender's paid platform is probably a better choice in a production environment for performance and reliability reasons, setting up your own is better for evaluation and instruction.*

A Prerender setup consists of two components. The first component is a standalone NodeJS server that acts as a thin wrapper for PhantomJS: Essentially, you can send this PhantomJS server an HTTP request with a URL in the path portion of the URL, and the server returns a static HTML version of the rendered page. This server is available on the NodeJS package manager, npm, as a package named `prerender`. To see this server in action, navigate to the directory containing this chapter's sample code, and run `npm install`. Then start the PhantomJS server by running `node ./node_modules/prerender/server.js`. Finally, open your browser and navigate to `http://localhost:3000/http://www.google.com`. You should see the familiar Google homepage. In the terminal, you should see approximately the following output:

```
2014-08-21T18:53:52.265Z getting google.com
2014-08-21T18:53:52.339Z got 200 in 74ms for google.com
```

There is one key difference between the prerendered Google homepage and the actual Google homepage you'll see in your browser: The prerendered version has no JavaScript and no `script` tags. It's simply a snapshot of the page's HTML state after the page is done loading (including all JavaScript).

> **NOTE** *Prerender's paid service essentially consists of a managed cloud version of the PhantomJS server described earlier. Because you can run the open source version locally, there is no reason to sign up for its paid service while you're evaluating it. The second component, described next, can be configured to make requests to any Prerender PhantomJS server, whether it be one you run locally or Prerender's managed server.*

The second component is *middleware* for your web server of choice (in the case of this chapter, a NodeJS-based web server) that intercepts search engine crawlers' requests and sends these requests to the PhantomJS server. This component is specific to your web server, but Prerender has guides to integrating this component into common web server tools like Nginx, Apache, and Ruby on Rails on `http://www.prerender.io`. The Prerender middleware for NodeJS is available on npm as `prerender-node`. You can install this package by running `npm install` from the directory containing this chapter's sample code. Unfortunately, the `prerender-node` middleware is currently only compatible with the Express web framework, which is currently the most popular web server framework in the NodeJS community. Express 4.8.5 is included as a dependency in the `package` `.json` for this chapter's sample code, so if you haven't run `npm install` yet, do so to install the two Prerender components and Express. Here's the web server that you will use to serve the HTML pages in this section:

```
var express = require('express');
var prerender = require('prerender-node');

var app = express();
app.use(prerender);
app.use(express.static('./'));

app.listen(8080);

console.log('Listening on port 8080');
```

If you're unfamiliar with Express, don't worry; all you really need to understand is that the preceding code creates a web server on port 8080 with two middleware functions: the Prerender middleware, and then the static middleware that returns static files from the current directory (that is, responds to `http://localhost:8080/foo.html` with the contents of `./foo.html`). Try starting this server with node `server_prerender.js` and navigating to `http://localhost:8080/part_iii_seo.html`. This page is the search-engine-friendly version of `part_iii.html`, and, as such, it has a couple of small additions. To understand what makes `part_iii_seo.html` special, you need to understand how Google's crawler handles AJAX-heavy pages.

The Google AJAX Crawling Spec

The Google AJAX crawling spec defines how search engine crawlers should handle JavaScript-heavy pages like AngularJS SPAs. You can read the full spec for enrichment at `http://developers` `.google.com/webmasters/ajax-crawling/docs/specification`, but for the purposes of AngularJS SPAs, the following brief summary should be sufficient.

The AJAX crawling spec exists to help crawlers identify JavaScript-heavy pages and account for the fact that, in SPAs, there are no page reloads. Essentially, when a crawler finds an a tag whose `href` starts with #! (the spec calls this a *pretty URL*), it assumes this link will cause JavaScript to transform the page. Note that a pretty URL must start with #!, to enable the crawler to distinguish between a link that indicates client-side routing and a link that simply saves the user's scroll position. The crawler then converts the pretty URL into a so-called *ugly URL*, which replaces the #! with `?_escaped_fragment_=`. For example, in the case of your book catalog SPA, the crawler will see a pretty URL similar to `part_iii_seo.html#!/book/5` and try to crawl the corresponding ugly URL `part_iii_seo.html?_escaped_fragment_=/book/5`. Because this transformation puts the hash portion of the URL into the query portion, your web server will actually receive the client-side route.

You may be wondering, now that your web server receives the client-side route in the `_escaped_fragment_` query parameter, how your server should handle it. The answer is, you've already done all the necessary work! The Prerender middleware handles this case by intercepting any requests that have the `_escaped_fragment_` query parameter and sending them along to the PhantomJS server. The PhantomJS server returns your SPA view as static HTML, your web server sends this static HTML to the crawler, and the crawler happily indexes your HTML.

Configuring AngularJS for Search Engines

Now that you've created your server setup for SPA search engine integration, you need to make a couple of minor tweaks to your AngularJS SPA. First of all, you need to add one line of code to your HTML head tag:

```
<head>
  <title>Part III: Basic SPA with SEO</title>

  <meta name="fragment" content="!">
</head>
```

This line of code enables Google to identify this page as an SPA right off the bat. Remember, search engine crawlers are good at following conventional HTML links and not much else. If the crawler couldn't identify this page as an SPA, it wouldn't know to add the _escaped_fragment_ query parameter; thus, the crawler would just see an empty page. With this meta tag, crawlers know to rerequest the page with an _escaped_fragment_ query parameter to get the prerendered page.

Also, you need to make a minor change to your AngularJS app configuration. Recall that AngularJS by default uses # instead of #! for client-side routing. Thankfully, AngularJS makes this easy to configure:

```
booksModule.config(function($routeProvider, $locationProvider) {
  $routeProvider.
    when('/', {
      templateUrl: 'part_iii_master.template.html',
      controller: BooksController
    }).
    when('/book/:id', {
      templateUrl: 'part_iii_detail.template.html',
      controller: BookDetailController,
      reloadOnSearch: false
    });

  $locationProvider.html5Mode(false);
  $locationProvider.hashPrefix('!');
});
```

The hashPrefix() function allows you to set any string to be placed between # and / in your client-side routes. This really only has one use case: inserting the ! necessary for search engine integration. The html5Mode() function enforces that AngularJS use its legacy URL configuration, which is necessary to get client-side routing to work in non-HTML5 browsers.

Search Engine Integration in Action

Congratulations! You've done all the work necessary to make sure your SPA is properly crawlable. The last step is putting it all together and seeing your SPA the way a crawler would see it. Open two terminals and navigate to this chapter's sample code. The Makefile contains two simple commands: make phantomjs-server starts the Prerender PhantomJS server, and make seo-web-server starts the Prerender-enabled web server. Run make phantomjs-server in the first terminal window and make `seo-web-server` in the second. Now you should be able to open `http://localhost:8080/part_iii_seo.html?_escaped_fragment_=/` in your browser and see the static HTML version of your book catalog!

Try clicking on the title of `Les Miserables`. The path in the browser address bar should change to `/part_iii_seo.html?_escaped_fragment_=/#!/book/1`. A properly configured crawler would replace this with `/part_iii_seo.html?_escaped_fragment_=/book/1`. Try navigating to that URL, and you should see your prerendered detail view for *Les Miserables*!

> **NOTE** *For a production application, you would preferably run your PhantomJS server on a different machine and leverage the Prerender PhantomJS server's caching ability. The setup you worked with in this section is ideal for instructional purposes, but there would be significant performance overhead in having your single production machine evaluating client-side JavaScript every time a crawler tries to crawl your page. If this performance impact would be unacceptable, you can either set up the PhantomJS server on a separate machine with a local Redis or MongoDB cache, or simply use Prerender's paid service.*

Introduction to Animations

AngularJS 1.1.5 introduced an exciting feature: the ability to use CSS3 animations to animate transitions between views! Transitions can make your UI much more intuitive by demonstrating navigation between pages through motion. For example, often mobile apps that utilize the master detail design pattern slide detail views in from the right and then slide them out to the right. This integrates particularly well with the common mobile browser convention that swiping left on a page functions effectively triggers the "back" button. AngularJS animations make it easy for you to integrate this functionality into your SPAs.

> **NOTE** *AngularJS animations require a browser that supports CSS3 animations. Recent versions of Chrome, Firefox, and Safari all support CSS3 animations. However, you need Internet Explorer 10 or greater for CSS3 animation support.*

Similar to the `ngRoute` module, AngularJS animation support is in a separate `ngAnimate` module. To use this module, you should download the version of `angular-animate.js` corresponding to your preferred version of the AngularJS core from `http://code.angularjs.org`. For your convenience, the version of `angular-animate.js` corresponding to AngularJS 1.2.16 is packaged with this chapter's sample code. Once you've included `angular-animate.js` using a `script` tag, you also need to add a dependency on the `ngAnimate` module:

```
var booksModule = angular.module('booksModule',
    ['ngRoute', 'ngAnimate']);
```

To effectively use the `ngAnimate` module, you need to understand the basics of the CSS3 `@keyframes` rule. The `@keyframes` rule is the primary building block for CSS3 animations: It allows you to define a transition from one set of CSS values to another. For instance, here is an example usage of the `@keyframes` rule that you'll use in this section to cause a view to gradually move on to the screen from the right:

```
@keyframes slideInRight {
    from    { transform:translateX(100%); }
    to      { transform: translateX(0); }
}
```

The most basic usage of the `@keyframes` rule uses the `from` and `to` keywords to indicate the starting and ending state for the animation, respectively. At the start of the animation, the browser applies the CSS styles corresponding to the `from` keyword and makes a linear transition to the styles corresponding to the `to` keyword. In the preceding case, when the animation starts, the associated element is translated off the far right of the screen, and at the end it is at its normal position. However, the `@keyframes` rule only defines an animation at a high level. To add concrete animations to your SPA, you need to use the CSS3 `animation` rule.

> **NOTE** *For more sophisticated animations, the* `@keyframes` *rule allows you to specify points in the animation by percentages. That is, you can tell the* `@keyframes` *rule that your animation should have a certain set of CSS properties 22 percent through the animation and another at 48 percent. The* from *keyword corresponds to 0 percent and the* to *keyword to 100 percent. However, this functionality is typically only useful for creating compound animation: for example, creating a bounce animation where an element slides to the left and then slides back to the right. In the context of transitions between views in AngularJS, however, this functionality is usually unnecessary, because an entry animation like a fade or a slide-in doesn't require multiple components.*

The CSS3 `animation` rule allows you to attach actual animations (that is, animations defined by the `@keyframes` rule) to CSS selectors. Here's an example of an `ng-enter` CSS class you'll be using in this section that enables you to use the `slideInRight` `@keyframes` rule:

```
.ng-enter {
    animation:slideInRight 0.25s both linear;
}
```

Any element that has this `ng-enter` CSS class is animated whenever it's created (or whenever it's marked with the `ng-enter` CSS class by JavaScript). Earlier, you specified four properties for the animation. The first argument, the `animation-name` property, is set to `slideInRight`, the name of the `@keyframes` rule to use. The second argument, the `animation-duration` property, is set to `0.25s`, meaning that the animation should take place over 0.25 seconds. The third argument, the `animation-fill-mode` property, is set to `both`, meaning that the `from` CSS styles of the keyframe should be applied before the animation starts and the `to` CSS styles of the keyframe should persist after the animation finishes. Finally, the fourth argument, the `animation-timing-function` property, is set to `linear`, meaning that the element should slide in at a constant speed.

Note that there's nothing special about the name `ng-enter` just yet. You can name this class whatever you want and see the same effect, but the significance of the name `ng-enter` will become clear once you start using the `ngAnimate` module.

The ngAnimate Module in Action

Now that you have a basic grasp of how the CSS3 `@keyframes` and `animation` rules work, you're ready to add some basic animations to your book catalog SPA. You're going to create a couple of basic transitions between the master view and the detail view. Specifically, when a user clicks on a book on the master view, the master view slides out to the left and the detail view slides in from the right. Conversely, when the user clicks on the back link on the detail view, the detail view slides out to the right and the master view slides in from the left. The overall effect is that the detail view is "to the right of" the master view. You can see this example in action in this chapter's sample code under `part_iii_animations.html`.

To achieve this effect, you're going to need four distinct animations. The master view needs to be able to slide in from the left and slide out to the left, and the detail view needs to be able to slide in from the right and slide out to the right. Thus, you're going to need four `@keyframes` rules:

```
@keyframes slideOutRight {
  to    { transform: translateX(100%); }
}
@-moz-keyframes slideOutRight {
  to    { -moz-transform: translateX(100%); }
}
@-webkit-keyframes slideOutRight {
  to    { -webkit-transform: translateX(100%); }
}

@keyframes slideOutLeft {
  to    { transform: translateX(-100%); }
}
@-moz-keyframes slideOutLeft {
  to    { -moz-transform: translateX(-100%); }
}
@-webkit-keyframes slideOutLeft {
  to    { -webkit-transform: translateX(-100%); }
}

@keyframes slideInRight {
  from { transform:translateX(100%); }
  to    { transform: translateX(0); }
}
@-moz-keyframes slideInRight {
  from { -moz-transform:translateX(100%); }
  to    { -moz-transform: translateX(0); }
}
@-webkit-keyframes slideInRight {
  from { -webkit-transform:translateX(100%); }
```

```
  to    { -webkit-transform: translateX(0); }
}

@keyframes slideInLeft {
  from  { transform:translateX(-100%); }
  to    { transform: translateX(0); }
}
@-moz-keyframes slideInLeft {
  from  { -moz-transform:translateX(-100%); }
  to    { -moz-transform: translateX(0); }
}
@-webkit-keyframes slideInLeft {
  from  { -webkit-transform:translateX(-100%); }
  to    { -webkit-transform: translateX(0); }
}
```

The -moz-keyframes and -webkit-keyframes rules are unfortunately necessary because, in current versions of Chrome and older versions of Firefox, plain old @keyframes is not supported. Similarly, you need to add -webkit-animation and -moz-animation to the actual CSS classes:

```
.master-view.ng-enter {
  z-index: 1;
  -webkit-animation:slideInLeft 0.25s both linear;
  -moz-animation:slideInLeft 0.25s both linear;
  animation:slideInLeft 0.25s both linear;
}
.master-view.ng-leave {
  -webkit-animation:slideOutLeft 0.25s both linear;
  -moz-animation:slideOutLeft 0.25s both linear;
  animation:slideOutLeft 0.25s both linear;
}

.detail-view.ng-enter {
  z-index: 1;
  -webkit-animation:slideInRight 0.25s both linear;
  -moz-animation:slideInRight 0.25s both linear;
  animation:slideInRight 0.25s both linear;
}
.detail-view.ng-leave {
  -webkit-animation:slideOutRight 0.25s both linear;
  -moz-animation:slideOutRight 0.25s both linear;
  animation:slideOutRight 0.25s both linear;
}
```

Note that the preceding CSS rules target multiple classes. That is, the .detail-view.ng-leave rule is only applied to elements that have both the detail-view class and the ng-leave class. The reason for targeting the detail-view class is so you can specify a different animation for the detail view than the master view. You can attach a CSS class to your views like so:

```
<div  ng-view="true"
      class="{{pageClass}}"
      style="position: absolute"
      autoscroll="true">
</div>
```

You can then assign a value to the `pageClass` variable in each of your view's controllers. For instance, here's what you can do in the master view's controller:

```
function BooksController($scope, $books) {
  $scope.pageClass = 'master-view';
  // ... rest of code
}
```

Now, the trickier question is, why the `ng-enter` and `ng-leave` classes? The `ngAnimate` module adds these classes to elements that are being created or destroyed, respectively. In the particular case of views in SPAs, when a view is about to be switched out, the `ngAnimate` module adds the `ng-leave` class and waits for the animations to finish before destroying the element. When a view is about to be switched in, the `ngAnimate` module adds the `ng-enter` class, waits for animations to finish, and removes the `ng-enter` class.

> **NOTE** *You may have noticed that, in this section, the* `ngView` *element is set to use* `position: absolute`*. One particularly tricky detail to get right with animations is making sure that, although both the entering and leaving* `ngView` *elements are visible, both elements are on the same level vertically. Typically, when you have two* `div` *elements with the same parent, the second appears below the first unless you reposition them with CSS. Using absolute positioning is typically the easiest way to make sure one view doesn't affect another's position during the animation process.*

And that's all the work you need to do to animate your SPA! Once you've included the `ngAnimate` module, most of the work comes down to creating CSS classes. When you have the CSS classes down, as long as your animations are well designed, you can make your app's UI considerably more intuitive.

CONCLUSION

Congratulations! You've just built your first AngularJS SPA, complete with search engine compatibility and animations. SPAs are a powerful paradigm that gives the developer more fine-grained control over the page's UX, as well as potentially better performance through a cleaner separation of templates and data. However, SPAs aren't the right choice for every application. For simple search-engine-dependent sites like blogs, an SPA may be overkill if a simple static HTML site is sufficient. In learning about SPAs, however, you also learned about AngularJS templates and the `$location` service, which can infuse powerful functionality into conventional multiple-page applications. Thus, even if you decide an SPA isn't the right choice for your application, you can still derive benefits from templates and the `$location` service.

7

Services, Factories, and Providers

WHAT YOU WILL LEARN IN THIS CHAPTER:

- ➤ The basics and benefits of dependency injection
- ➤ Inferred, annotated, and inline function annotation
- ➤ Tying your services into the dependency injector
- ➤ The three ways to create a service
- ➤ Common use cases for services
- ➤ Using providers to configure AngularJS

WROX.COM CODE DOWNLOADS FOR THIS CHAPTER

You can find the wrox.com code downloads for this chapter at http://www.wrox.com/go/proangularjs on the Download Code tab.

AngularJS is roughly equal parts library and framework. In addition to providing you with sophisticated tools, it provides a structure for organizing your code. In particular, AngularJS's dependency injection supplies a framework for writing code that is highly reusable, highly modular, and easy to unit test. If you've written an AngularJS controller before, you've used dependency injection. For instance, in the next example, $scope and $http are services that the dependency injector passes to the MyController function:

```
function MyController($scope, $http) {
  // Code here
}
```

You may have taken it for granted that AngularJS does some magic to pass the right parameters to MyController so that you can access the correct $scope and make HTTP requests with $http. This particular magic is known as *dependency injection*, and $scope and $http are services. A *service* is some JavaScript variable uniquely identified by its name that the dependency injector knows about. *Factories* and *providers* are two ways to construct services that you'll learn about in this chapter.

A BRIEF OVERVIEW OF DEPENDENCY INJECTION

Dependency injection is a design pattern first coined by Martin Fowler in 2004 to manage complexity in Java. Despite its beginnings in the Java community, dependency injection has spread to scripting languages like JavaScript. In particular, Google's emphasis on dependency injection internally made it a core AngularJS feature from the beginning.

The general idea of Google-flavored dependency injection is that business logic and dependency construction should never happen in the same block of code. Or, to put it in more concrete terms, the if keyword and the new keyword should never occur in the same function, with the exception of creating data-only objects. Although this principle is controversial, it is an integral part of how AngularJS works. To take full advantage of AngularJS, you should understand the reasoning behind this principle.

Typically, large JavaScript codebases break up their code into small manageable functions and objects. However, managing the interaction between these functions and objects becomes quite tricky as your codebase grows. For instance, in AngularJS 1.2.16, the commonly used $http service depends on six other services, and most AngularJS developers haven't used them directly. To make matters more confusing, some of these services have their own dependencies. The primary purpose of dependency injection is to wrap the process of constructing the $http service and its dependencies in a convenient way. This way, the end user doesn't have to worry about the internals of how the $http service is constructed, and someone working on the implementation of the $http service doesn't have to worry about how the underlying dependencies are constructed.

Of course, there is an alternative approach to using dependency injection: the *singleton* design pattern. Instead of explicitly declaring dependencies in function parameters, you can rely on the global state and create one instance of the $http service attached to the global window object. This may seem like an appealing approach, because constructing a single global $http object seems like it addresses the issue of abstracting away the $http object's dependencies. However, AngularJS's use of the admittedly more complex dependency injection pattern isn't born of a pedantic masochism: There are tremendous benefits to using dependency injection.

Like all approaches that rely on the global state, the singleton pattern is difficult to unit test and is inherently limited in its ability to adapt based on context. The reason the singleton pattern is tricky to unit test is fairly straightforward: To stub out the $http object for one test, you have to modify the global state and thus modify it for *all* tests. This puts extra onus on developers to clean up after themselves and can introduce difficult-to-diagnose failures into your tests. The singleton pattern's inability to adapt to different contexts becomes clearer when you consider the most common AngularJS service: the $scope service. Although it's often sufficient to consider the $http service as a singleton, the $scope service provides a different scope object for every controller. That's because the AngularJS dependency injector can inspect AngularJS's internal state and your app's configuration to provide the correct scope object based on context, whereas a singleton requires a separate indirection layer to make sure you got the correct scope.

> **NOTE** *If you are a devotee to the singleton design pattern, try not to use it too much in the context of AngularJS. Although the singleton design pattern has its merits, using it means you're fighting against one of AngularJS's core tenants and thus making your life more difficult by dividing your house against itself.*

The $injector Service

Interestingly enough, the dependency injector itself is available as a service. The $injector service provides access to the dependency injector object that AngularJS itself uses to create controllers, services, and directives. The $injector service is not used frequently in production code (although you will see a use case later in this chapter), but it is a convenient learning tool for exploring some of the more subtle features of dependency injection.

You may have noticed that, to tell the dependency injector that you wanted the $http services, you put it as a function parameter:

```
function MyController($http) {
  // Code here
}
```

Under the hood, AngularJS's $controller service creates this controller using the $injector service's invoke() function. The invoke() function handles figuring out what parameters need to be passed to the MyController function and executes the function. For instance, you can run the MyController function using this:

```
$injector.invoke(MyController);
```

Or you can simply inline the function that the $injector service should execute:

```
$injector.invoke(function($http) {
  // Use $http here
});
```

In the previous code snippet, $http is a service registered with the dependency injector. However, you'll notice that, in the code, the omnipresent $scope parameter is absent. That's because $scope isn't a service; it's a local. For reasons that you'll learn about when you start writing your own services, the way AngularJS uses $scope is incompatible with services. To make this work, the invoke() function actually takes three parameters. The second is a context (which you can ignore), and the third is a map of locals. To properly inject a $scope variable, you would do something like what follows. Once again, recall that this is an academic exercise to explain where the $scope variable comes from. You will probably never use this code in a real application:

```
$injector.invoke(
  function($scope, $http) {
    // Use $scope, $http here
  },
  null,
  { $scope: {} });
```

The `$injector` service is fairly simple, but there's one important point that these examples have glossed over: How does AngularJS know what parameters should be passed to the `MyController` function? In the previous examples, you've simply assumed that AngularJS can figure out which services and locals to pass in based on parameter names. Turns out, there are several ways to tell the dependency injector which services to pass to your controller or service.

Function Annotations

In the context of AngularJS, a *function annotation* is how you tell the dependency injector which services to inject into the function. The previous approach is called *inferred* function annotation, because the dependency injector infers the services from the function parameters. AngularJS does this by calling the `toString()` function: In JavaScript, calling `toString()` on a function returns a string containing the full function definition, including parameter names. Inferred function annotation is more intuitive and more commonly used than the other function annotation strategies.

Where the inferred function annotation strategy comes short, however, is when dealing with JavaScript *minifiers*. Because browser-side JavaScript is typically transferred over the Internet, developers are often tasked with keeping JavaScript file size small for improved page load times. A minifier performs operations like removing unnecessary whitespace to convert readable JavaScript into a form optimized for file size. Aggressive minifiers take advantage of a technique called *mangling*, which shortens commonly used variable names. For instance, if your code uses a variable called `$$__superInternalCache` very often, a minifier with mangling may replace that variable name with something shorter, like `a`.

Minifiers that mangle variable names can trip you up if you're using inferred function annotation, because your minifier may rename your `$scope` parameter to something else, say `b`. The dependency injector will then look for a service named `b` as opposed to `$scope`. Most AngularJS developers use *inline* function annotation to make sure the dependency injector knows which services to use even after mangling variable names:

```
myModule.controller('MyController',
  ['$scope', '$http', function($scope, $http) {
    // Code
  }]);
```

The preceding approach works because minifiers never mangle the contents of strings—imagine a minifier that mangled the text of error messages! The particulars of inline function annotation are clearer when illustrated using the `$injector` service—that is, the dependency injector service:

```
$injector.invoke(['$scope', '$http', function(s, h) {
  // Code
}]);
```

Inline function annotation is represented by passing an array to the `$injector.invoke()` function. When the `$injector.invoke()` function gets an array, it assumes that the last element in the array is the function to execute, and every element before that represents a parameter that should be passed into the function. Unlike inferred function annotation, inline function annotation doesn't rely on the function's parameter names (or even the number of parameters) at all, which is why the previous function can use `s` and `h` instead of `$scope` and `$http`.

> **NOTE** *Some of the AngularJS documentation uses inline function annotation without explaining the reasoning, so many AngularJS developers use inline function annotation by default. This is not necessarily a good idea, because inline function annotation is more difficult to read. Inline function annotation also opens the door to the questionable practice of using different names for AngularJS services, like* scope *instead of* $scope, *which further decreases readability.*

The third and oldest function annotation strategy is called $inject annotation. AngularJS veterans may recall that this was the only function annotation strategy in AngularJS 0.9.x. Similar to the inferred annotation strategy, you pass a function to $injector.invoke (or module.controller or module.service) but give it an $inject property like this:

```
function MyController(s, h) {}
MyController.$inject = ['$scope', '$http'];

$injector.invoke(MyController);
myModule.controller('MyController', MyController);
```

When you pass a function to $injector.invoke, AngularJS first checks for an $inject property. If it does not exist, the dependency injector falls back to inferred function annotation. This $inject annotation strategy is not typically used, because it requires an extra line to declare the $inject property and is thus more verbose. However, like inline function annotation, it does offer support for minifiers that mangle variable names.

That's all on function annotations. To recap, there are three strategies: inferred, inline, and $inject. Inferred is the simplest and most commonly used, but it doesn't behave well with minifiers that mangle variable names. Inline and $inject enable you to use dependency injection with minifiers that mangle variable names. They are essentially interchangeable, but inline function annotation is considerably more popular in the AngularJS community.

BUILDING YOUR OWN SERVICES

Now that you have a basic understanding of how AngularJS dependency injection works, it's time to write some real services. Over the course of this section, you'll use services to build a simple stock market dashboard using the Yahoo Finance application programming interface (API). You may notice that this code is similar to the Stock-Dog application that's used in other chapters. However, this section expands on the Stock-Dog code to demonstrate different ways of creating services, so if you've dug into the Stock-Dog code already, you'll have a small head start. The code presented in this section is available in this chapter's sample code. (It's independent of the Stock-Dog codebase.) You can run the sample code by simply opening the individual files in the browser using file:///. A server is not required to view the Hypertext Markup Language (HTML) pages in this chapter. However, one example utilizes a simple NodeJS web server (see provider_backend.js in this chapter's sample code), so if you have not installed NodeJS yet, you should go to nodejs.org and follow the installation instructions for your platform of choice.

AngularJS module objects have five functions that declare services to the dependency injector. The three most common ways are the `service()`, `factory()`, and `provider()` functions alluded to in this chapter's title. In this section, you'll first learn about the `service()` and `factory()` functions, which are the most commonly used approaches to define custom services. Then you'll learn about the `provider()` function, which allows you to configure your services in sophisticated ways. Finally, you'll learn a little about the `constant()` and `value()` functions, which are not used often but can be quite useful in certain situations.

The factory() Function

The first function you'll learn about is the `factory()` function. This is the simplest and most common way to create a service in AngularJS, and you will see it in virtually every AngularJS codebase. Fundamentally, a *factory* is a function that the dependency injector uses to create an instance of the service. Syntactically, a factory looks like this:

```
myModule.factory('$myService', function() {
  var myService = {};
  // Construct myService

  return myService;
});
```

The `factory()` function thus enables you to tell the dependency injector to use the given function to construct your arbitrary `$myService` service. The return value of the given function is injected into any function that lists `$myService` as a dependency. For example:

```
myModule.factory('$myService', function() {
  var myService = {
    foo: "bar"
  };

  return myService;
});

myModule.controller('MyController', function($myService) {
  console.log(myService.foo); // Prints "bar"
});
```

A factory can take parameters through dependency injection, so you can reuse services like `$http` (or even your own custom services) in your services. Many AngularJS codebases like to use services as wrappers around specific `$http` calls, so they don't need to reuse the same logic in different controllers. As a matter of fact, the factory you'll be writing for your stock market dashboard does precisely that. Just be careful not to introduce cycles in your dependency graph: If service A requests service B from the dependency injector, and service B then requests service A from the dependency injector, AngularJS throws an error.

Here's an example of constructing a service that actually does something useful. The task of building a stock market dashboard may seem daunting, but a good programmer always remembers the Chinese proverb that "a journey of a thousand miles begins with a single step." In that vein, your first service is the simplest unit of work for building such a dashboard: Your service loads the current Google stock price (Google's stock ticker is GOOG). You can find this code in this chapter's sample code as factory.html. Once again, there is no server component to this chapter, so you can just open this file directly in the browser or use your web server of choice:

```html
<div ng-controller="MyController">
    <h1>Google Stock Price: {{price.quotes[0].Ask}}</h1>
</div>

<script type="text/javascript" src="angular.js"></script>
<script type="text/javascript">
  var chapter7Module = angular.module('chapter7Module', []);

  chapter7Module.factory('$googleStock', function($http) {
    var BASE = 'http://query.yahooapis.com/v1/public/yql'

    var query = encodeURIComponent (
      'select * from yahoo.finance.quotes where symbol in (\'GOOG\')');
    var url = BASE + '?' + 'q=' + query +
      '&format=json&diagnostics=true&env=http://datatables.org/alltables.env';

    var service = {};
    service.get = function() {
      $http.jsonp(url + '&callback=JSON_CALLBACK').
        success(function(data) {
          if (data.query.count) {
            var quotes = data.query.count > 1 ? data.query.results.quote :
            [data.query.results.quote];
            service.quotes = quotes;
          }
        }).
        error(function(data) {
          console.log(data);
        });
    };

    service.get();
    return service;
  });

  function MyController($scope, $googleStock) {
    $scope.price = $googleStock;
  }
</script>
```

The preceding $googleStock service is a prototypical example of how factories are typically used: The factory creates a plain object, decorates it with some properties and functions, and returns the object. (In JavaScript parlance, *decorating* an object means adding properties and methods to make the object match a certain interface.) In addition, you will often see custom services as wrappers around an $http call or several closely related $http calls.

There is one subtle yet crucial fact about services that makes them indispensible for wrapping $http calls: Services are always *singletons* (although this term does not mean they use the global-state-dependent singleton design pattern!) in the sense that there is one instance of the service that's shared between all controllers and services that use it. In other words, if another controller on the same page depended on the $googleStock service, the service would only execute the initial $http call to the Yahoo Finance API once. This is extremely important for your app's performance, because typically the biggest bottleneck in AngularJS apps is $http calls, so you don't want to incur unnecessary round trips to the server. However, this is also why $scope isn't a service: $scope needs to be different in each controller, so having a $scope service wouldn't make sense.

One common pattern for services that wrap $http calls you'll see is demonstrated by the preceding $googleStock service and its get() function. In this case, there is only one $http call, whose sole responsibility is to load all the data from the API at once. That data can be hidden behind a function or, as in the preceding case, exposed as a simple property of the service. In this case, the $googleStock service loads a list of quotes from the Yahoo Finance API and exposes it as the quotes property. AngularJS's data binding (see Chapter 4) is sophisticated enough to know when the $http call has returned and the quotes property has been updated.

This design pattern has an inherent trade-off: Should the service itself handle reloading data, or should it delegate that task to the controller? Typically, a service that uses this design pattern has an initial call to load the data. Some services use the $interval service to periodically refresh the data or even use web sockets to update the data in real time. However, other services may choose to allow the controller to handle refreshing the data, perhaps whenever the user clicks a button. Both of these approaches are common, and either can be right depending on the situation. Handling refreshing in the service provides a convenient layer of abstraction and eliminates the possibility for accidental redundant requests from different controllers. However, you may need different refresh rules for different controllers, or you may need to tie the data refresh call into the user interface (UI), in which case, delegating responsibility to the controller may be the right choice.

The service() Function

The redundantly named service() function is another convenient way of creating a service. As you'll see, the service() function offers essentially the same functionality as the factory() function, with a few academic differences. Like the $inject function annotation strategy, the service() function is a vestigial remnant from AngularJS's experimental 0.9 versions. The factory() function provides essentially equivalent functionality in a more elegant and modern interface, but you will still see the service() function in use.

The difference between the service() function and the factory() function is that, whereas the factory() function requires you to construct an object in your code and return it, the function you pass to the service() function is executed using JavaScript's new operator. In other words, when using the service() function, you don't have to explicitly construct and return a new object; you simply need to attach properties to this. Here's how using the service() function looks in real JavaScript:

```javascript
myModule.service('$myService', function() {
  this.foo = "bar";
});

myModule.controller('MyController', function($myService) {
  console.log(myService.foo); // Prints "bar"
});
```

As you can see, the service() function is roughly equivalent to the factory() function. As a matter of fact, you can pass the functions you used with factory() in the previous section into the service() function and get the same result. The service() function is often more succinct. However, the this keyword is confusing and difficult to use properly in JavaScript, and many developers avoid using it out of principle. If you are going to use the service() function, be careful when using the this keyword in nested functions. In this section's sample code, you'll see one of the several approaches to minimizing your risk with using the this keyword.

> **NOTE** *Depending on your definition of an object-oriented programming language, JavaScript may or may not be object oriented. What is for certain is that common object-oriented paradigms like inheritance, constructors, and the* this *keyword exist in JavaScript, but they work in ways that will be completely alien to developers who are used to languages like C++ or Java. Thankfully, AngularJS doesn't force you into attempting to approximate object-oriented programming in JavaScript.*

In this section, you utilize the service() function to create a slightly more complex version of your stock market dashboard using another common service design pattern. The problem this service addresses is handling the case in which the user has a long list of stocks he wants prices for. In fact, you assume the list is so long that loading the prices all at once from the Yahoo Finance API is too slow. For the sake of convenience, assume that the following list of 11 technology stocks is sufficiently long:

```
var stocks = [
  'GOOG', // Google
  'AAPL', // Apple
  'MSFT', // Microsoft
  'YHOO', // Yahoo
  'FB',   // Facebook
  'AMZN', // Amazon
  'EBAY', // Ebay
  'ADBE', // Adobe
  'CSCO', // Cisco
  'QCOM', // Qualcomm
  'INTC'  // Intel
];
```

Instead of exposing a function to load the whole list and storing the last result like you did in the previous section, you expose a function to load more stock prices and store all the prices loaded so far. The user then has a convenient Load More button to request more data from the server. You can find this code in this chapter's sample code as service.html:

```
<div ng-controller="MyController">
  <h1 ng-repeat="quote in stocks.quotes">
    {{quote.Symbol}}: {{quote.Ask}}
  </h1>
  <span style="background-color: green" ng-click="stocks.getMore()">
```

```
      Load More
    </div>
  </div>

<script type="text/javascript" src="angular.js"></script>
<script type="text/javascript">
  var chapter7Module = angular.module('chapter7Module', []);

  chapter7Module.service('$stocks', function($http) {
    var BASE = 'http://query.yahooapis.com/v1/public/yql'
    var _this = this;

    var stocks = [...];

    var load = function(stocks) {
      var query = encodeURIComponent (
        'select * from yahoo.finance.quotes where symbol in (\'' + stocks.
      join(',') + '\')');
      var url = BASE + '?' + 'q=' + query +
        '&format=json&diagnostics=true&env=http://datatables.org/alltables.env';

      $http.jsonp(url + '&callback=JSON_CALLBACK').
        success(function(data) {
          if (data.query.count) {
            var quotes = data.query.count > 1 ?
            data.query.results.quote :
            [data.query.results.quote];
            _this.quotes = _this.quotes.concat(quotes);
          }
        }).
        error(function(data) {
          console.log(data);
        });
    };

    this.quotes = [];
    this.getMore = function() {
      load(stocks.slice(this.quotes.length, this.quotes.length + 5));
    };

    this.getMore();
  });

  function MyController($scope, $stocks) {
    $scope.stocks = $stocks;
  }
</script>
```

The preceding getMore() function is tied to the Load More button that allows the user to request the stock price of the next five technology stocks from the Yahoo Finance API. This design pattern may not seem terribly different from the one in the previous section, where you simply load all the data at once, but it is sufficiently common and sufficiently different to warrant its own discussion. The often-used master-detail design (in which you have a *master* view that lists items and a *detail* view for detailed information for a specific item) often benefits from using this pattern to load elements in batches, particularly if the master list is long. This way, you don't incur the massive overhead of loading all the stocks at once.

Another important detail worth noticing is the _this variable, which is set to be equal to this. If you're an experienced JavaScript developer, you may very well have seen something like this before, but the reasoning for this may not be clear to the uninitiated. The short answer is that, in JavaScript, this is a special variable that doesn't necessarily respect the scope hierarchy that JavaScript variables otherwise fall into. Note that the earlier load() helper function is declared using the var keyword. Because of the way this function is declared, in the load() helper function body, this refers to the global window object instead of to the service object. To make things more confusing, this behavior is environment dependent; if you're running tests in NodeJS, in the load() helper function body, this refers to the NodeJS global object. However, if you were to attach the load() helper function to the service—that is, this.load = function() {}—this would refer to the service in the function body. In other words, the JavaScript this keyword is surprisingly complex, and even seasoned JavaScript developers make mistakes with it.

One of the most common ways to sidestep the peculiarities of JavaScript's function context is to alias this as _this so you can use it as a conventional JavaScript object with normal lexical scoping. However, this (pun intended) is one of the primary reasons factory() is typically preferred to service(). In JavaScript, constructing an empty object and decorating it with various functions and properties is typically easier to write and understand than finagling with the this keyword.

> **NOTE** *JavaScript functions have a* lexical *scope, which behaves much like a scope in any programming language, and a* context, *which determines what* this *refers to. The context is completely independent of the function's lexical scope, and the built-in JavaScript functions* call(), apply(), *and* bind() *allow you to modify and call JavaScript functions with arbitrary contexts. In other words,* this *can refer to any object of any type depending on the function's context, and the object referred to by* this *doesn't have to be in the function's lexical scope hierarchy. This is why, although JavaScript technically can be called an object-oriented programming language, writing JavaScript as if you were writing Java or C++ is at best wasteful and at worst produces unmaintainable spaghetti code. Use the* this *keyword judiciously: If your code is confusing to you, odds are its also confusing to the next person who will work on it. In other words, remember legendary computer programmer Brian Kernighan's classic adage, "Debugging is twice as hard as writing the code in the first place. Therefore, if you write the code as cleverly as possible, you are, by definition, not smart enough to debug it."*

There is one more important detail about the relationship between the factory() and service() functions that's worth noting. Any service that you've registered using the factory() function can be registered using the service() function with no change. However, the opposite is absolutely *not* true: A service registered with the service() function probably won't work right when registered using the factory() function. This is due to one of JavaScript's myriad peculiar quirks: A JavaScript constructor can return a value, and, if that value is an object or an array, the resulting object of the new operator will be the return value. Here's a summary of JavaScript's quirky behavior with return values from constructors:

```
var Constructor1 = function() {
  this.value = "From Constructor";
  return { value: "From Return Value" };
};
console.log((new Constructor1()).value); // "From Return Value"

var Constructor2 = function() {
  this.value = "From Constructor";
  return;
};
console.log((new Constructor2()).value); // "From Constructor"

var Constructor3 = function() {
  this.value = "From Constructor";
  return 42;
};
console.log((new Constructor3()).value); // "From Constructor"

var Constructor4 = function() {
  this.value = "From Constructor";
  return [];
};
console.log((new Constructor4()).value); // undefined
```

Now that you've learned how to construct basic services using the mostly interchangeable `factory()` and `service()` functions, you're going to learn how to construct configurable services using providers. The `factory()` and `service()` functions create services the same way every time, but providers effectively enable you to switch which factory function the dependency injector uses to construct a given function. In this next section, you learn about how providers work and why they are useful.

The provider() Function

The `provider()` function is the most expressive way to create services, and, correspondingly, the most complex. At a high level, the `provider()` function lets you determine which service to register based on application-wide configuration. As a matter of fact, under the hood, the `factory()` and `service()` functions you just learned about are implemented as syntactic sugar on top of the `provider()` function. For most cases, the `provider()` function is overkill, and you often build out an entire AngularJS app without creating a single provider. However, as you'll see in this section, providers are extremely useful for testing and debugging. Furthermore, even if you don't need to write your own providers, many built-in services expose configuration options through providers. In this section, you'll create your own provider for your stock market dashboard. After you've written your own provider, you'll use the built-in `$httpProvider` and `$interpolateProvider` providers to tweak some core AngularJS features.

So far, you've learned that providers allow you to construct different services based on application-wide configuration. But where does the application-wide configuration come from? To answer this question, you need to learn about AngularJS modules' `config()` function. You may have used this function before to configure your single-page app routing (see Chapter 9, "Testing and Debugging AngularJS Applications") or set the maximum number of times a `$digest` loop should execute (see Chapter 4, "Data Binding"). These are just two examples of what the `config()` function can do. The primary purpose of the `config()` function is to configure the application's providers so the application uses the correct services. The contents of a `config()` function are typically called a *configuration block*. AngularJS runs your configuration blocks in order before any controllers, services, or directives are instantiated. Syntactically, a configuration block looks like this:

```
var app = angular.module('myApp', []);

app.config(function($httpProvider) {
  // Use $httpProvider here
});
```

Note that configuration blocks are the *only* place where you can access providers through dependency injection rather than the services themselves. For instance, you can't access `$httpProvider` in a controller:

```
app.controller('MyController', function($httpProvider) {
  // Error! $httpProvider can't be injected into a controller. Angular will
  // say it can't find $httpProviderProvider
});
```

In addition, you can *only* access providers in a configuration block, not concrete services. For instance, you can't access `$http` in a configuration block:

```
app.config(function($http) {
  // Error! AngularJS will say it can't find a provider
  // named $http
});
```

The preceding code represents roughly the extent of what you need to know about configuration blocks to develop your own providers. Although they may seem intimidating, configuration blocks are actually just a simple tool for interfacing with providers. Now that you understand how configuration blocks work, you're going to learn about providers by writing one.

A common application of providers is the ability to switch parameters like the server uniform resource locator (URL) without having to tweak your business logic. This is particularly useful for development and test environments. In particular, providers enable you to have your production JavaScript communicate with your production server and your test JavaScript communicate with your test server, without having to modify your business logic. As an example of this particular application, you're going to make the API endpoint that the `$googleStock` service uses. To see this in action, here is the code from `provider.html`, which will be your "production" application:

```
<body>
  <div ng-controller="MyController">
    <h1>Google Stock Price: {{price.quotes[0].Ask}}</h1>
```

```
    </div>

    <script type="text/javascript" src="angular.js"></script>
    <script type="text/javascript" src="provider.js"></script>
  </body>
```

And your "development" application, `provider_dev.html`, will be just slightly different. Note that to get `provider_dev.html` to work properly, you need to start the stubbed-out Yahoo Finance back end available in this chapter's sample code as `provider_backend.js` by running `node provider_backend.js`. This back end server mimics the Yahoo Finance API's output format but returns 42 for the stock price every time:

```
<html ng-app="chapter7Module">
  <head>
    <title></title>
  </head>

  <body>
    <div ng-controller="MyController">
      <h1>Google Stock Price: {{price.quotes[0].Ask}}</h1>
    </div>

    <script type="text/javascript" src="angular.js"></script>
    <script type="text/javascript" src="provider.js"></script>
    <script type="text/javascript">
      chapter7Module.config(function($googleStockProvider) {
        $googleStockProvider.setEndpoint('http://localhost:8080/?');
      });
    </script>
  </body>
</html>
```

As a matter of fact, the development environment is identical, except for one configuration block where you're telling the provider to use the fake back end running on port 8080 on your local machine. This setup is helpful for doing development work in a place where you have an unreliable internet connection, or if you want to write tests that are independent of the Yahoo Finance API.

Now that you've seen what the interface you want to provide looks like, it's time to look at how to actually implement this simple provider. This code is available in this chapter's sample code as `provider.js`:

```
var chapter7Module = angular.module('chapter7Module', []);

chapter7Module.provider('$googleStock', function() {
  var endpoint = 'http://query.yahooapis.com/v1/public/yql';
  var query = encodeURIComponent (
    'select * from yahoo.finance.quotes where symbol in (\'GOOG\')');
  var url = endpoint + '?' + 'q=' + query +
    '&format=json&diagnostics=true&env=http://datatables.org/alltables.env';

  this.setEndpoint = function(u) {
    url = u;
```

```
        };

        this.$get = function($http) {
          var service = {};
          service.get = function() {
            $http.jsonp(url + '&callback=JSON_CALLBACK').
              success(function(data) {
                if (data.query.count) {
                  var quotes = data.query.count > 1 ?
                    data.query.results.quote :
                    [data.query.results.quote];
                  service.quotes = quotes;
                }
              }).
              error(function(data) {
                console.log(data);
              });
          };

          service.get();
          return service;
        };
      });

      function MyController($scope, $googleStock) {
        $scope.price = $googleStock;
      }
```

As you can see, the `provider()` function works somewhat like a wrapper around the `service()` function. The actual function you pass to the `provider()` function is called using the `new` keyword, so you can attach properties using the `this` keyword. Every provider must define a `$get` function, which is what AngularJS uses to construct the actual service.

When constructing the service, the `$get` function is executed using the `new` operator, so you can use either `service()` function or `factory()` function semantics (decorating `this` versus creating an object, decorating it, and returning it). You'll notice that the `$get` function is virtually identical to the function you used to define the `$googleStock` factory. The only difference is the fact that the `url` and corresponding variables have moved up into the provider scope; the rest of the function is identical. Moving the `url` variable into the provider's scope enables you to create the `setEndpoint()` function. This function allows your configuration block to change the URL your server uses to load the stock price. You can think of a provider as enabling you to expose an API for configuring your service.

One particularly interesting application of providers is that, because JavaScript allows you to overwrite object properties, you can overwrite the provider's entire `$get` function in a configuration block. This lets you completely replace any service, whether your own custom service or a built-in service, in a configuration block. For instance, suppose you didn't want to have a version of this stock dashboard that didn't rely on network input/output (I/O) at all and instead displayed a fixed price. You can write a configuration block that overwrites the `$googleStock` service's `$get` function:

```
<body>
  <div ng-controller="MyController">
    <h1>Google Stock Price: {{price.quotes[0].Ask}}</h1>
```

```
    </div>

    <script type="text/javascript" src="angular.js"></script>
    <script type="text/javascript" src="provider.js"></script>
    <script type="text/javascript">
      chapter7Module.config(function($googleStockProvider) {
        $googleStockProvider.$get = function() {
          return { quotes: [{ Ask: 100 }] };
        };
      });
    </script>
  </body>
```

Here, at configuration time, you've overwritten the entire $googleStock service to simply return a hard-coded object. You could just as easily replace the $http service or the $compile service, although doing so is not recommended because AngularJS uses these built-in services internally, too.

So far, you've learned the basics of working with providers. Providers are a layer on top of services that enable you to define an API for configuring your services in configuration blocks. Although the technical details are fairly straightforward, there are myriad use cases for services and providers. In the next section, you explore a pair of use cases for services and providers and learn about their corresponding design patterns.

COMMON USE CASES FOR SERVICES

In this chapter so far, you have learned the technical details of how to create services and providers, but you've only scratched the surface of the benefits that services provide in the context of real application development. In this section, you build out more of your stock market dashboard, and, in the process, learn how to use services properly.

A common question AngularJS novices ask is, how do you share data between two controllers on the same page? Once your applications become sufficiently complex that you have multiple unrelated controllers in the same view, you still want to share certain pieces of information, like "what user is currently logged in?" between the controllers. Some developers ameliorate this difficulty by putting a top-level controller on every page that's responsible for loading common data and attaching it to the page's root scope. This may seem convenient, but this approach puts dependency management into your HTML templates (because all your controllers depend on the top-level controller). This is awful for readability and fails to take advantage of AngularJS's dependency injector. It's why, in general, services are the preferred approach for sharing state between controllers.

The most important reason services are so excellent for sharing state between controllers is that, as you saw earlier in this chapter, services are singletons. In the context of AngularJS, the term *singleton* means that there is at most one instance of a service at any time during your application's life cycle. (Once again, don't confuse this term with the common global-state-dependent singleton design pattern.) For instance, say one of your controllers used the $http service and set a property on the $http object, perhaps $http.foo = 5. After you do this, every other controller and service that uses the $http service can see that $http.foo is equal to 5, because $http is the same object in every controller and service.

The advantages of this may not seem clear when considering the $http service; however, think about the alternative example of a $user service that tracks the currently logged-in user. Suppose the purpose of this service is to load the currently logged-in user from an API endpoint and then enable the user to change her profile picture. Further, suppose you have two completely independent controllers—one that helps display your page's navigation bar and one that enables the user to change her profile picture. Both controllers depend on the $user service. Because the $user service is a singleton, there will be only one $http request to load the data about the logged-in user, and when one controller modifies the user's profile picture, the other controller's $user service reflects the change. In this next section, you apply this idea to build a minimal $user service for your stock market dashboard. You can find all the code for this section in the stock_dashboard.html file from this chapter's sample code.

Building a $user Service

In this chapter so far, you've only displayed the prices for a hard-coded list of stocks—either just the Google stock price or an array of 11 technology company stocks. In this section, you expand this functionality to allow an individual user to specify a list of stocks he's interested in tracking. Specifically, your $user service exposes an array of stock symbols, which your $stockPrices service uses to know which stocks' prices it should ask the Yahoo Finance API for. In this section, you don't create a server component to store and load the currently logged-in user, because setting up a server and a database adds a significant amount of complexity to this example and thus detracts from its usefulness as a learning exercise. Thus, the save() and load() functions on the $user service are stubs, but the design pattern is the same as if you had a real server. Here is what your $user service looks like:

```
chapter7Module.factory('$user', function() {
  var user = {
    data: {
      stocks: ['GOOG', 'YHOO']
    }
  };

  user.load = function() {
    // Stub for server call
  };

  user.save = function(callback) {
    // Stub for server call;
  };

  user.load();
  return user;
});
```

This service uses the factory() function, and, by default, the user is watching Google and Yahoo's stock prices. Furthermore, when the $user service is created, it automatically loads the currently logged-in user from the server. In this case, this operation is a stub, but converting it to a server call is straightforward. There is only one controller that interfaces with this service directly: a controller that enables the user to add new stocks to his watchlist:

```
function ModifyStockListController($scope, $user, $stockPrices) {
  $scope.addToStockList = function(stock) {
```

```
                    $user.data.stocks.push(stock);
                    $user.save();
                    $stockPrices.load();
                }
            }
```

This controller provides an interface for your HTML templates to be able to add a new stock to the user's watchlist, save the user's information, and reload all the stock prices so the user has an up-to-date snapshot. Here's how an HTML template that utilizes `ModifyStockListController` might look:

```html
<div ng-controller="ModifyStockListController">
    <h1>Add new stock:</h1>
    <input type="text" ng-model="newStock">
    <input type="submit"
            ng-click="addToStockList(newStock); newStock = '';">
</div>
```

This particular example has a simple input field and a submit button that calls the `addToStockList` function and empties the input field. These three code examples make up half of the services—controllers that are in your stock market dashboard. The other half, primarily based on the `$stockPrices` service, is responsible for actually loading and displaying the stock prices. This code is the subject of the next section.

Building the $stockPrices Service

The `$stockPrices` service loads and displays the prices for the stocks in the `$user` service's watchlist. Once again, services are singletons, so the `$stockPrices` service has the same `$user` object as the controllers. The `$stockPrices` service looks similar to the `$googleStock` service from previous sections, but it gets its list of symbols from the `$user` service's watchlist. Here's the `$stockPrices` service from `stock_dashboard.html`:

```javascript
chapter7Module.factory('$stockPrices', function($http, $user, $interval) {
  var service = {
    quotes: []
  };
  var BASE = 'http://query.yahooapis.com/v1/public/yql';

  service.loading = false;
  service.load = function() {
    service.loading = true;
    var query = encodeURIComponent('select * from yahoo.finance.quotes where '+
      symbol in (\'' + $user.data.stocks.join(',') + '\')');
    var url = BASE + '?' + 'q=' + query +
      '&format=json&diagnostics=true&env=http://datatables.org/alltables.env';

    $http.jsonp(url + '&callback=JSON_CALLBACK').
      success(function(data) {
        service.loading = false;
        if (data.query.count) {
          var quotes = data.query.count > 1 ?
```

```
              data.query.results.quote :
              [data.query.results.quote];
            service.quotes = quotes;
          }
      }).
      error(function(data) {
        console.log(data);
      });
    };

    service.load();
    $interval(service.load, 5000);
    return service;
});
```

This service has a `load()` function that loads the full list of stock prices from the Yahoo Finance API. Like many services that do asynchronous I/O, the `load()` function sets a `loading` flag to `true` when it's waiting for an HTTP request to return, so the UI can show a loading indicator to the user. In addition, this service uses the `$interval` service, which you may have never seen before. The `$interval` service is a convenience wrapper around JavaScript's `setInterval()` function, which schedules a function to execute repeatedly at a certain interval. The `$interval` service ties the `setInterval()` function into data binding, so you don't have to worry about calling `$scope.$apply()` in the function you pass to the `$interval` service. In the `$stockPrices` service, you called the `$interval` service to schedule the `service.load` function to execute every 5000 milliseconds (5 seconds).

Now that you have the `$stockPrices` service to load the prices for the stocks in the user's watchlist, it's time to tie this service into the UI. To do this, you need a simple controller:

```
function DisplayPricesController($scope, $stockPrices) {
  $scope.stockPrices = $stockPrices;
}
```

The HTML that utilizes this controller should look pretty familiar from previous sections. The only difference is that this HTML utilizes a simple loading indicator to inform the user when there's an outstanding HTTP request:

```
<div ng-controller="DisplayPricesController">
  <h1>My Stock Prices</h1>
  <em ng-show="stockPrices.loading">
    Loading...
  </em>
  <div ng-repeat="quote in stockPrices.quotes">
    {{quote.Symbol}}: {{quote.Ask}}
  </div>
</div>
```

Note that neither `DisplayPricesController` nor the HTML template have a dependency on the `$user` service. Good services build layers of abstraction on top of other services. One symptom of poorly designed AngularJS code is controllers and services with long dependency lists, because each dependency makes your controller or service more complex. Ideally, your controllers and services should have no more than five dependencies, and if you have a controller with more than 10 dependencies, you should strongly consider breaking up the controller into more manageable chunks. Services provide a nice framework for doing this: because they're tied in to dependency injection, you can create services that isolate complex pieces of functionality from controllers. In the stock market dashboard example, you can easily combine the functionality from `DisplayPricesController` and `ModifyStockListController` into a single controller. However, having them separate makes them simpler and more manageable. If your controllers are experiencing too much code bloat, you should split them into multiple controllers and services.

Now that you've learned of some use cases for services in the context of building real applications, you have all the information you need to write your own basic services. For the rest of this chapter, you switch gears and discover how you can use AngularJS's built-in providers to configure your application. These built-in providers allow you to tweak core AngularJS services in numerous, surprising ways.

UTILIZING BUILT-IN PROVIDERS

In the section on providers, you learned that providers enable you to configure services for use in different applications and different environments. AngularJS's built-in providers offer some limited yet exceedingly useful configuration options that enable you to tweak how AngularJS's core functionality works. In this section, you learn about three neat tricks you can do with built-in providers and configuration blocks. First you learn how to change the interpolation delimiters (that is, the {{ }} symbols that you've used to tie in to data binding). Second, you learn about a tool to protect your users from malicious links. Third and finally, you learn another way to extend the AngularJS expression language with custom functions and values.

Custom Interpolation Delimiters

In certain cases, the default {{ }} interpolation delimiters can be limiting. For instance, the Go programming language's server-side HTML templating package also uses {{ }} to delimit template code, and this option is not configurable. Fortunately, you can easily modify AngularJS's delimiters in a configuration block using the `$interpolationProvider` provider. Here's how you can use square braces (that is, `[[ ]]`) as interpolation delimiters:

```
var myModule = angular.module('myModule', []);

myModule.config(function($interpolateProvider) {
  // Use [[ ]] to delimit AngularJS bindings, because using
  // {{ }} confuses Go
  $interpolateProvider.startSymbol('[[');
  $interpolateProvider.endSymbol(']]');
});
```

Now you can write your HTML templates using square braces as interpolation delimiters. For example, here's the `custom_delimiters.html` example file from this chapter's sample code:

```
<div ng-controller="MyController">
  <h1>
    This app uses
```

```
      <em>[[delimiter]]</em>
      as interpolation delimiters
    </h1>
  </div>

  <script type="text/javascript" src="angular.js"></script>
  <script type="text/javascript">
    var myModule = angular.module('myModule', []);

    myModule.config(function($interpolateProvider) {
      $interpolateProvider.startSymbol('[[');
      $interpolateProvider.endSymbol(']]');
    });


    function MyController($scope) {
      $scope.delimiter = 'square braces';
    }
  </script>
```

The `startSymbol` and `endSymbol` functions allow you to set whatever custom delimiters you want. For example, the AngularJS documentation uses // as the start and end delimiter in its sample code. However, there's a couple of good reasons why most applications don't set custom delimiters. First, most AngularJS developers are used to using {{ }}. Even if this is a minor tweak, it's a minor tweak across all your HTML templates, which adds an extra hurdle to working effectively with your codebase. Second, curly braces have one big advantage over square braces or slashes: Curly braces are explicitly not allowed in URLs (at least according to RFC 3986, the technical specification on URLs). In other words, `google.com/[[]].html` is technically a valid URL, but `google.com/{{}}.html` is not. Therefore, when using curly braces, you don't have to worry about static URLs accidentally confusing AngularJS's interpolator.

In short, be careful with setting custom interpolation delimiters. The default delimiters are the right choice for most applications. However, for cases like using AngularJS with the Go programming language's server-side templating library, custom delimiters are indispensible.

Whitelisting Links with $compileProvider

AngularJS data binding is powerful, but its expressive nature has security implications. AngularJS is designed to avoid common vulnerabilities by default, but it is easy to override the default settings and unintentionally expose your users to malicious JavaScript if you aren't careful. For example, consider the following seemingly innocuous HTML:

```
<a ng-href="{{goodLink}}">This is a link!</a>
```

To the untrained eye, this may seem safe, but warning sirens should be going off in your head when you see code like this. The `goodLink` variable can redirect an unsuspecting user to *any* URL. If a malicious user could set the value of the `goodLink` variable, they could make your page execute arbitrary JavaScript by setting the `goodLink` variable to something like this:

```
hackerLink = 'javascript:window.alert(\'You just got hacked!\')';
```

This is a classic example of what web developers call a *cross-site scripting* vulnerability, or an XSS vulnerability for short. By default, AngularJS protects you from this by not allowing URLs to start with `javascript:`. Specifically, the `$compileProvider` has a regular expression that it uses to *whitelist* absolute URLs: Any URL that matches the whitelist regular expression is considered okay; any URL that doesn't is prefixed with `unsafe?` so clicking on it won't redirect the user or execute any JavaScript. Keep in mind that AngularJS converts URLs to absolute URLs (that is, `/path` to `protocol://domain/path`) before checking if the URL matches the whitelist regular expression, so your whitelist regular expression should assume an absolute URL.

You can get or set the whitelist regular expression using the `$compileProvider` provider's `aHrefSanitizationWhitelist()` function. The following code, from the `xss_vulnerable.html` file in this chapter's sample code, demonstrates what happens when you set the whitelist regular expression to accept any string:

```
<div ng-controller="MyController">
  <a ng-href="{{goodLink}}">Google!</a>
  <hr>
  <a ng-href="{{okLink}}">Not Google</a>
  <hr>
  <a ng-href="{{hackerLink}}">XSS Link</a>
</div>

<script type="text/javascript" src="angular.js"></script>
<script type="text/javascript">
  var myModule = angular.module('myModule', []);

  myModule.config(function($compileProvider) {
    $compileProvider.aHrefSanitizationWhitelist(/.*/);
  });

  function MyController($scope, $http) {
    $scope.goodLink = 'http://www.google.com';
    $scope.okLink = 'http://www.notgoogle.com';
    $scope.hackerLink = 'javascript:window.alert(\'You just got hacked!\')';
  }
</script>
```

Try clicking on the XSS link, and you'll see an alert pop up. Naturally, you don't want malicious users running arbitrary JavaScript in your users' browsers. By default, AngularJS 1.2.16 uses the following regular expression to whitelist URLs:

```
/^\s*(https?|ftp|mailto|tel|file):/
```

This regular expression does a reasonable job of preventing exploits like the XSS example from earlier. In particular, AngularJS blacklists any URLs that start with `javascript:`, which is the most common source of XSS vulnerabilities. When you open the `xss_default.html` file from this chapter's sample code in your browser, you see the first two links are whitelisted, and the third link, the XSS link, is prefixed with `unsafe:`.

```
<body>
  <div ng-controller="MyController">
    <a ng-href="{{goodLink}}">Google!</a>
```

```
      <hr>
      <a ng-href="{{okLink}}">Not Google</a>
      <hr>
      <a ng-href="{{hackerLink}}">XSS Link</a>
    </div>

    <script type="text/javascript" src="angular.js"></script>
    <script type="text/javascript">
      var myModule = angular.module('myModule', []);

      myModule.config(function($compileProvider) {
        // Use default a[href] whitelist
      });

      function MyController($scope, $http) {
        $scope.goodLink = 'http://www.google.com';
        $scope.okLink = 'http://www.notgoogle.com';
        $scope.hackerLink = 'javascript:window.alert(\'You just got hacked!\')';
      }
    </script>
  </body>
```

This default is sufficient for most applications, but you may want to be strict and ensure users can't link to another website. In this case, the whitelist regular expression is helpful. In fact, you can make it so that only links to, say, the google.com domain are allowed, and malicious users can't post links to Bing. Open the xss_extra_strict.html file from this chapter's sample code in your browser, and you'll see that both the XSS link and the "Not Google" link are marked as unsafe:

```
  <body>
    <div ng-controller="MyController">
      <a ng-href="{{goodLink}}">Google!</a>
      <hr>
      <a ng-href="{{okLink}}">Not Google</a>
      <hr>
      <a ng-href="{{hackerLink}}">XSS Link</a>
    </div>

    <script type="text/javascript" src="angular.js"></script>
    <script type="text/javascript">
      var myModule = angular.module('myModule', []);

      myModule.config(function($compileProvider) {
        console.log($compileProvider.aHrefSanitizationWhitelist());
          $compileProvider.aHrefSanitizationWhitelist(
            /^https?:\/\/(www\.)?google\.com(\/.*)?/i);
      });

      function MyController($scope, $http) {
        $scope.goodLink = 'http://www.google.com';
        $scope.okLink = 'http://www.notgoogle.com';
        $scope.hackerLink = 'javascript:window.alert(\'You just got hacked!\')';
      }
    </script>
  </body>
```

And now you've successfully made it impossible for links in your application to link to anywhere but Google. As you can see, providers let you do some useful high-level configuration. The defaults are sufficient for most applications, but you may find yourself needing to set custom delimiters or disallow certain URLs. Configuration blocks and providers enable you to make these configuration changes on a per-application basis.

Global Expression Properties with $rootScopeProvider

One of the most common sources of confusion with AngularJS is the fact that expressions don't have access to functions and properties that are in the global scope, such as encodeURIComponent. In Chapter 4, "Data Binding," and Chapter 5, "Directives," you learned that expressions are the JavaScript code that you put into your templates via directives like ngClick. You may have noticed that using the following code in your template won't work because AngularJS thinks encodeURIComponent is undefined:

```
{{ encodeURIComponent('A, B, & C') }}
```

In Chapter 4, you learned that you can ameliorate this issue by writing a filter to wrap the encodeURIComponent function. However, there is also a neat way to enable you to expose encodeURIComponent and any other value or function you may want to all your templates using providers and configuration blocks.

AngularJS has a service called $rootScope. As you might have guessed, this service gives you access to the root scope in your page's scope tree—that is, the scope that's an ancestor of every other scope. In particular, properties attached to $rootScope are available in every scope on your page. And, conveniently, AngularJS has a corresponding $rootScopeProvider that you can access in a configuration block.

However, this is where you run into a small difficulty: $rootScopeProvider exposes no configuration API in AngularJS 1.2.16. In other words, there's no officially documented way to configure $rootScopeProvider. Fortunately, as you learned earlier in this chapter, you can always overwrite the $get function on $rootScopeProvider and thus return your own service. Although this approach may seem hacky and impossible to maintain, the AngularJS dependency injector and the fact that functions in JavaScript are first-class members makes it possible to do this without needing to duplicate the actual implementation of $rootScopeProvider.$get:

```
<body>
  <div ng-controller="MyController">
    {{ encodeURIComponent(stringToEncode) }}
  </div>

  <script type="text/javascript" src="angular.js"></script>
  <script type="text/javascript">
    var chapter7Module = angular.module('chapter7Module', []);
    chapter7Module.config(function($rootScopeProvider) {
      var oldGet = $rootScopeProvider.$get;
      $rootScopeProvider.$get = function($injector) {
        var rootScope = $injector.invoke(oldGet);

        rootScope.encodeURIComponent = encodeURIComponent;
```

```
            rootScope.stringToEncode = 'A, B, & C';

            return rootScope;
        };
    });

    function MyController($scope) {
    }
    </script>
</body>
```

The fundamental idea in the preceding code is that the oldGet variable is a pointer to the original $rootScopeProvider.$get function. Once you have this pointer, you can overwrite the $rootScopeProvider.$get property to use the dependency injector to call the original $get function and attach some additional properties to the service. This enables you to extend AngularJS expressions in whatever way you choose in a configuration block.

> **NOTE** *The previous example demonstrates the most common application of the $injector service in real AngularJS applications. When the $injector service is used, often it's to achieve an "inheritance" effect like you see in the previous code, such as attaching properties to a provider by overwriting its $get function. Another application is simplified controller inheritance: running $injector.invoke on a controller function to attach that controller's functions and properties to the current controller's $scope.*

CONCLUSION

In this chapter, you learned about the AngularJS dependency injector, the three ways to register a service with the dependency injector, and some convenient tricks to configure AngularJS using providers. Services provide a convenient framework for breaking up complex code into smaller, more manageable chunks. In particular, because the dependency injector makes sure there is at most one instance of any service, services are extremely useful as wrappers around data loaded from a remote server via an HTTP request.

Providers are a layer on top of services that supply an API for configuring services using the config() function. They are useful for exposing options such as which server the service should load data from. In addition, built-in providers let you configure core AngularJS services.

Now that you have read the basics of how services are created and what they're useful for, you are ready to explore the internal structure of just about any AngularJS application. Services are used extensively in virtually any AngularJS application. If you find an app that doesn't use services, odds are it can be greatly simplified by adding a few well-designed services.

8

Server Communication

WROX.COM CODE DOWNLOADS FOR THIS CHAPTER

You can find the wrox.com code downloads for this chapter at http://www.wrox.com/go/proangularjs on the Download Code tab.

WHY WILL I LEARN?

Most modern web applications need to communicate with a server. Whether you're loading data from a public REST application programming interface (API) or sending data to your server for storage, server communication is the way your application acquires and persists data. In this chapter, you discover the mechanisms that AngularJS provides for loading data from APIs. You are exposed to basic best practices of RESTful APIs and generate a simple NodeJS back-end API server using StrongLoop's LoopBack framework. You also learn about AngularJS Hypertext Transfer Protocol (HTTP) interceptors, a powerful abstraction for handling errors. Finally, you will discover two mechanisms for using AngularJS to build real-time applications: web sockets and Google's Firebase framework.

> **NOTE** *You may have heard of the term* REST, *in phrases like* REST API *or* RESTful API. *REST, which stands for Representational State Transfer, is a paradigm for designing APIs that are accessed via HTTP. The most fundamental principle of REST is to use HTTP methods to describe specific actions on resources. Using the* POST *method tells the server to create a resource,* GET *to read an existing resource,* PUT *to update an existing resource, and* DELETE *to delete an existing resource. The operations create, read, update, and delete are commonly abbreviated as CRUD operations.*

This chapter's sample code uses NodeJS to serve as a back end for your HTTP requests and web sockets. If you have not installed NodeJS yet, please navigate to `nodejs.org/download` and follow the installation instructions for your operating system of choice. You will write a minimal amount of server-side JavaScript when you use LoopBack to generate a REST API. However, in the other sections, you will not need to write server-side JavaScript.

INTRODUCTION TO PROMISES

A *promise* is an object representing a value to be computed at some point in the future. In other words, a promise is an object-oriented construct for dealing with asynchronous operations. JavaScript HTTP requests are asynchronous, meaning that code that makes an HTTP request continues executing without waiting for the server to return a response. Promises provide a convenient alternative to callbacks or event emitters for handling asynchronous functions.

> **NOTE** *At the time of this writing, the two most common promise specifications are Promises/A+ and ECMAScript 6. The ECMAScript 6 specification is effectively a superset of Promises/A+. The two specifications are interoperable, except that the ECMAScript 6 specification specifies several extra functions, including* catch() *and* all()*. The promises returned by AngularJS'* $http *service support most of the features of the ECMAScript 6 standard, plus a few convenient helpers. Promises are currently a fragmented concept, so you should not write your code under the assumption that all ECMAScript 6 promises features are available.*

The core feature of promises is the `then()` function. This function is universal across the most popular JavaScript promises libraries. It takes two function parameters: `onFulfilled` and `onRejected`. Both parameters are optional: if `onFulfilled` or `onRejected` is not a JavaScript function, it is ignored. These two functions are handlers for the only state transitions allowed for a promise. Promises can be in one of three states: pending, fulfilled, or rejected. A promise starts out in the pending state and then can transition to the fulfilled or rejected state. Once a promise is fulfilled or rejected, it can't change state. Following is an example of the basic syntax of promises:

```
var promise = new Promise();

promise.then(function(v) {
  console.log(v); // Prints "Hello, world"
});

promise.fulfill('Hello, world');
```

> **NOTE** *One key feature of promises is that, if an* onFulfilled *function is attached after the promise is already fulfilled, that* onFulfilled *function must be called. In other words, if you surrounded the* then() *call in the preceding example in a* setTimeout() *function, the preceding code would still print "Hello, world," after a small delay. Contrast this behavior with the event emitter paradigm that is used heavily in Chapter 3, "Architecture." Any listener registered after you emit an event does not see that event. This contrast makes promises a better choice for wrapping single asynchronous calls.*

The then() function returns a new promise that wraps both the promise and the onFulfilled function you passed to then(). In particular, your onFulfilled function can return a promise that enables you to chain asynchronous calls. For instance, the following code prints out "hello, world" (all lowercase) after 1 second:

```
var promise = new Promise();

promise.
  then(function(v) {
    var newPromise = new Promise();

    setTimeout(function() {
      newPromise.fulfill(v.toLowerCase());
    }, 1000);

    return newPromise;
  }).
  then(function(v) {
    console.log(v);
  });

promise.fulfill('Hello, world');
```

Note that the first then() call returns a promise. Promises are smart enough to know that if then() returns a promise, the library should wait for the returned promise to be fulfilled before passing the value down the then() chain.

Promises are an integral tool for interacting with HTTP requests in AngularJS. Now that you have seen the basic concepts of promises, you will learn how HTTP requests work in AngularJS.

SERVICES FOR HTTP REQUESTS

As has already been stated, HTTP stands for Hypertext Transfer Protocol. You probably recognize this acronym from web addresses, such as `http://google.com`. HTTP is the most common mechanism for a web browser, like Google Chrome, to communicate with a server. For instance, every time you visit `http://google.com`, your browser makes an HTTP request to Google's servers and receives a response containing the HTML for Google's landing page. An HTTP response can contain virtually any type of content: HTML, images, or even JavaScript Object Notation (JSON).

The contents of an HTTP request are governed by an intricate standard. But for the purposes of this chapter, you are primarily concerned with four pieces of data associated with HTTP requests. The first piece of data is the *resource*, which is typically the part of the uniform resource locator (URL) after the domain name. For instance, when you navigate your browser to `http://google.com/maps`, the HTTP request to Google specifies the resource as `/maps`. The second piece of data is the *method* (sometimes referred to as the *verb*), which must be one of GET, HEAD, POST, PUT, DELETE, TRACE, OPTIONS, CONNECT, or PATCH. The method distinguishes between different actions you may want to take on a given resource. For instance, the POST method often means you want to create the resource you're requesting.

The third piece of information is the *headers*. The HTTP request headers are a set of key/value pairs that help the server interpret the request. The particulars of which HTTP headers you need depend on the server you are talking to. Finally, HTTP requests contain a *body*, which can hold additional data for the request. For instance, when using the POST method, the message body typically describes the resource you want to create. The HTTP requests you'll create in this chapter will send JSON in the message body.

The server responds to an HTTP request with an HTTP response. The response contains two pieces of information that will be important for this chapter. The first is the *status code*, which describes how the server handled the request. The particular semantics of individual status codes is a deep subject that isn't pivotal to understanding server communication in AngularJS. For the purposes of this chapter, it suffices to know that HTTP status codes consist of three numbers, and the first number indicates the high-level semantics of the response. Status codes that start with 2 (such as 200) indicate success. Status codes that start with 3 (such as 307) indicate that the requested resource moved. Status codes that start with 4 (such as 404) indicate that the request was invalid. Status codes that start with 5 (such as 500) indicate that the server experienced an error. Because status codes must be three digits, these status code classes are commonly abbreviated with the starting number followed by "xx." For instance, status codes that start with 2 are commonly abbreviated as "2xx status codes."

The second important piece of information is the response body, which, like the request body, contains additional data. In this chapter, the response bodies only contain JSON.

Browsers allow JavaScript to create and execute new HTTP requests (with some limitations that you'll learn about in this section). AngularJS has two services that wrap the native browser XMLHttpRequest class: $http and $resource. The $http service is comparatively low level and exposes a request and response abstraction around HTTP calls. The $resource service is more high level and provides an object-level abstraction—that is, loading and saving an object from the server as opposed to making requests directly. Both interact with the server via HTTP. In these next two sections, you learn the differences between $http and $resource and how to use them both effectively.

Note that the examples in this section utilize a NodeJS HTTP server to provide responses to your browser's HTTP requests. To run an example from this section's sample code, first run npm install from the root directory of this chapter's sample code. Then run node server.js to start an HTTP server on port 8080. Once you've started the HTTP server, you should be able to access the interceptor_example_1.html example by navigating to http://localhost:8080/interceptor_example_1.html.

$http

The $http service is AngularJS's low-level wrapper around native browser HTTP requests. In this section, you explore how to utilize the $http service to create HTTP requests, as well as how to configure the $http service using HTTP interceptors.

The semantics of the $http service are straightforward: The $http service exposes several functions to send an HTTP request to a server. These functions return a promise wrapper around the HTTP response from the server, which you use to capture the data that the server returns. Promises are the preferred mechanism of interacting with the $http service, which is why promises are important enough to have their own section.

Like many concepts in this book, the easiest way to learn about $http promises is by looking at a few basic examples. Typically, you will interact with the $http service by calling one of its HTTP method shortcuts. The $http service has methods corresponding to the GET, HEAD, POST, PUT, DELETE, or PATCH HTTP methods that create a new request with the given method. (There is also a helper function for JSONP, which you will learn about later.) For instance, to create a new HTTP request for the resource /maps with the GET method, you would use the following code:

```
$http.get('/maps');
```

The get() function returns an AngularJS HTTP promise that allows you to capture the eventual response from the server, as well as any error that might have occurred. You can attach handlers to the HTTP promise as shown here:

```
$http.get('maps').
  success(function(data, status, headers, config) {
    // data: parsed response body data
    // status: the response status code
    // headers: the HTTP response headers as a JavaScript map
    // config: the AngularJS http request configuration object
  }).
  error(function(data, status, headers, config) {
    // parameters have same semantics as earlier
  });
```

As you might have guessed, AngularJS executes the function passed to success() earlier when the HTTP request succeeded (that is, the server responded with a 2xx status code, such as 200). When the HTTP response indicates a failure (that is, the status code starts with 4 or 5, such as 404) AngularJS executes the function passed to error(). Browsers typically follow redirect responses

(responses with 3xx status codes, such as 307), so your AngularJS HTTP handlers should never see an HTTP 3xx status code.

Both the success and the error handler receive the same parameters. Typically, you will be most concerned with the `data` parameter, which contains the parsed response body. For the purposes of this chapter, the response body will always be JSON, and the `$http` service will automatically parse the JSON into a JavaScript object for you. The `status` parameter contains the HTTP response status code, which may be useful in interpreting the response. The `headers` parameter contains the HTTP response headers, which, like HTTP request headers, contain key/value pairs that may aid in interpreting the response. Finally, the `config` parameter contains the configuration of the original HTTP request, including the method, resource, and any custom headers you may have added.

Because JavaScript is flexible with the number of parameters a function should take, you can omit the last few parameters in your success and error handlers. For instance, success and error handlers that only take a `data` parameter are common:

```
$http.get('maps').
  success(function(data) {
    // Use data
  }).
  error(function(data) {
    // Use data
  });
```

This may seem heretical to developers who aren't familiar with JavaScript, but you can call any JavaScript function with any number of parameters. Even though AngularJS passes all four arguments to your handlers, your handlers can be functions that take a single parameter.

> **NOTE** *Note that, in the context of AngularJS's* `$http` *service, the term* promise *is used somewhat loosely. The* `$http` *service promises are typically used with different syntax than the promises you learned about in the "Introduction to Promises" section. However,* `$http` *service promises are technically compatible with both the Promises/A+ spec and ECMAScript 6 spec. For instance, given a function* `fn = function(data) {}`, *the usual* `$http.get('/test').success(fn)` *syntax is equivalent to* `$http.get('/test').then(function(res) { fn(res.data); })`.

Setting the HTTP Request Body

Typically, HTTP GET requests don't set a request body. However, in the RESTful paradigm, POST requests are used to create new resources. The preferred mechanism to describe the resource that a POST request wants to create is with JSON in the request body. The `$http` service makes setting the request body simple. Suppose you wanted to make a POST request with the JSON data `{ name: 'AngularJS' }` to the server. You could make the request as shown here:

```
var body = { name: 'AngularJS' };

$http.post('/test', body).
```

```
success(function(data) {
  // Handle response in the same way as get
});
```

Note that you must pass a JavaScript object as the second parameter to the `$http.post()` function, not a JSON string. The `$http` service takes care of converting the object to a string for you.

JSONP and Cross Site Scripting (XSS)

One important limitation on browser HTTP requests that often surprises new web developers is that you cannot make HTTP requests to different domains. For instance, if your JavaScript is executed on a page on the `foo.com` domain, you can only make HTTP requests to URLs on the `foo.com` domain. For instance, you can use the `$http` service to request `foo.com/resource1` or `subdomain1.foo.com/resource2`. This is a security restriction built into modern browsers.

However, there is a limited way to do cross-domain requests in JavaScript. JSONP, or "JSON with padding," utilizes the fact that you can load data from remote domains using HTML `script` tags. Fundamentally, JSONP inserts a `script` tag into the page, and the server responds with JavaScript code that contains the response data. AngularJS's `$http.jsonp()` function abstracts out the client-side code for implementing JSONP. As long as the remote server supports JSONP, you can use `$http.jsonp()` to make an HTTP request to the remote server in the same way you use other `$http` helpers. For instance, sample code in Chapter 7, "Services, Factories, and Providers," uses JSONP to load data from the Yahoo! Finance API, which runs on a remote domain:

```
$http.jsonp('http://query.yahooapis.com/v1/public/yql').
  success(function(data) {
  }).
  error(function(data) {
  });
```

Note that the remote server *must* be configured to support JSONP. Not all REST APIs support JSONP; the preceding example works only because the Yahoo! Finance API is configured to support JSONP.

HTTP Configuration Objects

So far in this chapter, you have used the `$http` service's helper functions, like `get()` and `post()`. However, the `$http` service exposes a much more general set of configurable parameters. In particular, you can use these configuration objects to set parameters like HTTP headers, the request body, and whether to use AngularJS's request cache. As a matter of fact, the `$http` service itself is a function that takes a single parameter: the request configuration object. For instance, the two HTTP calls in the following code are equivalent:

```
// Using the .get() helper...
$http.get('/test').
  success(function(data) {});

// is the same as passing a configuration option
// with 'method: 'GET'' to the $http() function.
$http({ method: 'GET', url: '/test' }).
  success(function(data) {});
```

The $http service supports numerous configuration options. The most commonly used ones are listed next:

➤ **method**—The HTTP method as a string, whether GET, POST, PUT, DELETE, HEAD, or JSONP.

➤ **url**—The absolute URL or the resource as a string. For instance, '/test'.

➤ **params**—A JavaScript object or string representing query parameters to be appended to the end of the URL in uniform resource identifier (URI)-encoded form. For instance, { a: 1, b: 2 } is appended to the end of the URL as "?a=1&b=2".

➤ **data**—The request body as a JavaScript object.

➤ **headers**—A JavaScript object that represents a map of HTTP headers. For instance, passing { a: 1, b: 2 } creates an HTTP request with two headers, a and b, with values 1 and 2, respectively. AngularJS ignores properties whose value is null or undefined.

➤ **timeout**—The number of milliseconds to wait for a response before triggering the error handler. Rather than specifying the number of milliseconds, you can set this property to a promise. The request times out when the promise is fulfilled unless it has already received a response.

In addition to passing the configuration to the $http() function directly, you can set configuration options in the $http service's helper functions. The $http.get() function takes a second parameter: the configuration object. For instance, you can set the GET request's query parameters and header information as shown next:

```
// GET /test?q=AngularJS, with "user" header set
// to "mobile"
$http.get('/test',
  {
    params: { q: 'AngularJS' },
    headers: { user: 'mobile' }
  });
```

The $http.post() and $http.put() functions take the configuration object as their third parameter, after the request body:

```
// POST /test?q=AngularJS, with "user" header set
// to "mobile", and "{ 'data': 'sample'}" as the body
$http.post('/test',
  {
    data: 'sample'
  },
  {
    params: { q: 'AngularJS' },
    headers: { user: 'mobile' }
  });
```

Setting Default HTTP Headers

Although you won't be relying on custom HTTP headers in this chapter's examples, many projects rely on headers for use cases like authentication. If your project requires sending custom headers, you should know that AngularJS gives you several mechanisms for automatically attaching headers to HTTP requests. Specifically, there are four ways that you can add headers to an HTTP request in AngularJS.

First, you can set headers on an individual HTTP request using the `$http` service. This is the most fine-grained way to set HTTP request headers:

```
$http.get('/maps',
  { headers: { myHeaderKey: 'myHeaderValue' } });
```

The `$http` service also has a `defaults.headers` object that defines headers that are added to *all* HTTP requests. Typically, you interact with this object in a `run()` block. For instance:

```
var myModule = angular.module('myModule');
myModule.run(function($http) {
  $http.defaults.headers.common.myCustomHeader =
    'myCustomHeaderValue';
});
```

This second method sets the `myCustomHeader` header for all HTTP requests, regardless of method. The `defaults.headers` object has several other properties, however. For instance, you can manipulate the `defaults.headers.get` object to set default headers for only those HTTP requests whose method is GET:

```
var myModule = angular.module('myModule');
myModule.run(function($http) {
  $http.defaults.headers.get.myCustomHeader =
    'myCustomHeaderValue';
});
```

The third mechanism you can use to set default HTTP headers is using the `$httpProvider` provider. If you want to learn more about the difference between services and providers, Chapter 7 includes a thorough discussion of the subject. For the purposes of this section, however, it suffices to know that you can only access the `$httpProvider` provider in a `config()` function. Otherwise, the semantics are identical to setting the `defaults.headers` object on the `$http` service. For instance, to set the `myCustomHeader` header for all HTTP requests with method POST with `$httpProvider`, you would use the following code:

```
var myModule = angular.module('myModule');
myModule.config(function($httpProvider) {
  $httpProvider.defaults.headers.post.myCustomHeader =
    'myCustomHeaderValue';
});
```

The fourth way to attach headers to an HTTP request involves AngularJS's ability to run functions on HTTP requests and responses before executing them. This functionality is exposed through HTTP *interceptors*, which enable you to define application-specific transformations at configuration time. Interceptors are the subject of the next section.

Using HTTP Interceptors

Interceptors are AngularJS's most flexible method for defining application-level rules for handling HTTP requests. This definition may sound vague, so consider the following task: Suppose you wanted to attach the HTTP response status to the body of every HTTP response so you could more easily tie the response status into your HTML. You could easily attach the status in every HTTP handler, as in the code that follows:

```
$http.get('/sample.json').
  success(function(data, status) {
    data.status = status;
    // Use data
  }).
  error(function(data, status) {
    data.status = status;
    // Use data
  });
```

However, you would have to remember to put the `data.status = status;` line in every HTTP handler, which is repetitive and error prone. Interceptors enable you to define a general rule for your application that attaches the HTTP status for you. You can find the following code in the `interceptor_example_1.html` file in this chapter's sample code. Don't forget that you need to start an HTTP server by running `node server.js` before opening this file in your browser as `http://localhost:8080/interceptor_example_1.html`:

```
<script type="text/javascript">
  var m = angular.module('myApp', []);

  m.config(function($httpProvider) {
    $httpProvider.interceptors.push(function() {
      return {
        response: function(response) {
          response.data.status = response.status;
          return response;
        }
      }
    });
  });

  m.controller('httpController', function($scope, $http) {
    $http.get('/sample.json').success(function(data) {
      console.log(JSON.stringify(data));
    });
  });
</script>
```

As in the preceding code, HTTP interceptors are defined as an array on the `$httpProvider` provider. Because providers can only be accessed in `config()` functions, interceptors must be defined in a `config()` function. An interceptor itself is a JavaScript object with an (optional) function `response` that defines how this interceptor transforms responses. This function takes a single parameter: a `response` object that contains all the information associated with the response, including the body, status, and headers. Following is the `response` object generated by the HTTP request in the `interceptor_example_1.html` example:

```
{
  "data": {
    "success": true
```

```
    },
    "status": 200,
    "config": {
      "method": "GET",
      "transformRequest": [
        null
      ],
      "transformResponse": [
        null
      ],
      "url": "/sample.json",
      "headers": {
        "Accept": "application/json, text/plain, */*"
      }
    },
    "statusText": "OK"
  }
```

The preceding highlighted snippets show where the body, status, and headers are defined. The body is accessed as `response.data`, the status as `response.status`, and the headers as `response.config.headers`.

> **NOTE** *The* `response` *object's* `statusText` *property contains the canonical (according to IETF RFC 2616 section 6.1.1) text equivalent to the numeric HTTP status. For instance, a response status of 200 means that* `statusText` *will always be* `OK` *and vice versa. Every other response status has a corresponding* `statusText`*; for instance, 404 corresponds to* `Not Found`*.*

Note that the `response` function *must* return the modified response; it provides an additional level of flexibility for interceptors. In other words, the `response` function can return an entirely new HTTP response. In fact, AngularJS supports the `response` function returning a promise, which means your interceptor can even make additional HTTP requests and utilize those responses. Be careful not to go overboard with making HTTP calls in interceptors, though: You can easily get stuck in an infinite loop because interceptors are executed on *all* HTTP requests.

Request Interceptors

Interceptors can transform HTTP requests as well as responses. Your interceptor can define a `request` function that takes the HTTP request configuration as a parameter. Like the `response` function, the `request` function must return the modified HTTP request.

A common use case for request interceptors is setting an HTTP `authorization` header for each request. In other words, you can use interceptors to attach credentials to each request (although whether you actually need to do so depends on your server). This use case highlights another important feature of interceptors: They are tied in to dependency injection, so your interceptors can access your services. This is particularly elegant because, as explained in Chapter 3, tracking the currently logged-in user is best done with a service. The following example code, which you can find in `interceptor_example_2.html`, defines a stubbed-out `userService` that your request interceptor uses to get credentials:

```javascript
var m = angular.module('myApp', []);

m.factory('userService', function() {
  return {
    getAuthorization: function() {
      return 'This is a fake authorization';
    }
  }
});

m.config(function($httpProvider) {
  $httpProvider.interceptors.push(function(userService) {
    return {
      request: function(request) {
        request.headers.authorization =
          userService.getAuthorization();
        return request;
      },
      response: function(response) {
        response.data.status = response.status;
        return response;
      }
    }
  });
});
```

The interceptor you defined earlier receives `userService` from the dependency injector and uses it to generate credentials. The interceptor then attaches these credentials to the request's `authorization` header. Thanks to the elegance of dependency injection, the `httpController` code from the `interceptor_example_1.html` example remains unchanged, even though the HTTP request now interacts with `userService`:

```javascript
m.controller('httpController', function($scope, $http) {
  $http.get('/sample.json').success(function(data) {
    console.log(JSON.stringify(data));
    $scope.data = data;
  });
});
```

Adding HTTP request headers is the most common use case for HTTP request interceptors. However, your interceptors can modify the request's method, body, or even its resource. Following is the request parameter that's passed to the request function in the `interceptor_example_2.html` example:

```javascript
{
  "method": "GET",
  "transformRequest": [
```

```
      null
    ],
    "transformResponse": [
      null
    ],
    "url": "/sample.json",
    "headers": {
      "Accept": "application/json, text/plain, */*"
    }
  }
}
```

The `method`, `url`, and `headers` properties shown earlier correspond to the request's method, resource, and headers. The request's body, if any, is contained in a `data` property that you can access with `request.data`. However, `GET` requests (as well as `HEAD` requests) typically don't have a body, so the `data` property is undefined in the preceding example.

> **NOTE** *In other tutorials, you may see the* `authorization` *header called the* `Authorization` *header. RFC 2616 section 4.2 specifies that HTTP header names are case insensitive, so these two are equivalent. Whether you prefer the capitalized version or not is a matter of personal preference. This chapter uses lowercase (that is,* `authorization`*) to be consistent with the book's JavaScript variable naming style.*

Error Interceptors

You can also use interceptors to capture HTTP errors. Your interceptor can specify `requestError` and `responseError` functions that are called upon to handle request errors and response errors, respectively. The `requestError` and `responseError` functions interact with promises rather than with requests and responses directly. However, these functions utilize AngularJS's `$q` service, which is a port of the popular NodeJS promises library Q. The `$q` service's syntax is more in line with the Promises/A+ spec, so don't be surprised that the syntax differs from the promises that the `$http` service generates.

> **NOTE** *The* `$q` *service is AngularJS's preferred mechanism of generating promises. Although interceptors are (in theory) compatible with other Promises/A+ conformant promises libraries, such as Q and Bluebird, the* `$q` *service is the safest choice for use with AngularJS.*
>
> *The primary mechanism you will be using to interact with the* `$q` *service in this chapter is the* `$q.defer()` *function. The* `$q.defer()` *function returns a* `promise` *object that your asynchronous operations can then call* `promise.resolve(value)` *or* `promise.resolve(error)` *on.*

Because the `requestError` and `responseError` functions can return promises, you can attempt to recover from the error with additional asynchronous calls. For instance, the example used in this chapter is recovering from a session timeout. Suppose your user left a browser tab open for several days and his session expired. The next time the user attempts to save his data, your server says that the user is not logged in. Many JavaScript apps either fail silently or fall back to redirecting the user. However, with the power of interceptors, your app can handle this more gracefully.

To use error interceptors to handle session timeouts gracefully, your `userService` needs to define an asynchronous function that prompts the user to log in. Promises don't necessarily need to wrap asynchronous HTTP calls. You can use promises to wrap any asynchronous behavior—even waiting for the user to enter a password. In this example, you tie your `userService` into a simple password prompt. You can find this example in the `interceptor_example_3.html` file in this chapter's sample code:

```
var m = angular.module('myApp', []);

m.factory('userService', function($q, $rootScope) {
  var password = '';

  var service = {
    getAuthorization: function() {
      return password;
    },
    authenticate: function() {
      var promise = $q.defer();

      $rootScope.promptForPassword = true;
      $rootScope.submitPassword = function(pwd) {
        $rootScope.promptForPassword = false;
        password = pwd;
        promise.resolve(pwd);
      };

      return promise.promise;
    }
  };

  return service;
});
```

The preceding code defines a simple asynchronous password prompt. Once any AngularJS code calls `userService.authenticate()`, the prompt is displayed. The `authenticate()` function returns a promise that is resolved when the HTML calls the `submitPassword()` function. Following is the HTML corresponding to the `authenticate()` function:

```
<div ng-if="promptForPassword">
  <hr>
  <h2>Please Enter the Password</h2>
  <form ng-submit="submitPassword(password)">
    <input type="text" ng-model="password">
    <input type="submit" value="Submit">
  </form>
</div>
```

To illustrate an HTTP error status, the `server.js` file you are using as an HTTP server defines a `POST /save` route. This route returns an HTTP 401 status (Unauthorized) if the HTTP `authorization` header is not equal to the string `"Taco"`. Following is the `httpController` code modified to make an HTTP `POST` request to the `/save` resource:

```
m.controller('httpController', function($scope, $http) {
  $http.post('/save').success(function(data) {
    console.log(JSON.stringify(data));
    $scope.data = data;
  });
});
```

Of course, you need to define an interceptor to set the `authorization` header. Thankfully, the request interceptor you defined in the "Request Interceptors" subsection is general enough that the changes to `userService` are sufficient. What ties all this code together and prompts the user for the password on an HTTP 401 is a `responseError` interceptor as shown here:

```
m.config(function($httpProvider) {
  $httpProvider.interceptors.push(function($q, $injector, userService) {
    return {
      request: function(request) {
        request.headers.authorization =
          userService.getAuthorization();
        return request;
      },
      response: function(response) {
        response.data.status = response.status;
        return response;
      },
      responseError: function(rejection) {
        if (rejection.status === 401) { // Unauthorized
          console.log('Rejected because unauthorized with password ' +
            userService.getAuthorization());

          return userService.authenticate().then(function() {
            return $injector.get('$http')(rejection.config);
          });
        }

        return $q.reject(rejection);
      }
    }
  });
});
```

As you can see, the interceptor utilizes the `$q` service to interact with the `rejection` object and return the correct promise. If the server returns an error that *isn't* an HTTP 401, the error interceptor ignores the error. Note that you still need to execute the `return $q.reject(rejection);` code to tell AngularJS that a given error interceptor does nothing.

When the server returns an HTTP 401, it is more interesting. In this case, the interceptor activates the password prompt and waits for the user to enter in a password. The interceptor returns an entirely new promise: the one returned by `userService.authenticate()`.

Note that you would normally use a modal (a JavaScript pop-up) to prompt a user to log in. The Angular-UI Bootstrap modals you will learn about in more detail in Chapter 10, "Moving On," are an excellent choice for integrating with the interceptor API. To integrate the Angular-UI Bootstrap $modal service with your interceptor, you only need to know two of its numerous features. First, the $modal service has an .open() function that takes a configuration object in which you can specify a template and a controller. Second, the return value from $modal.open() has a result property that is a promise wrapper around the user closing the modal. The following sample code demonstrates how you can utilize the $modal service's promise return value to integrate with HTTP interceptors. You can find the following example in the interceptor_example_modal.html file in this chapter's sample code:

```
m.factory('userService', function($q, $injector) {
  var password = '';

  var service = {
    getAuthorization: function() {
      return password;
    },
    authenticate: function() {
      var $modal = $injector.get('$modal');

      var modal = $modal.open({
        template: '<div style="padding: 15px">' +
                  '  <input type="password" ng-model="pwd">' +
                  '  <button ng-click="submit(pwd)">' +
                  '    Submit' +
                  '  </button>' +
                  '</div>',
        controller: function($scope, $modalInstance) {
          $scope.submit = function(pwd) {
            $modalInstance.close(pwd);
          };
        }
      });

      return modal.result.then(function(pwd) {
        password = pwd;
      });
    }
  };

  return service;
});
```

The error interceptor returns a promise that performs two actions. First, it calls userService .authenticate() and waits for the user to type in the password. Then, once the user has entered a password, the interceptor uses the rejection.config object to "retry" the original HTTP request. As long as the user keeps entering incorrect passwords, the server continues to return HTTP 401 errors, and the request interceptor continues to save the original HTTP request until your user enters the correct password. This means that your user doesn't have to leave the page to re-enter his password and thus doesn't have to lose his data if his session timed out. It's certainly a big improvement over redirecting the user to a login page and wiping out his form data!

The $resource Service

The $resource service is a high-level abstraction around $http that allows you to operate at the abstraction of objects loaded from the server rather than at the level of individual HTTP requests and responses. The $resource service allows you to create a convenient wrapper around a REST API enabling you to perform CRUD operations without directly creating HTTP requests. In other words, rather than creating a JSON object and then creating an HTTP request with method POST to persist the object to the server, you use the $resource service to create an object with a save() function that creates the correct HTTP POST request for you.

> **NOTE** *The* $resource *service is not part of the AngularJS core. To use it, you must include the* angular-resource.js *file and add a dependency on the* ngResource *module. For your convenience, version 1.2.16 of the* angular-resource.js *file has been included with this chapter's sample code.*

The $resource service itself is a function that creates these REST API wrapper objects. The $resource service uses strict REST conventions by default, but you can extend it to fit virtually any RESTful API. Many APIs use RESTful conventions without defining a full REST API. For instance, the Twitter API v1.1 (which you will use in this section) does not have a route to enable you to update a tweet. Furthermore, deleting a tweet requires a POST request rather than a DELETE request. In addition to scaffolding REST APIs, the $resource service enables you to create a layer of abstraction on top of quirky APIs like Twitter's.

The $resource function has the following signature. Note that square brackets mean the parameter is optional and may be omitted:

```
$resource(url, [paramDefaults], [actions], options);
```

This function returns a *resource* object that has a set of functions called *actions*. Each action corresponds to a different class of HTTP requests. In other words, you define an action by specifying an HTTP configuration (the argument to the $http() function). The key feature that makes actions so powerful is that their HTTP configurations are *parameterizable*. For instance, the following tweetService exposes a function called load() that loads a given tweet from the server. The following code is available in the resource_basic.html file in this chapter's sample code:

```
var m = angular.module('myApp', ['ngResource']);

m.service('tweetService', function($resource) {
  return $resource('/tweets/:id',
    {},
    {
      load: { method: 'GET' }
    });
});

m.controller('tweetController', function(tweetService) {
```

```
    // This performs an HTTP request: GET /tweets/123
    var tweet = tweetService.load({ id: '123' }, function() {
      console.log(JSON.stringify(tweet));
    });
  });
```

The preceding `tweetService.load()` function actually creates a `GET` request to `/tweets/123`. The `$resource` service enables you to specify *route parameters* in the URL. (The `:id` in `/tweets/:id` is a route parameter.) If you have used server-side frameworks like Ruby on Rails and Express, or you have read Chapter 6, "Templates, Location, and Routing," the `$resource` service's notion of route parameters should seem familiar. The `$resource` service searches URLs for route parameters and then pulls the corresponding values from the object you pass to the action function.

> **NOTE** *In the previous example, you set the* `tweet` *variable to the return value of the* `load()` *function. You then used the* `tweet` *variable in the* `load()` *function's callback. This is a design pattern that is common in AngularJS code. The action function returns an empty object and tracks a reference to that object. When the HTTP request returns, the* `$resource` *copies the properties from the server's response to the empty object.*

Beyond the route parameters in the URL, there are two additional ways you can parameterize your requests. The `$resource` service enables you to define rules for how query parameters and route parameter defaults are created.

> **NOTE** *Route parameter defaults, the second argument to the* `$resource()` *function, are used when you do not specify all the route parameters when you call the action function. For instance, in the following example, because the controller's* `send()` *call doesn't specify route parameters, the* `$resource` *service instead takes the default value for* `id`. *If the default value is a function, the* `$resource` *service executes it and uses the return value.*

You can define functions that the `$resource` service calls to set query parameters and URL parameter defaults:

```
m.service('tweetService', function($resource) {
  var count = 0;
  return $resource('/tweets/:id',
    {
      id: function() {
        return ++count;
      }
    },
```

```
    {
      send: {
        method: 'POST',
        url: '/tweets/:id/send',
        params: {
          counter: function() {
            return count;
          }
        }
      }
    });
  });

  m.controller('tweetController', function(tweetService) {
    // This performs an HTTP request: POST /tweets/1/send?counter=1
    var tweet = tweetService.send(function() {
      console.log(JSON.stringify(tweet));
    });
  });
```

To minimize boilerplate, the $resource service defines five default actions. Every resource you define gets the following actions free. These actions correspond to CRUD operations in a strict REST API:

```
{ 'get':    {method:'GET'},
  'save':   {method:'POST'},
  'query':  {method:'GET', isArray:true},
  'remove': {method:'DELETE'},
  'delete': {method:'DELETE'} };
```

There are two subtleties with the $resource service that the default actions illustrate. First, the query action's configuration has a mysterious isArray option. This option means you expect the server's response will be an array, so the object the query() function returns will be an empty array. When it receives an HTTP response from the server, the $resource service then copies that array into the array it returned. You typically don't have to use the isArray option because many APIs return objects that contain arrays as opposed to full arrays.

Second, $resource service returns objects that are more than just a set of static actions. Resources are semantically similar to classes in programming languages like Java: They have static methods, represented by the action functions you have used this far, but they can also be instantiated. Furthermore, instantiated resources have instance functions that serve as helpers for some of the action functions. In particular, the save(), remove(), and delete() functions (as well as any other actions whose method is *not* GET) are exposed as helper methods on resource instances. For instance, in the following example, the tweet resource instance has a $send() function that automatically performs a POST request with the tweet object as JSON in the request body. You can find the following code in the resource_instance.html file in this chapter's sample code:

```
var m = angular.module('myApp', ['ngResource']);

m.service('tweetService', function($resource) {
  return $resource('/tweets/:id',
```

```
          {},
          {
            load: { method: 'GET' },
            send: {
              method: 'POST',
              url: '/tweets/:id/send'
            }
          });
      });

      m.controller('tweetController', function(tweetService) {
        // This performs an HTTP request: GET /tweets/123
        var tweet = tweetService.load({ id: '123' }, function() {
          console.log(JSON.stringify(tweet));
          // This performs an HTTP request: POST /tweets/123/send
          tweet.$send({ id: tweet.id });
        });
      });
```

Now that you have seen the basic features of the `$resource` service, you will apply this knowledge to write your own resource. Specifically, you will write a resource that consumes a portion of v1.1 of the public Twitter REST API.

CONSUMING THE TWITTER REST API

In this section, you write a resource wrapper around part of Twitter's REST API. Specifically, you write a wrapper around five common Twitter API endpoints that correspond roughly to CRUD operations for a single tweet. These endpoints follow:

➤   `GET statuses/retweets/:id`

➤   `GET statuses/show/:id`

➤   `POST statuses/destroy/:id`

➤   `POST statuses/update/:id`

➤   `POST statuses/retweet/:id`

Building this resource wrapper gives you a deeper understanding of the `$resource` service. For the sake of simplicity (as well as the fact that the Twitter REST API doesn't support JSONP), the NodeJS server for this chapter's sample code includes a simple server-side implementation for these endpoints.

To build a resource that consumes this API, first you need to understand what each of these API endpoints does. These endpoints don't conform to strict REST (for instance, to delete a tweet you actually have to perform a `POST` request). Because of this, you need to do a little extra work to make the `$resource` service interface with this API:

➤   The `GET statuses/retweets/:id` endpoint returns an array of retweets.

➤   The `GET statuses/show/:id` endpoint loads a single tweet.

➤ The POST statuses/destroy/:id endpoint deletes a single tweet.

➤ The POST statuses/update/:id endpoint updates a single tweet.

➤ The POST statuses/retweet/:id endpoint creates a new retweet.

The resource wrapper for these five methods is shown next. You can find this code in the resource_twitter.html file in this chapter's sample code:

```
m.service('tweetService', function($resource) {
  return $resource('/statuses/',
    {},
    {
      retweets: {
        method: 'GET',
        url: '/statuses/retweets/:id',
        isArray: true
      },
      show: {
        method: 'GET',
        url: '/statuses/show/:id'
      },
      destroy: {
        method: 'POST',
        url: '/statuses/destroy/:id',
        params: {
          id: '@id'
        }
      },
      update: {
        method: 'POST',
        url: '/statuses/update/:id',
        params: {
          id: '@id'
        }
      },
      retweet: {
        method: 'POST',
        url: '/statuses/retweet/:id',
        params: {
          id: '@id'
        }
      }
    });
});
```

The preceding code has one new feature: the @id syntax. This syntax instructs the $resource service to set the id route parameter to the value of the id property in the request body. For instance, tweetService.retweet({ id: '123' }) would make a POST request to /statuses/retweet/123 with { id: '123' } in the body. You can now create a controller that loads a tweet and its retweets:

```
m.controller('tweetController', function($scope, tweetService) {
```

```
  $scope.load = function() {
    $scope.tweet = tweetService.show({ id: '123456' }, function() {
    });
  };

  $scope.loadRetweets = function() {
    $scope.retweets = tweetService.retweets({ id: '123456' },
      function() {});
  };
});
```

You may have noticed that the preceding controller doesn't expose wrappers for the `destroy()`, `update()`, and `retweet()` functions. Although you can use these functions directly, the `$resource` service exposes instance helper functions that you read about briefly in the "The $resource Service" section. Once you have a `tweet` instance, such as one returned from `tweetService.show()`, you can use the instance's `$destroy()`, `$update()`, and `$retweet()` helpers. Calling the `tweet.$destroy()` helper is equivalent to calling `tweetService.destroy(tweet)`. For instance, you can use the API exposed by `tweetController` to implement a "Retweet" button as shown here:

```
<button ng-click="tweet.$retweet()">
  Retweet
</button>
```

The `tweet.$retweet()` call translates to a POST request to `/statuses/retweet/123456` with the tweet instance's JSON representation in the body.

Congratulations! You've successfully implemented a resource wrapper around part of a real API! Now that you've seen how the `$resource` service makes it easy to consume APIs, you will take a brief look at a scaffolding tool that integrates with the `$resource` service: StrongLoop's LoopBack. LoopBack is a high-level tool for generating REST APIs. It automatically generates a NodeJS server for you and provides a question-and-answer interface for generating REST API endpoints. As you will see in the next section, LoopBack can even generate AngularJS resources that can consume the REST API endpoints it creates.

SCAFFOLDING A REST API WITH STRONGLOOP LOOPBACK

So far in this chapter, you have learned the basic concepts of HTTP requests in AngularJS. However, your code so far has interacted with trivial server back ends. That's because creating your own REST API is a more involved task, and focusing on building a REST API would detract from the AngularJS HTTP fundamentals. However, to really see these fundamentals in action, you're going to use StrongLoop's LoopBack framework to quickly scaffold a NodeJS-backed REST API. If you have not installed NodeJS yet, please navigate to `www.nodejs.org/download` and follow the instructions for your operating system of choice.

LoopBack is a NodeJS tool that automatically generates REST APIs for you. In other words, LoopBack generates NodeJS code, which utilizes the popular NodeJS web framework Express and provides a simple command-line interface to add models to your REST API. A *model* is an object representing a data schema. For instance, a user model would be an object that specifies what data will be stored about users, such as specifying that a user should have a string that represents his e-mail address. LoopBack creates API endpoints, general classes of HTTP resources that you can use to perform CRUD operations on model instances. Models are the server-side equivalent to the resources you built with the `$resource` service in the previous section.

Models are closely related to the concept of a table or a collection in a database. As a matter of fact, one key advantage of the LoopBack framework is that you can choose to persist instances of your models in one of four different databases: MongoDB, Oracle, MySQL, or Microsoft SQL Server. You can choose between databases on a per-model basis, so you can store users in MongoDB but financial transactions in MySQL, for instance. You can also choose to only store instances of your models in memory. For the purposes of this chapter, you will only use the in-memory storage option because installing and setting up a database is unnecessary overhead for this example. However, if you already have a MongoDB instance on your machine, you will be able to wire your REST API to persist data to your MongoDB instance. In practice, you typically want to store model instances in a database, but the in-memory storage option is sufficient for educational purposes.

Building a Simple API Using LoopBack

In this section, you use LoopBack to scaffold a real REST API for storing coffee shops. You create a server-side model using LoopBack and then build out the corresponding AngularJS `$resource` using LoopBack's AngularJS SDK. Finally, you create a simple HTML page that takes advantage of the `$resource` that the LoopBack AngularJS SDK generated for you.

To install StrongLoop LoopBack, you should run `npm install` in the `loopback-coffee` directory of this chapter's sample code. This installs the various LoopBack command-line tools under the `node_modules/strongloop/bin` directory. In this section, you focus on LoopBack as a means to an end, so you will only learn about LoopBack at a high level. You can learn about LoopBack in more detail at `http://loopback.io`. In this chapter, you utilize version 2.10.2 of the LoopBack framework.

Creating a New Application

The primary command-line tool you'll use to generate REST APIs with LoopBack is the `slc` command. To start the process of creating a REST API, run the `./node_modules/strongloop/bin/slc loopback` command from the root directory of this chapter's sample code. You should see the following prompt, which will enable you to scaffold a web server by answering a few simple questions. Name your application `loopback-coffee`:

```
[?] What's the name of your application? loopback-coffee
[?] Enter name of the directory to contain the project: loopback-coffee
```

With that one command, you have just created a trivial REST API. Your REST API has no models yet, but if you run the `./node_modules/strongloop/bin/slc run` command and navigate your browser to http://localhost:3000, you should see JSON data showing how long the server has been running, like the following output:

```
{"started":"2015-01-02T22:56:29.454Z","uptime":4.47}
```

Creating a LoopBack Model

You can run the ./node_modules/strongloop/bin/slc loopback:model command to create a new model. LoopBack asks you several questions to build your model. Call your model CoffeeShop (plural CoffeeShops). For the purposes of this section, your model will contain two properties—name and address—both strings:

```
? Enter the model name: CoffeeShop
? Select the data-source to attach CoffeeShop to: db (memory)
? Select model's base class: PersistedModel
? Expose CoffeeShop via the REST API? Yes
? Custom plural form (used to build REST URL): CoffeeShops
Let's add some CoffeeShop properties now.

Enter an empty property name when done.
? Property name: name
   invoke   loopback:property
? Property type: string
? Required? Yes

Let's add another CoffeeShop property.
Enter an empty property name when done.
? Property name: address
   invoke   loopback:property
? Property type: string
? Required? Yes

Let's add another CoffeeShop property.
Enter an empty property name when done.
? Property name:
```

That's all the work you need to do to create the CoffeeShop model and its corresponding REST API. Run the ./node_modules/strongloop/bin/slc run command to start your server and navigate your browser to http://localhost:3000/api/CoffeeShops. Because you haven't added any coffee shops, you should see an empty JSON array.

The API Explorer

LoopBack exposes a powerful documentation and configuration tool called the API Explorer by default. Navigate your browser to http://localhost:3000/explorer, and you should see a list of models defined in your server. You should see two: the Users model that LoopBack generates by default, and the CoffeeShops model you created in the previous section. When you click on the CoffeeShops model, you should see a list of all the operations your new REST API supports. For instance, you can do a POST request to /api/CoffeeShops to create a new CoffeeShop instance or do a GET request to /api/CoffeeShops to get a list of all coffee shops.

Generating Resources with Loopback AngularJS SDK

Now that you've created a REST API for coffee shops, you're probably wondering when AngularJS is going to make an appearance. One of the advantages of building REST APIs with LoopBack is the lb-ng executable, which generates AngularJS services for your models. In other words, the lb-ng executable automatically does for your API what you did for the Twitter API in the previous section.

To run the lb-ng executable, first create a js directory in the client directory. Then run the following command:

```
./node_modules/strongloop/node_modules/loopback-sdk-angular-cli/bin/lb-ng \
  ./server/server.js client/js/services.js
```

That's it! Open the client/js/services.js file and search for "CoffeeShop." You will see that LoopBack built a well-documented CoffeeShop service based on the $resource service for you. Don't worry about the fact that the services.js file has more than 1,600 lines of code; LoopBack produces an extraordinary number of comments. The CoffeeShop service looks like a lot of code, but the code is about 90 percent comments. Following is the CoffeeShop service without comments and formatted for readability:

```
module.factory(
  "CoffeeShop",
  ['LoopBackResource', 'LoopBackAuth', '$injector',
  function(Resource, LoopBackAuth, $injector) {
    var R = Resource(
      urlBase + "/CoffeeShops/:id",
      { 'id': '@id' },
      {
        "create": {
          url: urlBase + "/CoffeeShops",
          method: "POST"
        },
        "upsert": {
          url: urlBase + "/CoffeeShops",
          method: "PUT"
        },
        "exists": {
          url: urlBase + "/CoffeeShops/:id/exists",
          method: "GET"
        },
        "findById": {
          url: urlBase + "/CoffeeShops/:id",
          method: "GET"
        },
        "find": {
          isArray: true,
          url: urlBase + "/CoffeeShops",
          method: "GET"
        },
        "findOne": {
          url: urlBase + "/CoffeeShops/findOne",
          method: "GET"
        },
        "updateAll": {
```

```
              url: urlBase + "/CoffeeShops/update",
              method: "POST"
          },
          "deleteById": {
              url: urlBase + "/CoffeeShops/:id",
              method: "DELETE"
          },
          "count": {
              url: urlBase + "/CoffeeShops/count",
              method: "GET"
          },
          "prototype$updateAttributes": {
              url: urlBase + "/CoffeeShops/:id",
              method: "PUT"
          },
      }
  );

  R["updateOrCreate"] = R["upsert"];
  R["update"] = R["updateAll"];
  R["destroyById"] = R["deleteById"];
  R["removeById"] = R["deleteById"];

  R.modelName = "CoffeeShop";

  return R;
}]);
```

The preceding `Resource` service is a LoopBack-specific wrapper around the `$resource` service. The syntax is identical. Now that you've run the `lb-ng` command, you can use this `services.js` file to consume your homemade REST API.

To use the `services.js` file, you need to copy four files into your `loopback-coffee` app. First, the root directory of this chapter's sample code contains a `middleware.json` file. From your `loopback-coffee` directory, run the following command to copy this file into the right place:

```
cp ../middleware.json server/middleware.json
```

LoopBack's middleware configurations are a complex subject. For the purposes of this section, it suffices to know that this chapter's `middleware.json` file configures your LoopBack server to serve static files from the `client` directory. In other words, navigating to `http://localhost:3000/js/services.js` produces the contents of the `client/js/services.js` file, which happens to contain your `CoffeeShop` resource.

Once you've copied the `middleware.json` file, you also need to copy the `angular.js`, `angular-resource.js`, and `loopback_coffee.html` files into your `loopback-coffee` app. The `angular.js` and `angular-resource.js` files contain the AngularJS core and the `ngResource` module, respectively. The `loopback_coffee.html` file contains the actual HTML for your page. Run the following commands from your `loopback-coffee` directory to copy these files:

```
cp ../angular* client/js/
cp ../loopback_coffee.html client/
```

Now you're ready to see the `CoffeeShop` resource in action. Start your LoopBack server with the `./node_modules/strongloop/bin/slc run` command, and navigate your browser to `http://localhost:3000/loopback_coffee.html`. You should see a prompt to create a new coffee shop and a list of all coffee shops you've already saved. The `loopback_coffee.html` file contains one controller, `TestController`, that uses the `CoffeeShop` resource:

```
angular.module('myApp', ['lbServices']);

function TestController($scope, CoffeeShop) {
  $scope.newShop = new CoffeeShop();
  $scope.allShops = CoffeeShop.find();
  $scope.CoffeeShop = CoffeeShop;

  $scope.reset = function() {
    $scope.newShop = new CoffeeShop();
  };
}
```

Using the API exposed by `TestController`, you can create an HTML page that lists all coffee shops and lets you save a new coffee shop. Following is the HTML from the `loopback_coffee.html` file:

```
<div ng-controller="TestController">
  <h1>Create New Shop</h1>
  <input type="text" ng-model="newShop.name" placeholder="name">
  <br>
  <input   type="text"
           ng-model="newShop.address"
           placeholder="address">
  <br>
  <button ng-click="allShops.push(newShop); newShop.$create(); reset();">
    Save
  </button>
  <hr>
  <h1>Existing Shops</h1>
  <button ng-click="allShops = CoffeeShop.find()">
    Reload
  </button>
  <ul>
    <li ng-repeat="shop in allShops">
      {{shop.name}} ({{shop.address}})
    </li>
  </ul>
</div>
```

The preceding example uses two actions from the `CoffeeShop` resource. First, the `find()` function returns a list of all coffee shops by making a GET request to the `/api/CoffeeShops` route. Following is the `find()` action's definition from the `services.js` file:

```
"find": {
  isArray: true,
  url: urlBase + "/CoffeeShops",
  method: "GET"
}
```

The second action is represented by the $create() function. This function is an instance helper around the create action. The create action makes a POST request to /api/CoffeeShops to create a new CoffeeShop instance. Following is the create action's definition from the services.js file:

```
"create": {
  url: urlBase + "/CoffeeShops",
  method: "POST"
}
```

With these two basic actions, you have created an HTML wrapper around your REST API. Thanks to StrongLoop's LoopBack, you only had to run a couple of commands and produce a 51-line HTML file to create a simple REST API and its corresponding client code.

Congratulations! So far, you have learned how to use the $http and $resource services and used the latter to build two REST API clients. But you've only used HTTP to communicate with the server. Although HTTP is currently the most common mechanism for server communication, it is inherently limited. HTTP limits the server to responding to requests: It is not designed to allow the server to "push" updates to a client. This is why, for applications like browser-based real-time chat, web sockets are becoming popular. The next section introduces you to web sockets and shows how to use them with AngularJS.

USING WEB SOCKETS WITH ANGULARJS

In this chapter so far, you've become familiar with HTTP. However, HTTP is not the right fit for all use cases. The WebSocket standard is more flexible than the rigid request and response HTTP model, allowing the server to send updates to the client without waiting for a request. This is particularly useful for "real-time" applications. The term *real time* is often ill-defined, so consider this example. Suppose you had two browser windows open to the loopback-coffee app you built in the previous section, "Building a Simple API Using LoopBack." If you were to add a coffee shop in one window, it would not appear in the other window unless you clicked the Reload button to trigger another HTTP request. In a true real-time web application, the server would push an update to the client, and the other browser window would be updated immediately.

> **NOTE** *In computer science, a network socket is a low-level abstraction for communication between two programs (which may or may not be running on two separate machines). Sockets are an intricate topic, but for this chapter, you can consider a socket as a piece of code that provides a connection between two programs, enabling the programs to send messages to each other. Each program can read messages from the socket and write messages to the socket.*

Currently, the most common library for using web sockets in JavaScript is SocketIO. SocketIO is actually a layer on top of web sockets that enables you to send and receive events over web sockets. SocketIO utilizes the ubiquitous *event emitter design pattern* that pervades many JavaScript projects. In the event emitter design pattern, you can register a callback to an event, and you can emit an event. Suppose you emit an event named `connected`. The event emitter then calls any callbacks that are registered to listen for events named `connected`. When you emit an event, you can also attach data to that event. A common application of the event emitter design pattern is error handling, as demonstrated in the following pseudocode:

```
var emitter = new eventEmitter();

// Register a callback to listen for events named 'error'
emitter.on('error', function(message) {
  console.log(message); // Prints out 'woops!'
});

// Emit an event named 'error' with data 'woops!'
emitter.emit('error', 'woops!');
```

Event emitters typically only work within a program. SocketIO, however, provides an event emitter interface over web sockets, so the server can `emit()` events to the browser.

> **NOTE** *SocketIO is conceptually similar to Firebase, another real-time web development tool that you'll learn about in the next section. Both provide an event emitter interface over web sockets to allow you to update your clients in real time. The primary difference is that SocketIO has a server-side API that allows you to write your own SocketIO-enabled server. Firebase requires you to connect to Firebase's servers, which may be an advantage or a disadvantage depending on your skill set. In this chapter, you will not see much difference because this chapter's sample code has a SocketIO-enabled server.*

In this section, you will build out a simple real-time chat application with AngularJS and SocketIO. To run the example code in this section, all you need is the `server.js` script that all the examples from this chapter so far have used. When you run `node server.js`, you actually start a SocketIO server on port 8081, in addition to a static web server on port 8080. In this chapter, you will use version 1.3.3 of SocketIO.

In addition to the server component, you need the SocketIO client JavaScript file. For your convenience, version 1.3.3 of the SocketIO client has been included in this chapter's sample code in the `socket.io.js` file.

> **NOTE** *WebSockets are not supported in Internet Explorer 9 or earlier. SocketIO does support Internet Explorer 9, but through inelegant fallbacks. For best results, use a recent version of Google Chrome (version 16 or greater) or Mozilla Firefox (version 11 or greater).*

Using the SocketIO client is syntactically identical to your standard event emitter design pattern. The SocketIO client attaches a function called io() to the global window object. The io() function takes a single parameter, the URL to connect to, and returns an event emitter. This event emitter has several built-in events. The most important built-in events are connect and disconnect, which are emitted when the socket connects and disconnects, respectively. In addition, a client can emit arbitrary events to the server with the emit() function.

If the preceding description isn't clear, don't worry; SocketIO is easy to learn by example. Following is the JavaScript code from the socketio_chat.html file from this chapter's sample code. This is all the JavaScript necessary to create a real-time chat application with SocketIO:

```html
<script type="text/javascript"
        src="angular.js">
</script>
<script type="text/javascript"
        src="socket.io.js">
</script>
<script type="text/javascript">
  angular.module('myApp', []);

  function TestController($scope, $window) {
    $scope.messages = [];
    $scope.name = 'TestConnection';
    $scope.message = 'Test message';

    var socket = $window.io('http://localhost:8081');
    $scope.connected = false;
    socket.on('connect', function() {
      $scope.connected = true;
      $scope.$apply();
    });
    socket.on('disconnect', function() {
      $scope.connected = false;
      $scope.$apply();
    });

    socket.on('message', function(message) {
      $scope.messages.push(message);
      $scope.$apply();
    });

    $scope.sendMessage = function() {
      socket.emit('message', {
        name: $scope.name,
        message: $scope.message
      });

      $scope.message = '';
    };
  }
</script>
```

The most important parts of the preceding code are the `on('message')` event handler and the `sendMessage()` function. The `on('message')` handler is called whenever the SocketIO client receives an event named `message` from the server. The handler is responsible for aggregating all messages received from the server. Because SocketIO events are not part of AngularJS, you need to call `$scope.$apply()` to inform AngularJS that the scope's data has changed. (For more information on why this is necessary, see Chapter 4, "Data Binding.")

The other important part of the preceding example is the `sendMessage()` function. This function emits a "message" event to the server. This chapter's SocketIO server is configured to re-emit all "message" events on all connected sockets. Thus, when you call the `sendMessage()` function, SocketIO pushes the "message" events to every client that's connected.

To see this real-time chat example in action, open your browser and navigate to `http://localhost:8080/socketio_chat.html`. Open a second browser window and navigate to the same URL. You'll notice that when you click "Send Message" in one browser window, the other browser window updates automatically!

Now that you've seen SocketIO in action, you will create a similar chat application using Firebase, another real-time web development tool. Firebase makes developing real-time apps even more concise than SocketIO.

USING FIREBASE WITH ANGULARJS

Firebase is a hosted solution for developing real-time web applications. Firebase also has tight integration with AngularJS using the AngularFire connector. Because of these features, Firebase allows you to build AngularJS apps with minimum effort: no need to set up a server, and no need to worry about calling `$scope.$apply()`. You do need to sign up for an account, but as of this writing, Firebase offers a generous free tier that should be sufficient for this chapter's example. Sign up for an account, create a new app, and take note of your Firebase data URL. Your Firebase data URL should be of the form `<name>.firebaseio.com`.

To use Firebase, you need both the Firebase client and the AngularFire connector, which provides AngularJS bindings to the Firebase client. For your convenience, this chapter's sample code includes version 2.0.4 of the Firebase client (the `firebase.js` file) and version 0.9.2 of AngularFire (the `angularfire.js` file). As you'll see, once you've included these files, persisting your data to the server is trivial.

First, include AngularJS and the two Firebase files using `script` tags:

```
<script type="text/javascript"
        src="angular.js">
</script>
<script type="text/javascript"
        src="firebase.js">
</script>
<script type="text/javascript"
        src="angularfire.js">
</script>
```

Next, create a controller called `FirebaseController` that provides an identical API to the controller from the SocketIO section. AngularFire removes the need to listen for events, handles calling `$scope.$apply()` for you, and even persists data to the server for you. Following is the JavaScript from the `firebase_chat.html` file, which contains all the necessary code to create a real-time chat application with AngularFire:

```
angular.module('myApp', ['firebase']);

function FirebaseController($scope, $window, $firebase) {
  $scope.messages = [];
  $scope.name = 'TestConnection';
  $scope.message = 'Test message';

  var firebase = new $window.Firebase(
    'https://<name>.firebaseio.com/'); // Firebase Data URL here
  var sync = $firebase(firebase);

  $scope.messages = sync.$asArray();

  $scope.sendMessage = function() {
    $scope.messages.$add({
      name: $scope.name,
      message: $scope.message
    });

    $scope.message = '';
  };
}
```

The preceding example is shockingly concise. Other than the Firebase data URL, there is no code that resembles an HTTP call or socket connection. Nevertheless, try repeating the multiple browser window exercise from the previous section, "Using Web Sockets with AngularJS." Open `http://localhost:8080/firebase_chat.html` in two separate browser windows and start sending messages. You should see the messages you've sent in one browser window in the other, and vice versa.

The code that makes this real-time updating work in the preceding example is wrapped up in the `$asArray()` function and the `$add()` function. The `$asArray()` function returns an array-like object that has AngularFire-specific functionality. When you call the `$asArray()` function, the Firebase client handles loading all your messages from the server and maintains a web socket that continuously receives updates. On top of the Firebase client, AngularFire handles running `$scope.$apply()` for you, so you don't have to worry about the AngularJS digest loop.

The `$add()` function is Firebase's replacement of JavaScript arrays' `push()` function. The `$add()` function handles persisting data to Firebase. Note that you *must* use the `$add()` function; if you just use the `push()` function, your data will not be persisted to the Firebase server.

That's all for Firebase! Now you see how easy server communication can be. If maintaining a server and creating HTTP requests manually with the `$http` service seems too cumbersome for you, Firebase is an excellent alternative that lets you bypass all that work and get straight to building a great UI. Now you understand why AngularFire markets itself as "three-way data-binding." AngularFire abstracts out server communication in much the same way AngularJS's two-way data-binding abstracts out DOM manipulation. With two-way data binding, entering text in an input field automatically updates the state of a JavaScript variable. With AngularFire's three-way data binding, entering text in an input field updates the state of a JavaScript variable, which is, in turn, immediately persisted to the server.

CONCLUSION

In this chapter, you learned about the variety of tools the AngularJS community has for communicating with a server. These tools range from the relatively low-level $http service, which provides powerful features for managing individual HTTP requests, to AngularFire, which abstracts away server communication behind a "three-way data-binding" layer. You even used StrongLoop's LoopBack to generate your own REST API, as well as the corresponding REST API client.

You also learned about the difference between HTTP and web sockets. Although HTTP is still the dominant server communication protocol for browser JavaScript, web sockets are becoming increasingly popular because of the ability to push updates to the client. In particular, tools like SocketIO enable you to build powerful real-time apps on top of web sockets. Web sockets are likely the future of server communication in browser JavaScript, but HTTP will remain relevant for a long time.

9

Testing and Debugging AngularJS Applications

WHAT YOU WILL LEARN IN THIS CHAPTER:

➤ The testing pyramid as applied to AngularJS apps

➤ Unit testing with Mocha, Karma, and NodeJS

➤ Provisioning cloud browsers with Sauce

➤ Integration testing with ng-scenario and protractor

➤ Effectively utilizing the debug module

➤ The basics of the Chrome developer console

WROX.COM CODE DOWNLOADS FOR THIS CHAPTER

You can find the wrox.com code downloads for this chapter at `http://www.wrox.com/go/ proangularjs` on the Download Code tab.

ANGULARJS TESTING PHILOSOPHY

A little-known fact about AngularJS is that the original author, Misko Hevery, was a test engineer at Google when he first wrote <angular/>, as it was then called. His role as a test engineer involved educating Google engineers on utilizing practices like dependency injection to write modular code that was easy to unit test. Unsurprisingly, AngularJS was designed to make writing unit-testable code easy from day one. This is why AngularJS is known as a *framework* rather than simply a *library*: Controllers, services, and directives provide an opinionated structure for how code should be written. Libraries like jQuery simply provide helper functions for writing code any way you please.

The first step toward understanding AngularJS's testing philosophy is to understand what a unit test is. The term *unit test* is often tragically misused by software engineers; if you are already familiar with an alternative definition, please remember that the term has a different meaning when it comes to AngularJS. A *unit test* tests that a single block of code executes correctly *independent of all other blocks of code*. In particular, unit tests should not make any network requests or read any files, because input/output (I/O) is slow, adds setup overhead, and adds an additional implicit assumption that the I/O succeeds. Although I/O is unlikely to fail, it is several orders of magnitude more likely to cause a test failure than an in-memory operation.

An ideal unit test fails if and only if an assumption about how the module under test works is no longer valid. Thus, an extensive set of unit tests makes working with a module easier by making it simple to identify when a change is backward-breaking. In addition, focusing on unit tests in your day-to-day development practice encourages developing robust modular code, because writing unit tests requires thinking critically about assumptions inherent to a particular module, class, or function. As Misko Hevery has often said, if your code is difficult to unit test, it is not as good as it should be. Finally, unit tests should not require network or file I/O, so they should run extremely quickly—on the order of magnitude of thousands of tests per second—and provide a quick means of verifying basic functionality.

Here's an example of AngularJS code that's difficult to properly unit test:

```
function MyController($scope) {
  var xhr = new XMLHttpRequest();
  xhr.open('GET', '/api/v1/me');
  xhr.send();
  xhr.onreadystatechange = function() {
    if (xhr.readyState === 4) { // 4 means response received
      $scope.data = xhr.responseText;
    }
  };

  $scope.computeResultsFromData = function() {
    // Some manipulation of $scope.data here
  };
}
```

The preceding code is simple enough, but, upon careful inspection, it carries a lot of assumption baggage that makes it difficult to test. Note that to test the `computeResultsFromData` function, you first need to execute the `XMLHttpRequest` code, which makes a request to the server. In other words, this code requires a server with an `/api/v1/me` route, which can be quite difficult to set up. In addition, this introduces network latency (and the risk of network failure) to your test, which makes your test slow and unreliable. Of course, the preceding code is not representative of how HTTP requests are used in AngularJS. It would typically be implemented in AngularJS like this:

```
function MyController($scope, $http) {
  $http.get('/api/v1/me').success(function(data) {
    $scope.data = data;
  });

  $scope.computeResultsFromData = function() {
```

```
        // Some manipulation of $scope.data here
    };
}
```

In addition to being more concise, this implementation has a key advantage: `$http` is passed as a parameter to `MyController`, whereas in the first example, `MyController` had a hard-coded dependency on the `XMLHttpRequest` class. In the second implementation, `$http` can be mocked out easily—that is, replaced with a suitable object with the same interface for testing purposes. Depending on your testing needs, you can easily replace `$http.get()` with a function that returns a hard-coded result, a function that asserts its parameters are correct, or even a function that does a cross-site HTTP request to a staging server without modifying your code. In the context of unit tests, your `$http.get()` function should be replaced with something that's lightweight and runs in memory, so your tests execute quickly and without risk of failure due to network I/O issues.

> **NOTE** *You may be familiar with the notion of a spy. To effectively unit test code with nonmockable function calls, like the* `XMLHttpRequest` *example earlier, you may overwrite the* `window.XMLHttpRequest` *function with a spy. There are several modules, such as SinonJS, that provide sophisticated spy functionality. However, this approach suffers from the same problem as all global state: You can't run tests with global spies in parallel, and you need to be careful to clean up your global state so you don't pollute subsequent tests. AngularJS's code structure makes it easy to make mockable function calls, so, as a general rule of thumb, you should never have to use spies on global variables.*

The Testing Pyramid

Although unit tests are an indispensable tool for ensuring code quality and providing a fast test of code correctness, they are not the whole story when it comes to testing. Your individual modules may operate as expected, but the interaction between modules may still be incorrect. In code with high unit test coverage, bugs will usually happen in the interaction between modules rather than in the modules themselves. The general idea of the testing pyramid is to create a spectrum of tests, ranging from the most lightweight and simple unit tests to *end-to-end tests*, which interact with your application via the same code paths as your end users. The space between end-to-end tests and unit tests is called *integration tests*. See Figure 9-1. Because unit tests are blazing fast but cover small bits of functionality, you should have far more unit tests than end-to-end tests and thus form the base of the pyramid. End-to-end tests are typically bulky and slow, but each test covers large swaths of your codebase. You should have far fewer end-to-end tests than unit tests. The end-to-end tests form the top of the pyramid. To liken the testing pyramid to the USDA food pyramid, unit tests are like broccoli: You may not like writing them, but you should write them anyway if you want your codebase to grow up big and strong.

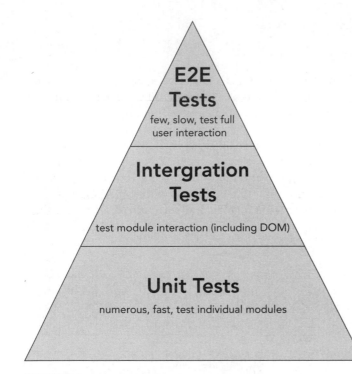

FIGURE 9-1

By mocking out appropriate modules, you can write higher or lower level integration tests as necessary. In this chapter, the integration tests you will be writing will look like end-to-end tests but will stub out the $http service with a mock HTTP back end. That is, these integration tests interact with your AngularJS code by interacting with HTML elements, but the server-side code is mocked out with an in-memory stub. This enables you to focus on testing AngularJS applications without having to worry about testing a server as well. Proper end-to-end tests look similar to these integration tests but don't stub out the server.

In particular, Figure 9-2 shows how unit tests, Document Object Model (DOM) integration tests, and end-to end tests relate to the architecture of an AngularJS app.

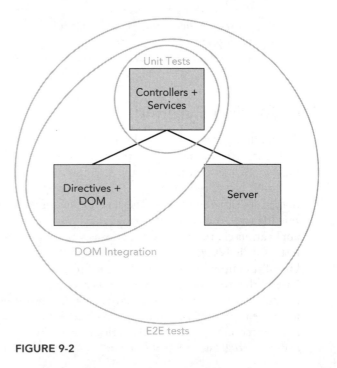

FIGURE 9-2

UNIT TESTING IN ANGULARJS

Up until fairly recently, unit testing JavaScript was difficult. With the advent of NodeJS, however, there has been an explosion of JavaScript testing tools. In addition, as a JavaScript interpreter available from the command line, NodeJS itself is an invaluable tool for JavaScript unit testing. NodeJS relies on the V8 JavaScript engine, so it is a reasonable approximation of how your JavaScript will run in the Google Chrome browser. For the first part of this section, you'll be writing tests in NodeJS exclusively, before exploring how to run these tests in actual browsers. If you have not yet installed NodeJS, please go to `http://www.nodejs.org` and follow the installation instructions for your platform of choice (OSX, Windows, or Linux). In this section, you also learn how to use tools available through the Node package manager, `npm`, to easily instrument live browsers for testing.

The Mocha Testing Framework

Mocha is a popular testing framework in both the NodeJS and AngularJS communities, written by the prolific NodeJS community contributor TJ Holowaychuk (who also wrote the `debug` module you'll use later in this section). Mocha is flexible and enjoys support from a wide array of testing tools. Jasmine is another testing framework that is quite popular in the AngularJS community, but Mocha has become the standard in the NodeJS community in addition to its AngularJS popularity. Furthermore, Mocha and Jasmine have virtually indistinguishable syntax; the differences between the two are mostly pedantic. The most significant difference is that Jasmine provides its own built-in assertion framework, whereas Mocha does not.

To get started with using Mocha, install it using `npm`:

```
npm install mocha -g
```

> **NOTE** *The* `-g` *flag specified tells* `npm` *to install Mocha globally, so the* `mocha` *command is accessible from your command line. Global installation is primarily useful for instruction and is not recommended for an actual project. The preferred method is to track Mocha as a dependency in your* `package.json` *file, the file that the* `npm install` *command uses to determine what it needs to install. You would also use a tool like Grunt, Gulp, or Makefile (see Chapter 2, "Intelligent Workflow and Build Systems") to run your tests. This ensures that you can install the correct version of Mocha with a single* `npm install` *command. Furthermore, a local installation of Mocha prevents version conflicts between different projects. You will use this approach later in this section.*

Mocha is heavily inspired by behavior-driven development (BDD) practices, so tests in Mocha have a slightly different structure than the usual `testCase` with `setUp()` and `tearDown()` structure you may be familiar with from JUnit, PyUnit, or similar frameworks. Mocha's test structure is more functional in nature; tests are structured using the describe() and it() functions. The it() function effectively describes a single test case. The describe() function wraps a suite of tests. Within the describe() function, you can define beforeEach() and afterEach() functions, which execute before each test in the suite and after each test in the suite, respectively.

If this is unclear, don't worry. Mocha's testing structure is easy to understand once you see an example. Suppose you have a simple controller that has functions to validate and save a form that asks the user for their name and e-mail address:

```
function MyFormController($scope, $http) {
    $scope.userData = {};
    $scope.errorMessages = [];

    $scope.saveForm = function() {
        $scope.saving = true;
        $http.
            put('/api/submit', $scope.userData).
            success(function(data) {
                $scope.saving = false;
                $scope.success = true;
            }).
            error(function(err) {
                $scope.saving = false;
                $scope.error = err;
            });
    };

    $scope.validateForm = function() {
        var validationFunctions = [
            {
                fn: function() {
                    return !!$scope.userData.name
                },
                message: 'Name required'
            },
            {
                fn: function() {
                    return !!$scope.userData.email
                },
                message: 'Email required'
            }
        ];

        $scope.errorMessages = [];
        for (var i = 0; i < validationFunctions.length; ++i) {
            if (!validationFunctions[i].fn()) {
                $scope.errorMessages.push(validationFunctions[i].message);
            }
        }
        return $scope.errorMessages;
    };
```

```
    }

    if (typeof module !== 'undefined') {
        module.exports = MyFormController;
    }
```

The check on `typeof module` in `MyFormController` is to enable `MyFormController` to be visible outside the `my_form_controller.js` file in NodeJS. NodeJS's JavaScript runtime has file-level scoping and requires variables to be attached to the file's `module` object to be visible outside the file. If you choose to test your AngularJS controllers in NodeJS, you should either build your code with a module like Browserify or use the `typeof module` check shown earlier.

Without further ado, here is an example of two corresponding unit tests for the `validateForm()` function:

```
var MyFormController = require('./my_form_controller.js');
var assert = require('assert');

describe('MyFormController', function() {
    describe('validateForm', function() {
        var $scope;
        beforeEach(function() {
            $scope = {};
            MyFormController($scope, null);
        });

        it('should succeed if user entered name and email', function() {
            $scope.userData.name = 'Victor Hugo';
            $scope.userData.email = 'les@miserabl.es';

            $scope.validateForm();
            assert.equal(0, $scope.errorMessages.length);
        });

        it('should fail with no email', function() {
            $scope.userData.name = 'Victor Hugo';
            $scope.userData.email = '';

            $scope.validateForm();
            assert.equal(1, $scope.errorMessages.length);
            assert.equal('Email required', $scope.errorMessages[0]);
        });
    });
});
```

When you run the preceding test from your command line with `mocha my_form_controller .test.js`, you should get the results in Mocha's default reporting format, dots:

```
    ..

    2 passing (4ms)
```

Note that the `MyFormController` code technically does not rely on AngularJS at all. These are strict unit tests; the code in `my_form_controller.test.js` doesn't have nonmocked dependencies and doesn't require access to a DOM.

The `my_form_controller.test.js` code demonstrates the flexibility of the `describe/it` syntax. You can nest calls to `describe()` to provide fine-grained separation between test suites while reusing variables from higher-level `describe()` calls. Even if a `describe()` call has only `describe()` calls within it, you can still use `beforeEach()` to run setup common to each nested test suite. You can also mix calls to `describe()` and `it()` at the same level. The `describe()` and `it()` calls execute in order, but all the `it()` calls execute before the `describe()` calls at the same level.

To quiz yourself on the order of execution in Mocha, figure out what the output will be if you run the following code in Mocha:

```
describe('', function() {
    console.log('Top level describe');

    beforeEach(function() {
        console.log('Top level beforeEach');
    });

    afterEach(function() {
        console.log('Top level afterEach');
    });

    describe('', function() {
        // The first describe has two it() calls
        beforeEach(function() {
            console.log('2nd level beforeEach from first describe');
        });

        afterEach(function() {
            console.log('2nd level afterEach from first describe');
        });

        it('', function() {
            console.log('test1');
        });

        it('', function() {
            console.log('test2');
        });
    });

    describe('', function() {
        // The second describe has one it call
        beforeEach(function() {
            console.log('2nd level beforeEach from second describe');
        });

        afterEach(function() {
            console.log('2nd level afterEach from second describe');
```

```
        });

        it('', function() {
            console.log('test3');
        });
    });

    it('', function() {
        console.log('test4');
    });
});
```

Because `it()` calls execute before same-level `describe()` calls, the output is as follows:

```
Top level beforeEach
Test4
Top level afterEach
Top level beforeEach
2nd level beforeEach from first describe
test1
2nd level afterEach from first describe
Top level afterEach
Top level beforeEach
2nd level beforeEach from first describe
test2
2nd level afterEach from first describe
Top level afterEach
Top level beforeEach
2nd level beforeEach from second describe
test3
2nd level afterEach from second describe
Top level afterEach
```

This concludes your dive into the basics of the Mocha testing framework. Executing tests in NodeJS is a quick way to validate individual module correctness from your command line. The next step is executing your unit tests against an actual browser.

Unit Testing in the Browser with Karma

Executing your Mocha unit tests on the command line with NodeJS is simple but has some significant limitations. Running your tests in NodeJS is likely sufficient if your users are only browsing using Google Chrome. However, there are an inordinate number of subtle differences between how different browsers execute JavaScript, so there is a clear advantage to running unit tests in live browsers. Luckily, there is a powerful tool called Karma that enables you to launch browsers, utilize them for tests, and see the results on your command line. In this section, you use Karma to enable yourself to run your tests in Google Chrome directly from your command line.

Karma is most easily installed and configured using `npm`. Karma is organized as a lightweight core surrounded by a massive confederation of plug-ins, so don't be surprised if you see a `package.json` file with an army of dependencies that start with `karma-`. You can install Karma globally using `npm install karma -g` as usual. However, this is poor practice in actual projects because it fails to take advantage of the ability to simply run `npm install` and install all the project's dependencies. Once again, the ideal JavaScript project requires only a single command to install all its dependencies. To make this a reality with your simple Karma tests, put your Karma dependencies in a `package.json` file:

```
{
  "name": "chapter-9",
  "version": "0.0.0",
  "description": "",
  "main": "index.js",
  "scripts": {
    "test": "make test"
  },
  "dependencies": {
    "mocha": "1.20.1",
    "karma": "0.12.16",
    "karma-chai": "0.1.0",
    "karma-mocha": "0.1.4",
    "karma-chrome-launcher": "0.1.4"
  },
  "author": "Valeri Karpov",
  "license": "ISC"
}
```

Notice that, even in this simple case of one simple test file and one browser, you had to install three Karma plug-ins. The `karma` package represents the lightweight core of Karma. The `karma-mocha` package enables Karma to integrate with Mocha, and `karma-chai` provides an assertion framework for your Mocha tests. Finally, `karma-chrome-launcher` enables Karma to launch and instrument a live Google Chrome browser. After you've run `npm install`, run `./node_modules/karma/bin/karma --version` to verify that the correct version of Karma is installed.

> **NOTE** *The node package manager,* npm, *is somewhat unconventional. Unless you use the* -g *flag,* npm *installs your dependencies into a* node_modules *directory in your current directory. Furthermore, each dependency within the* node_modules *directory is a directory that contains its own* node_modules *directory. The decision to represent dependencies in NodeJS as a tree is often contested for being wasteful of space and bandwidth, but it offers two key advantages. First, you don't have to worry about maintaining a* PATH *variable. Second, because each module has its own copy of its dependencies, you never have a conflict between two modules depending on two incompatible versions of the same module. As a consequence of this second fact, there is little benefit to not specifying exact version numbers for your dependencies—that is,* 0.1.4 *instead of* ~0.1.

The way to tell Karma how to run your tests is via a configuration file. Karma looks for a `karma.conf.js` file in your current directory by default. Although you can create a Karma configuration file manually, you will usually use Karma's convenient `init` helper to set up the basics of your configuration file. Run the following command in your shell to initialize a configuration file:

```
./node_modules/karma/bin/karma init
```

Karma then asks you a few questions. In your case, select Mocha as your testing framework and Chrome as the only browser you want to launch. Once you're done, your current directory should contain a karma.conf.js file that looks something like this:

```javascript
module.exports = function(config) {
  config.set({

    // base path that will be used to resolve all patterns (eg. files, exclude)
    basePath: '',


    // frameworks to use
    // available frameworks: https://npmjs.org/browse/keyword/karma-adapter
    frameworks: ['mocha', 'chai'],


    // list of files / patterns to load in the browser
    files: [
      './my_form_controller.js',
      './my_form_controller.test.js'
    ],


    // list of files to exclude
    exclude: [

    ],

    preprocessors: {},

    reporters: ['progress'],


    // web server port
    port: 9876,


    // enable / disable colors in the output (reporters and logs)
    colors: true,

    logLevel: config.LOG_INFO,


    // enable / disable watching file and executing tests whenever any file changes
    autoWatch: true,


    // start these browsers
    // available browser launchers: https://npmjs.org/browse/keyword/karma-launcher
```

```
browsers: ['Chrome'],


// Continuous Integration mode
// if true, Karma captures browsers, runs the tests and exits
singleRun: false
});
};
```

This configuration is almost enough to be able to properly run your `my_form_controller.test.js` tests in Chrome. There is one further change you need to make to the `my_form_controller.test.js` file itself. Karma loads the specified files as-is in the browser, so your `my_form_controller.test.js` file needs to make sure that it doesn't call `require()` when running in the browser. The `require()` function is specific to NodeJS and will not exist when Karma tries to run your tests in Chrome.

> **NOTE** *Tools like Browserify (see Chapter 3) enable you to compile NodeJS-style JavaScript into browser-friendly JavaScript, but the particulars of these tools are tangential to the subject of testing AngularJS applications. In the interest of minimizing complexity, you won't be using Browserify in this chapter.*

Here's the modified header code for the `my_form_controller.test.js` file:

```
if (typeof require !== 'undefined') {
  MyFormController = require('./my_form_controller.js');
  assert = require('assert');
}
```

Now, you should be able to start Karma by running `./node_modules/karma/bin/karma start`. Karma starts your local version of Google Chrome, executes your tests, and provides results on your command line.

If you intend to use Karma in your projects, you should use an automation tool similar to Grunt, Gulp, or Make (see Chapter 2) to simplify your testing workflow, in addition to saving you from having to type `./node_modules/karma/bin/karma` every time. For example, here's a simple rule you can add to your `Makefile` to enable you to start Karma with the more concise `make karma` command:

```
karma:
    ./node_modules/karma/bin/karma start
```

Browser Testing in the Cloud with Sauce

The Karma testing setup described in the previous section is rarely used in practice. Although it seems simple, your current Karma setup is limited by the fact that you need to install all browsers you want to test on each development machine. In all likelihood, you want to be able to test your application on multiple versions of Microsoft Internet Explorer and the myriad mobile browsers. Setting up an environment with these browsers on a development machine is tedious. Thankfully, there is a cloud solution to this problem: Sauce, `https://saucelabs.com`, provides the ability to provision live browsers to execute tests. In addition, Sauce provides good support for Karma. You don't need to use Karma for Sauce, but for the purposes of this section, you define a new Karma configuration that provisions browsers in Sauce.

First, go to https://saucelabs.com and sign up for an account. Sauce provides a paid service, but there is a free tier that provides a limited amount of test time. The free tier should be sufficient for the purposes of this chapter. Once you have signed up, remember your username and find your Sauce application programming interface (API) key. You need both of these. First, here are the contents of karma-sauce.conf.js, the configuration file for Karma and Sauce:

```
module.exports = function(config) {
  var customLaunchers = {
    sl_firefox: {
      base: 'SauceLabs',
      browserName: 'firefox',
      version: '27'
    },
    sl_safari: {
      base: 'SauceLabs',
      browserName: 'safari',
      platform: 'OS X 10.6',
      version: '5'
    },
    sl_ie_9: {
      base: 'SauceLabs',
      browserName: 'internet explorer',
      platform: 'Windows 7',
      version: '9'
    }
  };

  config.set({

    // base path that will be used to resolve all patterns (eg. files, exclude)
    basePath: '',


    // frameworks to use
    // available frameworks: https://npmjs.org/browse/keyword/karma-adapter
    frameworks: ['mocha', 'chai'],


    // list of files / patterns to load in the browser
    files: [
      './my_form_controller.js',
      './my_form_controller.test.js'
    ],

    exclude: [],

    preprocessors: {},

    reporters: ['dots', 'saucelabs'],


    // web server port
```

```
      port: 9876,


      // enable / disable colors in the output (reporters and logs)
      colors: true,

      logLevel: config.LOG_INFO,


      // enable / disable watching file and executing tests whenever any file changes
      autoWatch: true,

      // use these custom launchers for starting browsers on Sauce
      customLaunchers: customLaunchers,

      // start these browsers
      // available browser launchers: https://npmjs.org/browse/keyword/karma-launcher
      browsers: Object.keys(customLaunchers),


      // Continuous Integration mode
      // if true, Karma captures browsers, runs the tests and exits
      singleRun: true,

      sauceLabs: {
        testName: 'Web App Unit Tests'
      },
    });
  };
```

The changes highlighted in the previous code enable Karma to connect to Sauce and provision the desired browsers. The `customLaunchers` object defines a list of operating system (OS) and browser configurations you want Sauce to provision. In this case, you start Firefox 27 on Linux, Safari 6 on Mac OSX 10.6 Snow Leopard, and Internet Explorer 9 on Microsoft Windows 7. Because Karma runs forever watching for changes to files by default, the `singleRun` option is necessary for tests to terminate properly. Finally, the `sauceLabs.testName` field allows you to specify a human-readable identifier for your tests to allow you to find logs from your test runs in Sauce's resources dashboard.

You need two more minor changes to run Karma with the Sauce configuration. First, you need to modify your Makefile to run this new Karma configuration. The Karma executable treats the second command-line argument as the configuration file it should use, so running `karma start karma-sauce.conf.js` tells Karma to use this new configuration file. You should create a new rule in your Makefile to run Karma with the new config:

```
karma-sauce:
    ./node_modules/karma/bin/karma start karma-sauce.conf.js
```

In addition to the new make `karma-sauce` rule, you need to provide your Sauce username and API key. By default, `karma-sauce` looks for environment variables named SAUCE_USERNAME and SAUCE_ACCESS_KEY to know which credentials it should use. If you don't have experience using environment variables, don't worry; there are two very easy ways to set these variables.

> **NOTE** *An* environment variable *is a named variable that is global to your command-line session. The most well-known example of an environment variable is* PATH, *the variable that tells your shell which directories it should look for executables in. Some web developers use environment variables to configure servers and command-line tools. Debates between web developers over whether configuration files or environment variables are the appropriate way to handle server configuration are frequent.*

The first way to set an environment variable is using the env command. The env command creates a transient environment variable that only exists for the lifetime of the current shell command. For instance, running env SAUCE_USERNAME=vkarpov15 make karma-sauce properly exposes the SAUCE_USERNAME variable to the make karma-sauce command. However, if you run make karma-sauce again, the SAUCE_USERNAME variable isn't set unless you preface your command with env SAUCE_USERNAME=vkarpov15 again.

Using the env command every time can get repetitive, so you may choose to use the export command. Running export SAUCE_USERNAME=vkarpov15 sets the SAUCE_USERNAME environment variable until you close your terminal window. You can then run make karma-sauce without an extra configuration.

To highlight the effectiveness of Sauce, you run tests that are specifically designed to fail in different ways on Safari 5 and Internet Explorer 9:

```
describe('Tests that fail on different browsers', function() {
    describe('Safari 5 disallows non-UTC designators for ISO dates', function() {
        assert.ok(new Date('2007-04-05T14:30:00').toString() != 'Invalid Date');
    });

    describe('IE9 outputs weird date string format', function() {
        // IE9 outputs a date that looks like 'Thu Apr 5 14:30:00 UTC 2007'
        var d = new Date('2007-04-05T14:30:00').toString();
        assert.ok(d.indexOf('Thu Apr 05 2007') != -1);
    });
});
```

Now, when you run make karma-sauce, you should see something similar to the next output. The tests should succeed on Firefox 27 and fail on Safari 5 and Internet Explorer 9:

```
INFO [launcher.sauce]: firefox 27 session at https://saucelabs.com/tests/...
INFO [Firefox 27.0.0 (Linux)]: Connected on socket iDn0_bZOOKuYNovd-DoC...
..
Firefox 27.0.0 (Linux): Executed 2 of 2 SUCCESS (0.251 secs / 0.001 secs)
INFO [launcher.sauce]: safari 5 (OS X 10.6) session at ...
INFO [launcher.sauce]: internet explorer 9 (Windows 7) session at ...
INFO [Safari 5.1.9 (Mac OS X 10.6.8)]: Connected on socket UfV5ZJ01UhK38mA1-DoD...
Safari 5.1.9 (Mac OS X 10.6.8) ERROR
  AssertionError: expected false to be truthy
  at /Users/vkarpov/Desktop/Wiley/Sample/Chapter 9/node_modules/chai/chai.js:925
```

```
Safari 5.1.9 (Mac OS X 10.6.8) ERROR
  AssertionError: expected false to be truthy
  at /Users/vkarpov/Desktop/Wiley/Sample/Chapter 9/node_modules/chai/chai.js:925
Safari 5.1.9 (Mac OS X 10.6.8): Executed 0 of 0 ERROR (0.686 secs / 0 secs)
INFO [IE 9.0.0 (Windows 7)]: Connected on socket dxAxFkCbwzDSkIjx-DoE ...
IE 9.0.0 (Windows 7) ERROR
  AssertionError: expected false to be truthy
  at /Users/vkarpov/Desktop/Wiley/Sample/Chapter 9/node_modules/chai/chai.js:921
IE 9.0.0 (Windows 7) ERROR
  AssertionError: expected false to be truthy
  at /Users/vkarpov/Desktop/Wiley/Sample/Chapter 9/node_modules/chai/chai.js:921
IE 9.0.0 (Windows 7): Executed 0 of 0 ERROR (1.678 secs / 0 secs)
INFO [launcher.sauce]: Shutting down Sauce Connect
make: *** [karma-sauce] Error 1
```

At a high level, Karma provisions the desired browsers in Sauce and directs Sauce to point them to a lightweight web server that Karma starts on your local machine. When Sauce loads the page, Karma captures the browser, enabling Karma to run tests on that browser. An unfortunate side effect of this is that Karma may time out while trying to capture a browser, particularly if your local machine is on a slow Internet connection. Thus, your tests may fail simply because your Internet connection is too slow.

Evaluating the Unit Testing Options

The three unit testing approaches in this section—NodeJS, Karma, and Karma with Sauce—come with their own set of trade-offs. Running your tests with NodeJS on Mocha is easy to set up, reliable, and fast, but it doesn't account for different JavaScript execution engines. Running your tests in Karma against local browsers is fast, reliable, and does enable you to test multiple JavaScript engines, but it requires installing every browser you want to test on your local machine. Running your tests in the Sauce cloud with Karma is slow and unreliable but enables you to test multiple JavaScript engines without having to install additional browsers locally.

Which one of these approaches works best for you depends on your particular application's requirements. However, browser-specific bugs are becoming less and less frequent in the realm of pure unit tests. Browser-specific bugs usually occur when testing against an actual DOM. At the unit test level, most browser-specific bugs occur with the JavaScript Date object, but these difficulties are mitigated with libraries like moment. More often than not, NodeJS is sufficient for strict unit testing. However, as you'll see in the next section, Karma and Sauce are also incredibly useful for running DOM integration tests.

DOM INTEGRATION TESTS

Unit tests are quite powerful and an excellent tool for catching bugs before they break your production environment. However, unit tests don't capture everything that can go wrong. Even if your code has excellent unit test coverage, the integration between your modules or between your modules and the DOM may be broken. Thankfully, AngularJS provides two distinct powerful toolsets for running tests that integrate with the DOM: ng-scenario and protractor.

The first tool, ng-scenario, runs tests by taking over an `iframe` element. It is considered deprecated by the AngularJS team in favor of the second tool, protractor, due to the limitations inherent in the `iframe` approach. Specifically, as a security measure, JavaScript code in virtually every modern browser is not allowed to access the internals of an `iframe` element if its current URL is on a different domain. This means that your test code must be run on the same domain as the code under test, which is a significant limitation when you want to automate testing of a staging server. However, ng-scenario also offers advantages: It is easier to set up and is less tedious to work with.

Protractor, on the other hand, is based on Google's Selenium browser automation tool. Selenium is a powerful tool for starting and controlling various browsers, and protractor provides an AngularJS-friendly layer on top of Selenium. Although protractor does not suffer from the `iframe` limitations of an angular-scenario, it does suffer from the limitations and non-testing-oriented design decisions inherent in Selenium. One bug (or feature, depending on your perspective) that first-time Selenium users often find extremely frustrating is that Selenium throws an exception when you call `click()` on an element that Selenium doesn't think is visible. Although this behavior is considered correct from Selenium's point of view, in practice it puts a great deal of pressure on user interface/user experience (UI/UX) specialists to work within the confines of Selenium's quirks.

In the next couple of sections, you'll learn to write DOM-integrated tests with these two tools. The tests you will be writing will be integration tests that test the DOM interaction but not the server interaction. The server will still be stubbed out, using AngularJS's handy `$httpBackend` service. From an architectural perspective, these tests will look like Figure 9-3.

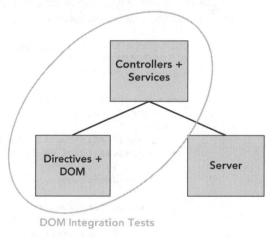

DOM Integration Tests

FIGURE 9-3

A Guide to $httpBackend

In the unit testing section, you created mocked-out stubs for AngularJS scopes. Scopes are simple objects, but mocking out the complex `$http` service can be tricky. Thankfully, AngularJS provides a convenience `$httpBackend` object that allows you to stub out `$http` for testing. The `$httpBackend` object provides numerous helpers that make stubbing out your server interactions much less verbose, which is key for integration tests that may do multiple server requests over the course of their execution.

The `$httpBackend` service is defined in the `ngMock` module. The AngularJS documentation specifies two different `$httpBackend` objects: one for unit testing in the `ngMock` module and one for integration testing in the `ngMockE2E` module; however, both are packaged in one file: `angular-mocks.js`. Therefore, you should download just the `angular-mocks.js` file, either using `bower install angular-mocks` or `code.angularjs.org`. For your convenience, `angular-mocks.js` for AngularJS v1.2.16 has been included with the sample code for this chapter. In this section's example, you will be using the one defined in the `ngMock` module; however, in your integration tests, you will be using the one in the `ngMockE2E` module. The difference between these two `$httpBackend` services is fairly trivial: The service in the ngMockE2E module has a passthrough function that enables you to specify certain routes that pass through the mock $http service and talk to a real server, whereas the service in the ngMock module lacks this function. Because you will not be using the passthrough function in this section, these two modules will be essentially interchangeable.

> **NOTE** *The* ngMock *module has a significant limitation: It is dependent on AngularJS being present in the global* window *object, and, in particular, can't be run in NodeJS without significant finagling. If you choose to run your unit tests in NodeJS, please make sure you write your own stub for* $http *rather than using* $httpBackend.

Learning to use $httpBackend is fairly straightforward from an example. Recall the MyFormController function from the unit testing section, which validates that a user entered in a username and e-mail:

```
function MyFormController($scope, $http) {
    $scope.userData = {};
    $scope.errorMessages = [];

    $scope.saveForm = function() {
        $scope.saving = true;
        $http.
            put('/api/submit', $scope.userData).
            success(function(data) {
                $scope.saving = false;
                $scope.success = true;
            }).
            error(function(err) {
                $scope.saving = false;
                $scope.error = err;
            });
    };

    $scope.validateForm = function() {
        var validationFunctions = [
            {
                fn: function() {
                    return !!$scope.userData.name
                },
                message: 'Name required'
            },
            {
                fn: function() {
                    return !!$scope.userData.email
                },
                message: 'Email required'
            }
        ];

        $scope.errorMessages = [];
        for (var i = 0; i < validationFunctions.length; ++i) {
            if (!validationFunctions[i].fn()) {
```

```
                    $scope.errorMessages.push(validationFunctions[i].message);
                }
            }
            return $scope.errorMessages;
        };
    }
```

Note that to make $httpBackend available in your tests, you need to make a small modification to your Karma configuration file to include both AngularJS and the ngMock module. This is because the ngMock module is dependent on AngularJS being present on the global window object.

```
// list of files / patterns to load in the browser
files: [
  './angular.js',
  './angular-mocks.js',
  './my_form_controller.js',
  './my_form_controller.test.js',
  './my_form_controller.http_backend.test.js'
],
```

The newly added my_form_controller.http_backend.test.js file contains a simple unit test for testing the saveForm function using $httpBackend:

```
describe('MyFormController', function() {
    describe('saveForm', function() {
        var $httpBackend, $rootScope, createController;

        beforeEach(inject(function($injector) {
            // set up the mock http service responses
            $httpBackend = $injector.get('$httpBackend');

            // get hold of a scope (i.e., the root scope)
            $rootScope = $injector.get('$rootScope');
            // the $controller service is used to create instances of controllers
            var $controller = $injector.get('$controller');

            createController = function() {
                return $controller('MyFormController', {
                    '$scope' : $rootScope
                });
            };
        }));

        it('should handle a successful server request', function() {
            createController();

            $httpBackend.when('PUT', '/api/submit').respond(200, {});

            $rootScope.saveForm();

            assert.ok($rootScope.saving);

            $httpBackend.flush();

            assert.ok(!$rootScope.saving);
```

```
            assert.ok($rootScope.success);
        });

        it('should handle server-side error', function() {
            createController();

            $httpBackend.when('PUT', '/api/submit').respond(
                500,
                { error: 'Oops' });

            $rootScope.saveForm();

            assert.ok($rootScope.saving);

            $httpBackend.flush();

            assert.ok(!$rootScope.saving);
            assert.ok(!$rootScope.success);
            assert.equal('Oops', $rootScope.error.error);
        });
    });
});
```

In the preceding code, $httpBackend provides a means of configuring a stubbed-out $http object, which is passed in to the controller via AngularJS's inject function. You may have never seen the inject function before, because it is rarely used outside of test code and the AngularJS core. The inject function executes AngularJS's name-based dependency injection manually. In this case, it executes the MyFormController function with $scope set to the $rootScope variable and a stubbed-out $http configured by $httpBackend. Note that you don't have to modify $http itself; modifying $httpBackend is sufficient.

The when function on $httpBackend enables you to specify the result of a server call with $http. The when function uses a fluent syntax designed for readability, such as the following call:

```
$httpBackend.when('PUT', '/api/submit').respond(200, {});
```

This tells $httpBackend that, when the code under test does an HTTP PUT request to the /api/submit route, the result will have HTTP status 200 (meaning that the request succeeded) and an empty body. If the code under test makes an HTTP request that $httpBackend hasn't been configured to handle using the when function, $httpBackend throws an error and your tests fail.

There is one more detail that is important about $httpBackend: It operates asynchronously, so you need to call the flush function to send responses to your code's HTTP requests. This is handy for testing intermediate state, for instance, testing that the saving variable is true after validateForm was called but before the HTTP response returns. This asynchronous behavior is also useful for testing long-running requests, such as if you want to test a time-out on an HTTP request. However, note that the flush function doesn't take parameters, so it is impossible to flush a specific request. The flush function causes *all* outstanding HTTP requests to receive their results.

Now that you understand how $httpBackend works, you're ready to use $httpBackend to write some sophisticated DOM integration tests with protractor and ng-scenario. Once again, recall how

DOM integration tests look in the context of AngularJS architecture. The DOM integration tests will interact with DOM elements on a page with a stubbed-out server, or, essentially, function as end-to-end tests with a fake back end.

The Page You'll Be Testing

In the next two sections, you're going to write a suite of DOM integration tests for an HTML page that uses the `MyFormController` code. First, take a look at the HTML page, `my_form.html`, that will be tested. This page may not be the most sophisticated AngularJS page out there, but writing tests for this page demonstrates the basic principles necessary to test sophisticated apps:

```html
<body ng-controller="MyFormController">
    <h1>This is a Form</h1>
    <hr>
    <h2>Name</h2>
    <input   type="text"
             ng-model="userData.name">
    <h2>Email</h2>
    <input   type="text"
             ng-model="userData.email">
    <hr>
    <input   type="submit"
             value="Save"
             ng-click="validateForm().length === 0 && saveForm()">
    <h2 ng-show="saving">Saving...</h2>
    <h2 ng-show="success">Saved!</h2>
    <div ng-show="errorMessages.length > 0">
        <h3>Errors occurred:</h3>
        <div ng-repeat="message in errorMessages">
            {{ message }}
        </div>
    </div>
</body>
```

In addition, running tests with ng-scenario and protractor requires a web server. There are myriad ways to set up a web server to serve static content using NodeJS, but for the purposes of this chapter, you use the `node-static` module and a simple `server.js` script:

```js
var static = require('node-static');

var fileServer = new static.Server('./');

require('http').createServer(function (request, response) {
  request.addListener('end', function () {
      fileServer.serve(request, response);
  }).resume();
}).listen(8080);
```

Now, running `node server.js` launches a web server on port 8080 that serves the contents of this chapter's source directory. Once you've started the server, navigate your browser to `http://localhost:8080/my_form.html` to see the simple form page in action.

DOM Integration Tests with ng-scenario

The ng-scenario framework is a simple E2E and integration testing tool. It operates by taking control of an `iframe` element and provides an API so you can manipulate the `iframe` element. The AngularJS team currently considers ng-scenario deprecated in favor of protractor; however, depending on your use case, it may be a better tool for you than protractor. Over the next two sections, you explore the trade-offs between these two frameworks, starting with ng-scenario.

Although you don't necessarily have to use Karma with ng-scenario, Karma makes using ng-scenario easier by handling launching browsers and providing output on the command line. Much like Mocha and Chai, ng-scenario is available as a Karma framework through npm. You can include `karma-ng-scenario` as a dependency in your `package.json` and run `npm install`:

```
"dependencies": {
    "mocha": "1.20.1",
    "karma": "0.12.16",
    "karma-chai": "0.1.0",
    "karma-mocha": "0.1.4",
    "karma-ng-scenario": "0.1.0",
    "karma-chrome-launcher": "0.1.4",
    "karma-sauce-launcher": "0.2.8"
},
```

Now that you've installed ng-scenario, you're going to create another Karma configuration file and another Makefile rule. Following is `karma-ng-scenario.conf.js`. This Karma configuration only needs to load one file, `my_form_controller.ng-scenario.test.js`, the suite of tests that the browser should run. It also needs to include the ng-scenario framework and establish a *proxy*. The proxy tells Karma where the local web server is, so when you tell ng-scenario to navigate to `my_form.html`, Karma knows that means (`http://localhost:8080/my_form.html`). Furthermore, ng-scenario comes with its own assertion framework that is much easier to use with ng-scenario than Chai, so you won't include the Chai framework:

```
module.exports = function(config) {
  config.set({
    basePath: '',


    // frameworks to use
    // available frameworks: https://npmjs.org/browse/keyword/karma-adapter
    frameworks: ['ng-scenario', 'mocha'],


    // list of files / patterns to load in the browser
    files: [
      './my_form_controller.ng-scenario.test.js',
    ],

    reporters: ['progress'],

    proxies : {
      '/': 'http://localhost:8080'
```

```
    },

    // web server port
    port: 8080,

    runnerPort: 9100,


    // enable / disable colors in the output (reporters and logs)
    colors: true,

    logLevel: config.LOG_DEBUG,


    // enable / disable watching file and executing tests whenever any file changes
    autoWatch: false,


    // start these browsers
    // available browser launchers: https://npmjs.org/browse/keyword/karma-launcher
    browsers: ['Chrome'],


    // Continuous Integration mode
    // if true, Karma captures browsers, runs the tests, and exits
    singleRun: true
  });
};
```

You run these integration tests only on Chrome and enable single-run mode, so Karma exits after tests run. The reason for using single-run mode is that integration tests are typically much slower than unit tests, so, in practice, you often don't want to run them after every save. In addition to this configuration file, add another rule to your Makefile:

```
karma-ng-scenario:
    ./node_modules/karma/bin/karma start karma-ng-scenario.conf.js
```

Unfortunately, $httpBackend has two significant limitations. First, for the purposes of testing, $httpBackend must be defined in the code that's under test, not in the test code. Second, $httpBackend stores when conditions in a private array, so once you set a when condition, there is no way to change it. These are significant limitations, but, as you'll see, there are a few reasonable workarounds to make $httpBackend behave.

Here's the header code for my_form.html, with included $httpBackend. Note the fact that the code attaches $httpBackend to the global window object. The reason for this decision will become clear when you actually write the test code.

```
<script type="text/javascript" src="/angular.js"></script>
<script type="text/javascript" src="/angular-mocks.js"></script>
<script type="text/javascript">
    var app = angular.module('domTest', ['ngMockE2E']);

    app.config(function($provide) {
        $provide.decorator('$httpBackend',
```

```
                        angular.mock.e2e.$httpBackendDecorator);
            });

            // define the fake back end
            app.run(function($httpBackend, $window) {
                $window.$httpBackend = $httpBackend;
            });
        </script>
        <script type="text/javascript" src="/my_form_controller.js"></script>
```

Now you need to write my_form_controller.ng-scenario.test.js. There are three scenarios you are going to test. First, you test that if the user enters their information correctly, they see a confirmation. Second, you test that the user sees error messages when they don't enter information. Third, you test that the appropriate error message shows up when there is an error on the server. Here are these three tests in ng-scenario:

```
describe('MyForm', function() {
    it('should submit successfully', function() {
        browser().navigateTo('/my_form.html');

        httpBackend(200, {});

        input('userData.name').enter('Victor Hugo');
        input('userData.email').enter('les@miserabl.es');
        element('input[type=submit]').click();

        expect(element('#saved').css('display')).not().toBe('none');
        expect(element('#saving').css('display')).toBe('none');
        expect(element('#errors').css('display')).toBe('none');
    });

    it('should show errors properly', function() {
        browser().navigateTo('/my_form.html');

        httpBackend(200, {});

        element('input[type=submit]').click();

        expect(element('#saved').css('display')).toBe('none');
        expect(element('#saving').css('display')).toBe('none');
        expect(element('#errors').css('display')).not().toBe('none');

        expect(repeater('.error-message').count()).toBe(2);
        expect(element('.error-message:nth-of-type(1)').html())
            .toContain('Name required');
        expect(element('.error-message:nth-of-type(2)').html())
            .toContain('Email required');
    });

    it('should handle server errors', function() {
        browser().navigateTo('/my_form.html');

        httpBackend(500, { error: 'Internal Server Error' });

        input('userData.name').enter('Victor Hugo');
```

```
        input('userData.email').enter('les@miserabl.es');
        element('input[type=submit]').click();

        expect(element('#saved').css('display')).toBe('none');
        expect(element('#server-error').css('display')).not().toBe('none');
        expect(element('#server-error').html())
            .toContain('Server Error: Internal Server Error');
      });
    });

  angular.scenario.dsl('httpBackend', function() {
    return function(code, response) {
      return this.addFutureAction('tweaking $httpBackend',
        function(window, document, done) {
          window.$httpBackend.when('PUT', '/api/submit').respond(code, response);
          done();
        });
    };
  });
```

Pay special attention to the preceding DSL code. DSL stands for *domain-specific language*. In the case of ng-scenario, a DSL allows you to define functions that operate on the `window` and `document` of the page under test. Because `my_form.html` exposes `$httpBackend` as a property of the `window` object, the DSL enables the test code to set the appropriate behavior for `$httpBackend`.

You may be wondering why these tests use the `expect` function to do assertions instead of `assert.equal`. It's because calls to ng-scenario's `element.css` function, such as `element('#saved').css('display')`, return a future rather than an actual string value. In other words, the return value of `element.css` is an object wrapper around an asynchronous operation, and the actual assertion should only be done when the asynchronous operation completes. The `expect` function wraps all the confusing asynchronous behavior and lets you write your test code as if it were synchronous.

> **NOTE** *The future design pattern is used for dealing with values that are computed asynchronously. It is closely related to the more well-known promise design pattern. A future is an object that serves as a placeholder for a value to be computed at some point in the future. For the purposes of ng-scenario, you don't need to know anything about futures beyond this one-sentence definition, because the* expect *function allows you to interact with futures as if they were simple numbers and strings.*

The `browser`, `input`, and `element` functions are all provided by ng-scenario. In fact, ng-scenario provides a rich set of tools for browser interaction. You can see a full list at code .angularjs.org/1.2.16/docs/guide/e2e-testing. However, the `browser`, `input`, and `element` functions are the most commonly used.

The `browser` function is primarily useful for the `navigateTo` function, which you used in the previous code to tell the browser to load `my_form.html` at the start of each test. The `input` function exposes a function called `enter`, which sets the value of a string input and calls `scope.$apply` in the page under test. The `element` function lets you use a subset of the jQuery API to query and modify elements in the page under test. For example, the `element('#saved').css('display')` function call returns a future representing the value of the cascading style sheets (CSS) `display` property on the DOM element with ID `saved`.

Now that you've looked at the test code, it's time to actually run the tests. Start the web server with `node server.js`, and, in a separate terminal window, run `make karma-ng-scenario`. You should see nice output that looks like this:

```
Chrome 35.0.1916 (Mac OS X 10.9.2): Executed 0 of 3 SUCCESS (0 secs / 0 secs)
DEBUG [proxy]: proxying request - /my_form.html to localhost:8080
DEBUG [proxy]: proxying request - /angular.js to localhost:8080
DEBUG [proxy]: proxying request - /angular-mocks.js to localhost:8080
Chrome 35.0.1916 (Mac OS X 10.9.2): Executed 2 of 3 SUCCESS (0 secs / 0.434 secs
Chrome 35.0.1916 (Mac OS X 10.9.2): Executed 3 of 3 SUCCESS (0 secs / 0.564 secs
Chrome 35.0.1916 (Mac OS X 10.9.2): Executed 3 of 3 SUCCESS (0.596 secs /
0.564 secs)
DEBUG [karma]: Run complete, exitting.
DEBUG [launcher]: Disconnecting all browsers
DEBUG [launcher]: Process Chrome exited with code 0
DEBUG [temp-dir]: Cleaning temp dir /var/folders/7h/...
```

The powerful part of using Karma for ng-scenario integration testing is easy integration with Sauce. Recall that you've already used Sauce to provision browsers in the cloud for running unit tests. You can do the same thing with ng-scenario tests! Karma even handles setting up a tunnel so the Sauce browsers can communicate with your local server. You don't need to make changes to the integration tests defined in `my_form_controller.ng-scenario.test.js`. You just need to create a new Karma configuration file: `karma-ng-scenario-sauce.conf.js`:

```
module.exports = function(config) {
  var customLaunchers = {
    sl_firefox: {
      base: 'SauceLabs',
      browserName: 'firefox',
      version: '27'
    },
    sl_safari: {
      base: 'SauceLabs',
      browserName: 'safari',
      platform: 'OS X 10.6',
      version: '5'
    },
    sl_ie_9: {
      base: 'SauceLabs',
      browserName: 'internet explorer',
      platform: 'Windows 7',
      version: '9'
    }
  };

  config.set({
```

```
    basePath: '',

    frameworks: ['ng-scenario', 'mocha'],

    // list of files / patterns to load in the browser
    files: [
      './my_form_controller.ng-scenario.test.js',
    ],

    reporters: ['dots', 'saucelabs'],

    proxies : {
      '/': 'http://localhost:8080'
    },

    // web server port
    port: 8080,

    runnerPort: 9100,

    // enable / disable colors in the output (reporters and logs)
    colors: true,

    logLevel: config.LOG_DEBUG,

    autoWatch: false,

    customLaunchers: customLaunchers,

    browsers: Object.keys(customLaunchers),

    singleRun: true,

    sauceLabs: {
      testName: 'Web App Integration Tests - ' + (new Date()).toString()
    },
  });
};
```

Congratulations! You've successfully used Karma and ng-scenario to run DOM integration tests on Internet Explorer 9, Safari 5, and Firefox. As you've seen, ng-scenario is powerful, simple, and requires minimal setup. In addition, with Karma's tunneling capabilities, it's possible to run tests on external browsers, such as in Sauce.

However, ng-scenario's approach of using an iframe comes with two significant limitations. First, users will not be running your page in an iframe, so your tests won't mirror the user's environment exactly. Second, you need to run your tests in ng-scenario from the same machine as your server is running on. This is not a significant limitation for development work, but what about testing a remote staging server deployed via Heroku, testing a server that you don't have SSH access to, or testing a server that you can't launch browsers on? It is quite possible to have a comprehensive testing strategy with ng-scenario and Sauce, but these limitations may be deal breakers in certain organizations. As you'll see in the next section, protractor lacks these limitations.

DOM Integration Testing with Protractor

Protractor provides an alternative to ng-scenario for DOM integration and E2E testing. Unlike ng-scenario, protractor has its own configuration method and should not be used with Karma. Protractor enables you to separate your tests from your server, so you can test a staging server or possibly even your production server from a script on your local machine. Protractor also uses the Jasmine testing framework exclusively, but Jasmine and Mocha are almost interchangeable, so you shouldn't be able to tell the difference.

Much like the other modules in this chapter, protractor is available via npm. You should add protractor as a dependency in your package.json and run npm install. In addition, it's necessary to run a web server to run tests with protractor, so you also need the node-static module that was introduced in the section "DOM Integration Tests with ng-scenario," earlier in this chapter.

```
"dependencies": {
    "mocha": "1.20.1",
    "karma": "0.12.16",
    "karma-chai": "0.1.0",
    "karma-mocha": "0.1.4",
    "karma-ng-scenario": "0.1.0",
    "karma-chrome-launcher": "0.1.4",
    "karma-sauce-launcher": "0.2.8",
    "node-static": "0.7.3",
    "protractor": "0.24.2"
},
```

Protractor is dependent on the open source Selenium project's WebDriverJS tool. WebDriverJS is not available via npm, but protractor comes with a tool to install and manage WebDriverJS. First, to install WebDriverJS, run the following:

```
./node_modules/protractor/bin/webdriver-manager update
```

Once that's done, start WebDriverJS:

```
./node_modules/protractor/bin/webdriver-manager start
```

Because protractor is Selenium-based and decoupled from the page under test, it lacks the DSL functionality that you saw in the "DOM Integration Tests with ng-scenario" section. As a consequence, you need to provide your own means of configuring your stubbed-out $httpBackend in the page under test. The simplest way to do this is to create a separate page, my_form .protractor.html, which configures the page's $httpBackend based on the query parameters provided. Here's what the $httpBackend setup JavaScript looks like on this new page:

```
var parseQueryString = function(queryString) {
    var params = {};
    pairs = queryString.split("&");

    for (var i = 0; i < pairs.length; ++i) {
        var pair = pairs[i].split('=');
        params[pair[0]] = decodeURIComponent(pair[1]);
```

```
    }

    return params;
};

var app = angular.module('domTest', ['ngMockE2E']);

app.config(function($provide) {
    $provide.decorator('$httpBackend',
        angular.mock.e2e.$httpBackendDecorator);
});

// define the fake back end
app.run(function($httpBackend, $window) {
    if ($window.location.href.indexOf('?') != -1) {
        var index = $window.location.href.indexOf('?');
        var queryParams =
          parseQueryString($window.location.href.substr(index + 1));
        var code = parseInt(queryParams.code || '200', 10);
        var result = JSON.parse(queryParams.response || '{}');
        $httpBackend.when('PUT', '/api/submit').respond(code, result);
        return;
    }
    $httpBackend.when('PUT', '/api/submit').respond(200, {});
});
```

This extra code enables you to configure your stubbed-out back end using a uniform resource locator (URL). For instance, by navigating the browser to my_form.protractor.html?code=500, $httpBackend returns an HTTP 500 with an empty response for PUT requests to /api/submit. Armed with this new code, you can write your first protractor tests.

The following tests the same three cases that the ng-scenario tests did. If you recall that section, these tests should look familiar. The first case is that, if the user enters valid information and the server responds with an HTTP 200, the user sees a confirmation message. The second case is that, if the user enters invalid information, they see an error message. The third case is that, if the user enters valid information but there is a server error, the user sees a message informing them of the server error. Here is how these tests look in protractor:

```
describe('MyForm', function() {
    var ptor;

    beforeEach(function() {
        browser.get('http://localhost:8081/my_form.protractor.html');
        ptor = protractor.getInstance();
    });

    it('should submit successfully', function() {
        element(by.model('userData.name')).sendKeys('Victor Hugo');
        element(by.model('userData.email')).sendKeys('les@miserabl.es');

        element(by.css('input[type=submit]')).click();

        expect(element(by.css('#saved')).
```

```
                    getCssValue('display')).
                        toBe('block');
        expect(element(by.css('#saving')).
            getCssValue('display')).
                toBe('none');
        expect(element(by.css('#errors')).
            getCssValue('display')).
                toBe('none');
    });

    it('should show errors properly', function() {
        element(by.css('input[type=submit]')).click();

        expect(element(by.css('#saved')).
            getCssValue('display')).
                toBe('none');
        expect(element(by.css('#saving')).
            getCssValue('display')).
                toBe('none');
        expect(element(by.css('#errors')).
            getCssValue('display')).
                toBe('block');

        expect(element.all(by.css('.error-message')).
            count()).toBe(2);
        expect(element(by.css('.error-message:nth-of-type(1)')).
            getText()).
                toContain('Name required');
        expect(element(by.css('.error-message:nth-of-type(2)')).
            getText()).
                toContain('Email required');
    });

    it('should handle server errors', function() {
        var response =
            '%7B%20"error"%3A%20\"Internal%20Server%20Error"%20%7D';
        var url = 'http://localhost:8081/my_form.protractor.html?' +
            'code=500&' +
            'response=' + response;
        browser.get(url);

        element(by.model('userData.name')).sendKeys('Victor Hugo');
        element(by.model('userData.email')).sendKeys('les@miserabl.es');

        element(by.css('input[type=submit]')).click();

        expect(element(by.css('#saved')).
            getCssValue('display')).
                toBe('none');
        expect(element(by.css('#server-error')).
            getCssValue('display')).
                toBe('block');
        expect(element(by.css('#server-error')).
            getText()).
```

```
                        toContain('Server Error: Internal Server Error');
        });
    });
```

Much like ng-scenario, protractor's syntax is designed to be very readable. Unfortunately, protractor's syntax is much more clunky and verbose. The preceding highlighted code shows several common patterns that appear in virtually every protractor test. Furthermore, most of the protractor tests primarily use combinations of these simple patterns. Here are these patterns explained in more detail:

```
// set the value of an input field with ngModel='userData.name'
// to 'Victor Hugo'
element(by.model('userData.name')).sendKeys('Victor Hugo');

// assert that the element matching the CSS selector '#saved'
// has its display CSS property set to 'block'
expect(element(by.css('#saved')).
    getCssValue('display')).
        toBe('block');

// click on an element matching the CSS selector
// 'input[type=submit]'
element(by.css('input[type=submit]')).click();

// assert that there are two elements on the page matching
// the CSS selector '.error-message'
expect(element.all(by.css('.error-message')).
    count()).toBe(2);

// assert that the text of the first div element with class
// 'error-message' contains 'Name required'
expect(element(by.css('.error-message:nth-of-type(1)')).
    getText()).
        toContain('Name required');
```

Because protractor doesn't use Karma, you need to use protractor's own configuration format. Here is the code for protractor_conf.js:

```
exports.config = {
  seleniumAddress: 'http://localhost:4444/wd/hub',

  // capabilities to be passed to the webdriver instance
  capabilities: {
    'browserName': 'chrome'
  },

  // spec patterns are relative to the current working directly when
  // protractor is called
  specs: ['my_form_controller.protractor.test.js'],

  // options to be passed to Jasmine-node
  jasmineNodeOpts: {
```

```
        showColors: true,
        defaultTimeoutInterval: 30000
    }
};
```

As you can see, protractor's configuration is usually fairly straightforward. One detail worth noting is the `seleniumAddress` variable, which is the uniform resource identifier (URI) for your Selenium server. The `webdriver-manager start` command you ran started a Selenium server on the default port, 4444. Protractor needs to be able to connect to this Selenium server to be able to run.

Another detail worth noting is that a protractor configuration file can launch only one browser at a time, specified in the `capabilities.browserName` field. You need separate protractor configurations for every browser you want to test.

Speaking of multiple browsers, you can also integrate protractor with Sauce. However, running tests against your local server with Sauce and protractor requires either setting up your own tunneling functionality or configuring a domain name for your local server. Unlike Karma, protractor doesn't automatically do tunneling for you. However, protractor's strength lies in being able to test remote servers rather than simply your local development server. To that aim, here is a standard protractor example, available in `angularjs.org_protractor.js`, that tests the `angularjs.org` homepage:

```
describe('angularjs homepage', function() {
    it('should greet the named user', function() {
        browser.get('http://www.angularjs.org');

        element(by.model('yourName')).sendKeys('Professional AngularJS');
        var greeting = element(by.binding('yourName'));

        expect(greeting.getText()).toEqual('Hello Professional AngularJS!');
    });
});
```

You can modify your protractor configuration a little bit to look like the `angularjs.org_protractor.conf.js` file:

```
// an example configuration file
exports.config = {
  //seleniumAddress: 'http://localhost:4444/wd/hub',

  // capabilities to be passed to the webdriver instance
  capabilities: {
    'browserName': 'chrome'
  },

  sauceUser: 'SAUCE USERNAME HERE',
  sauceKey: 'SAUCE API KEY HERE',

  // spec patterns are relative to the current working directly when
  // protractor is called
  specs: ['angularjs.org_protractor.js'],

  // options to be passed to Jasmine-node
```

```
  jasmineNodeOpts: {
    showColors: true,
    defaultTimeoutInterval: 30000
  }
};
```

Note that you removed the `seleniumAddress` field and instead specified `sauceUser` and `sauceKey`. Protractor comes with built-in support for Sauce and knows to connect to Sauce when `sauceUser` and `sauceKey` are specified but not `seleniumAddress`.

Evaluating ng-scenario and Protractor

Now that you've written basic tests for both ng-scenario and protractor, you should be aware of the trade-offs inherent in both systems. Protractor is a powerful utility for testing remote servers, particularly for end-to-end testing, but it doesn't make running DOM integration tests against your local server particularly easy. On the other hand, ng-scenario enables you to run tests against your local server easily, allows you to manipulate the page using DSL functions, offers a more elegant and concise syntax, and plugs in to the rich Karma plug-in community.

While the ng scenario is likely a better fit for most applications, protractor has certain significant advantages, particularly when you want to test and benchmark real servers. However, these advantages come at the cost of being more difficult to work with and less elegant. On the other hand, ng-scenario fills a different niche: testing on your local machine without having to worry about deploying to a real server. In general, ng-scenario itself and its surrounding tools are more mature and offer more diverse functionality than protractor. In the current paradigm of moving testing responsibility more toward the individual developer, ng-scenario continues to have a big role in testing AngularJS applications. Protractor is likely the future of AngularJS testing, but ng-scenario is the present, and a good AngularJS developer should be familiar with both.

DEBUGGING ANGULARJS APPS

AngularJS is built around a philosophy that automated testing should catch bugs before your users have a chance to run into them. However, end users are exceptionally good at finding bugs in your code, either by accident or with intent. Inevitably, every project has its bugs. Thankfully, there is an incredibly wide variety of debugging tools for JavaScript. In this section, you explore using the `debug` module and Chrome developer tools to debug applications.

The `debug` Module

Although there is no shortage of JavaScript debuggers, JavaScript also has a debug logging module that is so powerful and elegant that it warrants its own section. Debugging via print statements is controversial. Some developers think it is bad practice, and others haven't used a debugging tool beyond a print statement in years. This section stays neutral on the subject and presents tools for both approaches. After all, as the legendary computer scientist Brian Kernighan once said, "The most effective debugging tool is still careful thought, coupled with judiciously placed print statements." (*UNIX for Beginners*, Brian Kernighan, Bell Laboratories, 1978)

This approach is particularly relevant when you're debugging issues in older browsers that may not allow you to insert breakpoints or use other common debugger tools.

The debug module is available via npm. Although the module itself is built for NodeJS, the debug module also contains a file in dist/debug.js that is browser friendly. Unfortunately, this file doesn't come packaged with the npm module, so you have to download it from the GitHub repository at github.com/visionmedia/debug directly. For your convenience, the sample code for this chapter contains v1.0.2 of debug.js, which can be included in a browser via the script tag.

The debug module exposes a function, available globally in the browser as debug(), that generates a debug logger for a provided namespace. A *namespace* is a unique identifier string for that debug logger. Typically, your namespace is the name of the AngularJS controller, service, or directive you want to debug. Here's an example of how you can use the debug module for MyFormController. You can find this code in the sample code as my_form_controller.debug.js:

```
function MyFormController($scope, $http, $window) {
    if ($window.query && $window.query.debug) {
        debug.enable('MyFormController');
    } else {
        debug.disable('MyFormController');
    }
    var d = debug('MyFormController');
    d('loaded');
    $scope.userData = {};
    $scope.errorMessages = [];

    $scope.saveForm = function() {
        $scope.saving = true;
        d('saving form...');
        $http.
            put('/api/submit', $scope.userData).
            success(function(data) {
                d('save form success');
                $scope.saving = false;
                $scope.success = true;
            }).
            error(function(err) {
                d('save form failed: ' + err);
                $scope.saving = false;
                $scope.error = err;
            });
    };
};
```

If you run the preceding code with query.debug set—that is, by navigating to /my_form.debug .html?debug=true—you see something like the following output in your console:

```
MyFormController loaded +0ms
MyFormController saving form... +4s
MyFormController save form success +22ms
```

Each output line has the namespace first, then the log message, and then the time elapsed because the previous log message across all namespaces. The last part is particularly useful for finding slow

HTTP requests. In addition, the time elapsed output can help you identify which $apply calls are slow, which is the first step to debugging AngularJS performance issues.

Recall that the $http service conveniently wraps your success and failure handlers in a call to the scope.$apply function. This function executes a potentially slow loop, evaluating any registered expressions to see if they have changed. A common question to ask is how long a given $apply call takes. Because an $apply call executes in a blocking manner after your $http success handler, you can wrap a debug call in a setTimeout function so it executes immediately after $apply is finished:

```
$scope.saveForm = function() {
    $scope.saving = true;
    d('saving form...');
    $http.
        put('/api/submit', $scope.userData).
        success(function(data) {
            d('save form success');
            $scope.saving = false;
            $scope.success = true;
            setTimeout(function() {
                d('save form $scope.$apply() done');
            }, 0);
        }).
        error(function(err) {
            d('save form failed: ' + err);
            $scope.saving = false;
            $scope.error = err;
        });
};
```

The output in your console should look like this:

```
MyFormController saving form... +5s
MyFormController save form success +29ms
MyFormController save form $scope.$apply() done +2ms
```

Another important detail worth noting about debug is that you can enable or disable an individual debug logger. The debug.disable(namespace) function binds an empty operation to the debug logger. Keep in mind that you need to do this before instantiating the debug logger, because whether or not the debug logger actually outputs anything is determined when it's instantiated.

Overall, the debug module offers a simple and elegant set of functionality that provides insight into what your app is doing. Although it is not as powerful as a full debugger, it enables you to debug in older browsers that lack sophisticated developer tools. But, in browsers like Google Chrome, you can access some incredibly powerful developer tools that enable you to do debug more easily.

Debugging Using Chrome DevTools

Google Chrome's developer tools provide a rich toolset for debugging and analyzing what your code is doing. In addition to the ability to inspect the state of the DOM and read console output, Chrome allows you to perform more sophisticated debugging operations, such as breakpoints.

Launching Developer Tools

If you do not already have Google Chrome installed, you can install it from `https://google.com/chrome`. Even if you prefer an alternative browser for your day-to-day browsing, Chrome's built-in developer tools are indispensable for developing AngularJS applications. Once you have launched Chrome, you can access the developer tools, or DevTools for short, in one of four ways:

1. Open the Chrome menu, represented by the [▤] icon at the top right of the browser, and click on Tools ➪ Developer Tools.

2. Right-click anywhere on the page and click on Inspect Element. This opens the Elements tab in DevTools, which enables you to inspect the current state of the DOM.

3. The Ctrl+Shift+I keyboard shortcut (Cmd+Opt+I on Mac) opens the DevTools Elements tab.

4. The Ctrl+Shift+J keyboard shortcut (Cmd+Opt+J on Mac) opens the DevTools Console tab, which displays console log output.

Once you have launched DevTools, you see a pane at the bottom of your screen that has nine tabs: Elements, Resources, Network, Sources, Timeline, Profiles, Storage, Audits, and Console. Each tab has a different set of functionality useful for a different set of tasks.

Inspecting the State of the DOM

The most common task in DevTools is inspecting what the current state of the DOM is, such as what classes a `div` element has. For example, navigate to the `/my_form.debug.html` page in Chrome, right-click on the `h1` element at the top of the page, and click on Inspect Element. You should see a window that looks like Figure 9-4.

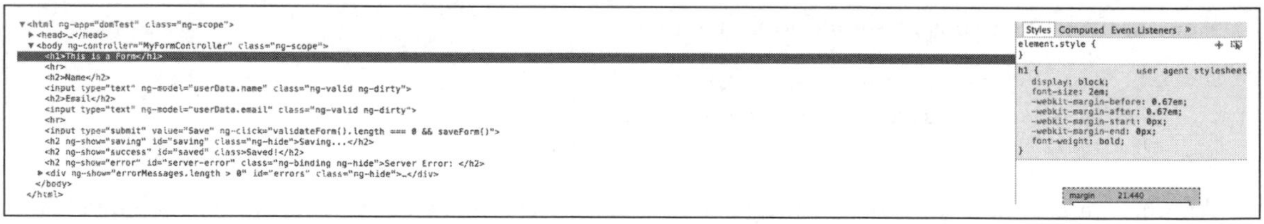

FIGURE 9-4

The Styles pane on the right side enables you to view and edit the styles associated with the selected element. Try clicking on the `element.style` text in the Styles pane and type in **color:red**. The `h1` element should turn red. Furthermore, you should see a check box next to `color:red` when you hover over the text. If you uncheck the check box, the `h1` element turns black again.

Using the Console Tab

The Console tab shows output from functions like `console.log` and `console.profile`. However, in addition to this simple task, the Console tab exposes a read-evaluate-print loop, commonly abbreviated *REPL*, that allows you to execute arbitrary JavaScript code against the page. For example, open the Console tab, click on the > there, and type **alert(window.location.href)**. You should see an alert window displaying the current URL.

Keep in mind, the Console tab's REPL evaluates JavaScript code against the global scope rather than any AngularJS scope. If you want to execute functions defined on an AngularJS controller, you need to expose them by attaching them to the `$window` object. For example, if you open the `my_form` `.html` page in this chapter's sample code, you see that this page attaches `$httpBackend` to the global `window` object. You can type the following code into the Console tab REPL to manually configure the page's `$httpBackend`:

```
$httpBackend.when('PUT', '/api/submit').respond(200, {});
```

Setting Breakpoints in the Sources Tab

Open the `my_form.html` page and navigate to the Sources tab in DevTools. Use the Ctrl+O (Cmd+O in Mac) shortcut to open a file in the Sources tab, and open the `my_form_controller.js` file. You should now see the source code for `my_form_controller.js` in the Sources tab. Right-click on line number 6 immediately to the left of the `$scope.saving = true;` line. Click on the Set Breakpoint option in the drop-down menu.

Now enter a name and an e-mail address, and click the Save button. You should see a Paused in Debugger overlay pop up over the screen and a new pane to the right of the source code, as shown in Figure 9-5.

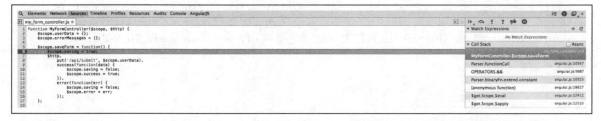

FIGURE 9-5

The pane on the right contains the current state of the JavaScript variables in the current scope. In particular, under the Scope Variables ⇨ Closure heading, you can see the current state of the `$scope` variable, including the `userData` values. See Figure 9-6.

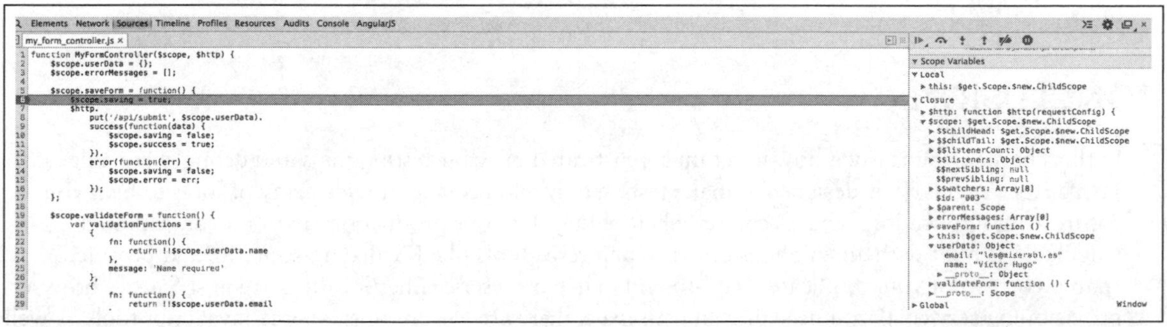

FIGURE 9-6

Debugging Network Performance

The Network tab provides a simple timeline visualization of server interaction: what requests are being made to the server and how long they took. Open the Network tab on the my_form.html page, and you should see something that looks like Figure 9-7.

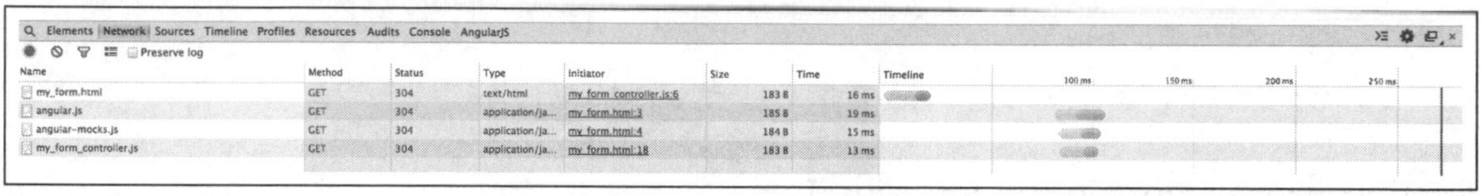

FIGURE 9-7

The Network tab shows that there were four server requests: one for my_form.html, and three for JavaScript files. All the requests took about 10 milliseconds, but the JavaScript files were requested in parallel about 80 milliseconds after the file my_form.html itself. The red and blue lines on the right side indicate when two important events happened: The red line indicates when the load event fired—that is, when all the page's resources were fully loaded. The blue line indicates when the DOMContentLoaded event fired—that is, when the HTML document was fully loaded and parsed.

The Network tab can also show you the contents of the HTTP response from the server. This is useful for bisecting bugs: Typically, the first step in debugging an AngularJS issue is determining whether the server is sending the correct response, so you can determine whether the issue is on the client or the server. Try clicking on the my_form_controller.js string in the Name column. The Network tab now shows a detailed breakdown of the HTTP request and HTTP response. See Figure 9-8.

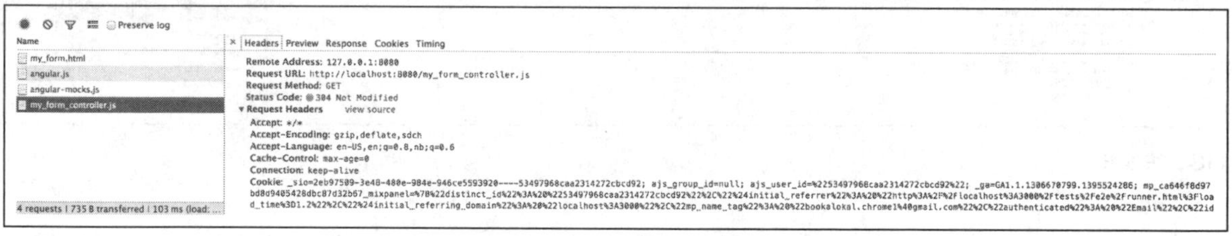

FIGURE 9-8

This panel shows that AngularJS sent an HTTP GET request for localhost:8080/my_form_controller.js, and received an HTTP 304 (Not Modified) in response. The Response tab shows the actual content of the response.

CONCLUSION

In this chapter, you learned how to set up sophisticated browser testing tools and debug client-side JavaScript. AngularJS is designed to make testing easy and provides a wide array of tools to help you ensure your application behaves correctly before bugs hit your production environment. Although AngularJS is built with an emphasis on basic unit tests, tools like Karma, ng-scenario, and protractor enable you to test your application end-to-end in live browsers, either locally or against Sauce's browser provisioning service. If you need to debug an issue, there are elegant open source JavaScript tools as well as Chrome's sophisticated DevTools to help you gain insight into why your code is misbehaving.

10

Moving On

WHAT YOU WILL LEARN IN THIS CHAPTER:

➤ Extending AngularJS with popular frameworks

➤ Using the Angular-UI Bootstrap module

➤ Building hybrid mobile apps with Ionic

➤ Manipulating dates using MomentJS

➤ Initializing and validating data with MongooseJS

➤ Using AngularJS and ECMAScript 6 (Harmony)

WROX.COM CODE DOWNLOADS FOR THIS CHAPTER

You can find the wrox.com code downloads for this chapter at http://www.wrox.com/go/proangularjs on the Download Code tab.

If you've made it all the way through this book, congratulations! The previous chapters contain all the information you need to use the AngularJS core to build and test sophisticated applications. However, because AngularJS is open source, there are myriad extensions, plug-ins, and frameworks that enable you to add powerful functionality to AngularJS. Furthermore, JavaScript itself has an extremely active open source community, and there are numerous modules that make writing applications in AngularJS easier. In this chapter, you'll expand beyond core AngularJS and learn how to use two popular AngularJS extensions (Angular-UI's Bootstrap project and the Ionic framework) and how to integrate two popular JavaScript modules (Moment and Mongoose) with AngularJS.

In addition, JavaScript itself is a rapidly evolving language. ECMAScript is the language standard underlying JavaScript, and its most recent iteration, ECMAScript 5 (ES5), added some exciting features. In addition, several browsers have already added support for some of the features in the proposed ECMAScript 6 (ES6) standard. Later in this chapter, you'll learn about how ES5 accessors integrate with AngularJS, as well as how to use ES6's `yield` keyword with the `$http` service.

USING ANGULAR-UI BOOTSTRAP

Bootstrap (`http://www.getbootstrap.com`) is a popular open source cascading style sheet (CSS) framework developed by Twitter with an attached JavaScript library. It offers a variety of features, including a flexible 12-column grid layout that adapts gracefully to small screens (that is, mobile devices). Its JavaScript component includes modals, drop-downs, and tooltips, but Bootstrap's JavaScript is intended to work with jQuery-style JavaScript. Although AngularJS can execute jQuery code, this doesn't take full advantage of features like data binding and directives. Thankfully, the Angular-UI team has created its own module, Angular-UI Bootstrap, which contains directives and services for integrating Bootstrap components into AngularJS data binding.

For your convenience, this chapter's sample code contains the four files necessary to use Angular-UI Bootstrap, in addition to AngularJS 1.2.16. The `bootstrap.css` and `bootstrap.js` files contain the unminified version 3.2.0 of Twitter Bootstrap. Bootstrap's JavaScript depends on jQuery, so jQuery 1.11.2 is included. In addition, the `ui-bootstrap-tpls-0.11.2.js` file contains version 0.11.2 of Angular-UI Bootstrap.

> **NOTE** *Angular-UI Bootstrap technically doesn't require the Bootstrap JavaScript file,* `bootstrap.js`*. Angular-UI Bootstrap implements its own components on top of Bootstrap's CSS. However, in practice, it is often helpful to have both. This is because, in some use cases in which data binding is not necessary, using AngularJS is wasteful and less convenient than vanilla Bootstrap JavaScript. For instance, if you need a simple drop-down whose state isn't tied to a JavaScript variable, using Angular-UI Bootstrap simply adds extra complexity and overhead to your* `$digest` *loops.*

Modals

One of the most common use cases for Angular-UI Bootstrap is creating AngularJS-enabled modals. Typically, the built-in JavaScript `alert()` and `confirm()` dialogs are jarring and look unprofessional. Bootstrap's modals are more elegant and customizable. In this section, you learn how to use the Angular-UI Bootstrap `$modal` service to create richly customizable modals for two use cases: a simple dialog asking the user to confirm an action, and a dialog that asks the user for input. This section's sample code is contained in the `bootstrap_modal` `.html` file.

The `$modal` service has one function, `open(options)`, which opens a modal based on the configuration specified in the `options` object. The `options` object has numerous options to tweak; however, three are necessary for almost all use cases. Unsurprisingly, the $modal service allows you to specify either a template or a templateURL option, which tells Angular-UI Bootstrap which template to render in the modal. (Recall that templates are strings that contain AngularJS-infused HTML.) In addition, the $modal service allows you to specify a scope option, which defines the parent scope for the $modal template's scope. Note that the $modal service always creates a new scope for its template. By default, that scope's parent is the page's root scope, represented by the $rootScope service. However, more often than not, you want to have the $modal service create a scope whose parent is the current controller's scope. This enables your modal to interface seamlessly with methods defined in your controller.

Now that you understand the basic options you can use to configure the $modal service, here's the implementation for a simple modal that asks the user to confirm an action:

```
// Need to add a dependency on the 'ui.bootstrap' module to use
// Angular-UI Bootstrap
var app = angular.module('myApp', ['ui.bootstrap']);

var confirmationTemplate =
    "<h3>" +
    " Are you sure you want to learn about" +
    " Angular-UI Bootstrap modals?" +
    "</h3>" +
    "<hr>" +
    "<button class='btn' type='submit' ng-click='confirm(true)'>" +
    " Yes" +
    "</button>" +
    "<button class='btn' type='submit' ng-click='confirm(false)'>" +
    " No" +
    "</button>";

app.controller('MyController', function($scope, $modal) {
    $scope.confirmed;
    $scope.modal;
    $scope.confirm = function(confirmed) {
        $scope.confirmed = confirmed;
        $scope.modal.close();
    };

    $scope.showConfirmation = function() {
        $scope.modal = $modal.
            open({
                scope: $scope,
                template: confirmationTemplate
            });
    };
});
```

The preceding controller exposes two functions through the controller's $scope: the showConfirmation() function, which uses the $modal service to open a modal whose template is the confirmationTemplate string, and the confirm() function, which the confirmationTemplate template calls to return a result and close the modal. Once again, the confirmationTemplate

template executes in a scope whose parent is the controller's $scope. Here's the HTML corresponding to this controller:

```
<div ng-controller="MyController">
    <button type="submit"
            class="btn"
            ng-click="showConfirmation()">
        Show Confirmation Modal
    </button>
    <h2 ng-if="confirmed === true">
        Confirmed
    </h2>
    <h2 ng-if="confirmed === false">
        Denied
    </h2>
</div>
```

You typically explicitly set the modal's scope option instead of using the default $rootScope to give the modal's template access to functions defined in the controller's $scope. The preceding code depends on the fact that the modal's template can call the confirm() function, which is attached to the controller's $scope, to communicate the user's choice back to the controller. In addition, because the $modal service creates its own scope, you can modify variables and functions in the modal's template without polluting the controller's $scope. Furthermore, you can attach a controller to the modal using the controller option for $modal.open(). The controller option enables you to write sophisticated modules that have their own internal state. For instance, here is the implementation for a modal that asks the user to select their favorite chapter from a drop-down:

```
$scope.favoriteChapter;
$scope.showSelectModal = function() {
    $scope.modal = $modal.
        open({
            scope: $scope,
            template: selectModalTemplate,
            controller: 'SelectModalController'
        });
};

$scope.setFavoriteChapter = function(chapter) {
    $scope.favoriteChapter = chapter;
};
```

Note that this modal uses the controller option you just learned about. Here's the implementation of the SelectModalController controller mentioned earlier:

```
app.controller('SelectModalController',
    function($scope, $modalInstance) {
        $scope.options = [];
        $scope.selectedOption;
        for (var i = 1; i <= 10; ++i) {
            $scope.options.push('Chapter ' + i);
```

```
        }
        $scope.select = function() {
            $scope.setFavoriteChapter($scope.selectedOption);
            $modalInstance.close();
        };
    });
```

Note that the `SelectModalController` controller uses a new local passed in through dependency injection: the `$modalInstance` object. Recall that a *local* is an extra object registered to the dependency injector in a given context. (The most common example of a local is `$scope`.) Much like `$scope`, it's not possible to register a service that depends on `$modalInstance`. Furthermore, if you try to use a controller that depends on `$modalInstance` in an `ngController` directive or outside of calls to `$modal`, AngularJS throws an error. For instance, the following HTML causes an `Unknown provider` error:

```
<div ng-controller="SelectModalController"></div>
```

The `$modalInstance` local exposes a convenient application programming interface (API) for manipulating the modal. In `SelectModalController`, you used its `close()` function to close the modal after the user selected their favorite chapter. There is also a `dismiss()` function, which behaves almost identically to the `close()` function. The only difference is that, semantically, a call to `dismiss()` is interpreted to mean that the modal was closed without the user performing the necessary actions. In particular, the `$modalInstance` object also has a result property, which is a promise that is fulfilled when the modal is closed and rejected when the modal is dismissed. (Recall that a *promise* is an object that provides syntactic sugar on top of an asynchronous request.) However, in this example you won't use promises, so the `close()` function and `dismiss()` function are interchangeable for the purposes of `SelectModalController`.

There is one more detail in `SelectModalController` that's worth noticing: the fact that `SelectModalController` can call the `setFavoriteChapter()` function, which is actually defined on its parent scope. You may recall from Chapter 4, "Data Binding," that scopes inherit from their parents; thus, you can call the `setFavoriteChapter()` function from any scope that is a descendant of the `MyController` scope. This inter-scope communication is precisely why you usually specify the `scope` option when calling `$modal.open()`. If you don't, the modal's template and controller are unable to access any properties defined on the `MyController` scope, so the modal can't communicate effectively with the controller.

Now that you've investigated the particulars of the modal's controller, you will use this controller's functions in the modal's template. The template for this modal, `selectModalTemplate`, looks like this:

```
var selectModalTemplate =
    "<h2>What's your favorite chapter?</h2>" +
    "<select ng-model='selectedOption'" +
    "        ng-options='x for x in options'>" +
    "</select>" +
    "<hr>" +
    "<button class='btn' ng-click='select()'>" +
    "  Submit" +
    "</button>";
```

The `selectModalTemplate` template only interfaces directly with properties defined in `SelectModalController`—namely, `options`, `selectedOption`, and the `select()` function. Typically, to maximize reusability, you want to minimize your modal's dependencies on its parent scope. In practice, you usually only use a given modal in a single controller, but you may want to have multiple controllers use a modal with the same template, same controller, or both. However, you're more likely to want to reuse the template than the controller, and AngularJS has no notion of template inheritance. Thus, in the interest of reusability, making sure your modal template doesn't interact with its parent scope is usually a good idea.

Datepicker

One common use case that the AngularJS core lacks coverage for is asking the user to select a date. AngularJS does interface well with the HTML5 "date" input field (which is similar to the familiar "text" input field), but that HTML5 element has poor cross-browser support. As a matter of fact, as of 2014, no version of Internet Explorer, Firefox, or Safari supports the HTML5 "date" input field. Thankfully, Angular-UI Bootstrap has a clean and simple `datepicker` directive that you can plug in to your application. For this section, the sample code is in the `bootstrap_datepicker.html` file. Suppose you have the following controller:

```
app.controller('MyController', function($scope) {
    $scope.date = new Date();
});
```

Plugging in the Angular-UI Bootstrap `datepicker` directive to allow your user to select a date is a one-liner:

```
<datepicker ng-model="date"></datepicker>
```

However, the `datepicker` directive, by default, shows a large calendar that doesn't do a good job of conveying to the user what the currently selected date is. (It highlights the currently selected date, but only if you're on the right month.) If you want to mimic the HTML5 `<input type="date">` element—that is, display the currently selected date in a text input and only show the calendar when the user clicks the input field—you can use the related `datepicker-popup` directive. This directive enables you to show a calendar equivalent to the `datepicker` directive in a pop-over when the user clicks on an input field:

```
<input   type="text"
         class="form-control"
         datepicker-popup="yyyy/MM/dd"
         ng-disabled="isOpen"
         ng-model="date"
         is-open="isOpen"
         ng-click="isOpen = true" />
```

The `datepicker-popup` directive attribute takes a format string. This string represents the format to be passed to AngularJS's `date` filter to determine how the date is rendered in the input field. In this example, for June 1, 2011, the date is rendered as "2011/06/01" in the input field.

Note that the open/closed status of the `datepicker` pop-over is controlled by the `isOpen` variable. Whenever the user clicks on the input field, the `isOpen` variable is set to `true`. The `datepicker` pop-over has some reasonable default rules for when it should be closed, such as whenever the user clicks on somewhere that isn't the pop-over, or whenever the user actually selects a date. In the preceding example, the input field is configured to turn "disabled" whenever the `datepicker` pop-over is open. This is a user experience (UX) decision to make sure the end user can't actually type in the input field. By default, when the pop-over is open, the user is actually allowed to type in the input field, which can lead to unpredictable behavior.

Timepicker

The `datepicker` directive allows you to modify only the date. The natural complement to the `datepicker` directive is a directive that enables the user to modify the time, so you can ask the user when a certain event is going to happen. Thankfully, Angular-UI Bootstrap has a corresponding `timepicker` directive that operates similarly to the `datepicker` directive. You can use both of these directives together:

```
<div ng-controller="MyDateController">
    <h2>Date</h2>
    <div style="width: 300px">
        <input   type="text"
                 class="form-control"
                 datepicker-popup="yyyy/MM/dd"
                 ng-disabled="isOpen"
                 ng-model="date"
                 is-open="isOpen"
                 ng-click="isOpen = true" />
    </div>
    <h2>Time</h2>
    <timepicker ng-model="date">
    </timepicker>
    <hr>
    <h2>
        Currently Selected Date: {{date | date:'medium'}}
    </h2>
</div>
```

The `timepicker` directive ties in seamlessly to two-way data binding, so you can simply specify an `ngModel` and let the directive handle all the user interaction. The `timepicker` directive also has some sophisticated user-input mechanisms. For instance, the user can use a mouse wheel to increment or decrement the current hours and minutes. Although the mouse wheel integration is typically the right choice, you can disable it using the `mousewheel` attribute. The code to disable mouse wheel integration looks like this:

```
<timepicker ng-model="date" mousewheel="false">
</timepicker>
```

Custom Templates

When using the `datepicker` and `timepicker` directives, you may have noticed that there is no way to modify the directive's user interface (UI) using the provided configuration options. That is, you weren't able to substitute your own template for the default `timepicker` directive template. Unfortunately, this is a limitation of how AngularJS templates work: Once AngularJS gets the directive's template, there is no way to change it. (That is, AngularJS only calls a directive function once.) Thankfully, Angular-UI Bootstrap lets you overwrite the template used for a given directive. (It overwrites the template used for *all* instances of that directive.) In this section, you build your own template for the `timepicker` directive you learned about in the previous section.

> **NOTE** *You may have been wondering why the Angular-UI Bootstrap JavaScript file is named* `bootstrap-tpls-0.11.2.js`. *The* `tpls` *means that this file contains templates for all the directives. Angular-UI Bootstrap also distributes* `bootstrap-0.11.2.js`, *which contains no templates, and thus requires you to specify your own templates for any directive you want to use. Typically, if you're just starting a new project, you will want to use the templates-included build of Angular-UI Bootstrap (that is, the* `bootstrap-tpls-0.11.2.js` *file) because, as you'll see in this section, you can easily overwrite existing templates. You may want to use the no-templates version (the* `bootstrap-0.11.2.js` *file) if your project doesn't use any of the built-in templates, and you want to reduce file size for the sake of performance.*

The easiest way to overwrite a built-in Angular-UI Bootstrap directive template is to use AngularJS's `script` directive. (AngularJS inspects your page's `script` tags to look for templates.) To replace the `timepicker` directive template with a simple template that just displays some text, use the following code:

```
<script id="template/timepicker/timepicker.html"
      type="text/ng-template">
   <h2>
      ==> I am a timepicker!
   </h2>
</script>
```

The preceding code tells AngularJS's template cache that it should not make an HTTP request for the `template/timepicker/timepicker.html` template; instead, it should use the contents of the `script` tag. If you're interested in learning more about AngularJS's template cache, Chapter 6, "Templates, Location, and Routing," contains more in-depth information. For the purposes of this section, however, it suffices to know that the template cache stores templates by ID (usually a uniform resource locator, or URL), and you can use `<script type="text/ng-template">` to overwrite an entry in the template cache. The `timepicker` directive uses the `template/timepicker/timepicker.html` template, so you can overwrite that with a `script` tag.

So far, all you've done is replace the `timepicker` directive with a "Hello, world" template. To make your custom template useful, you need to inspect and understand how the default `timepicker` directive template works. This is why, more often than not, you should just use the default Angular-UI Bootstrap template. To write a custom directive template, you need a more sophisticated understanding of how the `timepicker` directive works. That is, you need to know what functions to call and what scope variables to bind input fields to so you can make a functioning time picker. In many cases, this is simply unnecessary work. However, the `timepicker` directive is a common candidate; the default `timepicker` directive UI is a poor choice for many applications.

What follows is the default `timepicker` directive template from the `ui-bootstrap-tpls-0.11.2.js` file, reformatted for readability:

```html
<table>
    <tbody>
        <tr class="text-center">
            <td>
                <a  ng-click="incrementHours()"
                    class="btn btn-link">
                    <span class="glyphicon glyphicon-chevron-up">
                    </span>
                </a>
            </td>
            <td> </td>
            <td>
                <a  ng-click="incrementMinutes()"
                    class="btn btn-link">
                    <span class="glyphicon glyphicon-chevron-up">
                    </span>
                </a>
            </td>
            <td ng-show="showMeridian"></td>
        </tr>
        <tr>
            <td style="width:50px;"
                class="form-group"
                ng-class="{'has-error': invalidHours}">
                <input  type="text"
                        ng-model="hours"
                        ng-change="updateHours()"
                        class="form-control text-center"
                        ng-mousewheel="incrementHours()"
                        ng-readonly="readonlyInput"
                        maxlength="2">
            </td>
            <td>:</td>
            <td style="width:50px;"
                class="form-group"
                ng-class="{'has-error': invalidMinutes}">
                <input  type="text"
                        ng-model="minutes"
                        ng-change="updateMinutes()"
                        class="form-control text-center"
                        ng-readonly="readonlyInput"
                        maxlength="2">
            </td>
            <td ng-show="showMeridian">
                <button type="button"
                        class="btn btn-default text-center"
                        ng-click="toggleMeridian()">
```

```
                              {{meridian}}
                    </button>
                </td>
            </tr>
            <tr class="text-center">
                <td>
                    <a  ng-click="decrementHours()"
                        class="btn btn-link">
                        <span class="glyphicon glyphicon-chevron-down">
                        </span>
                    </a>
                </td>
                <td> </td>
                <td>
                    <a  ng-click="decrementMinutes()"
                        class="btn btn-link">
                        <span class="glyphicon glyphicon-chevron-down">
                        </span>
                    </a>
                </td>
                <td ng-show="showMeridian">
                </td>
            </tr>
        </tbody>
    </table>
```

In the preceding `timepicker` directive template code, the highlighted portions show examples of how to use the `timepicker` directive controller's "API" to manipulate the current time. Specifically, the `timepicker` directive controller exposes an `hours` variable and a `minutes` variable that are responsible for maintaining the `timepicker` directive's internal state. To make sure that changes to these variables are handled properly, there are corresponding `updateHours()` and `updateMinutes()` functions that you need to call after changing these variables. In addition, there are the helper functions `incrementHours()`, `incrementMinutes()`, `decrementHours()`, and `decrementMinutes()`, which call the corresponding update function for you. With this knowledge of the internal `timepicker` directive controller API in hand, it is simple to create a drop-down-based template for the `timepicker` directive. Here's a template that replaces the default `timepicker` directive template with a single drop-down:

```
<script id="template/timepicker/timepicker.html"
        type="text/ng-template">
    <div ng-init="showMeridian = false;">
        <select ng-model="myTime"
                ng-change="hours = myTime.hours; updateHours();
                  minutes = myTime.minutes; updateMinutes()"
                ng-options="t.value as t.display for t in 0 |
                  timepickerOptions">
        </select>
    </div>
</script>
```

The preceding code is succinct, but there are three subtle details in the code that merit further investigation. First, the `ngInit` code ensures that the `timepicker` directive is in 24-hour mode.

Otherwise, you would have to manipulate both the hours and the AM/PM setting, which, in this case, would make the directive more complicated than necessary. Second, because of a quirk in the internals of the `timepicker` directive's controller, the order of operations in `ngChange` is important: You need to change the `hours` variable and call `updateHours()` before you change the `minutes` variable; otherwise, the time doesn't update correctly. This is something you have to find out by carefully inspecting Angular-UI Bootstrap's code or by trial and error.

Finally, you might have noticed the `timepickerOptions` filter in the `ngOptions` directive. Because the `timepicker` directive is in an isolate scope, filters are the best way to bypass the scope hierarchy and insert data into the `timepicker` directive's scope. The filter implementation looks like this:

```
app.filter('timepickerOptions', function() {
    var timepickerOptions = [];
    for (var h = 0; h < 24; ++h) {
        timepickerOptions.push({
            display: h + ':' + '00',
            value: {
                hours: h,
                minutes: 0
            }
        });
        timepickerOptions.push({
            display: h + ':' + '30',
            value: {
                hours: h,
                minutes: 30
            }
        });
    }

    return function() {
        return timepickerOptions;
    }
});
```

As you can see, this filter returns a static array, regardless of the arguments passed in. This practice is for the sole purpose of getting around the `timepicker` directive's isolate scope; not even adding a variable to the root scope makes it accessible in an isolate scope. Thankfully, filters offer a way to bypass the scope hierarchy without directly modifying the directive controller's code.

Now that you've learned the basics of how to use custom Bootstrap-inspired components with Angular-UI Bootstrap, it's time to investigate another exciting AngularJS extension.

HYBRID MOBILE APPS WITH THE IONIC FRAMEWORK

You may have heard of Cordova and PhoneGap, which are tools for building "hybrid" mobile apps—that is, apps that are written as JavaScript running in a browser but are still distributed through the Android and iPhone app stores. These tools are extremely useful in that you can write one app in one language and distribute it to multiple app stores, rather than having to maintain a separate Android app written in Java and an iPhone app written in Objective-C. However, they are relatively bare compared to the sophisticated integrated development environments (IDEs) and built-in UI components that mobile developers typically use (Eclipse for Android and Xcode for iPhone). The Ionic framework, built on top of Cordova, includes a sophisticated command-line interface (CLI) to manage your app development, beautiful Bootstrap-like UI components, and, most importantly, integration with AngularJS. Using the Ionic framework, you can use concepts you learned about in this book to build mobile apps that you can then distribute through the app store of your choice. In this section, you'll write a simple Ionic framework application and get a high-level overview of how the Ionic framework works.

Setting Up Ionic, Cordova, and the Android SDK

Cordova and Ionic are most easily installed through the NodeJS package manager, npm. If you have not already installed NodeJS, please go to `http://nodejs.org` and follow the instructions to install NodeJS on your platform of choice. Once you have installed npm, you can install both Cordova and Ionic using `npm install cordova ionic -g`. Note that Cordova needs to be installed globally; Ionic requires Cordova to be on the system PATH.

For the purposes of this section, you'll set up the Ionic framework to build an Android application. Because the Ionic framework depends on the Android and iOS emulators to run, you need to install either the Android SDK or the iOS SDK. However, installing the iOS SDK is a troublesome process that requires signing up for an account and jumping through myriad legal hoops. Also, it is limited to OSX only. Getting started with the Android SDK is a simpler process and can be done on Windows, Linux, or OSX. If you have a choice of which operating system to use, it is probably easiest to set up the Android SDK on Ubuntu-flavored Linux. Please go to `http://developer` `.android.com/sdk/index.html` and follow the instructions for your platform. You also need to install the Java JDK (`http://www.oracle.com/technetwork/java/javase/downloads/index` `.html`) and the Ant build system (`http://ant.apache.org`). Be aware: The Android SDK is a bloated piece of software, and the download can take a long time.

Once you have installed Java, Ant, and the Android SDK, run the `android` command from your command line to start the Android SDK Manager. From there, check the box to install Android 4.4.2 (API Level 19) and click Install Packages to get yourself a reasonable version of Android. Next, you need to create an Android Virtual Device, or AVD. To create an AVD with your newly installed Android 4.4.2, run `android create avd -n android4 -t 1 –abi default/` `armeabi-v7a`.

Now that you've set up Android, you can create your first Ionic app and run it in the Android emulator:

```
ionic start myApp tabs
cd myApp
ionic platform add android
ionic build android
ionic emulate android
```

This creates a new Ionic app in the myApp directory, configures it to run on the Android emulator, and launches an Android emulator so you can see the app live. The app is created from Ionic's "tabs" starter application.

Using AngularJS in Your Ionic App

Ionic is so interesting because it allows you to write mobile apps using the same AngularJS principles you've learned about in this book. If you look closely at the code in the myApp directory you created in the previous section, you'll find some basic AngularJS controllers and services. The myApp/www/index.html file has the base Hypertext Markup Language (HTML) for the Android application that you saw in the previous section. Specifically, the following JavaScript files are included in the page:

```html
<!-- ionic/angularjs js -->
<script src="lib/ionic/js/ionic.bundle.js"></script>

<!-- cordova script (this will be a 404 during development) -->
<script src="cordova.js"></script>

<!-- your app's js -->
<script src="js/app.js"></script>
<script src="js/controllers.js"></script>
<script src="js/services.js"></script>
```

The ionic.bundle.js file includes the core angular.js file, along with various modules like angular-animate.js. The js/app.js file contains the module definition and client-side routing setup. The js/controllers.js file and js/services.js file contain the controllers and services that correspond to the client-side routes. Because this is a sample app, the controllers and services are stubbed out and not terribly sophisticated. The most complex part of this app is in the js/app.js file.

You may have noticed that the js/app.js file uses the Angular-UI Router module for client-side routing instead of the ngRoute module. Specifically, here is the code that defines the routes:

```javascript
config(function($stateProvider, $urlRouterProvider) {

  // Ionic uses the AngularUI Router, which uses the concept of states
  // Learn more here: https://github.com/angular-ui/ui-router
  // Set up the various states that the app can be in
  // Each state's controller can be found in controllers.js
  $stateProvider

    // Set up an abstract state for the tabs directive
    .state('tab', {
      url: "/tab",
      abstract: true,
      templateUrl: "templates/tabs.html"
    })

    // Each tab has its own nav history stack:

    .state('tab.dash', {
      url: '/dash',
      views: {
        'tab-dash': {
          templateUrl: 'templates/tab-dash.html',
```

```
         controller: 'DashCtrl'
      }
    }
  })
```

The Angular-UI Router module is essentially a more sophisticated version of the ngRoute module. Instead of having "routes," however, Angular-UI Router uses "states," which are similar to routes but allow you to handle more sophisticated navigation. For instance, in the myApp tabbed application, what would happen if you were on a "friends" detail view, switched to the dash tab, and then switched back to the friends tab? With the ngRoute module, all state is destroyed when you change routes, so when you navigate back to the friends tab, you see the master list of friends rather than the specific friend you were looking at. In mobile, this is not necessarily a good UX decision. Angular-UI Router provides a framework that enables you to either show the master list of friends or retain the particular friend the user was viewing, depending on your app's needs. (The myApp tabbed application, by default, takes you to the specific friend you were looking at.) However, the overall structure of Angular-UI Router is reasonably similar to the ngRoute module: You map a URL to a template and controller pair.

Another important detail to remember about the Ionic framework is that all your $http requests are cross-origin, because Ionic framework apps operate by launching a browser and navigating it to your HTML content using file://. For instance, if you were to log $window.location.href on the dashboard tab in the myApp application, you would see file:///android_asset/www/index.html. Thus, you need to make sure that any $http requests you make in your AngularJS code have a fully qualified URL, including domain name. You also need to ensure that any server you are making requests to is configured to accept cross-origin resource sharing (CORS) requests. CORS requests are HTTP requests from different domains.

Now that you understand some of the key differences between writing AngularJS for the Ionic framework and writing AngularJS for a standard desktop browser environment, it's time to make the myApp application do something useful. Specifically, you're going to adapt the Google stock price quoting service from Chapter 7 and plug it into the dashboard view so your app can show the current Google stock price. Here is the implementation of the $googleStock service:

```
factory('$googleStock', function($http) {
  var BASE = 'http://query.yahooapis.com/v1/public/yql'

  var query = encodeURIComponent('select * from yahoo.finance.quotes ' +
    'where symbol in (\'GOOG\')');
  var url = BASE + '?' + 'q=' + query + '&format=json&diagnostics=true&' +
    'env=http://datatables.org/alltables.env';

  var service = {};
  service.get = function() {
    $http.jsonp(url + '&callback=JSON_CALLBACK').
      success(function(data) {
        if (data.query.count) {
          var quotes = data.query.count > 1 ?
            data.query.results.quote :
```

```
            [data.query.results.quote];
          service.quotes = quotes;
        }
      }).
      error(function(data) {
        console.log(data);
      });
  };

  service.get();
  return service;
});
```

You can add this service to the myApp/www/js/services.js file. To finish plugging this service into the myApp application, you should add this service to DashCtrl in the myApp/www/js/controllers .js file:

```
.controller('DashCtrl', function($scope, $googleStock) {
  $scope.googleStock = $googleStock;
})
```

You should also add it to the actual dashboard template, in the myApp/www/templates/tab-dash .html file:

```
<ion-view title="Dashboard">
  <ion-content class="padding">
    <h1>Dash</h1>
    <h3>Current Google Stock Price: {{googleStock.quotes[0].Ask}}</h3>
  </ion-content>
</ion-view>
```

Now when you run the ionic emulate android command, you should see the current Google stock price on the dashboard.

Yeoman Workflow and Building for Production

Also worth mentioning is that, because Ionic framework applications are built using front-end technologies, their development process can benefit from the same workflow automation tooling described early on in this book. Specifically, the workflow promoted by Yeoman is also made available for assisting in the development and production compression of Ionic apps through the use of the generator-ionic Yeoman plug-in. To get started with the Ionic Yeoman Generator, run the following from the command line:

```
npm install -g generator-ionic
mkdir myApp && cd myApp
yo ionic
```

After running the yo ionic command in a newly created directory, you are presented with a similar set of prompts, as seen before when initially scaffolding the StockDog application from Chapter 1, "Building a Simple AngularJS Application." However, this time around you have the option of selecting from a list of popular Cordova plug-ins to install as well as selecting a starter template directly from the command line to help you scaffold an intelligent foundation for your application. Grunt supports the workflow created by this Yeoman generator, so you can achieve any modifications by changing the associated `Gruntfile.js`. The following are a few of the commands available out of the box:

➤ `grunt serve[:compress]`

➤ `grunt platform:add:<platform>`

➤ `grunt plugin:add:<plugin>`

➤ `grunt [emulate|run]:<target>`

➤ `grunt compress`

➤ `grunt build:<platform>`

Some of these commands use the official `ionic-cli` under the hood, so projects created using `generator-ionic` play nicely with the `ionic` tool. Running `grunt serve` launches your application in the browser for local development, whereas `grunt emulate:android --livereload` launches your application in the simulator with built-in livereload support. This is especially helpful because the only way to test integration with Cordova plug-ins is to run your app on a device, but constantly rebuilding and emulating for simple front-end changes can be extremely frustrating. It is important to realize that whereas the `dist/` directory was used for building compressed assets for StockDog, this generator compiles your application, using the `grunt compress` command, into the `www/` directory. This is because Cordova reads from that location to package your AngularJS application as a native app. You can find more information about the Ionic Yeoman Generator at `https://github.com/diegonetto/generator-ionic`.

Icons, Splash Screens, and Cordova Hooks

A common issue when working with Cordova and the Ionic framework is setting up your application's icons and splash screens. Properly configuring your app icons and splash screens to work with Cordova can be a pain to set up, so the generator has gone ahead and included an `after_prepare` Cordova hook that manages copying the appropriate resource files to the correct location within your current platform targets. To get started, you must first add a platform via `grunt platform:add:android`. Once you have a platform, the packaged `icons_and_splashscreens.js` hook copies over all placeholder icons and splash screens generated by Cordova into a newly created top-level `resources/` directory inside your project. Simply replace these files with your own resources (but maintain filenames and directory structure) and let the hook's magic automatically manage copying them to the appropriate location for each Cordova platform, all without interrupting your existing workflow. To learn more about hooks, check out the `README.md` file inside of the `hooks/` directory of your Ionic framework project.

That's it for the Ionic framework. The Ionic framework is a phenomenally deep subject, and this section provided only a brief high-level overview of how the Ionic framework works. The official Ionic framework website, `http://ionicframework.com`, contains more sophisticated tutorials and documentation.

INTEGRATING OPEN SOURCE JAVASCRIPT WITH ANGULARJS

One of JavaScript's most powerful features is its vibrant open source community. The NodeJS package manager, npm, is currently the largest package ecosystem in the world, with about 100,000 packages as of October 2014. And that's just one of JavaScript's package managers. There are numerous other package managers, such as NuGet and Bower, and some JavaScript packages are simply available as plain JavaScript files. If you are finding something difficult to do in JavaScript, usually there's an open source module that can solve your problem for you. In this section, you'll learn about integrating AngularJS with two common packages—Moment and Mongoose—that address two of JavaScript's weak points: date handling and schema validation.

Dates and Time Zones with Moment

You may have noticed that JavaScript's native `Date` objects are somewhat cumbersome and lacking in functionality compared to languages like Python. Indeed, native JavaScript dates have some significant limitations: They suffer from poor browser compatibility, their date arithmetic is limited, and there is no time zone support. Native JavaScript dates, by default, are specified in the browser's local time, but they have some convenience methods for modifying the date in Universal Coordinated Time (UTC). Although this is sufficient for many use cases, you may find yourself needing to manipulate dates in a more sophisticated way, including displaying dates in different time zones. Moment (`www.momentjs.com`) is the most popular open source date helper module for JavaScript. Moment and its extension, `moment-timezone`, have some extremely sophisticated date manipulation functionality that is indispensible for writing time-zone-aware AngularJS apps.

For your convenience, the `moment.js` and `moment-timezone.js` files have been included in this chapter's sample code. Moment exposes a single function, `moment()`, that you use to instantiate a Moment object, commonly referred to as a *moment*. The file `moment_examples.html` in this chapter's sample code contains a few common examples for manipulating dates with Moment outside of AngularJS:

```
<script type="text/javascript" src="moment.js">
</script>
<script type="text/javascript" src="moment-timezone.js">
</script>
<script type="text/javascript">
  // Moment representing current date
  moment();

  // Moment can also take a JavaScript date as a parameter
  moment(new Date());

  // Or a UNIX timestamp
  moment((new Date()).getTime());

  // Midnight GMT on June 1, 2011, in browser's timezone
  moment('2011-06-01T00:00:00.000Z');

  // Midnight GMT on June 1, 2011, in UTC
```

```
moment('2011-06-01T00:00:00.000Z').utc();

// Format: String representing June 1, 2011 12:00am GMT in browser's
// timezone. For example, will print 'May 31, 2011 8:00pm'
// if you run this in New York.
moment('2011-06-01T:00:00:00.000Z').
  format('MMMM D, YYYY h:ma');

// Format: Print out 'June 1, 2011 12:00am', because UTC
moment('2011-06-01T00:00:00.000Z').
  utc().
  format('MMMM D, YYYY h:mma');

// Add 42 days to 2011-06-01 (2011-07-13)
moment('2011-06-01T00:00:00.000Z').
  utc().
  add(42, 'days').
  format('MMMM D, YYYY h:mma');

// June 1, 2011 12:00am GMT in Los Angeles time (May 31, 2011 5:00pm)
moment('2011-06-01T00:00:00.000Z').
  tz('America/Los_Angeles').
  format('MMMM D, YYYY h:mma');

// Plain old JavaScript date object representing a moment
moment('2011-06-01T00:00:00.000Z').toDate();

// Current UNIX timestamp (milliseconds since Jan 1, 1970
// 12:00am UTC)
moment().unix();
</script>
```

In addition to providing date arithmetic, formatting, and sophisticated time zone support (which requires the `moment-timezone.js` file), Moment supports a fluid chaining syntax that allows you to write sophisticated date manipulations in a terse manner. Essentially, Moment does everything that JavaScript dates do poorly. However, Moment is not terribly compatible with vanilla JavaScript dates, and, in particular, the AngularJS `date` filter.

To learn how to integrate AngularJS and Moment, you use Moment's time zone functionality to display a list of international events. For instance, suppose your application displays a list of concerts in Europe. If you naively used native JavaScript dates, a date that appears as 8:00 p.m. in Paris would appear as 5:00 a.m. in Tokyo and 3:00 p.m. in New York. Someone browsing your app in a distant time zone would have trouble figuring out the actual time of the concert. In this case, the most sensible approach would be to display the concert's time in the time zone the event is taking place in, so your user will see "8:00 p.m. in Paris" whether they are in Paris, Tokyo, or New York.

The primary problem with integrating Moment and AngularJS is that you can't access the `moment()` function by default in AngularJS expressions (for example, the right side of an `ngBind` attribute). This means you either need to call the `moment()` function on every date in your JavaScript data from your controller or service, or you need to make the `moment()` function accessible in AngularJS expressions. The former case is simple, because then you can simply use Moment's chaining syntax in your expressions. However, doing so is often impractical, because you have to change your controllers as well as your HTML whenever the API you're loading data from changes. Also, because the `moment()` function can properly parse myriad inputs, including UNIX timestamps, JavaScript dates, and International Organization for Standardization (ISO) date strings, it's often convenient to simply convert server data to moments in expressions.

One common approach to integrating the `moment()` function into AngularJS expressions is using a filter:

```
app.filter('formatTz', function() {
    return function(input, timezone, format) {
        return moment(input).tz(timezone).format(format);
    };
});
```

Using the `formatTz` filter, you can employ standard AngularJS filter syntax and Moment's formatting library to format dates for the appropriate time zone. For instance, take the following sample list of concerts:

```
app.controller('ConcertsController', function($scope) {
    $scope.concerts = [
        {
            // GMT +1 => 9pm
            when: '2014-06-01T20:00:00.000Z',
            where: 'Europe/London'
        },
        {
            // GMT +2 => 6pm
            when: '2014-06-04T16:00:00.000Z',
            where: 'Europe/Oslo'
        },
        {
            // GMT +4 => 11pm
            when: '2014-06-22T19:00:00.000Z',
            where: 'Europe/Moscow'
        }
    ];
});
```

In HTML, you can render this list using the `formatTz` filter:

```
<div ng-controller="ConcertsController">
    <div ng-repeat="concert in concerts">
        Concert #{{$index + 1}}:
        {{concert.when | formatTz:concert.where:'MMMM D, YYYY h:mma'}}
    </div>
</div>
```

which gives you the desired output:

```
Concert #1: June 1, 2014 9:00pm
Concert #2: June 4, 2014 6:00pm
Concert #3: June 22, 2014 11:00pm
```

An alternative approach to this that enables you to use Moment's chaining syntax is using the overwriting $rootScopeProvider.$get trick that was introduced in Chapter 7. This puts the moment() function in the page's root scope and thus makes it accessible from any (non-isolate) scope on the page. Here's the JavaScript implementation of adding the moment() function to the page's root scope at configuration time. You can find this snippet in the moment_provider.html file in this chapter's sample code:

```
app.config(function($rootScopeProvider) {
    var oldGet = $rootScopeProvider.$get;
    $rootScopeProvider.$get = function($injector) {
        var rootScope = $injector.invoke(oldGet);

        rootScope.moment = window.moment;

        return rootScope;
    };
});
```

This JavaScript makes sure that the page's root scope always contains the moment() function. If you're interested in learning more about providers and the details of why the preceding code works, Chapter 7 includes a more detailed discussion of providers. With the previous configuration block in place, you can now use the moment() function in your AngularJS expressions:

```
<div ng-controller="ConcertsController">
    <div ng-repeat="concert in concerts">
        Concert #{{$index + 1}}:
        {{moment(concert.when).
            tz(concert.where).
            format('MMMM D, YYYY h:mma')}}
    </div>
</div>
```

These two approaches—using a filter and attaching the moment() function to the root scope—have some significant trade-offs. If you attached the moment() function to the root scope, you can't access the moment() function in isolate scopes, which limits your ability to utilize directives. Conversely, the filter syntax is limited: If you want to do date arithmetic, you have to write a separate filter. Another approach that ameliorates both of these difficulties (but is somewhat inelegant syntactically) is to use a filter that simply returns a moment:

```
app.filter('moment', function() {
    return function(input) {
        return moment(input);
    };
});
```

You can then utilize this filter to construct a moment, even in isolate scopes:

```
<div ng-controller="ConcertsController">
    <div ng-repeat="concert in concerts">
        Concert #{{$index + 1}}:
        {{(concert.when | moment).
```

```
        tz(concert.where).
        format('MMMM D, YYYY h:mma')}}
  </div>
</div>
```

This approach also removes the limitation inherent in the `formatTz` filter: You can use a moment's chaining syntax to take advantage of features like date arithmetic, rather than simply formatting a date. The downside of this approach, however, is that it adds complexity to your templates. Although you can use parentheses to chain extra operations on the result of a filter, it makes your code less readable and less easy to understand. However, all three approaches give the same output, so the decision of which of these is right for your development practice is up to you.

Schema Validation and Deep Objects with Mongoose

Mongoose is a popular object-document mapper (ODM) for NodeJS and MongoDB. Although it is primarily a server-side JavaScript module, its currently experimental 3.9 version includes the ability to run Mongoose's schema validation and safe navigation utilities in the browser. AngularJS's form validation code is powerful, but it is limited because the validation rules are specified in HTML. This means you have to maintain two separate sets of validation rules in two separate languages: one on your server and one on your client. If your server uses NodeJS and MongoDB, Mongoose allows you to utilize the same schema for server-side validation as well as client-side form validation. Even if you don't utilize NodeJS or MongoDB on the server side, Mongoose' schema validation tools and other object utilities are powerful and extensible.

For your convenience, this chapter's sample code includes the Mongoose client-side module (version 3.9.3) in the `mongoose.js` file. Mongoose is distributed through the NodeJS package manager, npm. If you install mongoose via npm, you can find the `mongoose.js` file in `node_modules/mongoose/bin/mongoose.js`. In addition, if you compile your client-side JavaScript using Browserify, you can include Mongoose's client-side module using `require('mongoose')`.

Mongoose's client-side module includes two data types that you'll primarily be interacting with: schemas and documents. A *document* is a possibly nested object that contains data. A *schema* is a set of rules for what fields a document should have, what types the fields should contain, and custom validation rules for each field. A document has exactly one schema that it uses for validation. Here are several examples of using schema validation and safe navigation with Mongoose in the browser. You can find these examples in this chapter's sample code in the `mongoose_examples.html` file:

```html
<script type="text/javascript" src="mongoose.js">
</script>
<script type="text/javascript">
  // Create a new Mongoose schema
  var schema = new mongoose.Schema({
    name: {
      first: String,
      last: String
    },
    email: {
      type: String,
      // E-mail needs to match given RegExp
```

```
      match: /.+@.+\..+/,
      // E-mail must be specified
      required: true
    },
    favoriteColor: {
      type: String,
      // Favorite color needs to be one of the enumerated
      // values
      enum: ['Red', 'Green', 'Blue']
    },
    age: {
      type: Number,
      // Age must be at least 21
      min: 21
    }
  });

  // Create a new empty document with schema
  var doc1 = new mongoose.Document({}, schema);

  doc1.validate(function(err) {
    // 'ValidatorError: Path 'email is required''
    console.log(err.errors['email']);
  });

  doc1.name = {
    first: 'James',
    last: 'Madison'
  };

  // 'James Madison'
  console.log(doc1.fullName);

  doc1.fullName = 'Thomas Jefferson';
  // 'Thomas'
  console.log(doc1.name.first);

  var doc2 = new mongoose.Document({}, schema);
  doc2.email = 'a@b.c';
  doc2.age = 20;
  doc2.validate(function(err) {
    // 'ValidatorError: Path 'age' (20) is less than minimum
    // allowed value (21)'
    console.log(err.errors['age']);
  });

  // Safe navigation
  console.log(doc2.name.first); // Undefined
</script>
```

The last example shows Mongoose's safe navigation in action. In reality, doc2.name is undefined, so trying to access doc2.name.first would normally trigger the dreaded TypeError: cannot read property 'name' of undefined JavaScript error. However, Mongoose does some work under the hood to make sure that you get back undefined if one of the parent objects is null or undefined.

In addition, a schema can define virtuals, which are pseudo-properties that are computed from other properties. You can access them using the dot syntax, and you can even set rules for modifying virtuals. For instance, you can store separate variables for first name and last name and have a virtual for the user's full name. When you set the user's full name, you can configure the virtual to set the user's first name and last name for you. Here are some examples of Mongoose virtuals in action, which you can find in the `mongoose_examples_virtuals.html` file in this chapter's sample code:

```javascript
<script type="text/javascript">
  // Create a new Mongoose schema
  var schema = new mongoose.Schema({
    name: {
      first: String,
      last: String
    },
    email: {
      type: String,
      // E-mail needs to match given RegExp
      match: /.+@.+\..+/,
      // E-mail must be specified
      required: true
    },
    favoriteColor: {
      type: String,
      // Favorite color needs to be one of the enumerated
      // values
      enum: ['Red', 'Green', 'Blue']
    },
    age: {
      type: Number,
      // Age must be at least 21
      min: 21
    }
  });

  // 'fullName' is a virtual: a pseudo-property composed of
  // other properties. When you assign a value to 'fullName',
  // it will split it up and set name.first and name.last
  schema.
    virtual('fullName').
    get(function() {
      return this.name.first + ' ' + this.name.last;
    }).
    set(function(v) {
      var s = v.split(' ');
      this.set('name.first', s[0]);
      this.set('name.last', s[1]);
    });

  // Create a new empty document with schema
  var doc1 = new mongoose.Document({}, schema);

  doc1.name = {
```

```
        first: 'James',
        last: 'Madison'
    };

    // 'James Madison'
    console.log(doc1.fullName);

    doc1.fullName = 'Thomas Jefferson';
    // 'Thomas'
    console.log(doc1.name.first);
</script>
```

As you can see, when you set the `fullName` property, Mongoose applies the virtual's `setter` function and updates the `name.first` and `name.last` properties accordingly. Of course, you don't have to define a `.set()` function at all, which makes the `fullName` property read-only. In practice, you'll see read-only virtuals more often than read/write virtuals, because the ability to read a computed property that's kept up to date with the underlying data is quite useful.

Mongoose relies on the `defineProperty()` function that's native to ECMAScript 5, the most recent accepted JavaScript language standard, to do safe navigation and create virtuals. Specifically, the `defineProperty()` function lets you define configurable properties on objects. Normally, JavaScript does not allow you to set properties as read-only, make them invisible to the `Object.keys()` function, or define custom getters and setters for them. The `defineProperty()` function allows you to tweak all these parameters for a given property, which makes syntactic sugar like safe navigation and virtuals possible. However, the downside is that Mongoose only works on browsers that support ECMAScript 5. This means that, in particular, Mongoose does *not* support Internet Explorer 8 or Safari 4.

Now that you understand how Mongoose's browser component is used, you'll learn how to integrate Mongoose with AngularJS. AngularJS interfaces seamlessly with properties created using the `defineProperty()` function, so you should be able to read and manipulate Mongoose document properties from within AngularJS directives (at least in browsers that support ES5). With that in mind, you can use the Mongoose browser component to implement the sophisticated validation functionality that has made it an indispensible part of so many NodeJS servers. You can find the following example in the `mongoose_validation.html` file in this chapter's sample code. First, you need to include `angular.js` and `mongoose.js` in `script` tags and define your schema. The schema used in this code is similar to the schema used in the previous examples but lends itself better to an actual HTML form. It contains four fields: the `name.first` and `name.last` fields, a `quest` string that must include the words *Holy Grail*, and a `favoriteColor` string that must be "Red," "Green," or "Blue."

```
<script type="text/javascript" src="mongoose.js">
</script>
<script type="text/javascript"
        src="angular.js">
</script>
<script type="text/javascript">
  var schema = new mongoose.Schema({
    name: {
      first: { type: String, default: '' },
```

```
        last: { type: String, default: '' }
      },
      quest: {
        type: String,
        match: /Holy Grail/i,
        required: true
      },
      favoriteColor: {
        type: String,
        enum: ['Red', 'Green', 'Blue'],
        required: true
      }
    });

    schema.
      virtual('fullName').
      get(function() {
        return this.name.first +
          (this.name.last ? ' ' + this.name.last : '');
      }).
      set(function(v) {
        var sp = v.indexOf(' ');
        if (sp === -1) {
          this.name.first = v;
          this.name.last = '';
        } else {
          this.name.first = v.substring(0, sp);
          this.name.last = v.substring(sp + 1);
        }
      });

    var app = angular.module('myApp', []);

    app.controller('MyController', function($scope) {
      $scope.doc = new mongoose.Document({}, schema);
      $scope.validating = false;
      $scope.err;
      $scope.validate = function() {
        $scope.validating = true;
        $scope.doc.validate(function(err) {
          $scope.validating = false;
          $scope.err = err;
          $scope.$apply();
        });
      };
    });
</script>
```

Note that the implementation of the fullName virtual changed. The simple implementation you saw in previous examples is a standard Mongoose demo but doesn't behave particularly well when it is plugged into the ngModel directive. Specifically, when you want to plug a Mongoose virtual into the ngModel directive, you usually need smooth handling of edge cases, such as when the input field is empty or when the user has only entered their first name. This is because AngularJS calls the setter to update the value while the user is typing, and then call the getter to get written value. You need to be careful that your virtual returns the same value the user typed for common edge cases; otherwise, the value of the input may change while the user is typing.

Also, note that Mongoose's browser component only includes an asynchronous `validate()` function in version 3.9.3. This is advantageous if you want to use HTTP calls or other asynchronous operations in your validation logic, but it adds the additional caveat that you must call `$scope.$apply()` in the `validate()` function's callback. Otherwise, AngularJS doesn't know that something in the scope changed.

Now that you have looked at the JavaScript for the `mongoose_validation.html` file, here is the HTML template:

```html
<body ng-controller="MyController">
  <h1>My Form</h1>
  <form ng-submit="validate()">
    <h3>What is your name?</h3>
    <input type="text" ng-model="doc.fullName" placeholder="Full Name">
    <div>
      <em>First: {{doc.name.first}}</em>
    </div>
    <div>
      <em>Last: {{doc.name.last}}</em>
    </div>
    <h3>What is your quest?</h3>
    <input type="text" ng-model="doc.quest">
    <h3>What is your favorite color?</h3>
    <input type="text" ng-model="doc.favoriteColor">
    <hr>
    <input type="submit" value="Validate">
    <br><br>
    <div ng-show="!validating && !!err">
      <div ng-repeat="(key, err) in err.errors">
        <b>Error validating path {{key}}:</b>
         {{err.message}}
      </div>
    </div>
    <div ng-show="!validation && !err">
      <h2>No Errors</h2>
    </div>
  </form>
</body>
```

There are a few important details worth noting about the preceding code. First, you can plug Mongoose values, and even virtuals, into the `ngModel` directive. Once again, when putting read/write virtuals into the `ngModel` directive, you want to make sure your virtual's getter always returns whatever the last setter call set the value to. There is no general guarantee of this behavior in virtuals, so the onus is on you to make sure the value doesn't change unexpectedly while the user is typing.

Another important detail to notice is that the `validate()` function is called only when the form is submitted. The core AngularJS validation directives, like `ngRequired`, run validation every time the input's model changes, which is not the right choice for every application. Mongoose's validate() function provides more fine-grained control over what fields are validated when. For example, you can add ngChange validation to the favoriteColor path. This code is demonstrated in the mongoose_validation_fine.html file in this chapter's sample code. First, you need to use the doValidate() function on schema paths to do potentially asynchronous validation on a single path:

```
$scope.validatePath = function(path) {
  $scope.validating = true;
  var schemaPath = $scope.doc.schema.path(path);
  schemaPath.doValidate($scope.doc.get(path), function(err) {
    $scope.validating = false;
    if (err) {
      if (!$scope.err) {
        $scope.err = { errors: {} };
      }
      $scope.err.errors[path] = err;
    } else {
      if ($scope.err && $scope.err.errors[path]) {
        delete $scope.err.errors[path];
      }
    }
  });
};
```

With this function in place, you can transparently tell Mongoose to validate only the favoriteColor path when the input field changes:

```
<h3>What is your favorite color?</h3>
<input  type="text"
        ng-model="doc.favoriteColor"
        ng-change="validatePath('favoriteColor')">
```

Finally, notice that there is no usage of AngularJS's validation directives, like ngRequired, in either of these examples. Mongoose is intended to be a replacement for AngularJS's form validation directives, rather than a supplement for them. AngularJS's form validation directives are embedded in the Document Object Model (DOM), so they are trickier to test and can be more difficult to maintain depending on your codebase. However, the one you use is a matter of personal preference and the requirements for your application. For simple forms and prototyping, AngularJS's form validation can be quite useful. However, Mongoose's form validation has some significant advantages: It offers incredibly sophisticated features that AngularJS form validation lacks, is independent of the DOM (and thus easier to test and reuse), and can be reused in your server if you're using NodeJS and MongoDB.

ANGULARJS AND ECMASCRIPT 6

At the time of this writing, the next version of the JavaScript language standard, ECMAScript 6, is still a work in progress. However, more and more developers are starting to utilize the powerful language features that ECMAScript 6 defines. Although ECMAScript 6 is not finalized yet,

Chrome and Firefox offer support for some ES6 features, so you can utilize them in AngularJS for experimental development and research purposes. However, using ES6 in a production AngularJS application is not a good idea because, as of this writing, no officially released version of Internet Explorer or Safari supports any of the topics you'll learn about in this section. As such, for the purposes of this section, you have to use either Google Chrome (version 37 or greater) or Mozilla Firefox (Version 31 or greater) to view the sample code. You also need to enable ES6 support in Chrome. (Firefox should have it enabled by default.) To do this on Google Chrome 38, navigate your browser to `chrome://flags/`, find and enable the Enable Experimental JavaScript flag, and restart Chrome.

Using yield for Asynchronous Calls

One exciting feature of ES6 that is taking the NodeJS community by storm is generator functions and the `yield` keyword. JavaScript's generators are fairly similar to Python's, so if you have experience with Python, ES6 generators should look familiar. In JavaScript, however, the `yield` keyword has some exceptionally elegant functionality when it comes to managing asynchronous function calls.

Experienced JavaScript engineers have likely heard of the term *callback hell* to describe code that has callbacks within callbacks within other callbacks. You may have experienced this pain in AngularJS when you realized that you had one HTTP call that had to use the result of another HTTP call. Organizing this through callbacks can lead to convoluted code. Generators provide an alternative to this approach that you'll learn about in this section.

You can find this section's sample code in the `http_yield.html` file. This file includes an open source module called `co` that provides a convenience wrapper for running generator functions.

How would you use the `yield` keyword to load the Google stock price from the Yahoo Finance API? Here's the implementation:

```
function convertToAPlusPromise($q, promise) {
  var deferred = $q.defer();
  promise.
    success(function(data) {
      deferred.resolve(data);
    }).
    error(function(err) {
      deferred.reject(err);
    });

  return deferred.promise;
}

function MyController($scope, $http, $q) {
  var BASE = 'http://query.yahooapis.com/v1/public/yql';
  var query = 'select * from yahoo.finance.quotes ' +
    'where symbol in (\'GOOG\')';
  var url = BASE + '?' +
    'q=' + encodeURIComponent(query) +
    '&format=json&diagnostics=true' +
    '&env=http://datatables.org/alltables.env' +
```

```
                    '&callback=JSON_CALLBACK';

        co(function*() { // The * is not a typo, marks this as a generator
          var result;
          try {
            result = yield convertToAPlusPromise($q, $http.jsonp(url));
            $scope.result = result;
          } catch(e) {
            console.log('Error occurred: ' + e);
          }
        })();
```

There are two important details to note about the preceding code. First, the `yield` keyword operates on a promise. A *promise* is an object that provides syntactic sugar around an asynchronous operation. In particular, the `yield` keyword expects a promise that conforms to the Promises/A+ standard, which unfortunately is entirely incompatible with the promises returned by the `$http` service. Thankfully, the AngularJS core contains a lightweight fork of the popular promises library "Q" as the `$q` service, which does conform to the Promises/A+ standard. The `convertToAPlusPromise()` function shown earlier converts a promise returned by the `$http` service to a promise returned by the `$q` service—that is, one that can be used with the `yield` keyword.

Second, there are no callbacks in the previous code. The `yield` keyword is smart enough to write the value returned in the `promise.resolve()` call above into the result variable when the asynchronous call is done. With the `co` library, you can execute JavaScript's fundamentally asynchronous HTTP calls in a manner that looks synchronous.

But what happens when there is an error, such as if the Yahoo Finance API is down? That's what the try/catch block is for! The `yield` keyword throws an error when its corresponding promise is *rejected* (the Promises/A+ standard's term for a promise raising an error). This means you can use the concise try/catch syntax to catch HTTP errors rather than having to specify an error handler function.

CONCLUSION

In this chapter, you explored several projects outside of the AngularJS core that enabled you to use AngularJS in new ways. In particular, you learned that you can build native mobile applications with AngularJS using the Ionic framework, utilize MomentJS for sophisticated date functionality, and integrate MongooseJS for schema-driven form validation. There are myriad other JavaScript modules that you can use to extend AngularJS: You can find more by searching for "AngularJS" on `www.npmjs.org` or `www.bower.io/search`.

APPENDIX

Resources

Many websites can help you learn more about AngularJS and connect with the AngularJS community. AngularJS's popularity has inspired a wide range of online content, ranging from simple blog posts to sophisticated screencasts, which can provide insight on most AngularJS questions and issues. Furthermore, several JavaScript module repositories enable you to find and install extensions for AngularJS:

➤ **AngularJS** (`http://www.angularjs.org`)—The official AngularJS site offers downloads, tutorials, forums, a Developer Guide, an application programming interface (API) reference, and much more. This is an ideal place to get basic information about AngularJS and to connect with the larger community.

➤ **Egghead.io** (`http://egghead.io`)—Egghead.io is currently the go-to source for AngularJS screencast tutorials. These tutorials are short (typically around 5 minutes) videos that demonstrate AngularJS concepts by showing a developer writing code in an integrated development environment (IDE). Egghead.io tutorials are ideal for quickly addressing a specific question that you have about AngularJS features.

➤ **Bower** (`http://bower.io`)—Bower is a package manager built for client-side JavaScript and cascading style sheets (CSS). Bower hosts numerous AngularJS packages, and the `bower.io` website has a convenient search engine so you can find specific AngularJS extensions.

➤ **npm** (`http://www.npmjs.org`)—npm originally started as a package manager for NodeJS, but thanks to modules like Browserify (see Chapter 3, "Architecture," for more information about Browserify) npm is now also a popular repository for client-side modules. The official npm website includes a convenient search engine to help you find useful AngularJS modules.

➤ **Thinkster** (`http://www.thinkster.io`)—Similar to Egghead.io, Thinkster provides screencast tutorials. However, Thinkster tutorials are typically organized as full courses rather than short standalone videos and focus more on full-stack development than AngularJS in isolation. If you are interested in learning about using AngularJS with Django, Ruby on Rails, Ionic, or as part of the MEAN stack, Thinkster is an excellent resource.

➤ **AngularJS-Learning** (`http://github.com/jmcunningham/AngularJS-Learning`)—The most popular community-curated list of AngularJS content includes links to numerous high-quality AngularJS articles, sample apps, and learning resources.

➤ **angular/angular.js** (`http://github.com/angular/angular.js`)—The official AngularJS code repository includes a mechanism to report issues and enables you to contribute to the AngularJS core through GitHub's Pull Requests feature.

➤ **AngularJS Code** (`http://code.angularjs.org`)—This page includes download links to all versions of AngularJS, including noncore modules like `angular-sanitize`. If you are comfortable digging into core AngularJS code or just want to download a specific module, this is the ideal location to find the file you're looking for.

INDEX

E